# Lecture Notes of the Institute for Computer Sciences, Social Informatics and Telecommunications Engineering 321

More information about this series at http://www.springer.com/series/8197

Jessica P. R. Thorn · Assane Gueye ·
Adam P. Hejnowicz (Eds.)

# Innovations and Interdisciplinary Solutions for Underserved Areas

4th EAI International Conference, InterSol 2020
Nairobi, Kenya, March 8–9, 2020
Proceedings

Springer

*Editors*
Jessica P. R. Thorn (iD)
African Climate and Development Initiative
University of Cape Town
Cape Town, South Africa

Department of Environment and Geography
University of York
York, UK

Adam P. Hejnowicz (iD)
Department of Animal and Plant Sciences
University of Sheffield
Sheffield, UK

Assane Gueye (iD)
Université Alioune Diop de Bambey
Bambey, Senegal

ISSN 1867-8211 ISSN 1867-822X (electronic)
Lecture Notes of the Institute for Computer Sciences, Social Informatics
and Telecommunications Engineering
ISBN 978-3-030-51050-3 ISBN 978-3-030-51051-0 (eBook)
https://doi.org/10.1007/978-3-030-51051-0

This Springer imprint is published by the registered company Springer Nature Switzerland AG
The registered company address is: Gewerbestrasse 11, 6330 Cham, Switzerland

# Preface

**Introducing InterSol 2020**

We are delighted to introduce the proceedings of the fourth edition of the 2020 European Alliance for Innovation (EAI) International Conference on Innovations and Interdisciplinary Solutions for Underserved Areas (InterSol 2020). This conference brought together African researchers from across 18 countries to focus on interdisciplinary and transdisciplinary solutions to the complex social-ecological challenges we face. A variety of key themes of InterSol2020 conference ranged from climate change adaptation and disaster risk preparedness; corporate environmental and social governance; land use change; nature-based solutions to infrastructure climate proofing; challenges and barriers faced by women in research; mitigating environmental pollution; information communication technology for overcoming the digital divide and improving health; e-readiness of marginalized communities; linking scientific and indigenous knowledge, and how is this evidence base translated into decision-making processes that result in flourishing biodiversity, and prosperous, meaningful livelihoods, amongst other topics. Accordingly, the overarching theme for this year's edition was "Nature-based solutions, gender equity and interconnectivity for climate resilience in Africa", with the first day celebrating International Women's Day, and the second investigating "Envisioning sustainable social-ecological futures." Drawing from case studies in Africa and Asia, the chapters in this book represent a subset of five of these key themes: (1) Feeding and securing healthy futures; (2) Mitigating environmental pollution and conservation beyond protected areas; (3) Climate change and energy efficiency; (4) ICT and innovative connectivity as an enabler for sustainable development; and (5) Computer science and its applications.

**What is InterSol?**

Today, there is a consensus that such challenges require solutions that are not amenable to separate single-discipline investigation, but require collaboration between many types of traditional disciplines. There is a need for more transdisciplinary practice: where research has a real-world impact. This is the essence behind InterSol; an international conference dedicated to the advancement of interdisciplinary research that addresses people's needs in underserved areas. It is intended to (1) encourage innovative interdisciplinary research, development, and education that focus on solving problems in underserved areas in Africa and beyond, and (2) create an international research and development community around "interdisciplinary solutions," which meets annually, publish in international fora, and incentivize members of the community to initiate interdisciplinary research projects that address needs. The first edition was held in Dakar. In 2017 Senegal, the second in Kigali, in 2018 Rwanda, the third in

Cairo, in 2019 Egypt, and the fourth edition of the conference was held in Nairobi, in 2020 Kenya.

## An Urgent Call for Innovation in the Climate Emergency

The year of 2020 is a momentous one for sustainability, biodiversity, and climate change policy. It represents the deadline for 21 Sustainable Development Goal (SDG) targets, the year a new post-2020 framework to replace the Aichi Biodiversity Targets will be agreed, and a turning point for climate change, according to the UNFCCC. This trilemma of policy issues represents a set of globally interlinked challenges, which are particularly significant for Africa.

According to UNEP, "no continent will be struck as severely by the impacts of climate change as Africa," a reality exacerbated by poverty and lack of adaptive capacity. By 2020, between 75-250 million people are projected to be exposed to increased water stress due to climate change, whilst changes in rainfall patterns and intensity will lead to severe flooding, and a wider distribution of vector-borne diseases. The 2018 Africa SDG Dashboards highlighted that Africa continues to face major difficulties in achieving the 2030 Agenda, with 13 out of the 15 goals showing little or no positive developments. In particular, health (SDG 3), infrastructure (SDG 9), peace, justice, and strong institutions (SDG 16), closely followed by food security and sustainable agriculture (SDG 2), energy access (SDG 7), and marine ecosystems (SDG 14). Moreover, the recent IPBES regional assessment highlighted Africa's extraordinary richness in biodiversity and ecosystem services, and wealth of indigenous and local knowledge, which collectively comprises a strategic asset for sustainable development. However, "the decline and loss of biodiversity is reducing nature's contributions to people in Africa, affecting daily lives and hampering the sustainable social and economic development."

At the same time, according to UN Habitat, the continent is undergoing widespread, rapid, and often unplanned urbanisation. By 2030, 50% of Africans are expected to live in urban areas, with the number of mega-cities also expected to grow over the next decade. In fact, recent projections suggest that the next 10 years will see Africa's 20 largest cities will expand by 50% and 6 of the world's 21 mega cities will be in Africa. However, as cited by the African Development Bank, in sub-Saharan Africa 62% of urban residents still live without or have poor access to water, sanitation, housing, and secure tenure. Indeed, 72% of the urban population lives in poorly planned settlements on city margins. Urban developments like these can have serious consequences for people's health and wellbeing as a result of air and water pollution and a lack of basic infrastructure. Moreover, they put increasing pressure on the natural resource base and are often associated with unregulated land cover transformations causing habitat loss, soil erosion, and degradation of water catchments. Activities that collectively undermine biodiversity and ecosystem services provision and the sustainability of peoples' livelihoods. In addition, according to the World Bank, Africa's levels of public debt and debt risk are increasing. And while the total labor force has increased, this has not been met by a similar increase in the availability of good jobs. Current estimates suggest the overall growth of Africa's economy is hindered by more fragile economies, which reduce annual growth by 0.5% (from 4% to 3.5% per annum). Meanwhile, structural and functional inequalities persist and ensure that poverty is still a wide-spread and recognizable reality for many.

Yet, concurrently the continent is witnessing widespread positive transformations, representing serious opportunities for securing sustainable development pathways. Africa's middle class is on the rise (expected to hit 210 million by 2020), expanding internal markets and increasing consumer spending to US$1.4 trillion. Sustainable manufacturing is being spurred by the African Continental Free Trade Area launched in 2018, that aims to grow business-to-business spending to US$666.3 billion in the next decade. Digitization of manufacturing and new human-machine interactions, "Industry 4.0," represent significant areas of innovation and investments for small and medium enterprises. By 2020, mobile technologies and services are expected to provide up to US$142 billion, or 8.6% of the continents GDP, with 500 million broadband connections. Indeed, in 2015, the African Development Bank (ADB) launched its High 5 program, focusing on enhancing industrial policies and programs, renewable energy investments, transport connectivity, capital flows through enterprise and strategic partnerships, and improving telecommunication platforms. The ADB's Feed Africa strategy attempts to develop inclusive agricultural growth pathways that account for youth and gender-based inequalities and climate resilience.

**Enter InterSol 2020**

Against this backdrop, this conference called for rigorous interdisciplinary and trans-disciplinary solutions. The purpose is to highlight the strong voices of African social, natural, and physical scientists.

The technical program of InterSol 2020 consisted of 20 full papers 3 keynote speeches, 6 technical workshops and tutorials. The keynote speeches were given by Dr. Rocio-Diaz Chavez, Stockholm Environment Institute, on peri-urban resilience; Charif Mahmoudi, Seimens, on intelligent systems; and Prof. Shem Wadiga, University of Nairobi, on climate change adaptation. Panel discussions related to the following questions: In a social and ecological compact, what is the role of the private sector? What are early career women's experience in navigating post PhD into academia and practice? What are conflicts across sectors in climate governance? And how do we bridge the gap in research and national planning and implement a policy making process? Six interactive workshops and tutorials were organized by co-hosts the Stockholm Environmental Institute, the Institute of Climate Change and Adaptation at the University of Nairobi, the Mawazo Institute, the University of Ngaoundere, and the Training Centre for Communication at the University of Nairobi. The following areas were addressed open source online modelling tools including Water Evaluation and Planning System (WEAP) and Long-Range Energy Alternatives Planning system (LEAP); how to measure science communication and write opinion editorials for policy and press; how to implement a distance training program in African universities; Interdisciplinary methods to understanding and navigating complex systems, and how to curb career attrition of women in STEM.

The conference program also included field excursions to Mathare Valley Slums to uncover community based disaster risk resilience, and to Nairobi National Park to observe the impacts of linear infrastructural developments on protected areas, together with a visit to the Masaai Manyatta village Bomas and performances by the Sarakasi Trust cultural dance troupe and acrobats as well as a Gala dinner. Collectively this offered a warm introduction to the rich history, diverse landscapes and people that Kenya has to offer.

Coordination with the steering chairs Jessica Thorn, Assane Gueye, Adam Hejnowicz, and Anderson Kehbila was essential for the success of the conference. It was also a great pleasure to work with the excellent Organizing Committee. We thank them, the conference manager Karolina Marcinova anonymous manuscript reviews, and the rest of the Springer publishing team, together with the authors who submitted their papers to the InterSol 2020 conference and workshops.

InterSol2020 was held partnership with the University of York Department of Environment and Geography, University of Cape Town African Climate and Development Initiative, Stockholm Environment Institute York and Africa, and University of Nairobi Institute for Climate Change and Adaptation. We give thanks to our sponsors, in particular the Next Einstein Forum, Canada International Development Research Centre, African Institute of Mathematical Sciences, and Google AI Africa. We further acknowledge funding from the UK Research and Innovation's Global Challenges Research Fund (UKRI GCRF) through the Development Corridors Partnership project (ES/P011500/1), and the Climate Research for Development Postdoctoral Fellowship CR4D-19-21 implemented by the African Academy of Sciences (AAS) in partnership with the United Kingdom's Department for International Development Weather and Climate Information Services for Africa (WISER) programme and the African Climate Policy Center (ACPC) of the United Nations Economic Commission for Africa (UNECA). Through the support of our sponsors, we sponsored 25 international presenters to attend the event—more than any previous event. Statements made and views expressed in this work are solely the responsibility of the author(s).

Intersol2020 attracted diverse, inter– and trans-disciplinary researchers from 18 countries across Africa, Europe and North America. Approximately 40% of these scientists are women. The conference represented a true confluence of diverse disciplines, from nuclear science, engineering, mathematics and physics, to geography, conservation, and climate change and onto religious studies, economics, gender, education, anthropology and many more. As in previous years, we hoped to showcase the best in research from across the continent to industry practitioners, government officials, think tanks, research organizations, NGOs, CBOs and private companies and African Institutions of Higher Education, Science and Technology.

We strongly believe that InterSol2020 conference provided an excellent interdisciplinary forum for researchers and practitioners to deeply engage in discourse around scientific, societal, environmental, technological and other components of complex systems relevant to addressing needs in underserved areas. It is an important gathering we hope fosters long term collaborations for evidence based decision making towards a sustainable African future. We expect subsequent additions of InterSol conference will be as successful and stimulating, as indicated by the contributions presented in this volume.

July 2020                                                      Jessica P. R. Thorn
                                                                        Assane Gueye
                                                                Adam P. Hejnowicz

# Organization

## Steering Committee

Assane Gueye      Univerity of Maryland, USA, and Université Alioune Diop de Bambey, Senegal

Imrich Chlamtac      University of Trento, Italy

## Organizing Committee

## General Chair

Jessica P. R. Thorn      University of York, UK, University of Cape Town, South Africa

## TPC Chairs

Assane Gueye      Université Alioune Diop de Bambey, Senegal

Jessica P. R. Thorn      University of York, UK, University of Cape Town, South Africa

Adam P. Hejnowicz      University of York, UK

## Local Chair

Anderson Kehbila      Stockholm Environment Institute Africa, Kenya

## Publications Chair

Adam P. Hejnowicz      University of York, UK

## Workshops Chair

Daniel Olago      Institute of Climate Change and Adaptation, University of Nairobi, Kenya

## Publicity and Social Media Chair

Yvonne Githiora      University of Nairobi, Kenya

# Web Chair

| | |
|---|---|
| Amayaa Wijesinghe | University of Cape Town, South Africa/<br>United Nations Environment Programme World<br>Conservation Monitoring Centre, UK |

# Posters and PhD Track Chair

| | |
|---|---|
| Hamidu Seki | University of York, UK, University of Dar es Salaam,<br>Tanzania |

# Panels Chairs

| | |
|---|---|
| Jessica P. R. Thorn | University of York, UK, University of Cape Town,<br>South Africa |
| Dieter Brandt | Advanced Environmental Design Initiatives, Germany |

# Tutorials Chair

| | |
|---|---|
| Narcisse Talla Tankam | University of Ngaoundere, Cameroon |

# Conference Manager

| | |
|---|---|
| Karolina Marcinova | EAI, Slovakia |

# Technical Programme Committee

| | |
|---|---|
| Mouhamadou Lamine Ba | Université Alioune Diop de Bambey, Senegal |
| Gaoussou Camara | Université Alioune Diop de Bambey, Senegal |
| Charif Mahmoudi | Siemens, USA |
| Melissa Densmore | University of Cape Town, South Africa |
| Abdelhamid Mambo | Nile University of Nigeria, Nigeria |
| Maimouna Diouf | Dakar American University of Science<br>and Technology, Senegal |
| Yvonne Githiora | University of Nairobi, Kenya |
| Bamba Gueye | Université Cheikh Anta Diop, Senegal |
| Assane Gueye | Université Alioune Diop de Bambey, Senegal |
| Anderson Kehbila | Stockholm Environment Institute Africa, Kenya |
| Alpha Lutta | University of Nairobi, Kenya |
| Malo Sadouanouan | UPB, Burkina Fasso |
| Maissa Mbaye | Université Gaston Berger de Saint-Louis, Senegal |
| Sidy Ndao | University of Nebraska, USA |
| Ababacar Ndiaye | Université Assane SECK de Ziguinchor, Senegal |
| Kara Nelson | UC Berkeley, USA |
| Solomon Njengah | University of Nairobi, Kenya |
| Joyojeet Pal | University of Michigan, USA |

| | |
|---|---|
| Narcisse Talla Tankam | Advanced School of Teachers Training, University of Ngaoundéré, Cameroon |
| Youssef Travaly | AIMS-NEI, Rwanda |
| Gertjan van Stam | Scientific and Industrial Research and Development Centre, Zimbabwe |
| Aminata Garba | CMU-Africa, Rwanda |
| Tembine Hamidou | NYU, USA |
| Ghada Bassioni | Ain Shams University, Egypt |
| Moustapha Diop | University of Maryland, USA |
| Adam P. Hejnowicz | University of York, UK |
| Amayaa Wijesinghe | University of Cape Town, South Africa/ United Nations Environment Programme World Conservation Monitoring Centre, UK |
| Hamidu Seki | University of York, UK, University of Dar es Salaam, Tanzania |
| Dan Olago | University of Nairobi, Kenya |
| Jessica P. R. Thorn | University of York, UK, University of Cape Town, South Africa |

# Contents

**Feeding and Securing Healthy African and Asian Futures**

Integration of Indigenous Knowledge, Climate Data, Satellite Imagery
and Machine Learning to Optimize Cropping Decisions by Small-Scale
Farmers. a Case Study of uMgungundlovu District Municipality,
South Africa.............................................. 3
    *John Nyetanyane and Muthoni Masinde*

A Multi-level Smart Monitoring System by Combining an E-Nose
and Image Processing for Early Detection of FAW Pest in Agriculture ..... 20
    *Sèmèvo Arnaud R. M. Ahouandjinou, Manhougbé P. A. F. Kiki,*
    *Prince E. N. Amoussouga Badoussi, and Kokou M. Assogba*

Indigenous and Scientific Knowledge of Soil Regulation Services,
and Factors Effecting Decision-Making in Agricultural Landscapes
in the Terai Plains of Nepal ................................. 33
    *Jessica P. R. Thorn*

Extraction of Relevant Data from Social Media Based on Termino-
Ontological Resources: *Application to Meningitis Surveillance via Twitter* ... 52
    *Wend-Panga Régis Cédric Bere, Gaoussou Camara,*
    *Sadouanouan Malo, Sylvie Despres, Moussa Lo, and Stanislas Ouaro*

Physiochemical, Mineralogical and Physical Properties of Overburden Over
Gneiss Basement Complex in Minna Metropolis, Nigeria.............. 64
    *Mohammed Mustapha Alhaji, Alhassan Musa,*
    *Abdulhameed Danjuma Mambo, Waheed Adejumo Taiye,*
    *and Abdullahi Yahaya Musa*

**Mitigating Environmental Pollution and Conservation Beyond
Protected Areas**

Mitigating the Impacts of Environmental Pollution in Lejweleputswa
District Through Integration of Local and Scientific Knowledge .......... 77
    *Mpho Mbele and Muthoni Masinde*

Environmental Protection in Nigerian Democracy: The Ogoni Clean-Up
in Perspective.............................................. 89
    *Harrison Adewale Idowu and Ismail Sano*

Mangroves Under Demographic Pressure and Salt Production Threats
in the Municipality of Ouidah (Benin) . . . . . . . . . . . . . . . . . . . . . . . . . . .     105
    *Sehouevi Mawuton David Agoungbome, Estelle Gbenontin,*
    *and Moussa Thiam*

**Climate Change and Energy Efficiency**

Hydroclimate Analysis Under 1.5 and 2 °C Global Warming in the Faleme
River Basin . . . . . . . . . . . . . . . . . . . . . . . . . . . . . . . . . . . . . . . . . . . . .     121
    *Mamadou Lamine Mbaye, Khadidiatou Sy, Bakary Faty,*
    *and Saidou Moustapha Sall*

Supervision Strategy of a Hybrid System PV with Storage for Injection to
the Electrical Network . . . . . . . . . . . . . . . . . . . . . . . . . . . . . . . . . . . . . . .     134
    *Amadou Ba, Alphousseyni Ndiaye, and Senghane Mbodji*

**ICT and Innovative Connectivity as an Enabler
for Sustainable Development**

Assessing the e-Readiness of Marginalised Communities for e-Government
Services: A Case of Oniipa, Namibia. . . . . . . . . . . . . . . . . . . . . . . . . . . . .     149
    *Karin Fröhlich, Marko Nieminen, and Antti Pinomaa*

Vulnerability Analysis in Mobile Banking and Payment Applications
on Android in African Countries. . . . . . . . . . . . . . . . . . . . . . . . . . . . . . . .     164
    *Didier Bassolé, Gouayon Koala, Yaya Traoré, and Oumarou Sié*

Stakeholder Relations and Ownership of a Community Wireless Network:
The Case of iNethi . . . . . . . . . . . . . . . . . . . . . . . . . . . . . . . . . . . . . . . . . .     176
    *Jaydon Farao, Monet Burse, Hafeni Mthoko, and Melissa Densmore*

Consolidating the Right to Data Protection in the Information Age:
A Comparative Appraisal of the Adoption of the OECD (Revised)
Guidelines into the EU GDPR, the Ghanaian Data Protection Act 2012
and the Kenyan Data Protection Act 2019 . . . . . . . . . . . . . . . . . . . . . . . . .     192
    *Rogers Alunge*

**Computer Science and Its Applications**

A Matrix Model to Analyze Cascading Failure in Critical Infrastructures . . . .     211
    *Assane Gueye, Babacar Mbaye, Doudou Fall, Alassane Diop,*
    *and Shigeru Kashihara*

Clusters Construction Mechanism for Strictly Linear Wireless
Sensor Networks. . . . . . . . . . . . . . . . . . . . . . . . . . . . . . . . . . . . . . . . . . . .     224
    *Abdourakhmane Fall, Moussa Dethié Sarr, and Cheikh Sarr*

On the Treewidth of Planar Minor Free Graphs .................... 238
    *Youssou Dieng and Cyril Gavoille*

BACP+: A More Efficient Beacon Analysis-Based Collision
Prevention Protocol....................................... 251
    *Sidiya Dieng, Youssou Faye, and Marius Dasylva*

Enriching Geolocalized Dataset with POIs Descriptions at Large Scale ..... 264
    *Ibrahima Gueye, Hubert Naacke, and Stéphane Gançarski*

Building Word Representations for Wolof Using Neural Networks ........ 274
    *Alla Lo, Cheikh M. Bamba Dione, Elhadji Mamadou Nguer,
    Sileye O. Ba, and Moussa Lo*

**Author Index** .......................................... 287

# Feeding and Securing Healthy African and Asian Futures

# Integration of Indigenous Knowledge, Climate Data, Satellite Imagery and Machine Learning to Optimize Cropping Decisions by Small-Scale Farmers. a Case Study of uMgungundlovu District Municipality, South Africa

John Nyetanyane[✉] and Muthoni Masinde

Department of Information Technology, Central University of Technology, Free State, Bloemfontein, South Africa
{jnyetanyane,emasinde}@cut.ac.za

**Abstract.** Despite being the backbone of food security in most African countries, small-scale farmers are overlooked during the implementation of many of developmental projects. These farmers are financially incapable of equipping themselves with irrigation systems and other agricultural technologies that can assist in improving their farm yields. One of the challenges facing them is that they rely heavily on rain-fed agriculture which makes them extremely vulnerable in the face of climate change. They have continued to consult their indigenous knowledge systems to predict the onset of rains and in making critical decisions such as when to prepare land for crop cultivation. Evidence shows that this knowledge is no longer as precise as it used to be – among other reasons, this is due to the effects of climate change and deforestation. The second problem is that the only sources of weather information these farmers have (e.g. the media) are general and not scaled down to the specific locations where they reside. On the other hand, most of the small-scale farmers are educationally and technologically semi-literate and are financially crawling when it comes to adoption of the likes of sensors and other technologies that could help in predicting and monitoring crop health. There is however opportunity in that most of these farmers are now using android phones. In this research, a model that utilizes the indigenous knowledge, climate data and vegetation index to foresee the onset of the favourable weather season for crop cultivation, crop monitoring and crop health prediction is proposed.

**Keywords:** Indigenous knowledge · Satellite imagery · Simple moving average · Weighted moving average · Linear exponential smoothing · Double exponential smoothing · Average ndvi

## 1 Introduction

Africa is considered to have less of crop lands in comparison with other continents such as America and Asia [11]. Increase in number as well as severity of droughts, coupled

© ICST Institute for Computer Sciences, Social Informatics and Telecommunications Engineering 2020
Published by Springer Nature Switzerland AG 2020. All Rights Reserved
J. P. R. Thorn et al. (Eds.): InterSol 2020, LNICST 321, pp. 3–19, 2020.
https://doi.org/10.1007/978-3-030-51051-0_1

with population growth, cause serious implication on vegetation lands in Africa [21]. Remote sensing technology such as satellite imagery to assess and monitor the vegetation health in Africa is not yet widely adopted. African farmers, majority of whom are small scale farmers, continue to rely on indigenous knowledge as opposed to conventional science and technology [23]. Factors that demotivate the use of technology such as satellite images, comes at high cost and need for massive processing before being readily available. Moreover, the requisition of complex and sophisticated software applications to manipulate the satellite images are adding on the complications to adopt to technology. Yes, we do have the satellite images that can be accessed at any time; however, these free satellite images have less spatial resolution of up to 100 to 1000 m. Among the well-known satellites, the National Aromatics and Space Administration (NASA)'s satellite called MODIS satellite provides images with the minimum spatial resolution of 250 m. Therefore, if one pixel of an image is covering a distance of 250 m by 250 m, it will be difficult to detect small objects from the ground. Even if Africa's small-scale farmers were to perceive the information from the satellite images, it will serve minimum or no interests on them because of the formats and language used to represent them. Moreover, in most cases it takes time to receive the updated versions of free-satellite images, making it difficult to track the changes in near-real-time.

Illiteracy and poverty level amongst most African farmers make it difficult for agricultural information dissemination and requisition of technological resources to aid on their farming growth [3]. However, farmers do need technology that can assist in optimising their cropping decisions, for instance, to monitor their crop growth. Even though, indigenous knowledge has been effective in the yesteryears, its usefulness has slowly been eroded, besides, it takes a human labour to physically and periodically monitor a huge portion of land. There are several attributes that can be detected using the machine as opposed to IK. These include Normalized Difference Vegetation Index (NDVI), level of gases in the atmosphere, precipitation, among others. Early detection of crop problems can assist in reducing financial losses, increase food security and reaching targeted yielding and profit margins [9]. In this paper, we argue that integrating the farmer's knowledge with mainstream scientific approach can improve the accuracy of crop yield prediction.

## 2  Literature Review

Different crops are cultivated in different seasons mainly during summer (Nov-Dec-Jan) and winter (May-June-July). The summer crops are harvested in autumn while the winter crops are harvested in spring. Summer crops need more rain and warm temperature during their life span while the winter crops need minimum of rain and cold temperature. The well-known summer crops are maize, sorghum, beans, peanuts, sunflower seed and so forth. Whereas wheat, peas, spinach, onions, carrots, lentils and so forth are planted during winter.

The dispersal of vegetation in African land is gradually becoming extinct [13]. According to [21] most studies have proved that Africa has experienced more frequent, intense and widespread of droughts from the last 50 years. South Africa depend highly on the availability of rain as it stands out as one of the most water-scarce countries [13].

According to [7], statistics showed that there was a decrease of agricultural households in South Africa from 19.9% in 2011 to 13.8% in 2016 due to severe drought in 2014 to 2015. Among other factors that aggravate the limitation of vegetation is escalating population and degradation of land and environment due to development of industries, mining sectors, houses and other premises [21]. Therefore, land is a limited resource and hence the present efforts should mainly rely upon increasing the productivity of the existing land [6].

Vegetation is the source of food, it must be well planned and monitored for sustainability. Contribution of land, vegetation and agriculture is the back bone of every country [28]. [36, 37] explained that crop production and yielding must be planned and accurately predicted through the use of technology. They further accentuate that being able to optimize cropping decisions and predict crop yields accurately will allow the government to plan production, distribution and food consumption more effectively, combat food insecurity, prepare for shortages and supply shocks well in advance. Additionally, [43] explain that efficient and effective vegetation monitoring can help preventing famine and support humanitarian efforts in light of climate change and droughts. According to [29], being able to monitor the crop health and predict the crop yield at a growing season, marketed prices can be forecasted, import and export can be planned, the socio-economic impact of crop loss can be minimized, and humanitarian food assistance can be planned.

Although there are some interesting aspects with vegetation monitoring, prediction of crop yield before harvest is a challenging aspect in the field of machine learning and artificial intelligence [44]. Developed countries such as USA and Japan are equipped with approaches such as comprehensive surveys of weather parameters and land cover types that are publicly available and greatly facilitate the crop yielding task [43]. However, the aforementioned technologies are not available in developing countries such as South Africa and yet reliable yield predictions are most needed [8]. As a solution, [8] introduce the use of remote sensing data such as free satellite images that is globally available, of good quality and relatively inexpensive. The use of remote sensing combined with other form of technologies can be quite helpful to the small-scale farmers especially those that do not enjoy the comfortability of having the irrigation systems and rely only on rain [17]. Most of the local farmers are making living from the rain-fed agriculture and at the onset of rainy season, farmers make crucial decisions about what, when and where to plant [13, 17, 34].

## 2.1 Remote Sensing Technology

Remote sensing is a technology of acquiring information above the earth surface without coming into contact with it [20]. Remote sensing technology has been used as an effective tool to track and monitor the crop vigour, density, health, development and growth [5]. Further, this technology can be used in computational sustainability such as species distribution modelling, poverty mapping, climate modelling and natural disaster prevention [43].

One of the main examples of remote sensing technology is satellite imagery system. It is a powerful tool equipped with powerful sensors and cameras used to collect images of the world surface [16]. These sensors can record the electromagnetic radiation emitted from the sun or any form of a solar and reflected from the ground and or objects on the ground [15].

## 2.2 Satellite Image Segmentation or Classification

Collected satellite images are also known as multispectral satellite images contains abundance of information visible and non-visible to the human eye that could be correlated with economic features, vegetation growth and agricultural outcomes [16, 43]. Because satellite images have high spatial graphics, data is high-dimensional and unstructured, deep learning and machine learning techniques come into operational when having to validate the image in to certain places of interest [16, 43]. Image segmentation also known as image classification is a process of classifying an image in to different groups or regions [9, 16, 43]. [40] define image classification as a part of computer vision that will help to classify pixels into finite set of individual classes based on their data values. It is a technique that will help to extract only useful data from a given image. Image classification is considered as a vital part of the remote sensing, image analysis and pattern recognition [38]. Object recognition and classification to extract meaningful insights from the large-scale image is considered as a challenging task by machines [16].

## 2.3 Vegetation Indices

When the features of interests such as crop lands have been extracted from the given satellite image using the machine vision algorithms, different types of indices specifically vegetation indices can be calculated. Among the existing indices, NDVI is a well-known index used to measure and assess the vegetation greenness, vegetation growth and vegetation health. According to [31], NDVI is a ratio based on the spectral reflectance from vegetation, fourthly it is from combined operations between red and NIR band regions of the multispectral light which is expressed mathematically as:

$$ndvi = \frac{I_{nir} - I_{red}}{I_{nir} + I_{red}} \tag{1}$$

NDVI values range between the scale of $-1$ and $+1$, healthy vegetation is presented by high NDVI values between 0.5 and $<1$. Non-vegetation surfaces such as soil and water bodies yield negative values considered as low NDVI values [2]. The healthiness of plants also depends on the health of the soil. A well-known index used to measure the soil health is Soil Adjusted Vegetation Index (SAVI). The formula is presented below whereby L represents the soil brightness correction that is traditionally 0 in the highly vegetation areas and 1 in a low vegetation areas

$$savi = \frac{I_{nir} - I_{red}}{(I_{nir} + I_{red} + L)} * (1 + L) \tag{2}$$

The historic and current vegetation data collected from the remote sensing technology can be fed to a time series models to predict the crop yield or future vegetation so to enlighten the local farmers, business or economical entities, agricultural, political developers and so forth with the future [14, 39, 42].

## 2.4  Machine Learning (Time Series Analysis)

Forecasting is the process of feeding the machine a historical data and allow the machine to learn the pattern or the trend from the data so that it can be able to predict new or future values. Most of the time series prediction approaches are based on the analysis of historical data and assume that past and current data patterns can be used to forecast future data points. Different types of models that are used are listed below. The researcher will dwell only on few models relevant to the paper.

### 2.4.1  Linear Exponential Smoothing (LES) Model

This model also known as exponential smoothing or single exponential smoothing (SES). From [33], exponential smoothing is one of the simplest and popular forecasting techniques that is included in popular forecasting software products. The algorithm automates the weight assignment process and it doesn't utilize the order movement and its forecasting mechanism doesn't ignore the past data. To automate the weight assignment, it utilises the summation of exponents and constant known as alpha that is assigned a value of $0 > a < 1$.

As presented below, the formula for linear exponential smoothing whereby ft + 1 represents the next forecasted value and alpha ($\alpha$) is constant value ranges between 0 and 1.

$$f_{t+1} = \alpha Y_t + (1 - \alpha)f_t \tag{3}$$

The formula can be expanded up until the $n^{th}$ period.

$$f_{t+1} = \alpha Y_t + \alpha(1 - \alpha)Y_{t-1} + \alpha(1 - \alpha)^2 Y_{t-2} + \ldots \alpha(1 - \alpha)^{n-1} Y_1 + (1 - \alpha)^n f_t \tag{4}$$

### 2.4.2  Double Exponential Smoothing (DES) Model

This model known as Trend Adjusted Exponential Smoothing (TAES) and "Holt-Winter's trend and seasonal method". It outperforms single exponential smoothing, especially when there is a non-stationery seasonal effect [30]. This model improves its accuracy level by adjusting the forecasted values based on a trend. The seasonal forecast is calculated as the previous forecast with trend added to the product of alpha and the difference of the previous actual value and the previous forecast with trend. The trend is calculated as the previous trend added to a product of a beta($\beta$) and the difference between the current seasonal forecasted value and the previous forecast with trend.

$$
\begin{aligned}
f_t &= fit_{t-1} + \alpha(A_{t-1} - fit_{t-1}) \\
T_t &= T_{t-1} + \beta(f_t - fit_{t-1}) \\
fit_t &= f_t + T_t
\end{aligned}
\tag{5}
$$

### 2.4.3 Simple Moving Average (SMA) Model

SMA model is the simplest method that perform forecasting by calculating an average from the past data towards the recent data. The model has to be parameterized with the number of steps it should take towards forecasting of the future values. The algorithm will start to calculate from the past data towards the recent data. [30] said the objective of SMA is to smooth the past data to estimate the trend cycle component by computing the moving average by dropping the oldest observations and including the next observation. The weakness of this model is that its forecasting mechanism focuses only on recent data ignoring the past data. This model assigns equal weights on the regressed subset data to predict for the next observation. The formula is presented below.

$$f_t = \frac{1}{k} \sum_{j=1}^{k} Y_{t-j} \tag{6}$$

Where k represents the order or the step of the moving average. The summation will start from the recent observation $(Y_{t-1})$ of the selected subset and move towards the old observation of $Y_{t-j}$ subset.

### 2.4.4 Weighted Moving Average (WMA) Model

This model is similar to SMA, it makes use of the order movement, and calculates the average from the selected subset of data. The predicted value is highly related to the subset of the previous values. However, each regressed subset is manually assigned a higher weight that is $0 > a < 1$, and it will decay towards the oldest observation in the subset. It is conventional that these weights are summed to 1. The formula is represented below.

$$f_t = \frac{1}{k} \sum_{j=1,r=1}^{k} Y_{t-j} W_r \tag{7}$$

Whereby $W$ is the vector of user defined weights based on the order process of the WMA.

### 2.5 Indigenous Knowledge

Even though the use of science and technology to monitor vegetation is escalating in every direction. In Africa, the use of machines and remote sensing technology has not been widely adopted and fully utilized due to poverty, educational level and cultural norms. Unemployment rate has been a trending concern in South Africa; education level is also dissatisfying, according to the statistics 18.6% of the South African farmers never went to school, while 56.3% never reached Grade 12 education [7].

Most African farmers still retain and maintain the use of indigenous knowledge than technology. Africa is the continent that still preserves, manage and share IK from generation to generation as it is crucial for social and economic development especially in rural Africa [26]. Over the course of history and up to this day, traditional local communities have continued to rely heavily on their own indigenous knowledge systems in observing the environment and dealing with natural disasters [27]. It is unique to a given culture or society and it is the basis for local level decision making in agricultural health care, food preparation, education and natural resource management [26]. It is a collection of a vast of body of knowledge on disaster prevention and mitigation, early warnings, preparedness and response acquired through observation and study, and is often based on cumulative experience handed down from generation to generation [27]. IK covers diverse areas of importance for society, spanning issues concerned with the quality of life from agriculture and water to health [41]. IK can also be defined as systematic body of knowledge acquired by local people through the accumulation of experiences and intimate understanding of the environment in a given culture [15]. It can also be explained as a formulation of expertise based on an observation of natural phenomena.

Although IK is considered as a valuable resource in sustainable development and peace building, it is not fully utilized by many domains such as government, donors, scientists and so forth [35]. According to [32] in western oriented academic circles and investigation, African voice is either side-lined or suppressed, and this is witnessed when IK and methods are ignored or not taken seriously. The notion of the static nature of indigenous knowledge has been disproved through numerous examples showing how IK can be changing continuously, especially as a culture or a community develops and grows, and is subject to changing environmental, cultural, physical and economical stressors [41].

Even though western science and technology are seen as a reliable resource, the use of scientific tools such as scientific weather forecasts in Africa is hampered by many technological challenges while their utilization is dismal [25].

As a way forward, [1] declare that IK and SK (scientific knowledge) can be merged together as long as IK is well collected and archived in a systematic manner. The integration of science, technology and indigenous knowledge as a way of performing information dissemination will help the farmers to respond to the forecast and cope with suboptimal climate impacts. In addition, [12] states that although the generation of knowledge has been confined by science alone, the emergence of a new contract between science and society has renewed knowledge management and production stakes. Evidence showed that local knowledge can and must be integrated with information and technology in efforts to improve the rural livelihoods ([10, 19, 24]). These researchers further enlighten that the integration of IK and science has proved its viability for the past decades and has expanded in the field of medicine, engineering, artificial intelligence, machine learning, social and economic sciences and other domains.

Some few researches are presented below: [27] explained the integration of both science and IK to diagnose types of hazards in diverse environmental and cultural settings. [22] proved the merge of IK and modern science as a bridge to forecast an early warning of drought, so to implement the strategies for preparations by the local communities. Further, [4] proposed a middleware that will integrates the heterogeneous data sources with IK based on a unified ontology for an accurate IoT-based drought early warning system (DEWS). [24] proposed the participatory geographic information systems as an organizational platform for the integration of traditional and scientific knowledge in contemporary fire and fuel management. Finally, [18] explained the integration of local knowledge and science to address the economic consequences of driftwood harvest in a changing climate.

# 3   Methodology

Mixed method approach was deemed most applicable because it enables elicitation of ideas and views of the phenomena in order to get descriptive and accurate findings. The sample of 50 farmers were interviewed while 100 surveys were distributed to the community of uMgungundlovu region in Pietermaritzburg South Africa. Among the selected farmers, 15 of them were growing sorghum and beans, 10 of them were growing wheat and peas and 25 were growing maize. The purposive sampling strategy was used, where by these farmers were selected on the basis that they are educationally and technologically illiterate, they are not equipped with irrigation systems and rely heavily on indigenous knowledge to perform cropping. During the interview, farmers were requested to state down the challenges that they are facing when using IK knowledge system alone to determine the onset of favourable weather season, crop monitoring and crop health and yield prediction. They accentuate on the impact of climate change on their crop health and yield and the impact of biotic (pests, crop diseases and other crop intruders) and abiotic (soil fertility) to their crop yield.

They were further requested to list the indigenous knowledge indicators that they use to foresee the onset of rains and winter season. Because IK indicators have different impacts towards the onset of favourable weather season, farmers were guided on scoring each indicator on a scale of 1 to 10.

The survey that was distributed to the local community was comprised of close and open-ended questions. The aim of the survey was to get the local insights about climate change, its impact on their vegetation and livestock, strategies that they use conserve water from rains and so forth.

The IK indicators and their associated weights together with local insights analysed from the surveys and interviews were documented for further processing.

# 4   Implementation

During the implementation phase, the system was developed based on the following domains.

- Determine the season onset
- Crop monitoring
- Crop health prediction

## 4.1   Determine the Season Onset

The indigenous knowledge, satellite imagery and machine learning were used to foresee the oncoming favourable weather season in the next three weeks. The summer season was identified with the successive rains and warm temperature while the winter season was identified with cold dry season (Fig. 1).

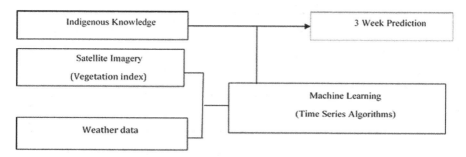

**Fig. 1.** Three-week prediction of season onset using three knowledge systems

### 4.1.1 Indigenous Knowledge

*Data Preparation.* Number of seasonal IK indicators associated with weights were obtained during the methodology phase. The indicators were clustered in to summer season and winter season. These indicators were stored in a file tagged with their appropriate weights. The weights were ranging between 0 and 1 where 0 represent no impact and 1 represents high impact.

*Data Processing.* The mobile app was developed whereby the user will first interact with the list of available IK indicators depending on the type of crop they want to cultivate and will be requested to select the indicators that they have observed from the environment in the last few days. The system will calculate the average percentage of the selected IK weights from the sum of all weights. The formula is presented below where $\sum_{b=1}^{k} L_b$ represents the selected weights and $\sum_{i=1}^{n} F_i$ represents the total weights.

$$AVG\_IK = \left( \frac{1}{\sum_{i=1}^{n} F_i} * \sum_{b=1}^{k} L_b \right) * 100 \qquad (8)$$

### 4.1.2 Satellite Imagery

*Data Preparation.* Previous years monthly Pietermaritzburg's satellite images were requested from MODIS satellite. The edge detection algorithms were used to extract uMgungundlovu region from each satellite image. From the extracted region, the average NDVI was calculated using the formula below where N represents the number of either NIR or Blue pixel values.

$$AVG\_NDVI = \left\{ \frac{1}{N} \sum_{i=1}^{n} \frac{NIR_i - B_i}{NIR_i + B_i} \right\} \qquad (9)$$

The aim of performing the above operation was to get one value that will represent the level of vegetation greenness on each extracted image. The average NDVI value which ranges between .1 and <1 was further converted in to percentage weight based on the type of crop needed to be cultivated (summer or winter crop) using the algorithm presented below (Fig. 2).

```
if(crop_type = 'summer') then
    if(avg_ndvi >0 AND avg_ndvi < 1) then
        percentage=((avg_ndvi)/.99)*100
    else then
            percentage=0
else then
    if(avg_ndvi > 0 AND avg_ndvi < 1) then
        percentage=(.1/avg_ndvi) *100
    else then
        percentage=0|
```

**Fig. 2.** An algorithm that assigns weight to average ndvi value

The calculated weights were sent to the time series models of machine learning. Four models were trained which are SMA, WMA, LES and DES. The RMSE (Root Mean Squared Error) formula was used to calculate the error rate of the models (Table 1).

**Table 1.** Representation of model evaluations

| Times series models | RMSE |
| --- | --- |
| SMA | 11.9 |
| WMA | 21.2 |
| LES | 15.6 |
| DES | 17.8 |

The SMA model outperformed other models, and it was used to perform four months' average NDVI predictions. The selection of four months was to cover the life span of the summer crops. The monthly predictions were converted into weeks so it will be easier to extract value based on a certain week. The values were sent to the cloud for further processing.

**Data Processing.** Immediately after the average percentage of the selected IK indicators is calculated, the system will extract the next three-week average NDVI percentage and integrate them together.

The main reason average NDVI is utilized on the prediction of favourable weather season is because number of researches showed that vegetation greenness increases during the onset of rains and depreciates during the onset of winter season. Therefore, tracking the vegetation greenness can give insight of the onset of the favourable weather season.

### 4.1.3   Climate Data

*Data Preparation.* The previous years' weekly rain and temperature data of Pietermaritzburg was obtained from South African climate data provider. These variables were analysed by the four-time series models which are WMA, SMA, LES and DES. The

WMA model outperformed other models with the error rate of 7.9. It was selected to predict the next four months 'weekly predictions to cover the life span of summer crops. The data was sent to the cloud for further processing.

*Data Processing.* Immediately after the average IK is calculated, the system will extract the next three-week rain and temperature predictions from the cloud and will be converted in to one weight. The following algorithm will be used to evaluate the type of crop needs to be cultivated (summer or winter crop), level of rains in millimeters and level of temperature in degree Celsius (Fig. 3).

```
if(crop_type = 'summer') then
  if(rain_level >= MIN_RAIN AND rain_level<=MAX_RAIN) then
    if(temp_level >= MIN_TEMP AND temp_level <= MAX_TEMP) then
      weight=((temp_level/MAX_TEMP)*40)+(rain_level/MAX_RAIN)*60
    else if(temp_level <MIN_TEMP) then
      weight=((temp_level/MAX_TEMP)*40)+(rain_level/MAX_RAIN)*60
    else then
      weight=√((temp_level/MAX_TEMP)*40) + √(rain_level/MAX_RAIN)*60
  else if (rain_level<MIN_RAIN) then
    weight=(rain_level/MIN_RAIN)*100
  else then
    weight=((rain_level/MIN_RAIN)*100)/2|
```

**Fig. 3.** An algorithm that assigns weight to climate data based on type of crop

In summary, the rain takes a high precedence when cultivating the summer crops while temperature takes a high precedence when cultivating the drought resistant crops.

### 4.1.4 Integration of Climate Data, Indigenous Knowledge and Satellite Imagery

The weights of all knowledge systems will be integrated together, and the average will be calculated. The user will receive the next three week forecast with a meaningful feedback.

$$FinalPrediction = \frac{\text{IK weight(\%)} + \text{climate data weight(\%)} + \text{vegetation index weight(\%)}}{3} \quad (10)$$

## 4.2 Crop Monitoring

The observation by an indigenous knowledge expert will be made on crops. The farmer will use the app to scale the health properties of the crops. These include crop greenness, leave size and stem size, soil health and fertility, level of crop pests and other crop intruders, crop diseases, and other properties. The system will calculate the average scaling done by the farmer. The results will be stored in a cloud. The farmer will monitor the crop health daily or at least 4 times per week. The scaling of each property ranges from 1 to 100, where 1 represent very weak health and 100 represents excellent health.

The formula below was used to obtain the average percentage of the monitored results where $\sum_{i=1}^{n} \frac{F_i}{100}$ represents the summation of weights scaled out of 100.

$$AVG_{Monitoring(\%)} = \frac{\sum_{i=1}^{n} \frac{F_i}{100}}{n * 100} \qquad (11)$$

### 4.3  Crop Health Prediction

During this stage, the system will extract monitored results from the cloud and send them to machine learning algorithms to perform three-week crop health prediction. The system will automate the models' training, error rate calculation, best model selection and three-week crop health prediction. To add more weight to the predicted results, we integrated the 3-week forecast of climate data and average NDVI (Fig. 4).

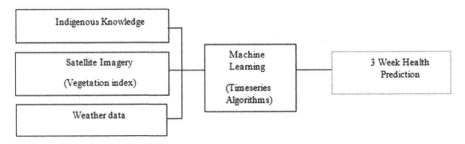

**Fig. 4.**  Three knowledge systems used to predict next three-week crop health

$$FinalPrediction = \frac{Prediction\ of\ Monitored\ Results(\%) + next\ 3\ week\ climate\ data(\%) + next\ 3\ week\ avg}{3}$$
$$(12)$$

## 5   Model Evaluation and Conclusion

For this paper we evaluated the system performance to foresee the onset of rains. For the system to perform forecasting, the weights of indigenous knowledge indicators observed from the environment need to be computed. The researchers with the help of indigenous knowledge experts analysed the rainy season IK indicators that were stated during the methodology phase. We categorised the IK indicators to months that they frequently appear. We further calculate the average weights of those indicators as shown on the table below (Table 2):

**Table 2.** Category of IK indicators

| Months | AVG_IK Indicators |
|---|---|
| January | 60% |
| February | 45% |
| March | 20% |
| April | 5% |
| May | 7% |
| June | 10% |
| July | 25% |
| August | 50% |
| September | 55% |
| October | 70% |
| November | 80% |
| December | 80% |

The data presented above was converted into weeks to perform weekly forecasts and was used as an input to the system. The 2019 weekly climate data (rain and temperature calculated percentage weights) was extracted. The 2019 satellite imagery data (percentages of average NDVI) was extracted. The system forecasts were tested against 2019 climate data as displayed below: We validated the system starting from week 1 of January to week 48 of December. The system forecasted the next three-week observations which were compared to the next three week climate data (Fig. 5).

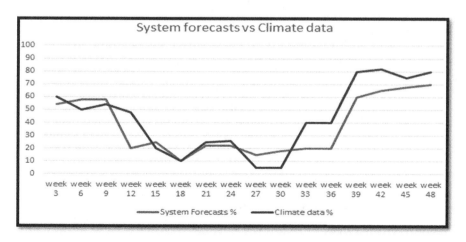

**Fig. 5.** System forecasts vs climate data chart

The mean percentage error(MPE) algorithm was used as modelled below.

$$mpe = \frac{100\%}{n} \sum_{j=1}^{n} \frac{a_j - f_j}{a_j}$$

The MPE of 15.35% was obtained. With the accuracy level of 84.65%. The system forecasts were again tested on 2019 satellite imagery data as displayed below (Fig. 6).

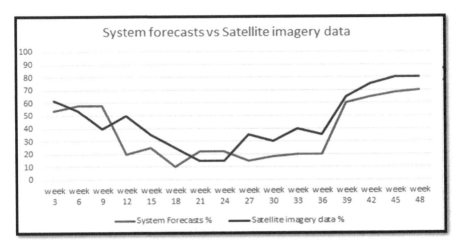

**Fig. 6.** System forecasts vs satellite imagery data chart

The MPE of 26.7% was obtained. With the accuracy level of 73.3%.

The system forecasts were tested against data from 2019 to 2017. The table shows the accuracy level of the prototype against climate data (Table 3).

**Table 3.** Accuracy measure against climate data

| Years | Accuracy measure against Climate data |
|---|---|
| 2019 | 85% |
| 2018 | 58% |
| 2017 | 62% |
| 2016 | 70% |
| **Average Accuracy** | **68.75%** |

The table below shows the accuracy level of the prototype's forecasts against satellite imagery collected data (Table 4).

**Table 4.** Accuracy measure against satellite imagery data

| Years | Accuracy measure against satellite imagery data |
|---|---|
| 2019 | 73% |
| 2018 | 61% |
| 2017 | 63% |
| 2016 | 69% |
| **Average Accuracy** | **66.5%** |

The correlation was calculated between the 2019 climate data and 2019 satellite imagery data. The 87.6% of the results was obtained. The correlation calculation was extended from 2019 to 2016.

From correlation statistics we conclude that the vegetation health is highly correlated with the rainy season. Therefore, we can analyse the vegetation health to infer to the onset of rains and suitable temperature (Table 5).

**Table 5.** Comparison of satellite and climate data

| Years | Satellite Imagery data vs Climate data (Correlation accuracy) |
|---|---|
| 2019 | 88% |
| 2018 | 81% |
| 2017 | 70% |
| 2016 | 83% |
| **Average Correlation** | **80.5%** |

The average system accuracy of approximately 70% was reached. Some of the factors that hampered the accuracy of the system are climate conditions on the satellite images, ever-green vegetation that cannot be related to any season, and some flaws observed from NDVI such as failure rate on highly saturated areas and so forth.

The model is easier and cheaper to use in contrast with other agricultural technologies. The paper valued the indigenous knowledge and emphasizes that indigenous knowledge can be mathematically calculated and integrated with the sophisticated technologies such as satellite imagery and machine learning algorithms. Although the model is not perfect, it is useful to many local farmers that mostly rely on rains for life.

# References

1. Agrawal, A.: Indigenous and scientific knowledge: some critical comments. Antropologi Indonesia (2014)

2. Ahmad, F.: Landsat ETM + and MODIS EVI/NDVI data products for climatic variation and agricultural measurements in Cholistan Desert. Global J. Hum.-Soc. Sci. Res. **12**(13), 1–11 (2013)
3. Aina, L.O.: Globalisation and small-scale farming in Africa: what role for information centres. In: World Library and Information Congress: 73rd IFLA General Conference and Council, pp. 1–8 (2007)
4. Akanbi, A.K., Masinde, M.: Towards semantic integration of heterogeneous sensor data with indigenous knowledge for drought forecasting. In: Proceedings of the Doctoral Symposium of the 16th International Middleware Conference, p. 2. ACM (2015)
5. Al-Kindi, K.M., Kwan, P., Andrew, N.R., Welch, M.: Remote sensing and spatial statistical techniques for modelling Ommatissus lybicus (Hemiptera: Tropiduchidae) habitat and population densities. PeerJ **5**, e3752 (2017)
6. Bringezu, S.: Visions of a sustainable resource use. In: Sustainable Resource Management, pp. 155–215. Routledge (2017)
7. Community Survey: Agricultural households. Statistics South Africa (2016)
8. Davey, J.: Sugar cane monitoring and analysis using remote sensing. Wooding Geospatial Solutions (2018)
9. Dhanachandra, N., Manglem, K., Chanu, Y.J.: Image segmentation using K-means clustering algorithm and subtractive clustering algorithm. Procedia Comput. Sci. **54**, 764–771 (2015)
10. Gerke, S., Evers, H.D.: Globalizing local knowledge: social science research on Southeast Asia, 1970–2000. J. Soc. Issues in Southeast Asia **33**(S), S242–S263 (2018)
11. Gibbs, H.K., Ruesch, A.S., Achard, F., Clayton, M.K., Holmgren, P., Ramankutty, N., Foley, J.A.: Tropical forests were the primary sources of new agricultural land in the 1980s and 1990s. Proc. Natl. Acad. Sci. **107**(38), 16732–16737 (2010)
12. Girard, N.: Knowledge at the boundary between science and society: a review of the use of farmers' knowledge in agricultural development. J. Knowl. Manag. **19**(5), 949–967 (2015)
13. Goldblatt, A.: Agriculture: Facts & Trends: South Africa. Ceo Wwf-Sa (2010)
14. Gomez, C., White, J.C., Wulder, M.A.: Optical remotely sensed time series data for land cover classification: a review. ISPRS J. Photogram. Remote Sens. **116**, 55–72 (2016)
15. Gupta, A.D.: Way to study indigenous knowledge and indigenous knowledge system. Cult. Anthropol. **373**, 393 (2012)
16. Jean, N., Burke, M., Xie, M., Davis, W.M., Lobell, D.B., Ermon, S.: Combining satellite imagery and machine learning to predict poverty. Science **353**(6301), 790–794 (2016)
17. Jiri, O., Mafongoya, P.L.: Managing vulnerability to drought and enhancing smallholder farmers resilience to climate change risks in Zimbabwe. In: Handbook of Climate Change Resilience, pp. 1–17 (2018)
18. Jones, C., Kielland, K., Hinzman, L., Schneider, W.: Integrating local knowledge and science: economic consequences of driftwood harvest in a changing climate. Ecol. Soc. **20**(1) (2015)
19. Kala, C.P., Farooquee, N.A., Dhar, U.: Prioritization of medicinal plants on the basis of available knowledge, existing practices and use value status in Uttaranchal. India. Biodiversity & Conservation **13**(2), 453–469 (2004)
20. Lei, L.I.U., Zhou, L.L., Bao, H.F.: Remote sensing image segmentation algorithm based on multiagent and fuzzy clustering. In: DEStech Transactions on Environment, Energy and Earth Sciences, (ICESEE) (2017)
21. Masih, I., Maskey, S., Mussá, F.E.F., Trambauer, P.: A review of droughts on the African continent: a geospatial and long-term perspective. Hydrol. Earth Syst. Sci. **18**(9), 3635 (2014)
22. Masinde, E.M.: Bridge between African Indigenous knowledge and modern science on drought prediction (Doctoral dissertation, UNIVERSITY OF CAPE TOWN) (2012)
23. Masinde, M., Mwagha, M., Tadesse, T.: Downscaling Africa's drought forecasts through integration of indigenous and scientific drought forecasts using fuzzy cognitive maps. Geosciences **8**(4), 135 (2018)

24. McBride, B.B., Sanchez-Trigueros, F., Carver, S.J., Watson, A.E., Stumpff, L.M., Matt, R., Borrie, W.T.: Participatory geographic information systems as an organizational platform for the integration of traditional and scientific knowledge in contemporary fire and fuels management. J. Forest. **115**(1), 43–50 (2016)

25. Mwagha, S.M. and Masinde, M.: Scientific verification of weather lore for drought forecasting– the role of fuzzy cognitive mapping. In: Proceedings of the IST-Africa 2015 Conference, Lilongwe, Malawi, pp. 6–8 (2015)

26. Owiny, S.A., Mehta, K., Maretzki, A.N.: The use of social media technologies to create, preserve, and disseminate indigenous knowledge and skills to communities in East Africa. Int. J. Commun. **8**, 14 (2014)

27. Pareek, A., Trivedi, P.C.: Cultural values and indigenous knowledge of climate change and disaster prediction in Rajasthan, India (2011)

28. Pavlovsky, G.: AGRICULTURAL RUSSIA: On the Eve of the Revolution. Routledge, London (2017)

29. Picchioni, F.: Monitoring the effects of changing food prices on food and nutrition security: the minimum calorie expenditure share (MCES) (Doctoral dissertation, SOAS University of London) (2017)

30. Prema, V., Rao, K.U.: Development of statistical time series models for solar power prediction. Renew. Energy **83**, 100–109 (2015)

31. Qiu, J., Wang, X., He, S., Liu, H., Lai, J., Wang, L.: The catastrophic landside in Maoxian county, Sichuan, SW China, on June 24, 2017. Nat. Hazards **89**(3), 1485–1493 (2017)

32. Owusu-Ansah, F.E., Mji, G.: African indigenous knowledge and research. African J. Disabil. **2**(1), 30 (2013)

33. Ravinder, H.V.: Determining the optimal values of exponential smoothing constants-does solver really work? Am. J. Bus. Educ. **6**(3), 347–360 (2013)

34. Roncoli, C., Ingram, K., Kirshen, P.: Reading the rains: local knowledge and rainfall forecasting in Burkina Faso. Soc. Nat. Resour. **15**(5), 409–427 (2002)

35. Ross, A., Sherman, K.P., Snodgrass, J.G., Delcore, H.D., Sherman, R.: Indigenous Peoples and the Collaborative Stewardship of Nature: Knowledge Binds and Institutional Conflicts. Routledge, London (2016)

36. Sabini, M., Rusak, G., Ross, B.: Understanding Satellite-Imagery-Based Crop Yield Predictions. Technical Report. Stanford University. http://cs231n.stanford.edu/reports/2017/pdfs/555.pdf. Accessed 23 Oct 2017

37. Silver, D., et al.: Mastering the game of Go with deep neural networks and tree search. Nature **529**(7587), 484–489 (2016)

38. Sowmya, D.R., Rao, S.A., Shenoy, P.D., Venugopal, K.R.: Generation of digital elevation map for steep terrain region using Landsat-7 ETM + Imagery. In: 2018 International Conference on Data Science and Engineering (ICDSE) (pp. 1–5). IEEE (2018)

39. Swain, K.C., Zaman, Q.U., Schumann, A.W., Percival, D.C., Bochtis, D.D.: Computer vision system for wild blueberry fruit yield mapping. Biosys. Eng. **106**(4), 389–394 (2010)

40. Thakur, N., Maheshwari, D.: A review of image classification techniques. Int. R. J. Eng. Technol. (IRJET) **4**(11), 1588–1591 (2017)

41. Tharakan, J.: Indigenous knowledge systems for appropriate technology development. In: Indigenous People, p. 123 (2017)

42. Verbesselt, J., Hyndman, R., Newnham, G., Culvenor, D.: Detecting trend and seasonal changes in satellite image time series. Remote Sens. Environ. **114**(1), 106–115 (2010)

43. You, J., Li, X., Low, M., Lobell, D., Ermon, S.: Deep Gaussian process for crop yield prediction based on remote sensing data. In: AAAI, pp. 4559–4566 (2017)

44. Zhao, Y., et al.: Genome-based establishment of a high-yielding heterotic pattern for hybrid wheat breeding. Proc. Natl. Acad. Sci. **112**(51), 15624–15629 (2015)

# A Multi-level Smart Monitoring System by Combining an E-Nose and Image Processing for Early Detection of FAW Pest in Agriculture

Sèmèvo Arnaud R. M. Ahouandjinou[1]([✉]), Manhougbé P. A. F. Kiki[2],
Prince E. N. Amoussouga Badoussi[1], and Kokou M. Assogba[2]

[1] Institut de Formation et de Recherche en Informatique (IFRI), Université d'Abomey-Calavi
(UAC), Cotonou, Benin
`ahou.arn@gmail.com, arnaud.ahouandjinou@uac.bj`
[2] Ecole Polytechnique d'Abomey-Calavi, Université d'Abomey-Calavi (UAC),
Laboratoire LETIA, EPAC, Cotonou, Benin

**Abstract.** Fall Armyworm whose scientific name is Spodoptera frugiperda is a pest which have a large destructive activity of cornfields in sub-Saharan Africa. Fall Armyworm is a pest causing significant economic harm in Africa. In this work, we proposed to develop a smart monitoring system through several level. Each level of the proposed monitoring system is used to control and to detect the pest early. The aim is therefore to develop a system for the early detection of fall armyworm, these eggs, larvae and its adult form on image in order to anticipate the damage it can cause and to prevent its proliferation. First of all, the proposed monitoring system is based on an e-nose to analyze the odors that are released in the environment by fall armyworm. Then, we use image processing techniques based on image segmentation to detect the presence of pest through the damage caused to the plants and leaves its environment. We offers through this work, a smart monitoring system for Early Detection of FAW (EDFaw) by combining an e-nose and the plant leaf image segmentation. Several experiments have been done to test the proposed system and the results of the image segmentation.

**Keywords:** Smart farming · Fall Armyworm (FAW) · Multi-level monitoring · Early detection · E-nose · Image processing

## 1 Introduction

West African countries benefit from climate and favorable terrain for agriculture. This agricultural potential enables the countries of this zone to cultivate a good number of seeds such as maize, cowpeas, rice, yams, pineapples, palm nuts [1]. Agriculture is an important pillar for development of countries despite the efforts that are made to secure it. It has many difficulties such as the invasion of insect pests. Pest control plays a crucial role in farming for without it, plants will die or not bear fruits. Pests are a natural enemy to farmers because they hinder farm production [1]. Farmers have to use different methods

© ICST Institute for Computer Sciences, Social Informatics and Telecommunications Engineering 2020
Published by Springer Nature Switzerland AG 2020. All Rights Reserved
J. P. R. Thorn et al. (Eds.): InterSol 2020, LNICST 321, pp. 20–32, 2020.
https://doi.org/10.1007/978-3-030-51051-0_2

of controlling pests. Common forms of pest control involves traps usage, field burning, air guns, hunting, using poisoned bait, natural rodent control, destruction of infected plants, poison spraying, sterilization, and eliminating breeding grounds through drainage of still water or proper management of waste. By implementing one of these methods, farmers can fully maintain the sound health of their farms and agricultural produces. However, these techniques are main factors in soil water contamination and soil depletion. Another solution is the use of Genetically Modified Organisms (GMOs) [1], which have proved to be very effective but with no impact on the environment. Thereby, apart from the various ethical problems they raise, they also lead to health complications for both consumers and farmers. Nevertheless, monitoring pest population is important and it is currently a key issue in crop protection. In a farm, it is fluently operated by repeated surveys by a human. This is a task and time consuming activity, and it would be important for farmers to have an efficient system of doing this work automatically. To fix this problem, we propose to design a smart sensor implanted in wireless network which uses an electronic nose architecture that is able to monitor the smells level characterizing the arrival of pests in the farm.

The main goal of this work is to propose smart systems for digitizing agriculture. All this contributes to the development of a smart, precise and ecological agriculture to address the harmful effects of climate change, depletion of agricultural production resources, environmental unfriendly methods struggling against pests. A review of different methods of fighting against pests and specifically the fall armyworm tells us that this problem is still relevant. No solution now offers a safe guarantee to farmers against pest attacks. Agricultural activities monitoring is an important tool in the early detection of plant diseases from symptoms at the parasite control stage during flowering and maturity. Indeed, in the phase of pest control in order to resist plant diseases in agriculture, the current solution requires the massive use of phytosanitary products that are dangerous for crops, the agricultural environment, and the health of both farmers and consumers [2].

Another purpose of this work is to respond to a new agronomic challenge in the context of agro-ecology through the development of a new method of pest control by using a smart crop monitoring system. Then, we propose a new approach to the fight against fall armyworm by proposing a multilevel monitoring strategy for the early detection of the pest on the cornfields. The proposed strategy is based on smart sensors by combining of a set of usual agricultural parameter measurement sensors (temperature, humidity) and electronic nose type sensors for the measurement of volatile substance in environment of the caterpillar using a brand new electronic system designed in order to detect caterpillar. The data provided by such sensors have to be collected in a way that reduce the energy consumption of the sensors as they could be in place for several month periods. An unmanned aerial vehicle will be used to fly over crops to gather sensors data such a detection method would contribute to the establishment of an effective control protocol against fall armyworm as soon as it is detected near crops. This would reduce the use of plant protection products, pesticides and the uses of GMOs, or considerably reduce the quantities usually used [4]. Also to use bio-pesticides at the appropriate time of the development of fall armyworm to annihilate it. This ecological method will therefore make it possible to fight efficiently against the fall armyworm while respecting the environment.

The paper is organized as follows. A Sect. 1 relates a context of this work and provides an overview of current methods of FAW control. In Sect. 2, we review the current computers tools for control fall Armyworm. Section 3 described the proposed a multilevel monitoring system for FAW early detection. Section 4 is devoted experiments results and discussion.

## 2    Current Struggle Methods Against Fall Armyworm

Many methods to control FAW are already being proposed and exploited. These approaches can be summarized in two broad categories: biological or biotechnological and behavioral approaches.

### 2.1    Biological or Biotechnological Approaches

**Genetically Modified Organisms:** To control pests, one of the recommended techniques is the use of genetically modified organisms (GMOs). Thus, although not developed for FAW, the trans-genic maize called "maize BT" has been controlled in Africa. Maize has been genetically modified by integrating genes from the Bacillus thurigiensis (BT) bacteria that produces insecticidal proteins that kill crop pests. The use of BT maize has in some cases, led to a reduction in insecticide use, pest control, and conservation of beneficial natural enemies and higher profits for farmers. However, these benefits may be short-lived because insect populations are able to adapt to BT proteins through the evolution of resistance [3]. Indeed, Spodoptera frugiperda has developed resistance to BT Maize in America and stem borers (Busseola fusca) have done the same less than two years after the deployment of BT Maize in the fields. Also, the ratio between the costs of supplying transgenic maize and the non-intensive production of most farmers makes it difficult to use this solution in the long term. It should also be noted that the consumption of products derived from transgenic plants is a cause of diseases such as cancer.

**Pesticides:** It involves the use of natural elements such as lime, salt, oil and soap as control measures to reduce the use of chemical pesticides. Lime and ash are very alkaline. Farmers also use local botanical pesticides (neem, chilli, local plants) [5]. However, this technique is expensive for people who do not always have the desired result. This leads to a high use of chemical pesticides with its disadvantages, which are soil contamination and groundwater contamination.

**Fertilizers:** Several studies have shown the effect of corn fertilization on the growth and mortality of FAW larvae and sometimes even the difference in the effects of FAW when using chemical fertilizer or organic fertilizer (manure). Differences between the two types of fertilizer were observed on: FAW larval growth, presence of natural enemies, FAW larval mortality, and cornfields infestation levels (percentage [%] of infested plants). However, in Brazil, chemical ferti-lizer resulted in significantly higher levels of FAW infestation in maize than treatments that did not use fertilizer, or organic fertilizer. The use of chemical fertilizers also impoverishes the soil and makes subsoil water unsuitable for consumption.

**Natural Enemies:** Some plants (e.g. beans and squash) are natural enemies of FAW because they emit chemicals that the caterpillar does not like. These volatile compounds are therefore natural "re-pellents". Also, some plants (Tagetes lucida, Coriandrum, Sonchus oleracea, Ruta, onions etc.) at-tract or facilitate the proliferation of insects that are predators for FAW. These animals harmful to FAW include predatory mite insects (Earwigs or Forficules, Terrestrial Beetles, Ladybugs, Spiders, Wasps, Bedbugs, Ants, etc.) that eat their prey, microbial parasites and pathogens (such as nematodes, fungi, bacteria, viruses and protozoa) that cause deadly infections and parasitoids. During inventories in the western hemisphere, nearly 150 different species of parasitoids have been found to be associated with FAW in various crops [6]. These natural enemies, although they are naturally present in agricultural areas, do not allow for a real control against FAW attacks. A deliberate increase in these natural enemies would also cause an imbalance in the ecosystem of the cultivation areas, thus posing a real ecological problem.

## 2.2 Behavioral Approaches

Managing FAW in maize fields begin with prevention. Some steps are recommended to farmers to reduce the impact of FAW on their fields.

**Crop Management:** Some approaches are recommended to farmers to reduce the impact of FAW on their fields.

**Harmonize the Sowing Date:** This method consists of harmonizing the sowing date, which means avoiding staggered sowing in the same area, as this would help to provide the FAW's favorite food locally, namely young maize plants. This is one of the most important recommendations for small producers. As mentioned above, in January 2018, some farmers in Kenya reported significant yield losses due to FAW on late planted maize plots compared to neighboring plots that had been planted earlier. This natural method only reduces the extent of damage to crops.

**Agricultural Diversity:** Diversity on the farm reduces the infestation of fall armyworm larvae and is favorable to natural enemies. Indeed, FAW females prefer to lay their eggs in corn. In a corn monoculture area, all the female has to do is fly over and lay these eggs and the contamination is done. But, when maize is grown in combination with other crops it is more likely to move, ignoring maize plants. Central American farmers have noticed that when they plant maize with other crops such as beans and squash (their traditional "milpa" systems), they have fewer pest attacks [7]. This method is also natural but does not protect farmers from attacks rather it just limits the damage.

**The Push-Pull Technique:** On the one hand, it consists of planting seeds around the cornfields that attract adult FAW females who leave their eggs there. On the other hand, insert seeds in maize plants that emit volatile compounds that repel FAW.

**Awareness Platform:** In order to raise awareness and keep the population informed about the various events related to the FAW, an awareness platform was developed by Bello-Bravo and collaborator in 2018. This platform is intended to be accessible to people with low literacy skills. Awareness platforms are very effective for sharing information. However, it does not allow us to be reactive enough and we are sometimes subject to false information from Internet users. The study of these different control techniques allows us to summarize their performance in Table 1.

**Table 1.** Performance summaries of FAW control systems.

| Control technique | Ecological | Cost | Speed of detection | Efficiency and effectiveness | Health problem | Autonomous | Production Quality for health |
|---|---|---|---|---|---|---|---|
| Pesticides | No | High | No | Average | Yes | No | Bad |
| GOM | No | High | No | Average | Yes | No | Bad |
| Fertilizers | No | High | No | Average | yes | No | Bad |
| Natural enemies | Average | Low | No | Average | No | No | Good |
| Crop management | Yes | Low | No | Average | No | No | Good |
| Awareness-raising platform | Yes | Low | Yes (average) | Average | No | No | Good |

# 3    Computer Tools Based Approaches for Struggle FAW

## 3.1    FAMEWS: FAW Monitoring and Early Warning System

The FAW Monitoring and Early Warning System (FAMEWS) is a free mobile application for Android cell phones from the Food and Agriculture Organization of the United Nations (FAO) for the real-time global monitoring of Fall Armyworm (FAW). This multi-lingual tool allows farmers, communities, extension agents and others to record standardized field data whenever they scout a field or check pheromone traps for FAW. Data from the app provides valuable insights on how FAW changes over time with ecology, to improve knowledge of its behaviour and guide best management practices. All collected data are used by FAO, countries and partners to map and monitor current infestations [10]. The app is designed to expand with the evolving needs of farmers, analysts and decision-makers, and can be used anywhere in the world. Fall Armyworm (FAW) (Spodoptera frugiperda), is an insect pest of more than 80 plant species. The larval stage of the insect causes dam-age to economically important cultivated cereals such as maize, rice, sorghum, and to vegetable crops and cotton. The pest is native to tropical and subtropical regions of the Americas. It was first detected in Central and Western Africa in early 2016, and has quickly spread across virtually all of sub-Saharan Africa. Because of trade and the moth's strong flying ability, it has the potential to spread further. Maize is the most infested crop in Africa.

### 3.2 Nuru

Nuru is an app that uses cutting-edge technologies involving machine learning and artificial intelligence. It runs on a standard Android phone and can work offline. "The new tool will help farmers recognize their new enemy and take immediate measures to stop it. Nuru becomes African farmers' newest ally against Fall Armyworm. Fall Armyworm first appeared in Africa in 2016, in West Africa, and then rapidly spread across all countries in sub-Saharan Africa in 2017, infecting millions of hectares of maize, and threatening the food security of more than 300 million people.

Many African farmers might have heard about Fall Armyworm but are seeing it for the first time, and are often unable to recognize it or unsure what they are facing. With the new application, they can hold the phone next to an infested plant, and Nuru can immediately confirm if Fall Armyworm caused the damage.

Nuru is a new tool will help farmers recognize their new enemy and take immediate measures to stop it. It complements FAO's recently launched Fall Armyworm Monitoring and Early Warning System (FAMEWS) mobile application [8], which builds knowledge on how and where the pest spreads, and what makes it less damaging," said Keith Cresman, FAO Senior Agricultural Officer who leads FAO's digital response to Fall Armyworm and other pests. An important feature on the new tool is that it can work offline so farmers can use it whenever they want it [9].

## 4  A Multilevel Architecture of a Smart Monitoring System for Early Detection of FAW

Through a study of different control methods of FAW, we can retain that the Fight against FAW is still relevant. Indeed, no solution at present offers a security guarantee to the farmer against FAW attacks. In this work, we propose a new approach to the control of FAW by build a multi-level monitoring strategy for the early detection of FAW on the field based on a combined set of agricultural parameter measurement sensors on one hand and electronic nose type sensors for the measurement of volatile substances in the track environment on the other hand. This technique represents a new approach in the fight against FAW because it uses an electronic system for automatic FAW detection. Such a detection method would contribute to the implementation of an effective control protocol for FAW as soon as it is detected in the vicinity of the crops. This would be achieved by no longer using pesticides and GMOs, or by significantly reducing the quantities usually used. But also to use biopesticides at the appropriate time in the development of FAW to annihilate it. This ecological method will therefore make it possible to control FAW effectively and in an environmental friendly way. The new approach to combating FAW comes from careful observation of FAW.

## 4.1  Level of Early Detection of FAW

Based on the life cycle and Behavior of the Fall Armyworm, we propose four level of fall armyworm detection.

**Detection Level 1:** The earliest phase to detect the presence of FAW in fields is the detection of adult FAW before it reaches the fields. We could then react (by setting up chemical barriers around crops for example) and prevent the intrusion of FAW into crops.

**Detection Level 2:** If it is not detected at the level 1, it must therefore be possible to detect the presence of FAW in the fields as soon as the intrusion occurs.

**Detection Level 3:** The third level consists of detecting the eggs laid on the leaves and this within a maximum of three days before the eggs hatch. This step is crucial in detection because FAW is at a stage in its life cycle that precedes the attack on crops. After hatching, we are the larval phase, which is the phase where the caterpillar creates the most damage. Its presence is materialized by the damage created on the plants. At this level, we used image-processing method to analyze the plant leaf images acquired by segmentation methods and to make a separation into several classes of images. This toil enables to detect the fall armyworm eggs, larvae and its adult form on images in order to anticipate the damage it can cause and to prevent its proliferation.

**Detection Level 4:** That is the last level of detection allows the caterpillar to be identified before it goes underground to become adult and proliferate. At this stage, Detection is no longer early, but it is still possible to react before the infection spreads and interrupt the life cycle of the first generation of FAW in the vicinity. The early detection level is therefore subdivided into four step summarized in the Table 2.

**Table 2.**  Different levels of FAW detection

| | Detection level | | | |
| | Early detection | | | Detection |
| Level | Very | Average | Few | Starting of the attack |
| Detection moment | Before adult FAW coming in the crops | Upon adult FAW entering in the crops | Detection of FAW eggs | Detection of larvae or attacks on leaves |

The below diagram (Fig. 1) related the proposed algorithm of fall armyworm multi-level detection. This diagram describes the sequence of different actions according to the monitoring system levels. Indeed, the first level of monitoring is based on the pheromone approach. At this step, the electronic nose is used to detect the volatile and odoriferous substances characterizing the early presence of the fall armyworm.

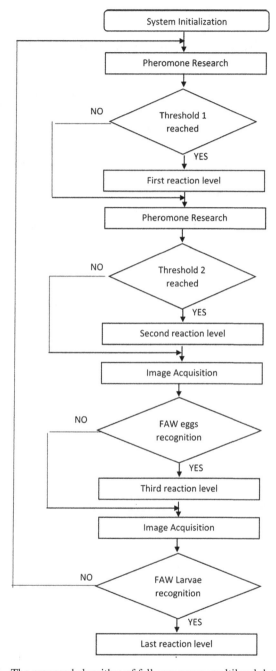

**Fig. 1.** The proposed algorithm of fall armyworm multilevel detection.

1. A deduction threshold is set in relation to the measurements of the chemical components performed by the electronic nose.
2. If the set threshold is reached, an early detection alarm of the caterpillar in the field is triggered so that more efficient control measures are triggered.
3. In the opposite case where the set threshold is not reached, the second level of monitoring is triggered which uses a computer vision system of image processing by the segmentation of the images of leaves of plants. At this stage, image segmentation can detect the presence of eggs or larvae of fall armyworm.

### 4.2 A Multilevel Monitoring System for Early Detection of FAW

The FAW first two detection levels are based on the identification of female FAW pheromone secretion. The density of pheromones identified help to know if the adult FAW is yet to be around crop or if it is already been there. This mainly involves the detection of (Z)-9-tetradecenyl acetate (Z-9-14: OAca) contained in the sexual pheromone of Spodoptera frugiperda. The last two detection levels are based on the volatile substances emitted by the plants when they enter into contact with adult FAW when plants are digested by FAW and when eggs are laid. At the fourth level of the system, we use image segmentation techniques to detect the damage and damage caused by caterpillar attacks on corn leaves.

**First and Second Levels. Electronic structure of the FAW detection system based on the Electronic Nose.** Fall Armyworm detection is based on an electronic nose and decision making system. The electronic nose is subdivided into three main parts. The proposed architecture for detection is shown in Fig. 2.

- **The air sampling system:** This is an important part of the system which allows the air sample to be taken for analysis. It is the mechanical part of the system that consists a metal enclosure equipped with solenoid valve and pump to control the air to be analyzed in the measuring enclosure.
- **The detection system:** This part is organized around of a group of sensors and signal conditioning circuits that are the reactive parts of the E-nose. It is mainly based on

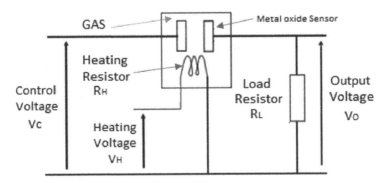

**Fig. 2.** Circuit diagram of the conditioning circuit of a metal oxide gas sensor.

semiconductor type metal oxide (MOSFET) transducer or resistive sensors that are installed in the measurement enclosure. Their electrical parameters (conductivity, resistivity) are modified as soon as they enter into contact with volatile substances such as pheromones. $V_0$ is the Output voltage of the E-nose of which is computed by Eq. (1) based on $G_{MOS}$ estimation through to use $V_c$ and $V_0$ with the resistor $R_L$ by Eq. (2). With GMOS the conductivity of the Metal oxide sensor.

$$V_0 = \frac{R_L}{R_L + \frac{1}{G_{MOS}}} V_C \tag{1}$$

$$G_{MOS} = \frac{1}{R_L} \times \frac{V_0}{V_C \times V_0} \tag{2}$$

- **The computer processing system:** Processor is a main component of this part. When the sensors detect a volatile substance, a specific response corresponding to the digital measurement of all sensors is recorded and accessible in one memory.
- **The decision system:** This part is very important in the detection system because it takes the data from the E-nose and compares them with specific signatures of the pheromones and volatile substances sought to identify the presence of FAW. Many methods can be used to realize pattern recognition, in our case signal profile recognition. The non-parametric method based on neural networks, for example, it is based exclusively on measured data for signal characterization. See in Fig. 3, the global architecture of the E-nose system to monitor the specific odor of the fall armyworm.

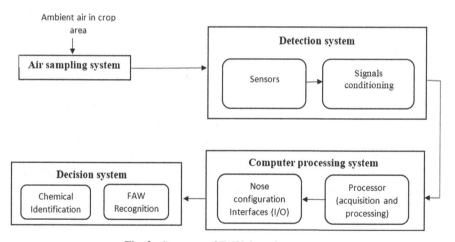

**Fig. 3.** Structure of FAW detection system.

**Levels Third and Four. Image processing Tools for Early Plant Diseases Detection on Leaf.** Fall Armyworm detection is also based on plant leaf image segmentation. We use region-based segmentation approach in a credibility context [2]. This approach has the advantage to take into account the segmentation model of all the sources of noise during the acquisition step. We proposed to use a new segmentation method which we develop in the context of plant disease leaf detection by combining three features and the potential noise source using TBM Framework. In our approach, we used the framework of transferable belief function to model the different potential sources of acquisition noise that are taken into account when extracting image features that have been negatively impacted by its noise. Hence, the robustness of the proposed technique against noise [2]. In addition, different features of the image were extracted and merged into one by exploiting the cautious information combination rules provided by the TBM tool to enhance the sowing performance and power of the segmentation algorithm. Experimental results show that the proposed method is appropriate for dealing with plant disease leaf image segmentation and has certain robustness for noise, and effective and accurate image 0segmentation method in the field of plant disease detection [12]. In the future, we will further compare the potential benefits and limitations of the other categories existing method against image segmentation methods and explore a fast disease leaf image segmentation method.

## 5  Experiments and Results

In a global tresholding algorithm, we use an arbitrary value for the threshold value. Therefore, how do we know that a value we have selected is good or not. The answer is, test method and error [11]. Nevertheless, consider a bimodal image (In simple terms, a bimodal image is an image which histogram has two peaks). For this image, we can roughly take a value in the middle of these peaks as a threshold value, right. This is what Otsu binarization does. Therefore, in simple terms, it automatically calculates a threshold value from the histogram of the image for a bimodal image (For images that are not bimodal, binarization will not be accurate) [11]. The Fig. 4, shows two results obtained as images of a FAW and its eggs (via the Otsu algorithm). To evaluate the proposed algorithm, we define and use two parameters which are Local Consistency Error (LCE) and Processing Time (PT in seconds). The measure of coherence between Martin's segmentations is based on two errors calculated in each pixel: an error of V with respect to R and an error of R with respect to V. If the pixels belongs to the region Vj in the truth-terrainand to the region Ri in the result image, these errors are: E (s) = card (Vj\Ri)/card (Vj) and E'(s) = card (Ri\Vj)/card (Ri). E (s) is 0 if Vj is a subset of Ri and is equal to 1 if the intersection of the two regions is reduced to pixels [11].

The dissimilarity between segmentation result and reference segmentation is then measured by the local error of coherence. The latter is estimated with Eq. 3.

$$LCE(R, V) = \frac{1}{A} \sum_{S} \min \left\{ E(s), E'(s) \right\} \tag{3}$$

| Type of image | Original image | ground truth image | Result | LCE | PT |
|---|---|---|---|---|---|
| Eggs 1 | 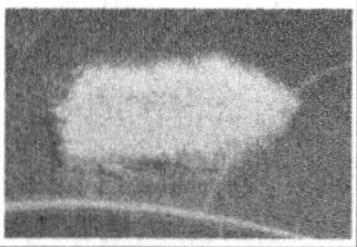 |  | 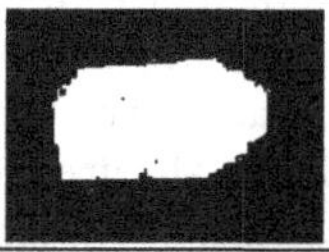 | 5.2726e-06 | 2 |
| Eggs 2 | 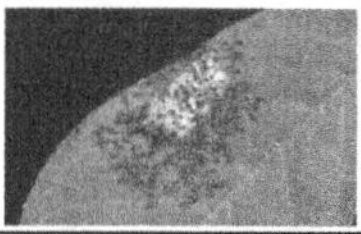 | 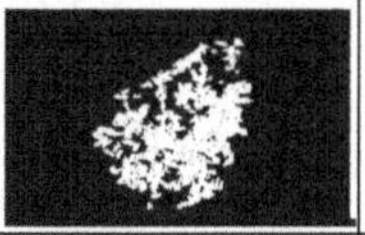 |  | 5.8576e-06 | 2 |
| larvae |  | 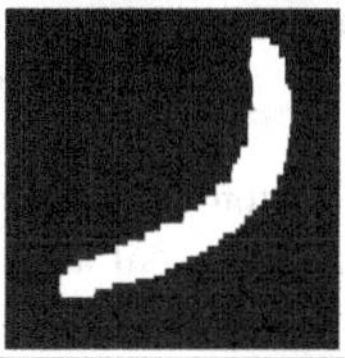 |  | 1.6693e-05 | 1 |
| Adult FAW | 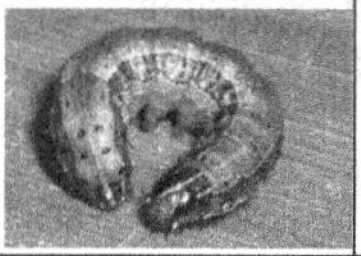 | 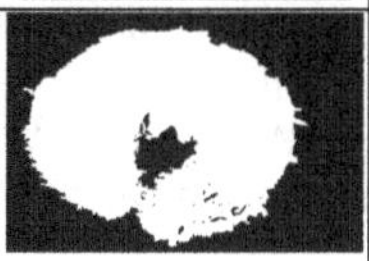 |  | 3.1335e-06 | 5 |

**Fig. 4.** Results of FAW detection image segmentation.

## 6   Conclusion

Fall Armyworm is a scourge of agriculture that must be eradicated. The multi-level early detection technique based on the electronic nose offers a better future for ecological control of FAW by avoiding the harmful effects due to the use of pesticides and GMOs. An integrated control method, using the different control techniques at the right time, will ensure efficient agriculture. Based on the results obtained, region based approach technique segmentation method is sensitive to noise but also the starting condition. In our approach, we used the framework of transferable belief function to model the different potential sources of acquisition noise that are taken into account when extracting image features that have been negatively impacted by its noise. Hence the robustness of the proposed technique to be robust against noise. In addition, three different features of the image were extracted and merged into one by exploiting the cautious information combination rules provided by the TBM tool to enhance the sowing performance and power of the segmentation algorithm. So, that our work can be a competing contribution of the NURU application, we deem it necessary to improve it, by:

- The addition of other segmentation techniques such as: region growth, split algorithm and merge and the bubble algorithm.
- Improvement of pre-processing operations (filtering, histogram equalization, etc.).
- Assessment of the infestation level of cornfields.

# References

1. Ahouandjinou, A.S.R.M., Kiki, P.M.A.F., Assogba, K.: Smart environment monitoring system by using sensors ultrasonic detection of farm pests. In: 2017 2nd International Conference on Bio-engineering for Smart Technologies (BioSMART), Paris, pp. 1–5 (2017)
2. Ahouandjinou, A.S.R.M., Motamed, C.: Robust Image Segmentation for Early Plant Diseases Detection on Leaf. In: 20ième Colloque CORESA, COmpression et REprésentation des Signaux Audiovisuels, CORESA 2018, Poitiers, France, 14 Novembre (2018)
3. Goergen, G., Kumar, P.L., Sankung, S.B., Togola, A., Tamò, M.: First Report of Outbreaks of the Fall Armyworm Spodoptera frugiperda (J E Smith) (Lepidoptera, Noctuidae), a New Alien Invasive Pest in West and Central Africa. PLoS ONE 11(10), e0165632 (2016)
4. Fatoretto, J.C., Michel, A.P., Silva Filho, M.C., Silva, N.: Adaptive Potential of Fall Armyworm (Lepidoptera: Noctuidae) Limits Bt Trait Durability in Brazil. J. Integr. Pest Manag. 8(1) (2017)
5. Bateman, M.L., Day, R.K., Luke, B., Edgington, S., Kuhlmann, U., Cock, M.J.W.: Assessment of potential biopesticide options for managing fall armyworm (Spodoptera frugiperda) in Africa. J. Appl. Entomol. 142(9), 805–819 (2018)
6. Food and Agriculture Organization of the United Nations, Integrated management of the fall armyworm on maize: a guide for farmer field schools in Africa (2018)
7. Midega, C.A.O., Pittchar, J.O., Pickett, J.A., Hailu, G.W., Khan, Z.R.: A climate-adapted push-pull system effectively controls fall armyworm, Spodoptera frugiperda (J E Smith), in maize in East Africa. Crop Prot. 105, 10–15 (2018)
8. Spodoptera frugiperda (fall armyworm). https://www.cabi.org/isc/datasheet/29810#toPictures
9. http://www.fao.org/news/story/en/item/1141889/icode/
10. Food and A. O. of the United Nations. Integrated management of the Fall Armyworm on maize. Food and Agriculture Organization of the United Nations (2018)
11. Bergounioux, M. (ed.): Introduction au traitement mathématique des images - méthodes déterministes. MA, vol. 76. Springer, Heidelberg (2015). https://doi.org/10.1007/978-3-662-46539-4
12. Thangaduraiand, K., Padmavathi, K.: Computer vision image enhancement for plant leaves disease detection. In: IEEE, World Congress on Computing and Communication Technologies, Trichirappalli, India, pp. 173–174 (2014)

# Indigenous and Scientific Knowledge of Soil Regulation Services, and Factors Effecting Decision-Making in Agricultural Landscapes in the Terai Plains of Nepal

Jessica P. R. Thorn[1,2]([⊠]) [iD]

[1] York Institute for Tropical Ecosystems, Department of Environment and Geography, University of York, Heslington, York, North Yorkshire YO10 5NG, UK
jessica.thorn@york.ac.uk
[2] African Climate and Development Initiative, University of Cape Town, Geological Sciences Building, Upper Campus, Level 6, 13 Library Road, Rondebosch 7700, South Africa

**Abstract.** Rapid degradation of soil regulation services is a growing concern for agricultural producers worldwide, with the potential for adverse impacts on agricultural productivity, food security, and livelihoods. Yet, data integrating observations of soil nutrient and physical status with farmers' knowledge of soil fertility is lacking, while landscape-level empirical assessments remain limited. In this paper, it is argued that a deeper understanding of the benefits and trade-offs of management practices currently employed by farmers to secure soil nutrients could help to promote improvements in natural resource management, agricultural productivity and efficiency. Using the case of the Central and Western Terai Plains of Nepal in 2012–2014, rice-cultivated soil parameters were estimated, and 354 respondents were interviewed to determine the cropping systems, soil nutrient status and risks, indigenous soil classification systems, and key biophysical, institutional, economic and risk perception factors effecting decision-making. Findings reveal farmers are acutely aware of the main causes of soil degradation and until today, these issues continue to be of critical importance. To counter this degradation, farmers employ a diversity of landscape-level practices to secure optimal crop yields and soil nutrients. However, farmers have limited access to agricultural extension services and scientific monitoring and apply fewer mineral fertilisers than previously reported. Additional investments are required to optimize farmers' practices and soil regulation services, such as cooperation for knowledge innovation systems, public/private extension, organisation for co-management, integrated nutrient management, and private forestry on farms. The case illustrates local knowledge and incremental efforts to adapt to emerging risks remain the foundation to implement spatially targeted conservation measures and design adaptive land use plans.

**Keywords:** Soil regulation services · Soil conservation · Indigenous knowledge · Agriculture · Decision-making · Soil fertility status

© ICST Institute for Computer Sciences, Social Informatics and Telecommunications Engineering 2020
Published by Springer Nature Switzerland AG 2020. All Rights Reserved
J. P. R. Thorn et al. (Eds.): InterSol 2020, LNICST 321, pp. 33–51, 2020.
https://doi.org/10.1007/978-3-030-51051-0_3

# 1 Introduction

## 1.1 A Subsection Sample

At the global scale, nearly 30% of terrestrial lands have agricultural crops or planted pastures as a dominant land use [1], which can profoundly impact environmental systems and ecological functioning across the whole landscape [2, 3]. Today, despite increased political attention in recent years and research investments in enhancing sustainable agriculture, land conversion to agriculture rapidly continues, modifying habitats and degrading ecosystems [4]. Many least developing countries still rely heavily on their primary sector (i.e., agriculture) as an engine of economic growth and food security [5]. Yet, the majority of actions largely do not take into account the need to customize recommendations to particular agro-ecological conditions, local knowledge systems and cultural preferences [6]. Land managers, planners, conservationists and community development practitioners require information on current practices, and factors influencing farmers' decision-making to secure optimum soil nutrients for sustainable yields and livelihoods.

Across Asia, there are potentially significant gains for improved soil management. Particularly in Nepal, 78% of the workforce depends on agriculture and demand continues to grow. However, in the last 20 years in Terai Plains of Nepal (hereon referred to as the Terai) - an area stretching 1360 km from East to West with the Himalayan Churia foothills to the North and India to the South [7], yields of rice have remained static or gradually declined, and soil fertility decline is a common concern of farmers [8–11]. Over-utilisation and erosion of marginal lands is widespread, given a growing population, rising land values, scarcity and fragmentation, tenure insecurity and short-term responses to productive needs [9, 12, 13]. Correspondingly, since 2000, the Ministry of Agricultural Development's financing in the agricultural sector has retracted by 30%, fertiliser subsidies have dropped by 55% [14], national fertiliser production is at a deficit (in 2010 the country required 100 000 metric tons, producing 30 000), and rural access to fertilisers is frequently restricted by cross-border strikes over fuel imports [16]. One consequence of these challenges and associated poverty faced by many rural farmers is that much of the young generation migrates to India, to East Asian or Persian Gulf countries, to supplement family incomes [13].

There have been suite of multi-stakeholder private-public partnerships, government, and international and non-governmental aid assistance projects aimed at implementing soil conservation initiatives, such as inter alia soil amendment and testing (e.g., via Nepal Agricultural Research Council (NARC), District Agricultural Development Offices, Ministries of Forest and Soil Conservation, cooperatives, and micro-credit institutions); planting woodlots, hedgerows, or set aside areas or bio-engineering for slope stabilisation (e.g., via LI-BIRD, CARE International and agroforestry extension services); terracing (e.g., International Centre for Integrated Mountain Development); improving irrigation efficiency (e.g., Institute of Development Enterprises); flood protection (e.g., International Water Management Institute); installing and maintaining canals (e.g., World Health Organisation); and rainwater conservation ponds (e.g., World Wide Fund for Nature, Community Forestry User Groups). However, many initiatives have not yielded expected results. This is in part due to difference between the expectations of farmers and managers of public programmes (including extension agents, trainers, conservationists) of the ability of these programmes to make yield improvements, along limited national ownership in programs, duplication of efforts, and affordability of capital and agricultural inputs [10, 16–18].

Research over the last 20 years in Nepal has studied soil fertility enhancement and conservation techniques such as green manuring [20], legume intercropping [21], crop residue retention and tillage [22]. Various studies have examined farm-level factors affecting the adoption of new technologies under different climate and socio-economic scenarios (e.g., [19, 23, 24]). Another significant body of literature has documented perceptions of soil fertility, soil classification systems [25–28], and indigenous knowledge [29], yet recent evaluations have not been conducted. Yet, the necessary data is not available for the Central and Western zones of the Terai Plains of Nepal. Few studies have– integrated observations of soil's nutrient status or physical characteristics with farmers' knowledge of soil regulation services [11]. Landscape-level assessments remain limited [30]. We also have an insufficient understanding of what influences farmers' actual decision-making processes in relation to programme participation and adoption of recommended practices [19].

To address this fundamental knowledge gap, this study aims to assess soil nutrient and physical status in combination with farmers' knowledge of soil fertility at the landscape-level and unpack what factors influence farmers' decision making in the Terai Plains of Nepal. Specifically, chemical and physical soil surveys were conducted on forty rice-cultivated farms. Farmer interviews (n = 100), and focus groups with 140 farmers (n = 354) were used to determine cropping systems (i.e., landholding sizes, crop combinations, stocking rates, and labour time), indigenous classification of soils. Finally, key informant interviews and focus groups were used to investigate current and potential soil conservation measures (i.e., perceived benefits, trade-offs, opportunities, and constraints for adoption and level of use), and key factors determining farmers' decision-making. Results offer recommendations for effective land-use planning.

## 2  Materials and Methods

### 2.1  Study Area

Sampling was carried out in four landscapes between May and September 2012 in 22 village district committees (VDCs) within 40 wards: (1) four VDCs in Madi Valley, Chitwan district (N27°28.305′ E084°17.244′, 204masl), (2) six VDCs in Rupandehi district (N27°35.414′ E083°31.180′, 138masl), (3) six VDCs surrounding Gohari, Dang district (N27°50.783′ E082°30.068′, 256masl) (referred to hereafter as Dang), and (4) six VDCs in the Deukhuri Valley, Dang district (N28°03.086′ E082°18.712′, 597masl) (referred to hereafter as Deukhuri) (Fig. 1, Appendix 1). The climate is a warm-temperate zone, with a mean annual temperature of 24.6 °C (min = 18.2 °C, max = 31 °C), and rainfall ranging from 1000 to 2100 mm/a [31]. Elevation ranges from 108 to 658masl, and the main soil type is Dystrochrepts [32]. The region hosts a population of 708,419, with notable geographic, climatic, ethnic and social diversity [33]. Land use is largely subsistence-based, including cultivation, home gardens, mixed crop-livestock systems, non-timber forest product harvesting, river boulder and gravel mining, aquaculture, residential, and tourism. Rice (*Oryza sativa L.*) is the main staple crop, grown predominantly for local consumption during the monsoon season, and holding high economic, social, and cultural importance [34, 35].

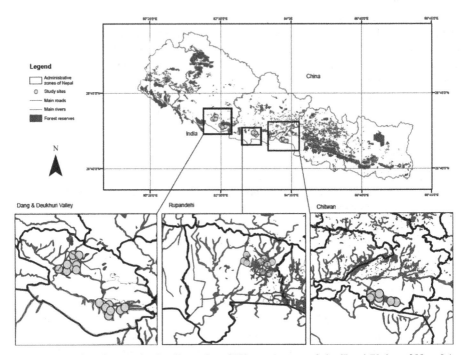

**Fig. 1. Map of study area in the Central and Western zones of the Terai Plains of Nepal (*n* = 40 villages).** Within each region, ten villages sampled were distributed across the hydroshed catchment within 200 km$^2$, surveyed using regional topographical maps of Nepal (1:25 000) sourced in 2012 from East View Cartographic Inc., Minneapolis in the USA, and the Ministry of Land Reform and Survey, Government of Nepal in Kathmandu. Farmers cultivate rice on 5.78 ± 2.33 ha (mean, SE) in the monsoon season (May – September) in terraced landscapes [43].

## 2.2   Cropping Systems

Data were available from farmers in forty villages and key informants (n = 354). Working with local partners, in each landscape the research team first met with the head of each village and key informants to describe the project objectives and obtain input on the study design[1]. The survey was then trailed with 40 respondents. One lead surveyor and three trained enumerators administered structured interviews with the self-identified

---

[1] Permissions to conduct the fieldwork from local communities were obtained, objectives were stated upfront to ensure respondents understood the purpose of the use of the information, and confidentiality/anonymity was ensured. Access to study sites was facilitated through NARC and a local organisation Friends Service Council Nepal, with ethical permissions rendered by the University of Oxford.

household head in each homestead or farm, in Nepali over 90 min between 06h00 and 09h00. To determine the cropping systems, questions were asked about landholding size, crop combinations, stocking densities, livestock use and fodder collection time and distance. As far as possible, the sample was stratified by age (25 to 67 years), sex (72.5% male, 27.5% female), caste (n = 9) and livelihood (n = 15). Representation by each caste group was taken into consideration during sampling, as traditionally there is some variation in farming practices following the Hindu caste system in Nepal (Tiwari, Sitaula et al. 2008). Respondents represented the castes of the Tharu (32.5%), Brahmin (27.5%), Chhetri (12.5%), Magar (7.5%), Dalit (7.5%), Gurung (5%), Sanyasi, Dura, and Teli (ea. 2.5%).

### 2.3 Soil Parameters

The procedure of in-situ soil analysis followed standard procedures using Hannah Instruments Professional Agricultural test kit (HI-3896, UK) [36, 37]. Abiotic chemical and physical indicators were used as proxies for soil regulation services. pH was measured using a colorimetric (halometric) indicator with a range of 4 to 9 pH (single increments). Available N was measured using a manual colorimetric method with Ned reagent. Available P was measured using a colorimetric method with ascorbic acid. Available potassium (K) was measured using a turbidimetric method using tetraphenulhorate reagent. Texture was assessed using a soil texture triangle test of particle size, indicating how much organic matter the soil can hold. Soil parameters were taken one month after planting and nutrient replenishment by manure or chemical fertilisers to the fields. Soil samples were taken randomly from ten fields in each landscape. Ten samples per field were obtained from the Ap horizon (0 to 15 cm) and amalgamated. To assess the indigenous soil classification system, farmers were asked to describe their system that forms the basis for crop selection, and agronomic cultural practices [32, 38, 39].

### 2.4 Perceived Factors Impacting Soil Quality Decline

We followed Bewket [40] and Vignola, Koellner et al. [23] by asking farmers about what they considered to be the salient risks to soil health, how this effects levels of production, erosion or input requirements, and if "general soil health" had changed in the last ten years. These factors were then ranked by importance. Salient risks were judged to be observable, well-known, to have an immediate effect, or high exposure on- or off-site [41, 42].

### 2.5 Strategies to Increase Soil Fertility, and Factors Determining Farmers' Decision-Making

Heads of households associated with the farms where ecological sampling was conducted, were asked to identify soil conservation practices, perceived benefits and trade-offs for soil regulation and production, opportunities and constraints for adoption, and level of use. Socio-economic, cropping system, and time-use data was also collected. Following interviews, transect walks were made on farms and the landscape within

250 m of homesteads to directly observe the soil's physical condition, and engage farmers in informal discussions about management practices. Informal interviews and focus group discussions with 140 farmers (a subset of the 354 respondents) provided additional information about farmers' perceptions, strategies and aided triangulation.

## 2.6 Policy Recommendations

A diverse range of interest groups ($n = 112$) were interviewed about constraints to soil conservation practices, the current role of local and extra-local institutions in promoting technologies, and effective policy recommendations. A total of 174 key informants were interviewed, including agricultural extension workers, academics, policy makers and conservation/development workers from the ward to international level (Table 1, Appendix 2, See [43]).

**Table 1.** Summary of representation from key informant interviews ($n = 174$), 14 operating internationally, 20 nationally, 11 regionally, 18 at the district level, 31 at VDC level, and 18 at the ward level. *(VDC: Village District Committees, INGOs: International non-governmental organisations).*

| Level | No. | % | Sectors | No | % | Institution type | No | % |
|---|---|---|---|---|---|---|---|---|
| Local (VDC) | 31 | 27.01 | Agriculture and food security | 40 | 35.71 | Community representative | 29 | 25.89 |
| National | 20 | 21.26 | Development | 36 | 32.14 | Government | 22 | 19.64 |
| Local (Ward) | 18 | 18.39 | Environment and climate | 20 | 17.86 | NGO | 17 | 15.18 |
| District | 18 | 12.64 | Risk reduction | 6 | 5.36 | Private sector | 15 | 13.39 |
| International | 14 | 12.07 | Finance and business | 6 | 5.36 | INGO | 14 | 12.50 |
| Regional | 11 | 8.62 | Education | 2 | 1.79 | Research | 12 | 10.71 |
| | | | Gender and health | 2 | 1.79 | Donor or media | 3 | 2.68 |

# 3 Results

## 3.1 Cropping Systems

Across the study area in the Central and Western regions of the Terai, the mean landholding is $5.12 \pm 4.78$ ha/household (mean, SE), and land has been continuously cropped for $6.56 \pm 1.63$ years. Twenty-three crop types were identified. Rice (*Oryza sativa* L.) comprises the main crop cultivated in 88% of fields, commonly intercropped with lentils *(Lens culinaris)* (45%), followed by maize (*Zea mays*) (65%), wheat (*Triticum aestivum*) (48%), and mustard (*Rassica juncea*) (38%). Seventy-eight per cent farm vegetables, herbs and trees are grown as cash crops[2]. Few farmers cultivate fruits, which are typically imported from India and sold in local markets. Crop variety selection depends on the grain and by-product yields (e.g., bedding for livestock stalls, feed or fuel). Alongside the cultivation of crops, the average household owns 12.55 livestock units, which is notably higher than that of the Mid-Hills (four livestock units) [44]. Goat and buffalo are the most common livestock, owned respectively by 53% and 50% of farmers, while 28% own cows and poultry, and 20% own oxen. Livestock are commonly reared for manure (by 73% of households), meat or milk (67%), manure for fuel (47%) and plastering using manure (43%), transport (20%), or risk insurance by sale (20%) (Table 2). Maintain livestock is a labour-intensive activity, on average, farmers walk 0.85 ± 0.9 km/day to collect fodder, specifically: 4.2 ± 2.39 h/day to collect fodder for goats, 2.71 ± 2.27 h/day for buffalo and 1.9 ± 0.89 h/day for cows. Livestock also have cultural value.

**Table 2.** Landholding and stocking density during the monsoon season in rice-based systems. Farmers cultivate the largest land area in Deukhuri (5.9 ± 4.93 ha), while farmers cultivate the smallest land area in Chitwan (3.6 ± 2.6 ha) *(M: mean; SD: standard deviation; SE: standard error)*.

| | Chitwan, Madi Valley | | | | Rupandehi | | | | Dang, near Ghorahi | | | | Deukhuri Valley, Dang | | | |
|---|---|---|---|---|---|---|---|---|---|---|---|---|---|---|---|---|
| | n | M | SD | SE | n | M | SD | SE | n | M | SD | SE | n | M | SD | SE |
| Farm size (ha) | 10 | 3.6 | 2.6 | 0.87 | 9 | 0.78 | 6.99 | 2.33 | 10 | 5.9 | 4.93 | 1.64 | 10 | 5.2 | 4.26 | 1.42 |
| *Livestock heads* | | | | | | | | | | | | | | | | |
| Buffalo | 10 | 13 | 1.42 | 0.45 | 10 | 110 | 1.15 | 0.37 | 10 | 6 | 1.07 | 0.34 | 10 | 23 | 2.21 | 0.7 |
| Small ruminant | 10 | 33 | 2.98 | 0.94 | 10 | 220 | 2.94 | 0.93 | 10 | 16 | 2.22 | 0.7 | 10 | 88 | 11.9 | 3.76 |
| Ox | 10 | 0 | 0 | 0 | 10 | 11 | 0.32 | 0.1 | 10 | 7 | 0.95 | 0.3 | 10 | 10 | 1.94 | 0.61 |
| Cattle | 10 | 4 | 0.97 | 0.31 | 10 | 88 | 1.4 | 0.44 | 10 | 7 | 1.25 | 0.4 | 10 | 4 | 0.7 | 0.22 |
| Pig | 10 | 0 | 0 | 0 | 10 | 00 | 0 | 0 | 10 | 1 | 0.32 | 0.1 | 10 | 5 | 0.97 | 0.31 |
| Poultry | 10 | 58 | 8.66 | 2.74 | 10 | 00 | 0 | 0 | 10 | 92 | 25.2 | 7.96 | 10 | 43 | 6.7 | 2.12 |
| Duck | 10 | 34 | 8.58 | 2.71 | 10 | 00 | 0 | 0 | 10 | 10 | 3.16 | 1 | 10 | 2 | 0.63 | 0.2 |

## 3.2 Soil Parameters

**Soil Texture, pH and Macronutrient Levels.** The mean soil pH in the wet season is 6.42 ± 0.81 (Table 3), meaning the soils are generally acidic, largely due to the acid-based parent material and inappropriate application of acidifying mineral fertilisers over

---

[2] For example, vegetables grown in the study area include potato, cauliflower, beans, cabbage, tomato, onion, ladyfinger, bitter guard, cucumber, bottle guard, carrot, lemon, garlic, peppermint, sunflower, chilli and coriander.

extended periods [45]. Nitrogen is typically at trace-low fine concentrations, with the lowest levels found in Rupandehi and the highest in Deukhuri. This can be attributed to continuous cropping of high N-feeding plants, and reduced fallowing [21]. Phosphorous is typically at low-medium concentrations, with the lowest levels found in Rupendehi and the highest in Chitwan. In most sites, potassium is at trace-low concentrations, except in Chitwan where it is medium grade. Physical analysis indicates soil texture is dominated with clay, except in Deukhuri where the soil is dominated by fine sand.

**Table 3.** Analysis of soil sampled (0–15 cm depth). Macronutrients are graded according to trace (1), trace-low (2), low-medium (3), medium (4), medium-high (5) and high (6). Values are represented as the mean and standard error.

| Parameter | Chitwan | Rupandehi | Deukhuri | Dang | All sites |
|---|---|---|---|---|---|
| Soil pH | 6.6 ± 0.07 | 6.61 ± 0.36 | 5.83 ± 0.3 | 6.8 ± 0.12 | 6.42 ± 0.15 |
| Soil total available Nitrogen (N) | 1.8 ± 0.29 | 1.33 ± 0.17 | 2.3 ± 0.42 | 1.5 ± 0.22 | 1.77 ± 0.16 |
| Soil total available Phosphorus (P) | 3.1 ± 0.41 | 1.89 ± 0.35 | 2.4 ± 0.36 | 2.67 ± 0.22 | 2.51 ± 0.2 |
| Soil total available Potassium (K) | 3.9 ± 0.1 | 2.33 ± 0.24 | 2.2 ± 0.34 | 2.67 ± 0.45 | 2.8 ± 9.18 |
| Stony texture (>2 mm) (%) | 2.00 | 4.00 | 12.00 | 0.00 | 4.50 |
| Coarse sand (2–0.02 mm) (%) | 17.50 | 1.63 | 8.50 | 5.00 | 8.16 |
| Fine sand (0.2–0.02 mm) (%) | 32.00 | 15.63 | 44.50 | 19.30 | 27.86 |
| Silt (0.02–0.002 mm) (%) | 15.50 | 10.63 | 14.00 | 33.80 | 18.48 |
| Clay (<0.002 mm) (%) | 33.00 | 68.13 | 21.00 | 41.80 | 40.98 |

**Indigenous Soil Classification System.** Farmers have their own criteria for distinguishing local soil types to evaluate production potential, species composition and agronomic cultural practices. Khrishna describe: *"It is not about the amount of land we have, it's the quality and the fertility of the land"* (27/05/2012, Beora, Rupandehi). Systems have been developed and transferred orally over many generations, as follows:

*Colour:* Colour is a partial indication of organic and mineral content, pH levels, age of the soil, parent material, and structural stability. For example, farmers typically consider darker or black soils more fertile, with a higher carbon and moisture content and cation-holding capacity. Red soils are generally considered high in iron and aluminum, low in P, and are an indication of a long-leaching process.

*Topsoil Texture:* Texture, the size of individual particles, is a partial indication of the supply of nutrients, water, and air, that are necessary for plant root development and soil workability. For example, heavy-textured and stony soils require higher labour inputs for ox/hand ploughing than light-textured soils. Land close to riverbanks is considered sandy and therefore unstable, with a higher risk of flooding and sedimentation. Silt is considered good for cultivation, as it is softer and fertile, but has poor water retention.

*Depth:* Farmers consider deep soils (>1 m) to generally have a higher water-holding capacity, and appropriate to plant crops with deeper roots.

*Slope and Altitude:* Flat lands often have lower likelihood to erode, and therefore are considered more suitable for cultivation, but low, waterlogged land is susceptible to nutrient leaching.

*Proximity to Forests:* Farmers consider land closer to densely or vegetated areas to have higher fertility.

### 3.3 Perceived Factors Driving Soil Fertility Decline

Seventy-four percent of respondents perceived a decline in soil fertility over the last ten years, according to indigenous soil classification attributes. The most highly ranked underlying reason reported by 89% of respondents for this was deforestation. Large-scale deforestation is driven by greater demand for building material, energy, agricultural use, and grazing. Deforestation causes severe soil erosion, reducing productivity in soils upstream, and sedimentation in water downstream [46]. Second, soil is contaminated by excess and indiscriminate application of mineral fertilisers (e.g., Murate of Potash (MOP), Diammonium Phosphate (DAP)) or pesticides (e.g., Goxamin, Thaitan, Krioloxy, Metacide). Excess inputs increase soil hardness, break down soil structure, reduce organic matter, and consequently cause long-term productivity decline. Much of the N applied to rice crops is lost by volatilisation, denitrification, and leaching [22, 47]. Third, organic fertiliser availability is declining. Livestock is less desirable to keep with increased direct costs. Fodder availability is declining with heightened land scarcity and forest restrictions. Moreover, urbanisation and international labour migration are lowering succession rates [9]. Consequently, farmers do not have a sufficient labour force and time to collect fodder or plough manually with oxen, buffalo, or hand. The majority of farmers (70%) are transitioning to mechanized tractors. Approximately 38% reported increased intensity of rainfall in short periods resulting in topsoil runoff, landslides and sedimentation of fields along river courses. Rainfall events are followed by extended periods of drought reducing vegetative cover, soil water infiltration capacity and moisture loss [48]. River-mining for building material exacerbates flooding intensity, widens river courses, increases agricultural land inundation, and irrigation water turbidity. Pests, pathogens and weed growth are other salient risks.

### 3.4 Strategies to Increase Soil Fertility

Farmers improve precision and manage risks through incremental adaptation and innovations, based on rich historical antecedents [49]. In total, 33 practices are employed individually or in combination. Appendix 3 lists the top 25 of these non-exclusive/interrelated practices. Beneficial practices are defined as those that supported the continued ability for the soil to sustain crop or animal growth over time through efficient recycling and provision of nutrients and water.

Nine methods of soil amendment are widely employed, using mineral fertiliser, farmyard manure (FYM), compost, green manures, decaying or living mulching, urine and faecal sludge, ash, vermicomposting, forest soil, or combined applications. To improve soil structure, stability, soil-water retention, slow water velocity and reduce nutrient loss, seven methods are used, i.e., farmers fallow, branch-pack, construct gabions, restrict river mining, post-harvest cover crop, and create ditches or bunds. To control erosion, farmers plant native woodlots and wildflower strips, contour hedgerows, or riparian buffer strips around farms, homesteads, riverbanks and communal areas. The most commonly grown plants to prevent erosion are *Dendrocalamus strictus, Leucaena leucocephala, Panax pseudo-ginseng, Cynodon dactylon* [50]. To increase soil organic matter (SOM), farmers reduce and amend the timing of tillage, or the ratio of chemical to organic fertiliser, retain crop residue, or selectively apply pesticides, fertilisers or herbicides.

To improve SOM levels, decomposition, and convert atmospheric N to usable ammonia N for plants many farmers intercrop (i.e., planting two or more temporary/permanent crops as a mixture of unstructured crops) [21, 51]. In 50% of cases a combination of at least three crops are cultivated, while in only 8% of cases one crop is planted. For example, farmers intercrop cereals with legumes, sesame, mustard or shade-grown crops between crop rows, underneath the main crop, or along farm boundaries.

Fifty-two percent of farmers rotate crops (i.e., cultivating single crops (type/variety) on a land parcel in one season, followed by another single crop in the following season [12]. For example, farmers rotate monsoon rice with winter wheat, cowpea, mustard, bamboo or chilli. Others rotate between land uses (e.g., crop-pasture-aquaculture). Rotation regenerates nutrients, reduces pest infestations, suppresses plant fungal and nematode pathogens in the soil, and allows farmers to cultivate crops with different water requirements. Farmers also commonly shift to new rice varieties every two to three years. In addition, 49% of farmers employ terracing with the land under irrigated *khet* or rainfed *bari* terracing being dependent upon the landform position and slope.

Consistent with evidence from other parts of Nepal (e.g., Pilbeam, Mathema et al. 2005, Paudel 2015), farmers traditionally place a high value on the use of FYM for organic fertiliser: 78% prepare and apply FYM. Farmers recognize the quality of the faeces of different animal species, and how the net movement of N from non-agricultural land to agricultural land varies according to fodder and livestock type. FYM is typically collected using household biogas compost pits, in-situ manuring, zero-grazing, and manually collecting untreated heaped compost.

Four of the seven types of chemical fertilisers used in Nepal are used in the study area [52]. Diammonium Phosphate (DAP) is most commonly applied by 60% of farmers at a rate of 0.11 kg/ha/season. Urea is applied by 53%, at a rate of 0.09 kg/ha/season, which is notably lower than reports of urea application in the Mid-Hills of 15 to 115 kg/ha/season [27]. Application rates of Murate of Potash (MOP) (0.004 to 0.034 kg/ha/season) and Zinc (0.014 to 0.027 kg/ha/season) are also much lower than previously reported [21]. Ammonium Sulphate (AS), Single Super Phosphate (SSP), Ammonium Phosphate Sulphate (APS) are not applied. However, these averages disguise the wide range of actual application rates, and fertiliser is often only applied to a portion of the total cropped area [27]. The ratio of organic to chemical fertiliser is 49:51, and is often combined (e.g., FYM with urea, DAP/MOP, residue, ash, green manure, or kitchen waste).

Ten species are used for green manuring (i.e., mixing plants into the soil), particularly on cultivated areas of rice and vegetables, which are considered to increase macronutrient levels. These include *Panax pseudo-ginseng, Bengal pogostemon, Achyranthes aspera,*

*Justicia adhatoda, Syzygium cumini, Albizia lebbeck, Artemisia indica/vulgaris, Leu-caena leucocephal,* and *Dendrocalamus strictus. Musa sapientum/paradisiac* is grown to increase the soil potassium content. *Sesbania* is a local grass grown to fix N and decompose quickly [50]. Previous studies have also shown the leaves of these plants have a higher macronutrient content than that of FYM compost (Table 4) [28].

**Table 4.** Estimated faeces voided, fertilizer applied and plant species used to enhance soil quality the monsoon season across all sites. **Adapted from Sthapit (1989); Khadka and Chand (1987); Subedi (1989).

| Estimated faeces voided | Kg/ha/day | Estimated fertiliser application rates | Kg/ha/season | Plant species commonly used to enhance soil fertility | Percentage (%) | | |
|---|---|---|---|---|---|---|---|
| | | | | | N | P | K |
| Buffalo | 45 | Diammonium Phosphate | 0.11 | *Justicia adhatoda* (Asuro) | 4.3 | 0.9 | 4.5 |
| Goat | 13.75 | Urea | 0.09 | *Artemisia indica/vulgaris* (Tite pate) | 2.1 | 0.2 | 4.1 |
| Cattle | 15 | Murate of Potash | 0.02 | *Albizia lebbeck* (Kalo siris) | 2.9 | 0.7 | 2.6 |
| Poultry | 0.74 | Zinc | 0.02 | *Sesbania sp* (Dhaincha) | 1.5 | 0.3 | 2 |
| | | | | Compost | 0.4 | 0.3 | 0.3 |

### 3.5   Factors Determining Farmers' Decision-Making in Soil Conservation Management

Farmers recognize the following interrelated factors to be most salient in determining the voluntary adoption of soil conservation interventions. There are many complex aspects of decision-making processes that evolve with changing societal values over time, but these are not addressed here [53].

**Perception of Risk:** Practices are adopted with benefits on-site (e.g., SOM, macronu-trients, macro/micro-fauna composition/activity, soil structural integrity, slope stabilisa-tion, texture, sediment profile) and off-site (e.g., reducing watercourse sedimentation or velocity) and which reduce risk (also shown in [54]).

**Knowledge and Experience:** Producers are more likely to take up a practice who have experience on their own land (territorial exposure) for a prolonged period of time (history of use), and if benefits are widely known. Access to new, clear technical knowledge that is crop/season/location-specific encourages adoption (also shown in [55, 56]).

**Biophysical Factors:** When determining conservation measures, farmers pay attention to crop requirements (e.g., seedling germination, crop growth rate, water), site-specific management history (e.g., origin of the land, seed bank, vegetation remnants), infrastructural access (e.g., roads, input suppliers, markets), and climatic conditions (e.g., precipitation, temperature, solar radiation, wind, evapotranspiration, soil moisture content) (also shown in [42]).

**Economic Factors:** Farmers are more likely to adopt practices which increase monetary utility or value, reduce production costs, or raise or stabilize yield of marketable goods (also shown in [56, 57]).

**Complementarity** (e.g., multiple uses such as shade, income generation with by-products or surplus products) and competitiveness (e.g., employing practices which minimize competition for nutrients, light, water or use) also determine whether practices will be adopted (also shown in [42]).

**Institutional Factors:** Practices are more likely to be adopted by farmers with good social capital for knowledge transfer, who participate in soil conservation programs, or have support from extra-local government agencies, NGOs, or communal institutions for technical training, demonstration, field visits, inputs, subsidies, financial transfers or enforcement of preventative legislation. Farmers with clear property rights or long-term rental agreements are more likely to adopt sustainable decisions regarding resource use (also shown in [58]).

## 4  Discussion

### 4.1  Comparison Between Indigenous Soil Classifications and Scientific Parameters

As this study has shown, Nepali farmers hold substantial knowledge on soil evaluation and classification, as revealed by their capability to categorize the soil's production potential based on various criteria (e.g., colour, texture, depth, slope, altitude, proximity to vegetated areas), and incrementally adapt to multiple stressors to improve the soil condition. Nepali farmers also have strong rationales for sustaining diverse soil conservation practices. It is critical to determine this knowledge because this it largely determines management approaches. However, despite knowledge and practice, more support is required to optimise soil fertility.

While some of farmers' observations were in close agreement with the level of the scientific observations, such as N and texture, for other parameters farmers lack accuracy, such as identifying the exact amounts of pH and minerals needed by their crops. Farmers do not have detailed information about the amounts of macro- and micronutrients in the soil, nor specific crops and appropriate inputs that are suited to particular soil types. Their diagnostic parameters are based mainly on visible, topsoil attributes of the soil. And changes in soil properties are only fully grasped when reductions in yield and growth performance are observed [59].

The limits to indigenous knowledge highlight the need for supplementation with scientific assessments, which can allow for the detection of changes not readily observable. In particular, scientific observations provide information on chemical properties and micronutrients below the soil surface. However, in the year prior to the survey, only 10% of respondents had access to scientific analyses of soil, partly because diagnostics are costly and time-consuming, and the diversity of soil classifications and taxonomies are difficult to grasp. Moreover, only 20% of farmers had contact with extension agents representing the District Agriculture Development Office, mandated to provide information of soil quality measurements and appropriate application of fertilisers. Therefore, beyond post hoc annual assessments of yield and soil regulation service, the effectiveness of conservation practices is not clear. For farmers who do have information access, blanket recommendations for fertiliser application often disregard soil type, or vary greatly depending on sources [60]. Meanwhile, NARC suggests most farmers do not adhere to recommended rates, timing and type of fertiliser application, and many do not have access to inputs: in the study area, application rates of fertiliser are lower than found in previous studies (e.g., [27, 61]).

Recognizing these barriers to information access and appropriate management practices, local knowledge can advance the scientific knowledge and vice versa. Indigenous classifications should be seen to complement, and not substitute scientific methods [59, 62]. Complementarity of the two knowledge systems can develop new paradigms for sustainable development. Looking forward, cooperation between researchers, government extension agents, agrovets, and farmers needs to be enhanced to improve diagnostic tools. To be successful, on-farm adaptive research needs to use a participatory approach, employing simple local or regional language when measuring soil parameters [59].

### 4.2   How Do We Incentivize Soil Conservation Practices at the Farm and Landscape Scale?

Farmers in the Terai require more scientific assessments of soil, and training in composting practices, integrated nutrient management, FYM production, cultivation of N fixing crops, and drainage techniques for saturated soil. To increase the uptake of soil fertility management practices, and woodlot cultivation, pluralistic approaches to extension services (e.g., volunteer extension agents, agrochemical dealers, commercial outgrower schemes, e-extension) could address strained staffing and financing, and should be accompanied by demonstration (e.g., [63]).

Although farmer-to-farmer learning is considered helpful [64], surveys indicated the exchange of information between farmers could be improved. Membership to farmer organisations has been shown to have a positive effect on adopting new practices via access to social capital, labour-sharing and credit [65]. However, technical assistance is needed to build in organisational, literacy and financial capacity, and meet registration requirements [66]. Shared learning and analyzing trade-offs within/across communities, can be promoted via knowledge sharing days, farmer exchanges, or experimental plots [67].

Cash and other livelihood incentives for soil management practices need to be at least equivalent or higher than other livelihood options. For example, farmers need to understand the economic benefits of using FYM for organic fertiliser, rather than for plastering, sale or fuel. To increase cash incentives, the sale of organic-certified products has potential to promote healthy soil, rich in organic matter, nutrients and microbial activity. Communities are organizing themselves to reduce marketing costs, centralize sales, lobby government, or independently construct roads, bridges, irrigation systems and storage systems. However, technical assistance is needed to promote local multi-product markets, link producers directly to national/international buyers, manage commercial contracts, improve product quality, credit access, post-harvest processing and handling [68]. Developing local markets to procure livestock can increase stocking rates and FYM production, as could zero-grazing zones, stall-feeding and fencing, distributing fodder seedlings, and installing cement troughs [69]. Furthermore, integrating private forestry on farms into the national forestry program could reduce pressure on forest and soil resources (and reduce respiratory/eye ailments associated with indoor fuel wood usage), as could up-scale decentralized renewable energy (e.g., biogas, solar energy) [70]. At the same time, community conservation concessions could encourage communal woodlot cultivation, with appropriate attention paid to compliance and enforcement.

All of these interventions and associated diverse actors operate within particular institutional and regulatory contexts. For example, bilateral negotiations between the Nepali and Indian governments could help control the import and use of low-grade chemical fertilisers, currently sold on the black market [14]. However, an analysis of which goes beyond the scope of this paper. At the same time, there is a need to ensure that financial incentives do not crowd-out intrinsic motivations for good soil management practices or lead to perverse outcomes, such as in the case of the Northeastern Chinese Sloping Land Conversion Programme which resulted in unintended impacts such as afforestation in marginal lands [71]. Aligning national food security and conservation aims is one way to reduce perverse subsidies that harm ecosystem service provisioning [72, 73].

Given the retraction of public spending in agriculture, innovative mechanisms are clearly needed to source additional streams of capital. Benefits have been shown in the coexistence of diverse public, private and mixed funding streams. Taxes are unlikely to be available, given that 48.4% of Nepal's population lives on less than $3.10/day (2011), while collection is challenging [74]. Payments to farmers for ecosystems service provision via tradable rights could offer some funding, and have been around for some time[3]. However, the nature of spatially heterogeneous landscapes in the Terai, with high temporal variability, means quantifiable regular tracking and verification at a national scale is complex, requiring specialized equipment, expertise and clarification of property rights.

---

[3] For example, the Gold Standard Biogas Voluntary Emissions Reduction pilot project, implemented by WWF since 2015, and the Reduced Emissions from Deforestation and Degradation plus (REDD+) readiness process was implemented by the Ministry of Forests and Soil Conservation and others since 2010.

# 5   Conclusion

This study aimed to assess soil nutrient and physical status in combination with farmers' knowledge of soil fertility at the landscape-level and unpack what factors influence farmers' decision making in the Terai Plains of Nepal. Evidence presented provides local indigenous knowledge and scientific information at the landscape scale of a wide range of soil fertility management practices currently employed in the Terai Plains of Nepal. The combination of knowledge systems may provide a means to engender participatory agricultural land use planning and agro-technology transfer [62, 75]. Incremental adaptation and innovations to emerging changes are based on rich historical antecedents. Decision-making is informed by risk perception, knowledge, experience, complementarity and competitiveness, as well as multiple economic, biophysical and institutional qualities valued by farmers, who form part of social-ecological systems. This study provides a deeper understanding of the suite of soil management practices currently employed, to help to optimise precious resources and time, and incorporate flexible, adaptive land management, and recognition of the contribution that farmers make to conservation. Initiatives could be replicated in other areas with similar contexts – thereby contributing to the reconciliation of food production and conservation and the ability of farmers in the Terai Plains of Nepal to meet multiple Sustainable Development Goals, such as 2 (zero hunger), 3 (health and wellbeing), 12 (responsible consumption and production),13 (climate action), and 15 (life on land).

Future longitudinal research is needed to evaluate the effectiveness of practices both in terms of landscape-outcomes and specific interventions, including soil amendment technologies that are affordable, reduce dependence on external inputs and are appropriate for changing climatic conditions (e.g., bio-char, bacteria/fungi, vermiculture). Future research could investigate the information farmers require regarding landscape configurations for intercropping, contour planting, planting native woodlots, or set-aside habitat in farmed landscapes. Research could also study targeted "fit-for-purpose" practices that, inter alia, reduce erosivity, increase nutrient cycling, efficiently use space, improve water retention and slope stabilisation, and suppress weeds and pests. Additionally, research could also investigate the information farmers require on the most appropriate types/lengths of crop rotation, or crop cultivars (e.g., genetically modified organisms, wild relatives. Finally, future research could explore relationships between farmer age, education, exposure to training, access to government subsidies, and the uptake of new or short-/long-term practices.

**Acknowledgements.** We are grateful to the farmers who took part in the survey, particularly Bhim Chaudhury, Rhada Chaudhury, Mangu Chaudhury, Shem Narayan Chaudhary, Laksmi Chaudhury, Jhup Lal Bhudhathoki, Chandra Kumari Mahata, Hiramati Grau, Kopila Paudel, the Garima Farmers' Cooperative and Sagarmatha's Women's Group. Research assistance was provided by Anita Bake, Dev Kala Dumre, Renu Shakya, Binay Mahargen, Sindhu Sapkota, Raju Acharey, Dharma Raj Ghimre and Asma K.C. Thanks are due to the advisory support of Thomas F. Thornton, Kathy J. Willis and Ariella Helfgott and the comments of anonymous reviewers. Friends Service Council Nepal and Nepal Agricultural Research Council provided in-country institutional support.

**Funding.** This work was supported by Climate Change Agriculture and Food Security (CCAFS) research program on Systemic Integrated Adaptation of the Consultative Group of International Agricultural Research, the Long-term Ecology and Resource Stewardship Lab, and Merton College at the University of Oxford.

# References

1. Ramankutty, N., Mehrabi, Z., Waha, K.: Trends in global agricultural land use: implications for environmental health and food security. Ann. Rev. Plant Biol. **69**, 789–815 (2018)
2. Clark, M., Tilman, D.: Comparative analysis of environmental impacts of agricultural production systems, agricultural input efficiency, and food choice. Environ. Res. Lett. **12**, 064016 (2017)
3. FAO, WFP, and IFAD: The state of food insecurity in the world 2012. FAO, Rome (2012)
4. Willis, K.J., Gillson, L., Knapp, S.: Biodiversity hotspots through time: an introduction. Philosoph. Trans. Roy. Soc. London B **362**, 169–174 (2007)
5. FAO: The role of agriculture in the development of Least-Developed Countries and their integration into the world economy. Commodities and Trade Division. Rome, FAO (2002)
6. Pingali, P.L.: Green revolution: impacts, limits, and the path ahead. Proc. Natl. Acad. Sci. United States of America **109**(31), 12302–12308 (2012)
7. Ministry of Agriculture and Cooperatives: Statistical information on Nepalese agriculture. Singh Durbar, Kathmandu, Nepal, His Majesty's Government, Ministry of Agriculture and Cooperatives, Agribusiness Promotion and Statistics Division (2004)
8. Government of Nepal: National Adaptation Programme of Action (NAPA) to Climate Change. Kathmandu, Nepal, Ministry of Environment (2010)
9. Bhandari, B.S., Grant, M.: Analysis of livelihood security: a case study in the Kali-Khola watershed of Nepal. J. Environ. Manag. **85**, 17–26 (2007)
10. Maskey, N.L., Bhattarai, S., Peoples, M.B., Herridge, D.F.: On-farm measurements of nitrogen fixation by winter and summer legumes in the Hill and Terai regions of Nepal. Field Crops Res. **70**, 209–221 (2001)
11. Desbiez, A., Matthews, R., Tripathi, B., Ellis-Jones, J.: Perceptions and assessment of soil fertility by farmers in the Mid-Hills of Nepal. Agricult. Ecosyst. Environ. **103**, 191–206 (2004)
12. Government of Nepal: Agriculture district summary National Census 2011/12. Kathmandu, National Planning Commission Secretariat Central Bureau of Statistics (2012)
13. Devkotaa, S., Upadhyay, M.P.: Agricultural productivity and poverty reduction in Nepal. Faculty of Research and Creativity 6 (2013)
14. Joshi, K.D., Conroy, C., Witcombe, J.R.: Agriculture, seed, and innovation in Nepal: Industry and policy issues for the future. Washington D.C, International Food Policy Research Institute (2012)
15. Dixon, A.: World Bank can help build Kathmandu-Terai fast track. The Kathmandu Post. Kathmandu, Ekantipur (2016)
16. Bista, D.B.: Fatalism and Development: Nepal's Struggle for Modernisation. Sangam Books Ltd., Kathmandu (1991)
17. Shrestha, B., Maskey, S.L., Shrestha, R.K., Tripathi, B.P., Khadka, Y.G., Munankarmi, R.C., et al.: Soil fertility management: farmers' practices and perception in the hills of Nepal. Lumle Technical Paper No. 2000/4. Pokhara, Lumle Agriculture Research Station (2000)
18. Ghimire, L.S.: Main problem is design stage of foreign aid projects in Nepal. New Spotlight New Magazine. Kathmandu. 8 (2014)
19. Illukpitiya, P., Gopalakrishnan, C.: Decision-making in soil conservation: application of a behavioural model to potato farmers in Sri Lanka. Land Use Policy **21**(4), 321–331 (2004)

20. Ali, M.: Quantifying the socio-economic determinants of sustainable crop production: an application to wheat cultivation in the Terai of Nepal. Agricult. Econ. **14**, 45–60 (1996)
21. Shreshtra, G.: Role of legume intercropping in sustainable farming in Mid-Hills of Nepal. Third SAS-N Convention, Kathmandu (2008)
22. Sah, G., Shah, S.C., Sah, S.K., Thapa, R.B., McDonald, A., Sidhu, H.S., et al.: Tillage, crop residue and nitrogen level effects on soil properties and crop yields under rice-wheat system in the Terai region of Nepal. Global J. Biol. Agricult. Health Sci. **3**(3), 139–147 (2014)
23. Vignola, R., Koellner, T., Scholz, R.W., McDaniels, T.L.: Decision-making by farmers regarding ecosystem services: factors affecting soil conservation efforts in Costa Rica. Land Use Pol. **27**(4), 1132–1142 (2010)
24. Lamarque, P., Artaux, A., Barnaud, C., Dobremez, L., Nettier, B., Lavorel, S.: Taking into account farmers' decision-making to map fine-scale land management adaptation to climate and socio-economic scenarios. Landscape and Urban Planning **119**(Supplement C), 147–157 (2013)
25. Tamang, D.: Indigenous soil fertility management in the Jhihku Khola watershed: soil fertility and erosion issues in the middle mountains of Nepal. In: Proceedings of the Workshop on the Jhikhu Kola Watershed, Nepal (1991)
26. Tamang, D.: Indigenous soil fertility management in the hills of Nepal: lessons from an east–west transect. Report No. 19, Kathmandu, HMG Ministry of Agriculture/Winrock International Research (1992)
27. Pilbeam, C.J., Mathema, S.B., Gregory, P.J., Shakya, P.B.: Soil fertility management in the Mid-Hills of Nepal: practices and perceptions. Agricult. Hum. Values **22**(2), 243–258 (2005)
28. Paudel, K.C.: Implication of forage and livestock production on soil fertility. FAO, Rome (2015)
29. Thapa, B., Walker, D.H., Sinclair, F.L.: Indigenous knowledge of the feeding value of tree fodder. Anim. Feed Sci. Technol. **67**, 97–114 (1997)
30. Uddin, K., Murthy, M.S.R., Wahid, S.M., Matin, M.A.: Estimation of soil erosion dynamics in the Koshi Basin using GIS and remote sensing to assess priority areas for conservation. PLoS ONE **11**(3), e0150494 (2016)
31. Lumbini Crane Conservation Centre: Lumbini crane conservation centre (2011). http://lumbinicrane.org. Accessed 26 Dec 2011
32. Pariyar, D.: Nepal Country Pasture/Forage Resource Profiles. FAO, Rome (2006)
33. Government of Nepal: Nepal Census of Agriculture 2001/2 (2002). http://www.cbs.gov.np. Accessed 26 Dec 2014
34. Malla, G.: Climate change and its impact on Nepalese agriculture: review paper. J. Agricult. Environ. **9**, 62–71 (2008)
35. Rana, R.B., Garforth, C., Sthapit, B., Jarvis, D.: Influence of socio-economic and cultural factors in rice varietal diversity management on-farm in Nepal. Agricult. Hum. Values **24**(4), 461–472 (2007)
36. Larson, W.E.: The dynamics of soil quality as a measure of sustainable management. Defining soil quality for a sustainable environment. In: Doran, J.W., Coleman, D.C., Bezdicek, D.F., Stewart, B.A. (eds.) Soil Science Society of America, Madison, WI, USA, vol. 35, pp. 7–51 (1994)
37. Kim, H.-J., Kenneth, A.S., Hummel, J.W.: Soil macronutrient sensing for precision agriculture. J. Environ. Model. **11**, 1810–1824 (2009)
38. Paudel, B.R., Udawatta, R.P., Kremer, R.J., Anderson, S.H.: Soil quality indicator responses to row crop, grazed pasture, and agroforestry buffer management. Agrofor. Syst. **84**(2), 311–323 (2012)
39. van der Ploeg, J.D.: Peasant-driven agricultural growth and food sovereignty. J. Peasant Stud. **41**, 999–1030 (2014)

40. Bewket, W.: Soil and water conservation intervention with conventional technologies in north-western highlands of Ethiopia: acceptance and adoption by farmers. Land Use Policy **24**(2), 404–416 (2007)
41. Grothmann, T., Patt, A.: Adaptive capacity and human cognition: the process of individual adaptation to climate change. Glob. Environ. Change **15**, 199–213 (2005)
42. Wossink, A., Swinton, S.M.: Jointness in production and farmers' willingness to supply non-marketed ecosystem services. Ecol. Econ. **64**(2), 297–304 (2007)
43. Thorn, J.P.R.: Adaptation "from below" to changes in species distribution, habitat and climate in agro-ecosystems in the Terai Plains of Nepal. Ambio **48**, 1482–1497 (2019)
44. Dahal, G.R.: Community forestry in Nepal: Decentralized forest governance. Lessons from forest decentralization, London, Earthscan, pp. 67–81 (2008)
45. Carson, B.: The land, the farmer and the future: a soil fertility management strategy for Nepal. ICIMOD Occasional Paper No. 21. Kathmandu, International Centre for Mountain Development (1992)
46. Sharpe, R.R., Harper, L.A., Giddens, J.E., Langdale, G.W.: Nitrogen use efficiency and nitrogen budget for conservation tilled wheat. Soil Sci. Soc. Am. J. **86**, 1394–1398 (1988)
47. FAO: Agricultural extension services in Nepal. Pulchok, FAO (2010)
48. Thorn, J.P.R.: Ecosystem services, biodiversity and human wellbeing along climatic gradients in smallholder agro-ecosystems in the Terai Plains of Nepal and Northern Ghana. DPhil, University of Oxford (2016)
49. Vermeulen, S.J., Challinor, A.J., Thornton, P.K., Campbell, B.M., Eriyagama, N., Vervoort, J.M., et al.: Addressing uncertainty in adaptation planning for agriculture. Proc. Natl. Acad. Sci. U.S.A. **110**(21), 8357–8362 (2013)
50. Thorn, J.P.R., Thornton, T.F., Helfgott, A., Willis, K.J.: Indigenous uses of wild and tended plant biodiversity maintain ecosystem services in agricultural landscapes of the Terai Plains of Nepal. J. Ethnobiol. Ethnomedicine (in review)
51. Prasad, R.B., Brooke, R.M.: Effect of varying maize densities on intercropped maize and soybean in Nepal. Expl. Agric. **41**, 365–382 (2005)
52. Diwakar, J., Prasai, T., Pant, S.R., Jayana, B.L.: Study on major pesticides and fertilisers used in Nepal. Sci. World **6**(6) (2008)
53. Brunner, S.H., Grêt-Regamey, A.: Policy strategies to foster the resilience of mountain social-ecological systems under uncertain global change. Environ. Sci. Policy **66**, 129–139 (2016)
54. Dale, V.H., Polasky, S.: Measures of the effects of agricultural practices on ecosystem services. Ecol. Econ. **64**(2), 286–296 (2007)
55. McDowell, C., Sparks, R.: Multivariate modeling and prediction of farmer's conservation behaviour towards natural ecosystems. J. Environ. Manage. **28**, 185–210 (1989)
56. Tiwari, K.R., Sitaula, B.K., Nyborg, I.L.P., Paudel, G.S.: Determinants of farmers' adoption of improved soil conservation technology in a middle mountain watershed of Central Nepal. Environ. Manage. **42**(2), 210–222 (2008)
57. Leyva, J.C., Martinez, J.A.F., Gonzalez-Roa, M.C.: Analysis of the adoption of soil conservation practices in olive groves: the case of mountainous areas in Southern Spain. Spanish J. Agricult. Res. **5**(3), 249–258 (2007)
58. Ervin, D.E.: Constraints to practicing soil conservation: land tenure relationships. Conserving Soil: Insights from Socioeconomic Research. S.B. Lovejoy, and T. L. Napier. Ankeny, Iowa, Soil Conservation Society of America (1986)
59. Martin, H.T., Santos, E.P.: Comparison of indigenous and scientific knowledge on soil classification among farmers in Imhugan, Nueva Vizcaya, Phillipines. J. Environ. Sci. Manag. Spec. Issue **2**, 71–83 (2016)
60. Khadka, D., et al.: Assessment of soil fertility status and preparation of their maps in National Wheat Research Program (NWRP), Bhairahawa. In: Conference Proceedings (2015)

61. Shrestha, R.K.: Soil fertility status of rice field in Paundi watershed, Lamjung District, Nepal. Am. J. Agricult. Forestry 3(3), 120–123 (2015)
62. Gowing, J., Payton, R., Tenywa, M.: Integrating indigenous and scientific knowledge on soils: recent experiences in Uganda and Tanzania and their relevance to participatory land use planning. Uganda J. Agricult. Sci. 9, 184–191 (2004)
63. Zhang, Y., Babu, S.C.: Knowledge driven development: private extension and global lessons. Public Policy and Global Development (2015)
64. Shikuku, K., et al.: Support farmer-to-farmer and community-wide social learning. International Center for Tropical Agriculture (CIAT). Cali. CO. (2017). 4 p.
65. Nkegbe, P.K., Shankar, S.: Adoption intensity of soil and water conservation practices by smallholders: evidence from Northern Ghana. Bio-based Appl. Econ. 3(2), 159–174 (2014)
66. Lipper, L., Mann, W., Meybeck, A., Sessa, R.: "Climate-smart" agriculture: policies, practices and financing for food security, adaptation and mitigation. Rome, FAO (2010)
67. David, S.: Learning to think for ourselves: knowledge improvement and social benefits among farmer field school participants in Cameroon. J. Int. Agricult. Extension Educ. 14, 2 (2007)
68. Scherr, S.J., McNeely, J.A.: Biodiversity conservation and agricultural sustainability: towards a new paradigm of 'eco-agriculture' landscapes. Philosoph. Trans. Roy. Soc. B: Biol. Sci. 363(1491), 477–494 (2008)
69. WWF Nepal: Annual report 2016. Kathmandu, Nepal WWF (2016)
70. Acharya, K.P.: Linking trees on farms with biodiversity conservation in subsistence farming systems in Nepal. Biodivers. Conserv. 15(2), 631–646 (2006)
71. Wang, C., Maclaren, V.: Evaluation of economic and social impacts of the sloping land conversion program: a case study in Dunhua County. China. Forest Policy Econ. 14(1), 50–57 (2012)
72. Mattison, E.H.A., Norris, K.: Bridging the gaps between agricultural policy, land-use and biodiversity. Trends Ecol. Evol. 20(11), 610–616 (2005)
73. Butsic, V., Kuemmerle, T.: Using optimization methods to align food production and biodiversity conservation beyond land sharing and land sparing. Ecol. Appl. 25(3), 589–595 (2015)
74. World Bank: Poverty headcount ratio at $3.10 a day (2016). http://data.worldbank.org/indicator/SI.POV.2DAY?locations=NP. Accessed 7 Dec 2016
75. Braimoh, A.K.: Integrating indigenous knowledge and soil science to develop a national soil classification system for Nigeria. Agric. Hum. Values 19, 75–80 (2002)

# Extraction of Relevant Data from Social Media Based on Termino-Ontological Resources: *Application to Meningitis Surveillance via Twitter*

Wend-Panga Régis Cédric Bere[1,5]([⊠]), Gaoussou Camara[2],
Sadouanouan Malo[3], Sylvie Despres[4], Moussa Lo[5], and Stanislas Ouaro[1]

[1] LAMI, Université Joseph Ki-Zerbo, Ouagadougou, Burkina Faso
cedric.bere@gmail.com,ouaro@yahoo.fr
[2] EIR-IMTICE, Université Alioune Diop de Bambey, Bambey, Senegal
gaoussou.camara@uadb.edu.sn
[3] Université Nazi Boni, Bobo-Dioulasso, Burkina Faso
sadouanouan@yahoo.fr
[4] LIMICS, Université Paris 13, Paris, France
sylvie.despres@univ-paris13.fr
[5] LANI, Université Gaston Berger, B.P. 234 Saint-Louis, Senegal
moussa.lo@ugb.edu.sn

**Abstract.** In this paper, we present a process for collecting and filtering relevant data for epidemiological surveillance of meningitis. We focus on the African meningitis belt stretching from Senegal to Ethiopia. This study aims to fill the data gap for the early detection of epidemics based on the analysis of social media. Our approach is based on previous work that showed that social media analysis contributes significantly to the surveillance of epidemics. It uses IDOMEN (Infectious Disease Ontology for MENingitis) a meningitis domain ontology and a SKOS resource meningVocab (meningitis vocabulary). IDOMEN is an extension of the Infectious Disease Ontology (IDO). The SKOS resource meningVocab is built from a corpus of meningitis tweets from social media. We align the IDOMEN ontology and the SKOS resource meningVocab for collection and filtering tweets containing data relevant to meningitis in a perspective of epidemiological surveillance. Tweets are collected via the Twitter API on the basis of a list of terms related to meningitis. They are then annotated using these two resources and filtered using the rules of the domain (for example, the rules characterizing situations suggestive of bacterial meningitis: *fever* AND *purpura* AND *headache*).

**Keywords:** Ontology · SKOS Resource · Social media · Epidemic intelligence · Meningitis

© ICST Institute for Computer Sciences, Social Informatics and Telecommunications Engineering 2020
Published by Springer Nature Switzerland AG 2020. All Rights Reserved
J. P. R. Thorn et al. (Eds.): InterSol 2020, LNICST 321, pp. 52–63, 2020.
https://doi.org/10.1007/978-3-030-51051-0_4

# 1   Introduction

The advent of social media is contributing to a significant increase in the generating of digital data. Using of this data offers new opportunities in several disciplines and provides many applications in various fields such as biology and health.

Infodemiology is a combination of the words: *"information"* and *"epidemiology"*. This term refers to a science based on Information and Communication Technologies (ICT) to achieve population health monitoring and guide public health policies [7]. Infodemiology exploits various data sources: websites, social media such as "micro-blogging" sites (Twitter, Tumblr etc.). These data are collected and analyzed in real time in order to predict and warn about risks of epidemics.

For more than two decades, meningitis epidemics have not been effectively contained. Meningococcal meningitis is an infectious disease that causes inflammation of the meninges surrounding the brain and spinal cord. This disease is caused by a Gram-negative bacterium called ***Neisseria meningitidis***. The World Health Organization (WHO) recorded nearly one million suspected cases of meningitis and more than 100,000 deaths reported in the African meningitis belt. In 2017, Nigeria and Niger experienced a major epidemic with more than 18,000 registered cases[1]. The detection of the first cases of meningitis is crucial for taking appropriate measures to contain a possible epidemic. This identification requires the collection and rapid integration of data and events related to risk factors for its propagation. However, in sub-saharan African countries, there is usually no real-time data collection tool for disease surveillance systems. Therefore, there are difficulties in early detection of the meningitis epidemic.

The work of [3] has shown that the use of ontologies can be an appropriate tool for epidemiological surveillance. A meningitis domain ontology could be an effective way to accomplish the task of filtering tweets. Indeed, ontologies provide both domain terminology and axioms describing relationships between domain concepts. In this paper, we present a process of collecting and filtering relevant data for the epidemiological surveillance of meningitis in the African meningitis belt stretching from Senegal to Ethiopia. As part of this work, we use the terminology associated with IDOMEN [1] and meninVocab to implement the process of collecting and filtering tweets containing relevant meningitis-related data. IDOMEN being built from the knowledge of medical experts, the use of a controlled SKOS vocabulary aims to capture tweets posted by communities of non-expert users using their own vocabulary that does not necessarily correspond to the technical terms of the medical field of disease. This controlled vocabulary is constructed from terms used in a manually processed sample of tweets.

The purpose of this work is to propose a collection and filtering process for the early detection of meningitis epidemics using real-time data from the Twitter social media. Our strategy consists in collecting and filtering messages from Twitter using termino-ontological resources (IDOMEN, meningVocab). Then we annotate the

---

[1] WHO: Controlling Meningitis Epidemics in Africa: A Quick Reference Guide for Health Authorities and Caregivers, http://www.who.int/csr.

tweets collected. The annotation allow to identify the terms contained in the Tweets and go back through the relationships in the termino-ontological resources. We perform matching of the annotated elements with IDOMEN concepts that appear in the rules of diagnosis of a *"suspected case"* of meningitis.

In the following of this paper, we draw up a state of the art relating to the extraction of data in social networks. In the second section, we describe the termino-ontological resources (*IDOMEN, meningVocab*) used in our approach. Then we present the methodology of collection and filtering adopted and based on the use of termino-ontological resources. Finally, we discuss the results of filtering on the social network Twitter.

## 2    Related Works

Social networks are web-based technology platforms that allow organizations or individuals to produce and share text, image, video, or audio content. These social networks are new modes of electronic communication but the volumetry of the data produced and the diversity of their format make their exploitation complex. Indeed, the data is mostly unstructured, which makes it difficult for them to be used immediately by machines. The reuse of this data requires an extraction guided by needs of use. The purpose of extracting data from social networks is to analyze them in order to predict a situation, to understand user behavior and to explain societal phenomena.

In this part, we draw up a state of the art focused on health surveillance in social networks. Some works has been done on the health surveillance of diseases such as influenza, dengue and other diseases with high epidemic potential. Most of these studies were conducted in countries in Europe, America and Asia.

In the context of influenza surveillance, there are two types of approaches those based on supervised classification [4] and those based on unsupervised classification [2]. It is possible to combine these approaches with message localization techniques [6] associated with the dynamics of disease propagation, but also with the frequency of the keywords related to the disease studied.

In [6], they are interested in monitoring influenza on Twitter. The tweets ranked according to the relevance of the infection. They combines a tweets location to focus the study on 10 countries from 4 continents having English as the official language. The results of this work show strong correlations between the number of tweets related to an influenza infection and the number of influenza cases recorded by the health surveillance services in these 10 countries.

[10] shows that the social network Twitter can serve as a complementary tool for seasonal surveillance of influenza in France. The authors base their approach on the use of keywords relating to the human flu. They use the Twitter streaming API to collect tweets related to their keyword vocabulary. The tweets relating to the animal flu are automatically deleted from the corpus obtained. To filter relevant tweets, they use a machine-learning algorithm based on SVMs (Support Vector Machine). Subsequently, the analysis of these data consists in comparing the data obtained on Twitter with data from two networks of hospital emergency

structures. Indeed, by using Spearman's correlation coefficients and significance tests according to regions in France, [10] manage to establish that there is a link between the weekly number of tweets relating to influenza and the weekly number of influenza cases recorded in these two networks of health structures.

This work shows that the tools offered by automatic language processing (standardization, lemmatization, N-gram, etc.) constitute the common base for all this work to analyze the content of tweets. The approaches presented are generally based on the use of keywords. Other works show the interest of using an ontology. Indeed an ontology provides a more complete terminology of the field than the keywords. Moreover the exploitation of the relations between the concepts and the axioms make it possible to refine the filtering or the classification of the tweets.

The ambition of the ontology is to provide a conceptual model describing the concepts of the domain, the relations that exist between these concepts, while specifying the nature and the mode of use of these relations.

In this paper, we propose to use termino-ontological resources to enrich the annotation process and take into account the particular nature of tweets.

## 3   Use of the Termino-Ontological Resources

In this section we present the termino-ontological resources (IDOMEN, meningVocab), we use for collecting and filtering the tweets. Termino-ontological resources refer to a model that has both a conceptual component described/represented by an ontology and a lexical or terminological component associated with the ontology. The terminological component is linguistic in nature and therefore in the vocabulary used in the communities that employ them.

These termino-ontological resources will be used to support the semantic annotation of messages from Twitter.

### 3.1   The IDOMEN Ontology

The purpose of IDOMEN ontology [1] is to allow the annotation of texts to assist in the extraction of data from social media text messages related to meningitis. IDOMEN will also serve as a support for data integration, sharing of knowledge in the field and contributing to effective communication between the actors of the epidemiological surveillance system. IDOMEN is an extension of IDO ontology, IDO is a core ontology that is common to infectious diseases, it does not address specificities related only to a given disease. IDOMEN deals with meningitis, this ontology covers clinical aspects, biological aspects but above all climatic and social economic aspects which are linked to the risk factors of epidemics. The methodology that IDOMEN ontology uses is based on the NeOn methodology [8]. IDOMEN implements the OBO recommendations advocated by the *Open Biomedical Ontologies*, which correspond to proven good practices that promote interoperability, reusability and good ontology construction. The architecture of the IDOMEN ontology is structured in three modules: the biological perspective, the clinical perspective and the epidemiological and public health perspective. Each 3 modules divided into sub-modules linked together by the semantic relations existing between a concept of a sub-module with a concept of another sub-module.

In this paper, our collection application is mainly based on the clinical perspective (aspects related to the symptoms) Fig. 2 and the epidemiological perspective (aspects related to risk factors, epidemic emergence factors of meningitis) Fig. 1. These figures show the main hierarchies of IDOMEN concepts whose associated labels will be used in this collection. Patients discuss on social media (forums, web site, microblog site, ) and share their experience and history of the disease by explaining the different manifestations of the disease. The manifestations of the disease are most often referred to as symptoms: fever, migraine, convulsion, etc. Figure 1 illustrates the emergence risk factors that characterize the climatic environment and promote the spread of meningitis. Figure 2 shows the main clinical factors related to meningitis.

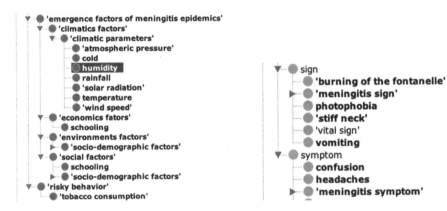

**Fig. 1.** Concepts related to epidemiological and public health aspects

**Fig. 2.** Concepts related to clinical aspects

### 3.2   Annotation of the Corpus with IDOMEN Vocabulary

In this part we use only IDOMEN's vocabulary to annotate tweets to evaluate IDOMEN coverage on a corpus of tweets related to meningitis. Our corpus consists of 1413 tweets related to meningitis. We use GATE (General Architecture for Text Engineering,) [5] to make the annotations of the corpus. Figure 3 illustrates the annotation performed, and Table 1 the result of the annotation process. We note that we have 1780 annotations on the 1413 tweets.

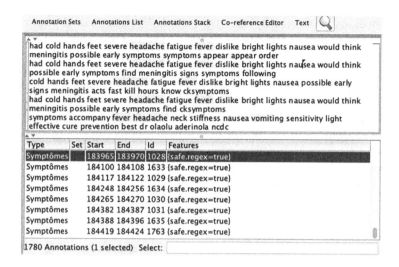

**Fig. 3.** Annotation of the corpus in GATE with IDOMEN vocabulary

**Table 1.** Table of annotation results with IDOMEN vocabulary.

| #Concepts | rdfs:Label | Number of occurrences |
|-----------|-----------|-----------------------|
| IDOMEN_0000026 | Vomiting | 97 |
| IDOMEN_0000028 | Photophobia | 14 |
| IDOMEN_0000029 | Stiff neck | 215 |
| IDOMEN_0000031 | Headache | 294 |
| IDOMEN_0000031 | Burning of the fontanelle | 0 |
| IDOMEN_000032 | Confusion | 93 |
| IDOMEN_000040 | Fever | 1031 |
| IDOMEN_0000041 | Convulsion | 22 |
| IDOMEN_0000044 | Purpura | 9 |
| IDOMEN_0000045 | Neurological signs | 5 |
| **Total** | | **1780** |

The results highlight the low coverage of the IDOMEN vocabulary on the tweets corpus. Indeed, manually exploring the tweets it appears that some symptoms common to meningitis are expressed in terms different from those used by the experts domain. The Fig. 3 presents two examples of terms used in Twitter to designate symptoms that are not in the IDOMEN vocabulary. Indeed, Twitter users do not necessarily know the experts terminology and use terms that express the form or nature of the manifestation of this symptom in the language they are familiar with. Thus, to express "photophobia", users will tend to use these expressions "eye sensitity" or "light dislike" earlier than the term "photophobia". The nature of IDOMEN ontology justifies the findings, IDOMEN is built by the semantic concepts and relationships of the field used by experts: clinicians, epidemiologists of meningitis, biomedical practitioners. In the perspective of keeping this ontology to use later the decision rules determining if a tweet is likely to describe a case of meningitis and which are constructed from IDOMEN's concepts and relationships, we have built a terminological resource gathering the terms used in Twitter to designate manifestations corresponding to meningeal symptoms. In this section, we present the SKOS resource named "meningVocab" and developed from a sample of meningitis-related messages from the Twitter social media (Fig. 4).

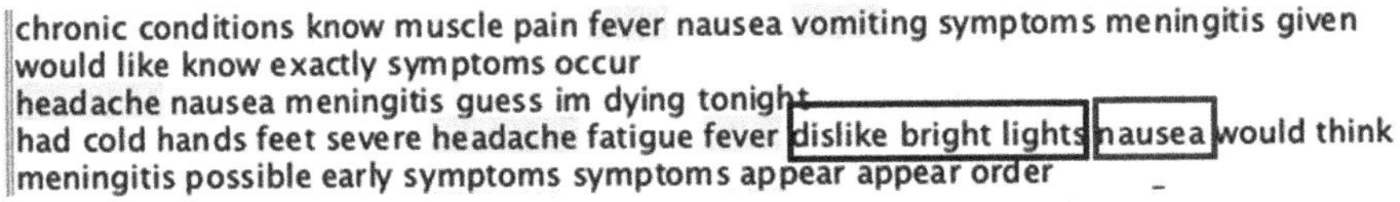

chronic conditions know muscle pain fever nausea vomiting symptoms meningitis given would like know exactly symptoms occur
headache nausea meningitis guess im dying tonight
had cold hands feet severe headache fatigue fever dislike bright lights nausea would think
meningitis possible early symptoms symptoms appear appear order

**Fig. 4.** Example of a symptomatic manifestation found in tweets

Its purpose is to improve the annotation based on the ontology IDOMEN. It is built to be scalable, which will take into account the specificity of expression of social media. MeningVocab resource was built by collecting tweets related to meningitis. We have adopted the OWL-compliant Simple Knowledge Organization System (SKOS) formalism to develop this resource. This resource is built independently of IDOMEN which will make it easier to manage the evolution of the vocabulary. An alignment will be done with the labels of the ontology IDOMEN. After analyzing the collected tweets, we note (manually scrolls through the corpus of tweets) some terms are closed to the clinical symptoms (used as concepts in IDOMEN ontology).

In this version of the SKOS meningVocab vocabulary we have 10 *concepts*, 20 *prefLabel* (in English and French), and 60 *altLabel*. We made two collections in the SKOS resource: a disease-related collection called *"Symptoms"* and a context-bound collection called *"Contexts"*.

### 3.3   The Resource *"hybrid"* : IDOMEN Aligned with meningVocab

The alignment of the two resources and their alignment allows us to have a hybrid resource that we use. Indeed, we have 2 types of IDOMEN ontology concepts that are used. These are concepts related to clinical symptoms and concepts related to socio-climatic aspects. These concepts are aligned with the skos resource using the altLabel of these concepts that we match with the prefLabel of the meningVocab concepts (Table 2).

**Table 2.** Extract from The resource *"hybrid"* : IDOMEN aligned with meningVocab

| IDOMEN | | meningVocab | | | |
|---|---|---|---|---|---|
| Concept | altLabel | skos:Concept | skos:prefLabel@en | skos:prefLabel@fr | skos:altLabel@en |
| IDOMEN_0000040 | fever | vocmen0101 | fever | fièvre | high temperature; hot body, high body temp, body temp, acute fever |
| IDOMEN_0000031 | headache | vocmen0102 | headache | mal de tête | severe headache, migraine |
| IDOMEN_0000029 | stiff neck | vocmen0103 | stiff neck | raideur de la nuque | unable move neck, neck pain |
| IDOMEN_0000032 | confusion | vocmen0104 | confusion | confusion | lethargy, hallucination, irritability |
| IDOMEN_0000041 | convulsion | vocmen0106 | convulsion | convulsion | spasm, muscle pain, convulsing |
| IDOMEN_0000026 | vomiting | vocmen0107 | vomiting | vomissement | vomited, nausea, vomit |
| IDOMEN_0000028 | photophobia | vocmen0108 | photophobia | photophobie | dislike light, light sensitivity, eye sensitivity, sensitivity light |

# 4    Strategy of Collecting and Filtering

In this section, we propose a strategy for collecting and filtering relevant messages from social networks as part of the health monitoring of meningitis epidemics based on termino-ontological resources. It is based on 4 steps: (1) collection and filtering, (2) pre-processing, (3) annotation of tweets and matching, and (4) enforcement of rules. The main challenge is to be able to extract relevant and meaningful terms related to meningitis from the huge amount of data produced on Twitter (Fig. 5).

## 4.1    Step 1: Collect and Filter Messages from Twitter

**The collection:** the daily tweets flow is estimated at just over 500 million tweets per day [9]. The Twitter Python API used to access tweets in real time. The streaming of tweets is then analyzed by retrieving those that are related to the vocabulary of IDOMEN ontology.

**The filtering:** we use the vocabularies of aligned resource to filter messages related to meningitis. The labels of ontology concepts are aligned with the terms of the SKOS resource. All the terms designating the concepts of the domain are collected in a list of term candidates using the Owlready API. Message filtering is carried out using two categories of filters that we apply sequentially:

1. Filter on clinical aspects;
2. Filter on the climatic aspects of meningitis.

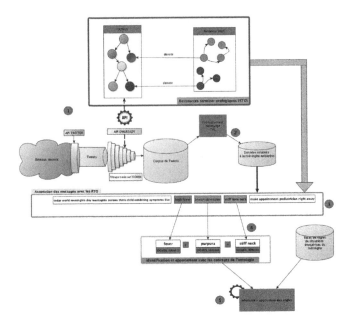

**Fig. 5.** Processing chain

## Filter on Clinical Aspects

The filter based on the symptoms and signs of meningitis is a filter consisting of candidate terms related to the symptoms of meningitis. All subclasses of parent classes: "meningitis symptom" and "meningitis sign" in the ontology will serve as a filter on the clinical aspects. The subclasses are: "vomiting", "burning of the fontanelle", "photophobia", "stiff neck", "fever", "headache" and "purpura".

## Filter on the Climatic Aspects Related to Meningitis

The evolution of meningitis (appearance, development, and intensity) is strongly linked to socio-demographic, economic, climatic and environmental factors [11]. It is therefore appropriate to consider these dimensions in the context of meningitis surveillance to detect events that may be risk factors for the spread of meningitis. We use filtering based on climatic and environmental events. The filter is based on the subclasses "climatic" and "environmental factors". We therefore find the following terms: "humidity", "wind speed", "cold", "rainfall", "solar radiation", "atmospheric pressure", "temperature", "dust", "cloud dust".

### 4.2    Step 2: Pre-treatment and Cleaning

NLP pre-processing techniques are then used to clean tweets from artifacts such as emoticons, RT (ReTweet) statements, URLs, unnecessary punctuation, etc. The decomposition of tweets into sentences is called tokenization. This operation allows us to split the tweet into sentences from which we delete the stopwords.

Some examples of stopwords in english ("by", "than", "could not", "re", "is not", "on", "my", "would", "up", "we", "doesn", "is", "doing", "haven", "an", etc.) are words that do not add value to our analysis. We use the N-Gram technique, to break down tweets into N-gram. To do this, we use the Python TextBlob library, which allows us to process text data such as partial tagging, extraction of nominal phrases, sentiment analysis, classification, translation, etc. Each N-gram passes through the filters described above. If there is a match with one of the filter terms then it will be considered a relevant tweet.

### 4.3   Step 3: Annotation with RTOs

The annotation process consists of annotating the corpus of tweets based on the two resources: the IDOMEN ontology vocabulary and the controlled vocabulary of meningVocab. The purpose of this step is to identify a term or phrase and to be able to match it with an ontology concept using the SKOS resource "meningVocab". We use existing relationships between terms to associate them with a symptom of meningitis.

### 4.4   Step 4: Application of the Domain Rules

As part of the medical diagnosis of meningitis, [12] have established rules to recognize situations suggestive of meningitis. These rules have been translated into SWRL using the IDOMEN ontology. After identifying or matching the symptoms contained in a tweet, the 5 rules below are applied to qualify and select the tweets to be processed (Fig. 6).

- Rule 1 : Fever + stiff neck + confusion $\Rightarrow$ *suspectedCase*;
- Rule 2 : Fever + stiff neck + headache $\Rightarrow$ *suspectedCase*;
- Rule 3 : Fever + purpura + headache $\Rightarrow$ *suspectedCase*;
- Rule 4 : Fever + focal neurological signs $\Rightarrow$ *suspectedCase*;
- Rule 5 : Fever + convulsions $\Rightarrow$ *suspectedCase*;

```
autogen1:IDOMEN_0000023(?symA, ?y) ^ autogen1:IDOMEN_0000040(?symA) ^
autogen1:IDOMEN_0000023(?symB, ?y) ^ autogen1:IDOMEN_0000041(?symB) ->
autogen1:IDOMEN_0000021(?y)
```

**Fig. 6.** Rule 4 in IDOMEN : Fever + focal neurological signs = suspected case

## 5   Discussion and Conclusions

The Table 3 gives the results of the new annotations made on the same corpus of 1413 tweets with the SKOS meningVocab resource. At step 3 of our processing we will have 1780 annotations (with IDOMEN) and 324 additional terms

**Table 3.** Results of the annotation with the vocabulary of resources aligned

| Terms of resources aligned | Number of occurrences |
| --- | --- |
| Hot body | 0 |
| High body temperature | 0 |
| Acute fever | 2 |
| Severe headache | 58 |
| Migraine | 22 |
| Unable move neck | 1 |
| Lethargy | 10 |
| Irritability | 11 |
| Hallucination | 5 |
| Focal neurologic | 5 |
| Spasm | 3 |
| Muscle pain | 13 |
| Dislike bright light | 17 |
| Light sensitivity | 3 |
| Eye sensitivity | 4 |
| Sensitivity light | 17 |
| Stain blood | 13 |
| Rash | 52 |
| Nausea | 86 |
| **Total** | **324** |

(with meningVocab specific terms missing from IDOMEN), that is a total of 2104 annotations using the two termino-ontological resources . This result is not surprising since terms used by users are already in IDOMEN. The 324 annotations identify symptoms that are not usually designated by scientific terms such as *"photophobia"* appears very rarely while terms such as *"dislike bright light"*, *"light sensitivity"*, *"eye sensitivity"* or *"sensitivity light"* are used to describe it. Using the two resources, we obtained 2104 annotations.

In this article we have presented a strategy for collecting and filtering data related to meningitis using two termino-ontological resources: IDOMEN and meningVocab. Our approach takes advantage of the complementarity of these two resources. The use of the SKOS resource allows to enrich the one obtained from IDOMEN. We plan to evaluate the relevance of tweets selected. In a first approach, the choice of terms used to build the meningVocab vocabulary was done manually by going through the initial corpus. In future work we will use automatic learning techniques (including a lexical extension model on the corpus) to propose better term candidates for the SKOS resource .

# References

1. Béré, W.R.C., Camara, G., Malo, S., Lo, M., Ouaro, S.: IDOMEN: an extension of infectious disease ontology for MENingitis. Stud. Health Technol. Inform. **264**, 313–317 (2019). https://doi.org/10.3233/SHTI190234. http://europepmc.org/abstract/med/31437936

2. Broniatowski, D.A., Paul, M.J., Dredze, M.: National and local influenza surveillance through Twitter: an analysis of the 2012–2013 influenza epidemic. PLoS ONE **8**(12), e83672 (2013). https://doi.org/10.1371/journal.pone.0083672. https://dx.plos.org/10.1371/journal.pone.0083672

3. Camara, G., Després, S., Djedidi, R., Lo, M.: Vers une ontologie des processus de propagation des maladies infectieuses. In: 23èmes journées francophones d'ingénierie des connaissances, pp. 99–114. IC 2012, June 2012

4. Culotta, A.: Towards detecting influenza epidemics by analyzing Twitter messages. In: Proceedings of the First Workshop on Social Media Analytics, pp. 115–122. SOMA 2010, Association for Computing Machinery, Washington D.C., District of Columbia, July 2010. https://doi.org/10.1145/1964858.1964874

5. Cunningham, H., Tablan, V., Roberts, A., Bontcheva, K.: Getting more out of biomedical documents with GATE's full lifecycle open source text analytics. PLOS Comput. Biol. **9**(2), e1002854 (2013). https://doi.org/10.1371/journal.pcbi.1002854. https://journals.plos.org/ploscompbiol/article?id=10.1371/journal.pcbi.1002854

6. Dredze, M., Paul, M., Bergsma, S., Tran, H.: Carmen: a twitter geolocation system with applications to public health. In: AAAI Workshop - Technical Report, pp. 20–24, January 2013

7. Eysenbach, G.: Infodemiology and infoveillance framework for an emerging set of public health informatics methods to analyze search, communication and publication behavior on the internet. J. Med. Internet Res. **11**(1), e11 (2009)

8. Gomez-Perez, A., Fernández-López, M., Corcho, O.: Ontological Engineering: with examples from the Areas of Knowledge Management, e-Commerce and the Semantic Web. Springer, London (2006). https://doi.org/10.1007/b97353

9. Liu, S., Young, S.D.: A survey of social media data analysis for physical activity surveillance. J. Forensic Legal Med. **57**, 33–36 (2018). https://doi.org/10.1016/j.jflm.2016.10.019. https://linkinghub.elsevier.com/retrieve/pii/S1752928X1630141X

10. Vilain, P., Menudier, L., Filleul, L.: Twitter: a complementary tool to monitor seasonal influenza epidemic in France? Online J. Public Health Inform. **11**(1), e296 (2019). https://doi.org/10.5210/ojphi.v11i1.9724. https://journals.uic.edu/ojs/index.php/ojphi/article/view/9724

11. Yaka, P., Sultan, B., Broutin, H., Janicot, S., Philippon, S., Fourquet, N.: Relationships between climate and year-to-year variability in meningitis outbreaks: a case study in Burkina Faso and Niger. Int. J. Health Geograph. **7**(1), 34 (2008). https://doi.org/10.1186/1476-072X-7-34. http://ij-healthgeographics.biomedcentral.com/articles/10.1186/1476-072X-7-34

12. Zender, H.O., Olivier, P., Genné, D.: Méningites bactériennes communautaires aiguës chez l'adulte (2009). https://www.revmed.ch/RMS/2009/RMS-220/Meningites-bacteriennes-communautaires-aigues-chez-l-adulte

# Physiochemical, Mineralogical and Physical Properties of Overburden Over Gneiss Basement Complex in Minna Metropolis, Nigeria

Mohammed Mustapha Alhaji[1], Alhassan Musa[1], Abdulhameed Danjuma Mambo[2(✉)], Waheed Adejumo Taiye[1], and Abdullahi Yahaya Musa[1]

[1] Department of Civil Engineering, Federal University of Technology,
PMB 65, Minna, Niger, Nigeria
[2] Department of Civil Engineering, Nile University of Nigeria, Abuja, Nigeria
a.mustapha@futminna.edu.ng

**Abstract.** Soil engineers pay very little or no attention to variation in the mineralogical and consequently, the geotechnical properties of overburden with depth on basement complexes, a situation which can lead to sudden failure of civil engineering structures. Soil samples collected at depths ranging from 0.5 m to 4.0 m at 0.5 m intervals, from a trial pit dogged manually to depth of 4.0 m on an overburden over gneiss basement complex, was evaluated for physiochemical, mineralogical and physical properties. This is to determine the variation of these properties with depth within the profile of the strata. Results showed that sodium amphibolite and feldspar, which are both primary minerals dominate the overall profile of the over-burden. Carbon which dominates the lower profile of the strata was observed to alter to gregorite at upper section of the profile. Organic matter contents and cation exchange capacity reduces with increase in depth while lost on ignition and pH were relatively constant with depth. The index properties as well as natural moisture contents increases from 0.5 m to between 1.0 m to 1.5 m depth after which the values reduced to constant values at 3.0 m depth. The grain size analysis shows high composition of sand sized particles with silts of low to non-plasticity. The maximum Dry Density (MDD) values are generally relatively high and increases from 2.262 g/cm$^3$ at 0.5 m depth to 2.410 g/cm$^3$ at 4.0 m depth while the Optimum Moisture Content (OMC) reduced from 9.8% at 0.5 m depth to 6.7% at 4.0 m depth.

**Keywords:** Gneiss basement complex · Mineralogical properties · North Central Nigeria · Physiochemical properties · Physical properties · Overburden soil

## 1 Introduction

Tropical soils represent the most heavily weathered soils on earth, because the climate is characterized by high temperatures and rainfall patterns promoting extreme alteration of minerals from the parent rock resulting in the formation of new minerals [1]. Soil

J. P. R. Thorn et al. (Eds.): InterSol 2020, LNICST 321, pp. 64–74, 2020.
https://doi.org/10.1007/978-3-030-51051-0_5

mineralogy plays an important role in forming the character of a soil, such that the key features employed to differentiate soils at the highest level depend on mineralogy [2]. These properties are responsible for all the physical properties of the overburden soils and consequently, the engineering properties of such soils [3]. Mineralogical and physiochemical analysis conducted on overburden soils proves to be useful in understanding the physical properties of these soils and consequently, its engineering properties [4].

Geologists over the years have proved that basement complexes differs from one position to the other over the entire earth crust depending on the rock underlying the complexes. The common basement complexes identified are the Granitic, Gneiss and schist basement complexes. However, the most common of these basement complexes is the granite complex whose overburden has received some level of study [5]. Little studies have been carried out specifically on Schist and Migmatite Gneiss basement complexes. Soil engineers borrow the overburden soil on these complexes for construction of structures or construct heavy structures on the overburden over these complexes without considering possible differences in the physical properties and consequently, the engineering properties of these soils. Ignoring the variability of mineralogical and physiochemical characteristics on these residual weathering profiles with depth is denying the different formation factors of these soils and may lead to misleading results and consequently, serious failure to engineering structures erected on them. This work is therefore, aimed at studying the variation with depth in the physiochemical, mineralogical and the physical properties of the overburden on Migmatite Gneiss complex in Minna metropolis.

## 2    Location and Geological Setting of the Studied Area

The location of the study area lies within 9° 23' 01.0"N and 6° 22' 01.78"E and in geological sheet 184 of Nigerian Geological Sheet which span from Gidankwanu to Kataeregi along Minna-Bida road, Niger State, Nigeria. This sheet has been studied geologically by Olose et al. [6] (Fig. 1).

Some other authors that worked on geology of Nigeria regional sheets includes Ekweme [7], who carried out extensive study on the geochemistry of the schist and metasedimentary phyllites of South-West UGEP, Nigeria. The study revealed that the metasediment contains substantial amount of silica, alumina and Zr but lacking in Nickel. The presence of 0.033% and 0.144% of Titanium oxide and alumina respectively confirms that metasediment in this region originated from bedrocks containing substantial amount of quartz and clay. Dambata and Garba [8] worked on the geochemistry and petrogenesis of the Zuru schist belt of Nigeria. The amphibolite in this region consists mainly of green hornblende, plagioclase and quartz as well as the occurrence of pyroxene, quartz and epidote in small quantity.

The schist belt of Igara in Southwestern Nigeria was studied by Adepoju and Adekoya [9] to investigate the geochemical characteristic of the area. When the anomalous values obtained for the mean of the geological materials are compared, the result suggests that anomalous values for Au, Hg, U, Cu, Pb, Zn, Th and La shows that these minerals can be explored. There also exists amphibolite and pegmatite in the schist belt. Alabi [10] worked on Environmental impact assessment and geology of granitic rocks of Minna area. The result of the field study carried out by the researcher showed eight granitic masses termed Paiko and Minna Batholiths with height of 350 m above sea level. The geochemistry and geology of Zungeru amphibolite was studied by Agbo [11]. Twelve samples of amphibolite rocks were collected for the study. The result of XRF test showed major oxides including silica, alumina, iron oxide, calcium oxide and magnesium oxides. The geology of Paiko in Niger State of Nigeria which covers part of sheet 185 was extensively studied [12]. The result of the study revealed that the major rocks occupying this region are granitic rocks which can be separated into leucocratic and biotite granites.

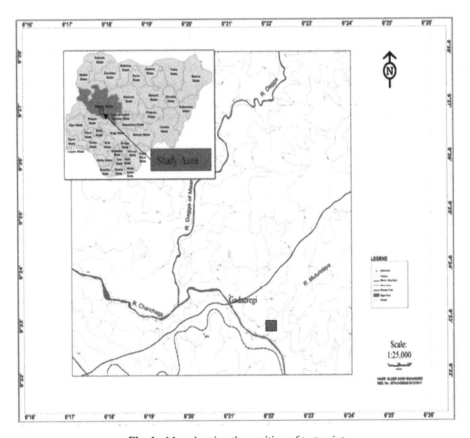

**Fig. 1.** Map showing the position of test point

The Geophysical study, hydrogeological and geological studies of Niger State was carried out to evolve a ground water development of the region [13]. The result of the studies revealed crystalline and sedimentary rocks existing in the same proportion in the state. The crystalline rocks encountered were mainly granites, gneisses, Migmatite and schists while the sedimentary rocks are clay, shale and sandstone. The basement rocks around Bishewa-Ologoma area was studied in view of knowing the major and trace elements in the rocks [14]. Results from the study showed that there is presence of granite which was interpreted to have been of igneous source with some sedimentary mixtures. Biotite granite, quartz-mica schist and biotite-hornblende granite of this area was observed to be well developed. The geology of the area under consideration which forms part of sheet 184 was studied extensively by Olose et al. [6]. The geochemical properties of amphibolite schist in Gadaeregi area of North Central Nigeria were studied. The paper concluded that the three major theological units predominant in this region are Migmatite-Gneiss, Amphibolite-Schist and Granite rocks. The geochemical and geological characteristics of the rocks on sheet 164 around Kuta town in Niger State, Nigeria were investigated [15]. The study has shown that the studied area is underlain majorly by quartz, phlogopites, paragonite, muscovite, kyanite, kaolinite, topaz and magnetite.

OlaOlurun et al. [16] worked on the geochemistry of amphibolite from schist belt of Egbe-Isanlu in south-west Nigeria. Results of the study showed uniformity of minerals in some areas and variation of minerals in some other areas. Tremolite, actinolite, quartz, plagioclase and hornblende are the abundant minerals in the thin shell of the complex.

All these authors considered basement rocks and not the overburden soil on the rocks. The work by Alhaji [5] is one of the early studies that consider the variation of geotechnical properties of overburden on granitic rock with depth. The researcher observed significant variation in geotechnical properties of residual profile on granitic rock with depth. Geotechnical and geological study was also conducted within a gully site along River Bosso in Niger State, Nigeria [17]. Field results showed that granite-Gneiss, granite and schist are the rocks that form the basement complex in this region. The index test results generally revealed high sand content and low plasticity index which was reported to have been the cause of erosion in the soil deposit.

# 3 Materials and Methodology

The materials used in this study involve disturbed soil samples collected in one trial pit. The trial pit was manually dogged to depth of 4.0 m where manual digging became almost impossible. Disturbed soil samples were collected at depths of 0.5, 1.0, 1.5, 2.0, 2.5, 3.0, 3.5 and 4.0 m. These samples were air-dried and pulverized using the method highlighted in BS 1377 [18]. Representative specimen taken from each of the samples were prepared and sent to iThemba laboratories, Somerset West, 7129, South Africa, for X-ray Diffraction (XRD) tests. The test uses a Bruker AXS D8 X-ray diffractometer system coupled with Cu-Kα radiation of 40 kV and a current of 40 mA. This is to obtain the major minerals contained in the specimens. The physiochemical tests (cation exchange capacity, Calcium carbonate, organic matter, loss on ignition and pH values) were carried out using the method highlighted in BS 1377 [18]. The physical properties of the overburden soils were determined using the method highlighted in BS 1377 [18].

# 4 Results and Discussion

## 4.1 Mineralogical Characteristics of the Soil Collected

The mineralogical analysis results for weathering profile on Gneiss Basement Complex are shown in Fig. 2 and Table 1. From the results, four distinct strata are observed: The first lowest stratum from 3.5 to 4.0 m is the closest to the intact base rock and possesses major minerals including quartz, feldspar (albite), amphibole (sodium amphibole) and carbon. The second stratum from 3.0 to 3.5 m consists of all the minerals in the first stratum with introduction of mica (phlogopite and biotite) in the stratum. The third stratum from 2.0 to 3.0 m consists of the same minerals as first stratum except that carbon is completely absent. The fourth stratum ranging from 0.0 to 2.0 m consists of same minerals as in the first stratum except with the introduction of gregoryite and disappearance of carbon. Except for carbon and gregoryite, all these minerals are primary silicate minerals while the secondary silicate minerals (clay minerals) are completely absent. This is an indication of a very poor weathering profile which can lead to absence or minimal plasticity of the overburden soils.

The presence of amphibole mineral spanning through the whole profile agrees with the findings from geological study carried out on sheet 184 [6]. The formation of gregoryite in the fourth and upper stratum is probably due to reaction between carbon that existed in the lower stratum and dissolved oxygen from rain water which leached from the surface through the soil profile to form dissolved carbon dioxide. The carbon dioxide in turn reacts with sodium from sodium amphibolite to form the gregoryite mineral.

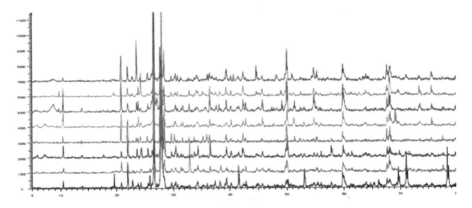

**Fig. 2.** X-ray Diffractogram for Gneiss basement

### 4.2  Physiochemical Properties of the Soils

The physiochemical properties determined from the soils are the cation exchange capacity, organic matter content, pH and loss on ignition. Their variation with depth of the weathering profile is presented in Fig. 3. The cation exchange capacity was observed to decrease from 77.0 at 0.5 m depth to 52.0 cmol/kg at 2.5 m depth after which the values increased to 67.0 cmol/kg at 4.0 m depth. These values are generally low compared to values obtained with clay soils. This is an indication that secondary minerals are minimal in the overburden soil on this basement complex. The organic matter decreased from 0.45% at 0.5 m depth to 0.34% at 3.0 m depth after which the values increased to 0.68% at 4.0 m depth. This trend is in agreement with literature where organic matter was observed to reduce with depth. The later increase must have resulted from the presence of carbon at the lower part of the profile. The pH was observed to be relatively constant at neutral to basic with value of between 7.15 to 7.77. The loss on ignition shows similar trend with organic matter content. The values reduced from 7.2% at 0.5 m depth to 3.8% at 4.0 m depth. These values are generally low and indicate low availability of fine soils.

### 4.3  Physical Properties of the Soils

Variation of natural moisture content, liquid limit and plasticity index with depth of the weathering profile is presented in Fig. 5. The natural moisture content increased from 9.7% at 0.5 m depth to maximum of 13.8% at 1.5 m depth after which the values reduced to 8.3% at 3.0 m depth and thereafter the values reduced to constant values of 7.6%. This trend is in agreement with Alhaji [5] who attributed this trend to residual profiles where water table is relatively far from the base of the excavation pit and the surface water percolating from the ground surface has its maximum accumulation at depth of 1.5 m. The trend for liquid limit and plasticity index is similar to that of natural moisture content except that the maximum values of liquid limit and plasticity index occurs at 1.0 m depth. This indicates that, even though rate of weathering is observed to me minimal within the profile, the highest weathering stratum must have occurred at depth of 1.0 m.

The grain size analysis (Fig. 5) shows high composition of sand size particles and silt of low to non-plasticity. This grain analysis is a clear indication of lack of clay soils from secondary minerals which would have resulted in to higher plasticity. The grain size analysis curves showed that the curve is capped at the top by soil at 1.0 m depth and covered from the bottom by soil at 3.0 m depth. The soils beyond 3.0 m depths showed increase in grading probably because of inclusion of freshly weathered rocks (Fig. 4).

The trend of the maximum dry densities with depth (Fig. 6) showed increase from $2.262 \text{ g/cm}^3$ at 0.5 m depth to $2.41 \text{ g/cm}^3$ at 4.0 m depth. These values are generally high

**Table 1.** The mineralogical composition of Gneiss basement with depth

| Depth (m) | Mineral name | Chemical formula |
|---|---|---|
| 0.5 | Quartz | $SiO_2$ |
|  | Albite (Plagioclase feldspar) | $KO.2NaO.8AlSi_3O_8$ |
|  | Magnesioarfvedsonite (Na-amphibole) | $Na_3(Mg,Fe)_5Si_8O_{22}(OH)_2$ |
|  | Gregoryite (Carbonate) | $Na_2CO_3$ |
| 1.0 | Quartz | $SiO_2$ |
|  | Albite (Plagioclase feldspar) | $KO.2NaO.8AlSi_3O_8$ |
|  | Magnesioarfvedsonite (Na-amphibole) | $Na_3(Mg,Fe)_5Si_8O_{22}(OH)_2$ |
|  | Arfvedsonite (Na-amphibole) | $(Na,K)_2.6Fe_5(Si,Al)_8O_{22}(OH)_2$ |
|  | Gregoryite (Carbonate) | $Na_2CO_3$ |
| 1.5 | Quartz | $SiO_2$ |
|  | Albite (Plagioclase feldspar) | $KO.2Na0.8AlSi_3O_8$ |
|  | Magnesioarfvedsonite (Na-amphibole) | $Na_3(Mg,Fe)_5Si_8O_{22}(OH)_2$ |
|  | Arfvedsonite (Na-amphibole) | $Na,K)_2.6Fe_5(Si,Al)_8O_{22}(OH)_2$ |
|  | Gregoryite (Carbonate) | $Na_2CO_3$ |
|  | Hydrobiotite (Mica) | $K(Mg,Fe)_9(Si,Al)_8O_{20}(OH)_4.4H_2O$ |
| 2.0 | Quartz | $SiO_2$ |
|  | Albite (Plagioclase feldspar) | $KO.2NaO.8AlSi_3O_8$ |
|  | Magnesioarfvedsonite (Na-amphibole) | $Na_3(Mg,Fe)_5Si_8O_{22}(OH)_2$ |
| 2.5 | Quartz | $SiO_2$ |
|  | Albite (Plagioclase feldspar) | $K0.2NaO.8AlSi_3O_8$ |
|  | Magnesioarfvedsonite (Na-amphibole) | $Na_3(Mg,Fe)_5Si_8O_{22}(OH)_2$ |

*(continued)*

**Table 1.** (*continued*)

| Depth (m) | Mineral name | Chemical formula |
|---|---|---|
| 3.0 | Quartz | $SiO_2$ |
| | Albite (Plagioclase feldspar) | $KO.2NaO.8AlSi_3O_8$ |
| | Arfvedsonite (Na-amphibole) | $(Na,K)_2.6Fe_5(Si,Al)_8O_{22}(OH)_2$ |
| | Phlogopite (Mica) | $KMg_3(Si_3Al)O_{10}(OH)_2$ |
| | Biotite (Mica) | $KMg_3(Si_3Al)O_{10}(OH)_2$ |
| | Carbon (Carbon) | C |
| 3.5 | Quartz | $SiO_2$ |
| | Albite (Plagioclase feldspar) | $KO.2Na0.8AlSi_3O_8$ |
| | Arfvedsonite (Na-amphibole) | $(Na,K)_2.6Fe_5(Si,Al)_8O_{22}(OH)_2$ |
| | Carbon (Carbon) | C |
| 4.0 | Quartz | $SiO_2$ |
| | Albite (Plagioclase feldspar) | $KO.2NaO.8AlSi_3O_8$ |
| | Arfvedsonite (Na-amphibole) | $(Na,K)_2.6Fe_5(Si,Al)_8O_{22}(OH)_2$ |
| | Carbon (Carbon) | C |

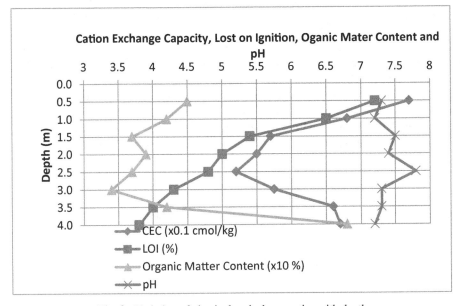

**Fig. 3.** Variation of physiochemical properties with depth

compared to other values in literature. This trend suggests that magnitude of weathering reduces with depth within this residual profile which postulates that, primary minerals increases with increase in depth and consequently, the MDD increase with depth in the profile. Conversely, the optimum moisture content (Fig. 7) reduces with increase in depth, a trend which is in agreement with literature.

The trend of specific gravity with depth is shown on Fig. 8. The trend showed decrease in specific gravity from 2.77 at 0.5 m depth to 2.58 at 2.0 m depth after which the values increases to 2.71 at 4.0 m depth.

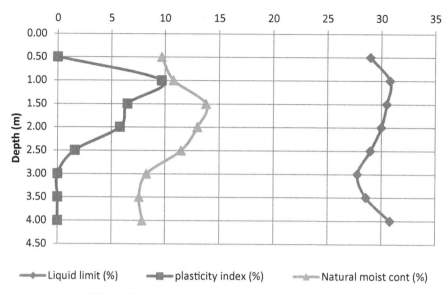

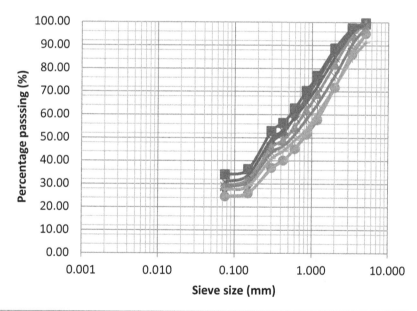

**Fig. 4.** Variation of Atterberg limit and NMC with depth

**Fig. 5.** Grain size analysis of soils within the profile

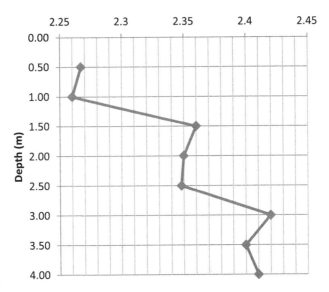

**Fig. 6.** Variation of Maximum Dry Density with depth

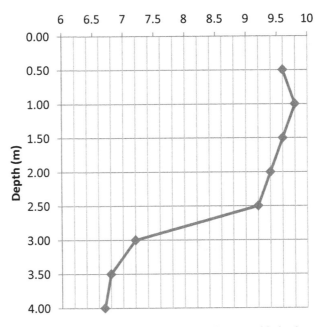

**Fig. 7.** Variation of Optimum Moisture Content with depth

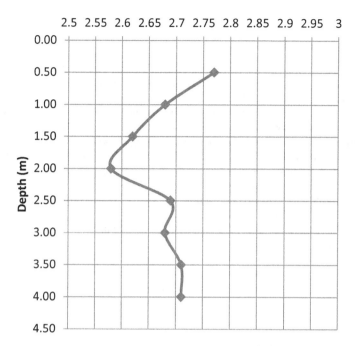

**Fig. 8.** Variation of specific gravity with depth

## 5  Conclusion

The mineralogical characteristics of overburden soil on gneiss basement complex with depth consist basically of amphibolite and feldspar within the entire profile with little alteration of carbon element contained at lower stratum of the profile to gregorite at upper stratum.

The natural moisture content as well as the Atterberg limits increases to between 1.0 to 1.5 m depth after which the values reduced to a constant value at 3.0 m depth.

The result of the grain size analysis coupled with the Atterberg limits classified most of the soil within the profile as silty sand (SM) based on Unified Soil Classification test. The general grain size distribution curves is capped on the top by soil at 1.0 m depth and covered at the base by soils from 3.0 m depth. Beyond 3.0 m depth, the grading began to increase again.

The MDD values were observed to be relatively high and increases from 2.262 g/cm$^3$ at 0.5 m depth to 2.410 g/cm$^3$ at 4.0 m depth while the OMC reduced from 9.8% at 0.5 m depth to 6.7% at 4.0 m depth.

From all the forgoing conclusions, structures sited on this basement complex are not susceptible to catastrophic collapse resulting from foundation failure.

# Reference

1. Yakubu, M., Ojanuga, A., Pedogenesis, G.: Weathering status and mineraloy of the soils on ironstone plateau (Laterites), Sokoto, Nigeria. In: Fasina, A.S., et al. (eds.) Management of Nigerian soil Resources for Enhanced Agricultural Productivity. Proceedings 33rd Annual Conference Soil Science Social Nigeria, pp. 26–37 (2009)
2. Uehera, G., Gillsman, G.: The minerology, chemistry and physics of tropical soils with variable charge clays, Westview Tropical Agriculture Series No. 4. Published in the United States of America by, Westview Press, Inc. (1981). ISBN 0-89158-484-6
3. Shafique, U., Khan, M.S., Mustafa, A., Arif, S.: Engineering geological characterization of Lahore soil, based on geotechnical testing and mineralogical composition using X-ray diffraction. Pakistan J. Sci. 64(3), 191–195 (2012)
4. Mahalinger-Iyer, U., Williams, D.J.: Properties and performance of lateritic soil in road pavements. Eng. Geol. 46, 71–80 (1997)
5. Alhaji, M.M.: Physical properties of residual profile found in minna. AU J. Technol. 11(3), 91–98 (2008)
6. Olose, M.A., Abdulkadir, H., Chaanda, M.S., Alaku, I.O., Omanayan, Y.A., Iyah, R.O.: Litho-Geochemistry, petrogenesis and minerilization potential of amphibolite schist around gadaeregi area, North-Central Nigeria. J. Environ. Earth Sci. 7(12), 83–90 (2017)
7. Ekwueme, B.N.: Geochemistry of crystalline basement rocks, SW UGEP, Nigeria, Global. J. Geol. Sci. 1(2), 143–157 (2003)
8. Dambata, U.A., Garba, M.L.: Geochemistry and petrogenesis of precambrian amphibolite in the zuru schist belt, North Western Nigeria. J. Min. Geol. 43(1), 23–30 (2007)
9. Adepoju, M.O., Adekoya, J.A.: Reconnaissance geochemical study of a part of igarra schist belt, Southwestern Nigeria. Ife J. Sci. 13(1), 75–92 (2011)
10. Alabi, A.A.: Geology and environmental impact assessment and benefit of granitic rocks of minna area, Northwestern Nigeria. Ethiopian J. Environ. Stud. Manage. 4(4), 39–45 (2011)
11. Agbor, A.T.: Geology and geochemistry of zungeru amphibollites, North Central Nigeria. Universal J. Geosci. 2(4), 116–122 (2014)
12. Pius, E., Omoboriowo, A.O., Adiela, U.P.: The geology of part of paiko sheet 185 (North West), Nigeria, Int. J. Sci. Eng. Sci. 1(5), 35–39 (2017)
13. Idris-Nda, A., Abubakar, S.I., Waziri, S.H., Dadi, M.I., Jimada, A.M.: Groundwater development in a mixed geological terrain: a case study of niger state, Central Nigeria. WIT Trans. Ecol. Environ. 196, 77–87 (2015)
14. Ajadi, J.: Geochemistry and petrogenetic evolution of rocks around bishewa-ologomo area, part of lafiagi sheet 203, Northcentral Nigeria. Int. J. Sci. Eng. Res. 8(4), 1333–1343 (2017)
15. Muhammed, A., Shehu, O.U., Agbor, A.T.: Geological and geochemical characterization of kyanite-bearing rocks around kuta part of minna sheet 164, North Central Nigeria. Asian J. Geol. Res. 1(2), 1–22 (2018)
16. OlaOlorun, O.A., Oyinloye, A.O., Adeleye, A.R.: Geochemistry and petrology of guguruji amphibollites from egbe-isanlu schist belt, Southwestern Nigeria. Geoscinces 8(1), 14–20 (2018)
17. Okunlola, I.A., Abdulfatai, I.A., Kolawole, L.L., Amadi, A.N.: Geological and geotechnical investigation of gully erosion along river bosso, Minna, North Central Nigeria. J. Geosci. Geomatics 2(2), 50–56 (2014)
18. BS 1377: Methods of test for soils for civil engineering purposes. British Standards Institution, London (1992)

# Mitigating Environmental Pollution and Conservation Beyond Protected Areas

# Mitigating the Impacts of Environmental Pollution in Lejweleputswa District Through Integration of Local and Scientific Knowledge

Mpho Mbele$^{(\boxtimes)}$ and Muthoni Masinde

Centre for Sustainable SMART Cities, Central University of Technology, Private Bag X20539, Bloemfontein 9300, Free State, South Africa
mmbele@cut.ac.za

**Abstract.** South Africa is home to extensive mining activities, although it is good for the economy it is also one of the more serious environmental problems such as air pollution, which is a major contributor to health issues and inability to grow crops within mining communities. Though the concerned industries (such as mining) and governments have developed environmental management systems/plans to identify, prevent/mitigate the impacts the mining activities have on the society, the effects of these plans have done little to redress the threats facing the community. The main reason for this is the lack of appropriate and comprehensible air pollution monitoring systems that are specifically targeted to the at-risk local communities. Sustainable, timely, and relevant air pollution monitoring systems enables communities to mitigate the negative impacts easily. Current pollution systems are fraught with challenges of not having adequate coverage by air quality monitoring stations, hence leaving small-rural communities unattended. These communities are left with only one option; consulting their own local knowledge to observe and mitigate air pollution. In this paper, we demonstrate the integration of scientific and local knowledge in monitoring air pollution for the district of Lejweleputswa, Free State, South Africa. Fuzzy Cognitive Maps was utilized as a tool to analyze, verify or validating local knowledge whereas Wireless Sensor Network (WSN) was used as a scientific approach to collect pollutants.

**Keywords:** Fuzzy Cognitive Maps (FCMs) · Local knowledge · Pollution monitoring system · Wireless Sensor Networks (WSN) · Lejweleputswa

## 1 Introduction

Mining contributes to the economy of South Africa, resulting in positive impacts such as employment and enrichment of community members' lives. Though there are positive impacts, negative impacts still exist, as their operations are unsettling to the environment; they often pollute our natural resources, and thus have led to adverse impacts on surrounding communities as well as wildlife [1]. For the purposes of this paper, pollution can be defined as "addition of undesirable material into the environment because of

J. P. R. Thorn et al. (Eds.): InterSol 2020, LNICST 321, pp. 77–88, 2020.
https://doi.org/10.1007/978-3-030-51051-0_6

human activities". Throughout the years, substantial metals have been discharged from mines into the earth leaving enormous measures of mine dumps and corrosive mine waste [2]. This has left mining networks in the locale of Lejweleputswa helpless against tuberculosis (TB) [3]. The greatest test confronting the mining business is to demonstrate that it adds to the government assistance and prosperity of the present age without trading off the personal satisfaction of people in the future [4]. Regions, for example, Mangaung Metropolitan and Vaal Triangle, have conventional contamination checking stations that report to contamination observing frameworks, for example, South African Air Quality Information System (SAAQIS). Notwithstanding, the quantity of these stations is generally extremely little and there is no satisfactory information assembled for assessment in little networks, for example, Lejweleputswa. Besides, the utilization and importance of SAAQIS, is new to the semi-unskilled and ignorant mining networks in Lejweleputswa. Their strategies for getting to and spreading results make it increasingly hard for the networks to comprehend. In this manner, these networks keep on relying more upon their neighborhood information for watching and checking air contamination; they have watched and encountered the progressions throughout the years. Neighborhood information is depicted as "information that individuals in a given network have created after some time, and keep on creating; it depends on understanding, regularly tried over hundreds of years of utilization, adjusted to the local human progress and condition, implanted in network rehearses, organizations, connections and customs, held by people or networks and it is dynamic and ever evolving" [5].

Local information is indispensable with regards to having a reasonable human race, everybody's information and association is required for dynamic in regards to the earth. Individuals' view of and disposition towards environmental change, dry season or natural contamination is basic in diminishing introduction among individuals and can likewise impact the reaction to mediation that are planned for empowering deportment change [6]. This information helps to guarantee that strategy and correspondence systems accomplish change in open mentalities, subsequently recognizing the significance of the mind that individuals have about the earth. Right now, examine approach was received because of the idea of the investigation. This methodology was regarded appropriate on the grounds that it investigates the exploration question and it is applied to get a firm comprehension of the objective respondent(s) information, conclusions and conduct related with the examination.

Local people accept that present logical arrangements like those that are referenced here don't generally address their issues, reason being that these arrangements are simply "transfer of innovation" from logical specialists to them. Concerned local people enduring the most extreme dangers and wellbeing impacts by mining exercises are requesting a more prominent job in examining, portraying, and upholding answers for alleviate the nearby risk's they face. One of the exploration question was, "To what expand can an air pollution monitoring framework that coordinates local information alleviate impacts related with pollution and be satisfactory by mining areas of Lejweleputswa District?" The central objective of this examination was to build up a versatile air pollution observing model that incorporates local with scientific information to report about pollution to the mining areas of Lejweleputswa District.

## 2   Related Literature

### 2.1   An Overview of Air Pollution by Mines

There are different forms of environmental pollution; air, soil, water, light, noise, thermal and visual; this study focuses on air pollution. Air pollution occurs when gaseous substances, dust, fumes, or odor in high volumes, which could be harmful to the health or comfort of humans, cause damage to fauna and flora, affects air. Air pollution in Africa is estimated to exceed the limits set by of World Health Organization by 10 to 30 times [7]. Since the discovery of gold in the Witwatersrand Goldfields in 1886 (the Goldfields consists of 7 basins including Lejweleputswa), gold mining resulted in the establishment of more than 270 mine dumps, containing more than 6 billion tons of tailings(waste) and some 600 000 tons of uranium, and covering 400 km$^2$ [8].

Dust from mine dumps is known to be an irritant especially during windy seasons, and it is a health risk to communities living near them; this has necessitated the need to find appropriate coping mechanisms to protect themselves [9]. Trying to eliminate the impact that mine dumps have on the communities, Harmony Gold (one of the mining companies) started rehabilitating the dumps to reduce the level of pollution and also try and reclaim the land that the dumps are sitting on to economic account rather than just restores it to open field as the mine laws dictates [3]. This has decreased the number of dumps around Matjhabeng, but there are many more still remaining.

### 2.2   Local Knowledge and ICTs

To manage the scope, density and ambiguity of global environmental problems, it is important to take into account different types and sources of knowledge to form an adaptive co-management approach [9]. Researchers today agree that local knowledge and modern science complement each other for example, ITIKI a drought prediction tool that bridges a gap between indigenous and modern science [10]. Integrating local and indigenous knowledge with science for hydro-meteorological disaster risk reduction and climate change adaptation in coastal and small island communities [11].

Local knowledge has been a useful tool for the community in terms of mitigating the impacts of pollution and coming up with coping mechanisms. The issue has always been the level of effectives and usability but careful integration of local knowledge present opportunities especially in the dissemination process of monitored pollution to mining communities in Lejweleputswa because this supports ways that are appropriate and locally relevant to the people. The cost of installing a single pollution monitoring station is around thousands of rands. In contrast, local knowledge is cheap and time-saving. However, with ICT revolution and climate change it is impossible to talk about local knowledge in isolation. The ICT component with highest potential as compared to monitoring station is wireless sensor network. WSNs are fully scalable, cost effective and they do not depend on any preexisting infrastructure and can be redeployed or expanded easily [12]. Once deployed, the nodes are able to detect pollutants and monitor parameters that contribute to environmental pollution with better accuracy as compared to distant monitoring stations. WSNs can be deployed in large numbers in order to accurately measure parameters such as temperature, methane ($CH_4$), ethylene ($C_2H_4$), ammonia

(NH$_3$), benzene (C$_7$H$_8$), LPG (C$_4$H$_{10}$), CO$_2$, CO and nitrogen oxides (NO$_x$). These readings can then be used, together with other less obvious aspects of local knowledge (such as observed Particles from mine dumps/Closed mine shafts/Acid mine drainage) to improve monitoring.

### 2.3  Fuzzy Cognitive Maps (FCMs)

Originally developed by Kosko (1986) as a semi quantitative and dynamic method to structure expert knowledge, FCM has historical roots in cognitive mapping (Axelrod 1976). Similar to other cognitive maps, FCMs are graphical representations of a system that visually illustrate the relationships or edges between key concepts, or nodes, of the system, including feedback relationships [13]. FCMs enables creation of concepts out of people's perceptions and integrating them into the system; this is a better way of getting a broader view of how the community understands their environment.

**FCM Model for Air Pollution Monitoring System.** Local communities depend or trust information they learned for themselves, information that is based on what they have seen or experienced over time. For the monitoring system to be acceptable and understood by locals, it must be adaptive. The system should be able to cater for the already available knowledge from the locals, knowledge on how to observe, monitor and cope with air pollution around them. FCMs were used as a tool to collect, verify and validate this local knowledge in order for it to be integrated within the system. The concepts identified during local knowledge understanding and analysis (white dust, orange water, black soil, white soil, gaseous smell, air moisture, foul smell, particles from mine dumps, rain, wind and acid mine drainage) were uniquely structured by their respective positions. Each indicator represents a concept in an FCM model (C1…Cn); these concepts are linked by weights to determine the causality of one concept to the other. The causal effects between the concepts (local knowledge indicators) were declared using values, in a closed set of range [−1, 1]. These values are represented in linguistic values: {strong positive (1), medium positive (0.5), low positive (0.25), none (0), low negative (−0.25), medium negative (−0.5) and strong negative (−1)} from the mental modeler tool being used. This section provides more clarity about the concepts and their dependencies. In this portion, a matrix is designed as show in Table 1. This matrix is called as weight matrix. The names of all the concepts are written as row heading and concepts symbol like C1, C2, etc., are written as column headings were each cell contains a value.

During a scenario simulation, changes are made to the matrix to see how the system might react to plausible changes of health or environmental components within the system. From the 18 concepts represented in Table 1, the matching relationships were graphically represented as shown in Fig. 1. These relationships describe the impact of one concept on the other concept. If the relationship is directly proportional, then a positive value on the arc is written. Directly proportional means that a concept is directly affecting on the other. This effect may be either increasing or decreasing order. For example, wind has direct relation with particles from mine dumps, meaning that when it is windy the particles form of dust make way into the environment resulting in air pollution. If the relationship is inversely proportional, then negative value on the arc is written. Inversely proportional means that concept is inversely effecting the other. For example, if it is

**Table 1.** Causal effects representation

| Concepts | Symbol | $C_1$ | $C_2$ | $C_3$ | $C_4$ | $C_5$ | $C_6$ | $C_7$ | $C_8$ | $C_9$ | $C_{10}$ | $C_{11}$ | $C_{12}$ | $C_{13}$ | $C_{14}$ | $C_{15}$ | $C_{16}$ | $C_{17}$ | $C_{18}$ |
|---|---|---|---|---|---|---|---|---|---|---|---|---|---|---|---|---|---|---|---|
| Rain | $C_1$ | 0 | −1 | 1 | 0 | 0 | 0.25 | 0 | 0 | 0 | 0 | 0 | 0 | 0 | 0 | 0 | 0 | 0 | 0 |
| White dust | $C_2$ | 0 | 0 | 0 | 0 | 0 | 0 | 0 | 0 | 0 | 0 | 0 | 0 | 0.5 | 0.5 | 0.5 | 0.5 | 0.5 | 1 |
| Acid mine drainage | $C_3$ | 0 | 0 | 0 | 0 | 0 | 0.5 | 1 | 0 | 0 | 0 | 0 | 0 | 0 | 0 | 0 | 0 | 0 | 0 |
| Wind | $C_4$ | 0 | 0 | 0 | 0 | 1 | 0 | 1 | 0 | 0 | 0 | 0 | 0 | 0 | 0 | 0 | 0 | 0 | 0 |
| Particles from mine dumps | $C_5$ | 0 | 1 | 0 | 0 | 0 | 0 | 0 | 0 | 0.25 | 0 | 0 | 0 | 0 | 0 | 0 | 0 | 0 | 0 |
| Black soil | $C_6$ | 0 | 0 | 0 | 0 | 0 | 0 | 0 | 0 | 0 | 0 | 0 | −1 | 0 | 0 | 0 | 0 | 0 | 0 |
| Orange water | $C_7$ | 0 | 0 | 0 | 0 | 0 | 0 | 0.5 | 1 | 0 | 0 | 0 | 0 | 0 | 0 | 0 | 0.5 | 0 | 0 |
| Foul smell | $C_8$ | 0 | 0 | 0 | 0 | 0 | 0 | 0 | 0 | 0 | 0 | 0 | 0 | 0.25 | 0.25 | 0 | 0 | 0 | 0 |
| White soil | $C_9$ | 0 | 0 | 0 | 0 | 0 | 0 | 0 | 0 | 0 | 0 | 0 | −1 | 0 | 0 | 0 | 0 | 0 | 0 |
| Gaseous smell | $C_{10}$ | 0 | 0 | 0 | 0 | 0 | 0 | 0 | 0 | 0 | 0 | 0.5 | 0 | 0 | 0 | 0 | 0 | 0 | 0 |
| Atmospheric moist | $C_{11}$ | 0 | 0 | 0 | 0 | 0 | 0 | 0 | 0 | 0 | 0 | 0 | 0 | 0 | 0 | 0 | 0 | 0 | 0 |
| Soil fertility | $C_{12}$ | 0 | 0 | 0 | 0 | 0 | 0 | 0 | 0 | 0 | 0 | 0 | 0 | 0 | 0 | 0 | 0 | 0 | 0 |
| Asthma | $C_{13}$ | 0 | 0 | 0 | 0 | 0 | 0 | 0 | 0 | 0 | 0 | 0 | 0 | 0 | 0 | 0 | 0 | 0 | 0 |
| Eczema | $C_{14}$ | 0 | 0 | 0 | 0 | 0 | 0 | 0 | 0 | 0 | 0 | 0 | 0 | 0 | 0 | 0 | 0 | 0 | 0 |
| Eyes irritation | $C_{15}$ | 0 | 0 | 0 | 0 | 0 | 0 | 0 | 0 | 0 | 0 | 0 | 0 | 0 | 0 | 0 | 0 | 0 | 0 |
| Skin irritation | $C_{16}$ | 0 | 0 | 0 | 0 | 0 | 0 | 0 | 0 | 0 | 0 | 0 | 0 | 0 | 0 | 0 | 0 | 0 | 0 |
| Lung cancer | $C_{17}$ | 0 | 0 | 0 | 0 | 0 | 0 | 0 | 0 | 0 | 0 | 0 | 0 | 0 | 0 | 0 | 0 | 0 | 0 |
| Tuberculosis | $C_{18}$ | 0 | 0 | 0 | 0 | 0 | 0 | 0 | 0 | 0 | 0 | 0 | 0 | 0 | 0 | 0 | 0 | 0 | 0 |

rainy, we have less particles from mine dumps resulting in less air pollution. No arc is drawn if there is no relation between two concepts. Even in weight matrix value, zero (0) is written. Zero represents no relation between concepts. For example, there is no relation between foul smell ad gaseous smell.

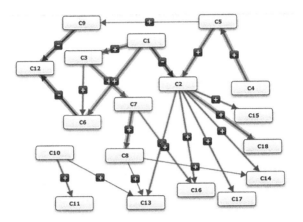

**Fig. 1.** Relationship between indicators

Scenarios were embraced to decide how the framework may respond to conceivable changes to wellbeing or environmental parts inside the framework. The Scenario interface of Mental Modeler permits the dynamic impacts of interchange the board intercession situations, given the present degree of gathering comprehension of the framework, to be assessed. For example, as a result of building a mutual network model of the air monitoring framework, focus groups in Lejweleputswa region built up a speculation that restoring mine dumps may ease air contamination. A few situations could be proposed and run progressively to perceive the adjustment of the air observing framework and what should be possible to diminish the degree of effect pollution has in the Nyakallong area.

## 3   Integration Framework

The framework comprises of three elements (data collection, monitoring, and visualization) that work together to produce an integrated system. It is designed around the generic early warning system framework developed by the United Nations Office for Disaster Risk Reduction (UNISDR) [14] (Fig. 2).

### 3.1   Architecture Design

**Capturing Sensor Data.** Remote sensors dependent on the Libelium gas sensor board introduced in chosen areas measure the accompanying natural parameters: temperature, carbon monoxide, carbon dioxide, and methane. At present, the sensors take readings each 30 min and the qualities put away in a removable memory card. In corresponding

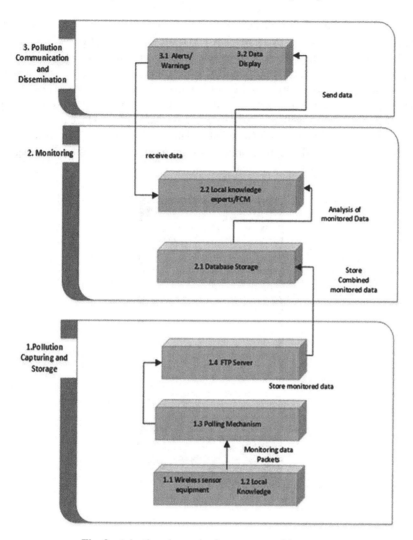

**Fig. 2.** Adaptive air monitoring system architecture

with this technique, the sensors send hourly normal readings (figured from the 30 min interim readings) to the server as instant messages (SMS). Information from the Secure Digital (SD) cards are physically transferred to the server after at regular intervals. The sensor readings are naturally transmitted as instant messages (GPRS/GSM) to the database at foreordained interims. The biggest bottleneck to the sensors 'operation is the GPRS module that frequently fails and cuts-off the communication between the sensors and the system, this is as a result of the antenna not functioning well as well as the depletion of airtime by the SIM card used by the module. For future deployments, this will be resolved by use of the XBee Radio and XBee Antennas in replacement of GPRS module.

**Capturing Local Knowledge.** The system was developed to work with local knowledge collected and processed by FCMs. LK was retrieved from FCMs and pre-stored in MySQL database as indicators to be observed. For the community targeted, an intermediary person (who understands both English, local language as well as ICT and LK) was identified and used as the interface to the community. Using a mobile smart phone application (Fig. 3), the intermediary keys in all the observations about the LK provided by the identified respondents as well as any extreme events taking place. Once the information is stored on the phone, it will be sent to MySQL database via the phone's internet facility. When internet is not available, the phone stores information on its internal storage and uploads it later when internet is available.

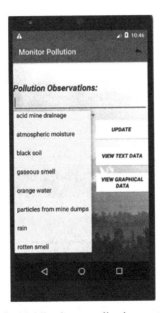

**Fig. 3.** Mobile phone application prototype

## 4    Implementation and Testing

### 4.1    Pollution Monitoring

The integration framework was implemented as a set of three components:

Sensor data that is received by the FTP server is sent to MySQL database after every 30 min for monitoring and then compared to the already provided quality standards. Local knowledge experts send in monitored observations into the system by using android mobile application (observations that relate to the already stored local knowledge indicators). For local knowledge, FCMs are used to bring together all the indicators from the focus group and produce a single FCM. Scenarios are created based on the changes being made to the indicators. The output of the scenarios is then formatted into readable form for storage in the database.

## 4.2 Pollution Knowledge Dissemination

**Android Mobile Application and SMS Ability.** The system provides three methods for dissemination based on user preference: The application takes in input from the end users such as any extreme event-taking place at that time, the event can then be disseminated to other registered users via SMS. The option of viewing graphical points of where pollution comes from is also available by Google Maps integration into the application (Fig. 4a). The system sends SMS alerts or warnings on current pollution status to registered users; this also caters for people with no smartphone. The users can also send in extreme events to the system using SMSs, the events are distributed to registered users of the system. The intermediary person is responsible for keying them in the android mobile application for storage on the database, then registered users are able to receive the extreme events by SMS receive the extreme events (Fig. 4b).

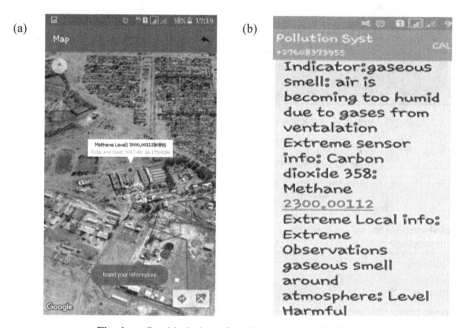

**Fig. 4.** a. Graphical view of monitored data. b. SMS alert

**Web Portal.** The web portal shows the status of pollution, the warnings, as well as extreme events. The option of viewing graphical points of where pollution comes from is also available by Google Maps integration (Fig. 5).

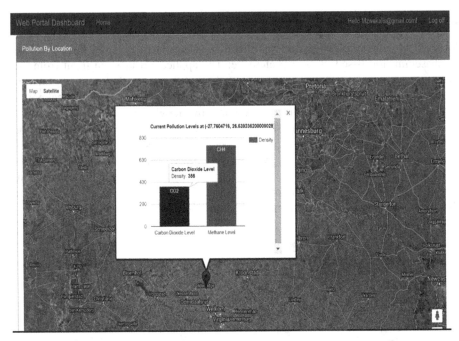

**Fig. 5.** Graphical view of monitored data on a web-portal

**Table 2.** Importance of System's Prototype Functionalities

|  | Not important | Fairly important | Neutral | Important | Very Important | No response |
|---|---|---|---|---|---|---|
| Monitoring with sensors | 0% | 0% | 0% | 20% | 80% | 0% |
| Monitoring with indicators | 0% | 0% | 10% | 20% | 70% | 0% |
| Google Map feature | 0% | 0% | 20% | 50% | 30% | 0% |
| Discussion board feature | 0% | 10% | 30% | 60% | 0% | 0% |
| SMS notification | 0% | 0% | 0% | 30% | 70% | 0% |

### 4.3   Feedback on the System's Prototype Functionalities

Table 2 above summarizes the respondent(s) views regarding the functionalities provided by the prototype. Based on the results it is evident that the group found the use of monitoring pollution with sensors and indicators very important and the option of them receiving SMS notifications. The researcher demonstrated the system to the group and allowed them to interact with the prototype. Moreover, majority of the group (60%) rated the system as very important while 30% deemed the system as important and 10% were neutral to their response.

## 5  Conclusion and Further Work

In this paper, we have portrayed continuous research work that involves a system for coordinating from one perspective local knowledge and on the other scientific knowledge on air contamination utilizing cell phones, FCMs and WSNs. We have likewise depicted a framework model that actualizes this structure. So as to test the framework model in a genuine domain, it was conveyed in Nyakallong Allanridge in the Lejweleputswa locale.

Our pollution monitoring framework offers a special and promising arrangement that is versatile and reasonable. The utilization of local information contamination pointers, which are incorporated with pollution information read from remote sensors is a novel commitment. Further, through the spread segment, our answer gives significant pollution cautions to partners, particularly unskilled and semi-ignorant ranchers in the provincial regions of Africa. In addition, the utilization of less expensive cell phones (than proficient pollution stations) for pollution information assortment and for contamination dispersal makes the arrangement increasingly maintainable and moderate for mining networks. However, during meetings with the focus group members, the researcher learned of the most critical factors affecting the community, the air around the community is mostly affected by heavy metals and dust, their water, and soil are affected by heavy metals and acid. Our system did not provide all the necessary solutions for these problems. For that to happen, more sensor boards are being acquired and will be placed in mining communities. The required boards have to cater for the above-mentioned pollutants. In particular, Smart Water sensor board as well as agriculture sensor board will be acquired, this would aid the communities not just Nyakallong but across the district.

## References

1. Mabiletsa, M., du Plessis, W.: Impact of environmental legislation on mining in South Africa. Constitution and Law IV: Developments in the Contemporary Constitutional State, p. 153 (2001)
2. Singh, N., Li, J.H.: Environmental impacts of lead ore mining and smelting. Adv. Mater. Res. **878**, 338–347 (2014)
3. Mbele, M., Masinde, M.: Development of adaptive environmental management system: a participatory approach through fuzzy cognitive maps. In: 2016 IST-Africa Week Conference, pp. 1–13. IEEE (2016)
4. Azapagic, A.: Developing a framework for sustainable development indicators for the mining and minerals industry. J. Cleaner Prod. **12**(6), 639–662 (2004)
5. Singh, A., Devine, M. (eds.): Rural Transformation and Newfoundland and Labrador Diaspora: Grandparents, Grandparenting, Community and School Relations. Springer, Heidelberg (2013). https://doi.org/10.1007/978-94-6209-302-7
6. Muindi, K., Egondi, T., Kimani-Murage, E., Rocklov, J., Ng, N.: We are used to this: a qualitative assessment of the perceptions of and attitudes towards air pollution amongst slum residents in Nairobi. BMC Public Health **14**(1), 226 (2014)

7. Mbele, M.: development of an adaptive environmental management system for Lejweleputswa District: a participatory approach through fuzzy cognitive maps. Masters Dissertation, Bloemfontein: Central University of Technology, Free State (2017)

8. National Pollutant Inventory. http://www.npi.gov.au/resource/particulate-matter-pm10-and-pm25. Accessed 27 Feb 2020

9. Wright, C., Matooane, M., Oosthuizen, M., Phala, N.: Risk perceptions of dust and its impacts among communities living in a mining area of the Witwatersrand. South Africa Clean Air J. **24**(1), 22–27 (2014)

10. Masinde, M., Bagula, A.: ITIKI: bridge between African indigenous knowledge and modern science of drought prediction. Knowl. Manag. Dev. J. **7**(3), 274–290 (2011)

11. Hiwasaki, L., Luna, E., Syamsidik Shaw, R.: Process for integrating local and indigenous knowledge with science for hydro-meteorological disaster risk reduction and climate change adaptation in coastal and small island communities. Int. J. Disaster Risk Reduct. **10**, 15–27 (2014)

12. Nelson, C., Paine, T.: The Making of Common Sense. New England Rev. (1990) **27**(3), 228–250 (2006)

13. Gray, S.A., et al.: Using fuzzy cognitive mapping as a participatory approach to analyze change, preferred states, and perceived resilience of social-ecological systems. Ecol. Soc. **20**(2) (2015)

14. UNISDR. Developing early warning systems: a checklist. In: Third International Conference on Early Warning (EWC III). United Nation/International Strategy for Disaster Reduction (UN/ISDR) (2006)

15. Axelrod, R.: Structure of Decision: The Cognitive Map of Political Elites. Princeton University Press, Princeton (1976)

16. Kosko, B.: Fuzzy cognitive maps. Int. J. Man-Mach. Stud. **24**, 65–75 (1986). https://doi.org/10.1016/S0020-7373(86)80040-2

# Environmental Protection in Nigerian Democracy: The Ogoni Clean-Up in Perspective

Harrison Adewale Idowu[1](✉) ⓘ and Ismail Sano[2]

[1] Adekunle Ajasin University, Akungb-Akoko, Nigeria
idowuadewale88@yahoo.com
[2] Obafemi Awolowo University, Ile-Ife, Nigeria
sanohusman@gmail.com

**Abstract.** This paper examines the progress made thus far on the Ogoni clean-up exercise in Nigeria. Over the years, the people of Ogoniland, a local community in the Niger Delta region, has suffered severe environmental crisis. Despite the fact that Ogoni has produced and continue to produce the country's largest export resources – petroleum, its environment has suffered from mining activities and the people continue to wallow in environmentally induced sicknesses and diseases. Governments (military and democratic) have neglected the community for long. Nonetheless, in 2016, the democratic government of President Buhari set in motion, the environmental clean-up of Ogoniland. Relying on exploratory research design, qualitative method and primary data sourced from semi-structured interviews, the paper critically appraises the Ogoni clean-up exercise. Findings show that although little progress has been made, the progress has been slow and insignificant over the past three years; the project continues to face series of challenges and that the prospect does not look bright. The paper concludes that Ogoni clean-up is best described as an abstraction at the present. Recommendations were directed to the government, HYPREP, Shell and the Ogonis.

**Keywords:** Environmental protection · Democracy · Ogoni · Niger delta · UNEP · Nigeria

## 1 Introduction

The Niger Delta region of Nigeria is the country's most endowed region in terms of mineral resources deposits. The region contributes the largest quota to the country's annual GDP, owing to the fact that it houses the country's economic base – crude oil. Paradoxically, however, the region has remained devastated owing to the side effects and remains of mining activities. Not misplaced therefore, that Nworu [17: 31] posits that "no nation, no people had suffered so terrible in the petroleum quest than the Ogonis." The region consistently endures oil spillage, gas flaring, oil bunkering and militancy, all products of mining activities in the region. These mining aftermaths have resulted in polluting land, water and air, so much so that much of the people suffer one form of ailment or the other. Furthermore, the land in the region suffers from excessive chemical

J. P. R. Thorn et al. (Eds.): InterSol 2020, LNICST 321, pp. 89–104, 2020.
https://doi.org/10.1007/978-3-030-51051-0_7

emissions that most of the land have lost Agricultural value and nutrients, thus, making farming and fishing – the major occupations of the region, a moribund enterprise. The Niger Delta region, thus, suffers from oil exploration by way of taking jobs (farming and fishery) away from them, sickness and diseases, insecurity, among others. Ogoniland, a small community in Rivers State has been the worst hit of the environmental challenges in the Niger Delta region.

For instance, the report of the United Nations Environment Programme [22] shows that there is an unimaginably dangerous concentration of benzene in the air and drinking water in Ogoniland. The report also shows that Ogale in Eleme local government area of Ogoniland, had in its air and drinking water, a benzene concentration which is 900 times higher than World Health Organization's minimum requirement. The report further revealed a high concentration of hydrocarbons in the drinking water, up to the tone of 1,000 times higher than the recommended level for Nigeria [22]. Given the severity of the environmental issues in Ogoniland, UNEP averred that it will take up to 30 years to clean up the land and it recommended an initial injection of US$1billion into the clean-up project. Despite the weight of the environmental situation in Ogoniland, the Nigerian government made no attempt to salvage the situation.

While Ogoniland continues to suffer severe and devastating environmental challenges, year-in-year out, both military and civilian (democratic) governments have abandoned and pay deaf ears to the plight of the people. In fact, the agitations from the people on the need for government to respond to their plight led to the famous killing of the Ogoni nine, including the murder of Ken Saro-Wiwa, a renowned environmental activist in the region. Albeit, in 2016, the President Muhammadu Buhari's democratic government set the pace for the comprehensive clean-up of Ogoniland. To kick start the clean-up project, the Nigerian government set up the Hydrocarbon Pollution Remediation Project (HYPREP) to ensure the implementation of UNEP recommendations. Since 2016, it has been three years down the lane, how has Ogoni clean-up fared under a democratic government which ideally, is supposed to guarantee the human rights of the people? What are the challenges and prospects of the clean-up exercise? These are the questions this paper seeks to provide tenable answers. While a lot has been said on the clean-up exercise by government officials, private stakeholders, public analysts alike, and reports written, it remains to be empirically examined from the perspectives of the very indigenes and residents of Ogoniland who are the direct victims of these environmental challenges, on what the actual situation is with respect to the Ogoni clean-up exercise. This is the very thrust of this paper.

The paper is structured into six sections. Following this introductory section, the next section presents the literature review. Section three presents the research methods, while the subsequent section presents the research results. The two last two sections are on the discussion of findings; and conclusion and recommendations respectively.

## 2  Literature Review

Environment could be referred to as the entity which houses humans, plants and aquatic lives, including other molecular elements. It is the habitat of man and animal. A democratic government is one which exists solely for the good, interest and benefit of the people. It is the government of the people, by the people and for the people [16]. Environmental security refers to a state of preserving and protecting the environment against all forms of activities capable of disrupting or deteriorating the environment. It is ensuring the safety of the environment from all sorts of hazards which could prove dangerous to the environment and the inhabitants. According to Barnett [4], environmental security entails the proactive measures put in place to minimize all sort of threats to the entire components of the environment; human and other organisms inclusive. The US Department of Defense [23] posits that environmental security entails acts of compliance to environmental laws, restoration of lost values, prevention of environmental pollution, environmental conservation, among others. Environmental security is to guard against environmental degradation so as to protect natural resources, humans and other materials within the environment [5]. Environmental security is germane and very critical to the human existence. To this end, Zurlini and Muller [26: 1351] posit that "the environment is the most transnational issue, and its security is an important dimension of peace, national security, and human rights." Ratner [19] presents the four dimensions of environmental security according to the perspective of the Global Environment Facility (GEF) in Fig. 1 below.

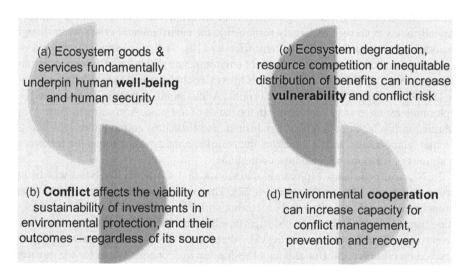

(a) Ecosystem goods & services fundamentally underpin human **well-being** and human security

(c) Ecosystem degradation, resource competition or inequitable distribution of benefits can increase **vulnerability** and conflict risk

(b) **Conflict** affects the viability or sustainability of investments in environmental protection, and their outcomes – regardless of its source

(d) Environmental **cooperation** can increase capacity for conflict management, prevention and recovery

**Fig. 1.** Dimensions of environmental security. **Source:** Ratner [19: 6]

When the environmental situation in Ogoniland is examined within the context of Ratner's [19] dimensions of environmental security, then is it easier to deduce whether indeed, Ogoniland is environmentally secured or not. In terms of the ecosystem which Ratner posits underpins human well-being and human security, the ecosystem in Ogoniland has been largely bastardized, thus, constituting huge threat to human wellbeing and security [17, 22: 30–33]. With respect to conflicts, which Ratner avers have negative effects on investments in environmental protection, among others, Ogoniland and indeed, the entire Niger Delta region has been known for various violent conflicts, militancy, kidnappings and other forms of insecurity [7, 25]. Ecosystem degradation can result in vulnerability and increase conflict risks. This dimension of Ratner's environmental security explains the vulnerability of Ogoniland to sicknesses, diseases [14: 17] and conflicts [7, 17], as a result of ecosystem degradation in the region. Lastly, where there is cooperation with the environment, the prospects for conflict management, prevention and recovery are increased. For Ogoniland, the reverse has been the case as there is outright lack of environmental cooperation in the region [14], hence, the incessant proneness to conflicts. Against Ratner's dimensions of environmental security, it is evident that Ogoniland suffers largely from environmental insecurity.

The drive, passion and desire for more wealth by corporations and individuals alike, has resulted in serious environmental crises across the globe [12]. The spread of capitalism and industrialization and the quest for capitalists to accumulate excessive resources and profits, had, according to Dobson [8], resulted in environmental destruction. This explains the activities of Shell Petroleum in the Niger Delta region of Nigeria. Data collated from UNEP, US Environmental Protection Agency (EPA) and the Toxic Release Inventory (TRI) Program show that a total of 5,374,060 tons of toxic chemicals has been released into the environment globally as of July 20 2019 [24]. This has manifested in air and water pollution, acid rain, land degradation, erosion, depletion of the ozone layer, global warming, among other environmental insecurities. Marx and Weber had first foreseen this when they warned against the rift between human beings and the earth [6]. Capitalism has been seen as largely responsible for environmental crises, even though corporations pretend to be environment friendly [10]. The petroleum industry and oil exploration, one of the prominent means of environmental degradation, have gone a long way in history. Ihunwo [14] avers that this history could be traced to few decades ago in the United States and Western Europe origins. At this point, petroleum industry and oil exploration exercise were exclusively in the hands of the state. According to Parra [18], the relationship between petroleum industries and their host communities was that of colonial relationships. In that situation, the petroleum industries dictated the terms and conditions of relations with the host communities.

In Nigeria, petroleum exploration dates back to 1908 when Tar Sand was being explored in South Western Nigeria [14, 22]. This process was however brought to an abrupt end during World War I, only to resume in 1938. In 1946, after WWII, oil exploration began in Niger Delta region of Nigeria, where in 1956, oil was discovered in commercial quantity at Iloibiri and Afam [15]. Since then, the Nigerian economy has largely survived on oil proceeds. But although this has led to economic boom for the country, the Niger Delta region remains highly devastated and environmentally deteriorated. The role of oil in Nigeria's economy has been explained in that the sector contributes over 95% of the country's foreign exchange earnings and 80% of the resources needed to run the government [1]. The Niger Delta region has contributed over US$600 billion since the 1960s [15].

Quite in sharp contrast to what obtains in most parts of the globe where oil exploration has driven development in host communities, the Niger Delta of Nigeria has been bedeviled with underdevelopment, poverty, sicknesses, diseases, environmental degradation, among others [14, 22]. Petroleum is formed largely from hydrocarbon which is highly detrimental to the environment, and constitutes serious health hazard to the soil, water, vegetation, aquatic and terrestrial wildlife and on people [14, 22, 25]. While hydrocarbon products are highly economical, they have been found to have serious environmental consequences, especially during spills [22]. The main sources of severe exposure to petroleum and hydrocarbon which include oil exploration, production and processing, among others, are common in Ogoniland. Also, some environmental degradation and insecurity issues have the capacity to trigger conflicts in host communities. Furthermore, where there are scarce resources, unequal access/distribution of resources and environmental degradation, these result in environmental-related security risks [26]. Ogoniland could be best described as the epitome of these latter descriptions.

The Fig. 2 below presents the model of the various dimensions of environmental exposure to oil spills.

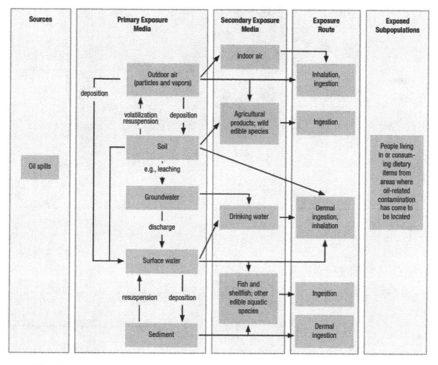

**Fig. 2.** Model of environmental exposure to oil spills. **Source:** UNEP [22: 40]

Ogoniland suffers significantly from all the above dimensions of environmental exposure to oil spills. This is correct to the extent that the region continues to be exposed to oil spills which result in water, land, air and soil pollution, thereby, causing serious harm to human lives, aquatic species, agricultural produce and wildlife [17, 22: 30–33]. Ogoniland is located in Rivers State, in the Niger Delta region of Nigeria. It has a population of approximately 832,000 people [22]. The community has a population density of 1250 km$^2$ [3]. Ogoniland is made up of four local governments of Eleme, Gokana, Khana and Tai [22]. It approximately covers about 100,000 km$^2$ of Rivers State and naturally endowed with rivers, creeks and streams [25]. The Fig. 3 below shows the map of Ogoniland for clearer description.

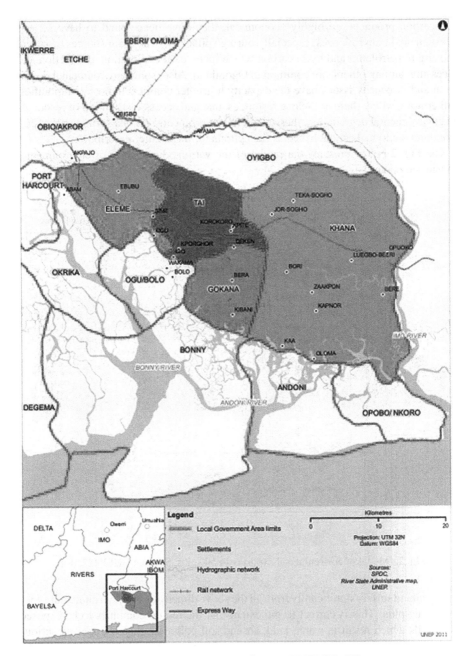

**Fig. 3.** Map of Ogoniland. **Source:** UNEP [22: 23]

Because of the environmental setting of Ogoniland, the people are predominantly engaged in farming and fishery. The Ogonis hold the belief that they are intrinsically intertwined with their environment, as such, they do all they can to resist any form of environmental abuse and violation. The environmental activist, Saro-Wiwa [20: 12] paints the picture of the Ogonis thus:

The Ogoni consider the land on which they lived and the rivers which surrounded them very important. They not only provided sustenance in abundance, they were a spiritual inheritance. The land is a god and is worshipped as such. The fruit of the land, particularly yams, are honored in festivals and indeed, the Annual Festival of the Ogoni is held at the yam harvest. The planting season is not a mere period of agricultural activity: it is a spiritual, religious and social occasion.

The above explains the series of struggles, protests and solidarity marches that Ogoni people have committed themselves in order to preserve and protect their environment in the face of environmental threats. Such struggles and agitations against environmental degradation had led to the execution of the Ogoni nine by the military government in 1995, including the renowned environmental activist, Ken Saro-Wiwa. The environmental devastation in Ogoniland is difficult to describe (see appendices for goring scenes from the community). Given the severe environmental conditions in Ogoniland, the Federal Government of Nigeria invited the United Nations Environment Program in 2008 to conduct an independent assessment of the environmental situation in Ogoniland. The UNEP report recommended among other 27 items, the urgent clean-up of the land with initial startup funds of up to US$1billion. The Fig. 4 below summarizes UNEP's recommendations.

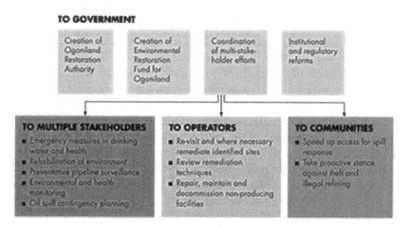

**Fig. 4.** Summary of key recommendation in UNEP Report. **Source:** Shell [21]

Environmental protection in Nigeria is ensured by the Ministry of Environment, Department of Petroleum Resources (DPR) and the National Oil Spell Detection and Response Agency (NOSDRA), via the instrumentality of the Environmental Guidelines and Standards for Petroleum Industry in Nigeria [9]. The role of these government institutions in ensuring environmental protection/security in Ogoniland, remains largely inefficient.

## 3    Research Method

The study adopts the exploratory research design, using the qualitative method. It relies on primary and secondary data sources. Primary data were sourced from semi-structured interviews. Interviews were conducted with 20 purposively and randomly selected key informant respondents (KIRs) drawn from among residents of Ogoniland who constitute the local population (10), social justice crusaders and environmental activists (4) conversant with Ogoni clean-up, officials of HYPREP (3), and executive members and leaders of Ogoni community (3). While social justice crusaders and environmental activists, officials of HYPREP and executive members and leaders of Ogoniland were purposively selected, residents of Ogoniland who participated in the interviews were randomly selected. The purposive sampling was based on the experience, practical involvement and interest of respondents in the environmental issues in Ogoniland. Interviews were conducted from July 18 to July 22, 2019. Interviews lasted for between 5 to 25 min. Secondary data were collected from relevant literature and official gazettes and documents. Data were analyzed using content analysis.

## 4    Research Results: The Progress, Challenges and Prospects of Ogoni Clean-Up

From the data gathered, most of the respondents alluded that there has been little or no progress in the Ogoni clean-up exercise. According to a resident, "The performance has been abysmally poor…I would not say that they [government] are not sincere [with the clean-up], I would say they have not really been committed to the execution of the project." Also, some of the residents averred that while there are remediation sites already set up in Tai and Eleme local government areas, none has been set up in places like Khana and Gokana. According to a community leader, some environmental activists and residents, the operations of the federal government do not show any sincere commitment to the clean-up. This is as most of the critical and 'emergency' recommendations of UNEP like provision of portable water; provision of medical examination and treatment; establishment of the Center for Excellence and an Integrated Soil Management Center; advice to stop all sources of pollution, especially artisanal refining; all of which are germane for the clean-up, have not been put in place. What seems glaring however, as some environmental activists and residents posited, is that there is so much talking and politicking with the exercise, whereas, there is nothing actually going on three years down the lane.

Also, a community leader observed that even though money up to the tone of US$187 has thus far been released for Ogoni clean up, not a single borehole has been sank in any of the four local government areas of Ogoni. The quality of work currently being done in Ogoni clean-up is also a cause for concern. In the words of another community leader, "The site I visited at Ogolo in Eleme local government area, one of the sites HYPREP claims they are cleaning, they are pouring sharp sand on the pollution to cover it up, and that is what they are calling clean up." With respect to the pace of work, although HYPREP claims that they are currently doing soil testing and that this could take a very long process, some social justice crusaders, human rights activists and residents are of the opinion that at least, the UNEP emergency recommendations should first be put in place.

On the other hand, however, HYPREP's account differs significantly from the account of ordinary Ogoni residents, environmental activists, human right fighters and independent stakeholders and observers alike. According to HYPREP, Ogoni clean-up is work in progress and between 2016 and 2019, significant progress has been made. Some members of HYPREP Governing Board aver that all the structures necessary for the success of the clean-up have been put in place, including the HYPREP which was part of the recommendations of UNEP; and a total of 21 contractors have so far been deployed to various clean-up sites. With respect to the health recommendations, a member of HYPREP Governing Board posits that "health studies are being carried out-...some health outreaches have been done, where some members of Ogoni community have been treated. Over 20,000 Ogonis have been treated, about 400 of them have had medical operations."

It is pertinent to state that although HYPREP lays claims to these achievements, none of the on-sight assessment by various independent stakeholders so far corroborates with HYPREP's claims. What is glaring however, is that there has been success with setting up so much structures which are grossly non-functional, an Ogoni community leader and some residents lament. While procurement is currently been made to start work on another 30 sites, some members of the HYPREP Governing Board concur with the fact that UNEP's recommendations on the establishment of Center for Excellence, Center for Soil treatment and the [very paramount and pressing need of] provision of drinking water have not been met. The Center for Excellence is to be converted into a University of Environment and Agriculture and the bill is currently undergoing its second reading at the National Assembly.

On the challenges currently besetting the Ogoni clean-up exercise, respondents also aired their opinions. According to some environmental activists and residents, government's insincerity/politicking and insecurity in the Niger Delta region continue to pose threat to the clean-up exercise. Another challenge also identified by respondents is that of corruption and misappropriation of funds. A community leader avers that "187 million [US] dollars thus far released, upon all this money, a borehole has not been sank in any of the four local government areas of Ogoni. HYPREP went behind us inducing some of our executives with monetary gains." Also, some community leaders, social justice crusaders, rights activists and residents added that lack of transparency in the clean-up exercise, including in terms of financial dealings, lack of accountability on the part of government and HYPREP, absence of any key performance indicator and bureaucratic bottlenecks are some of the challenges besetting the clean-up.

Furthermore, some residents are of the view that some of the challenges facing Ogoni clean-up are distrust and lack of mutual understanding between HYPREP and the locales of Ogoniland; and the challenge of finance, where only US$187 has thus far been released out of the US$1billion required for the first trench of the clean-up exercise. On the other hand, on the part of government and HYPREP, one major challenge besetting the clean-up exercise is that of lack of patriotism and pursuit of personal and selfish interest, rather than that of the community. According to some members of the HYPREP Governing

Board, the selfish desire of certain members of the community to share the money allotted the project and also secure the clean-up contracts for their personal companies without the requisite qualification, have made some to resort to media blackmail and unnecessary litigations. For them [members of HYPREP Governing Board], all of these struggles, agitations, blackmail and litigations serve as distractions for the project. Another serious challenge to the clean-up exercise is the issue of re-pollution, "as we are cleaning, people are re-polluting the place", a member of the HYPREP Governing Board laments.

The prospects for Ogoni clean-up exercise look bleak. Most of the respondents alluded that with the current situation on ground, if there is no redress, the prospects for actualizing the Ogoni clean-up is very slim. A community leader posits that "with the current model on ground, if we follow it, there is no model whatsoever and it poses a danger not just for the Ogoni environment, but the entire environment of the Niger Delta." Most other respondents' accounts corroborate with this position. According to some social justice crusaders, rights activist and residents, except the government and indeed, HYPREP show more commitment and come out straight with their plans for the clean-up, the exercise will not see the light of the day. However, a resident of Ogoniland begged to differ when he posited that "at least this government has tried to flag it [clean-up exercise] off, whereas other governments [military and democratic] have simply ignored the land, even killing those who stood up for Ogoni people." Interestingly, however, a democratic government should ordinarily exist to protect the lives and rights of its citizens, they owe this to the people.

## 5  Discussion of Findings

The study found that although a little progress has been made, on a larger scale, the progress of work done since the inception of the Ogoni clean-up has been significantly slow and lacks quality. It seems to be that the clean-up exercise is continuously being politicized. The quality and pace of work in Ogoni is abysmally poor. To this extent, none of the UNEP's 27 recommendations, among which are emergency recommendations, have been fully implemented. Not even the most critical and needing urgent attention – the provision of drinking water has been met. Three years down the lane, not a single borehole has been dug in Ogoni, the government and HYPREP claim they are still working out the modalities. The fact that sharp sand is being laid to cover up messy and polluted land, speaks to the quality of work going on in Ogoni. While the government and HYPREP keep canonizing the clean-up exercise, the study finds that virtually nothing is going on with respect to the clean-up exercise. There seems to be a persistent loss of human wellbeing and spiritual values [cf. 20: 12] due to continuous activities that are unfriendly to the environment (like artisanal refining, gas flaring and oil spillage) still going on in Ogoniland in the midst of the clean-up exercise. This finding aligns significantly with various reports on the clean-up exercise [cf. 2, 11, 25]. As a matter of fact, the report by the Friends of the Earth International [11] shows that progress has been "painfully slow."

Also, the study finds that challenges such as embezzlement of funds, corruption, insincerity on the part of government and its agency- HYPREP, and the distrust and lack of mutual understanding between HYPREP and the locales of Ogoni, continue to pose serious threat to the clean-up. Furthermore, insecurity in the Niger Delta, lack of transparency in the award of contracts, lack of accountability from HYPREP and the government, constitute other challenges currently besetting the exercise. The study also found that bureaucratic bottleneck and red-tapizm, lack of finance, unpatriotic behavior of some members of Ogoni community, and re-pollution, are major threats to the clean-up. Some of these challenges have also been buttressed in the reports given by Friends of the Earth International [11]; and Alabi [2].

With respect to the prospects of the Ogoni clean-up, the study finds that should the current situation persist, there is no future prospects for the clean-up. Although the current democratic government has made a major stride over the past military and democratic governments by flagging off the clean-up exercise, the clean-up may not see the light of the day if its current challenges are not nipped in the bud. Friends of the Earth International's [11] lamentation of the pace of work does not portray bright prospects for the clean-up exercise.

## 6  Conclusion and Recommendations

The paper has been able to appraise the Ogoni clean-up exercise promised in 2015 and flagged off in 2016 by the current federal and democratic government of Nigeria. Although a little progress has been made over the clean-up exercise, but preponderance of opinion suggests that the clean-up could best be described as an abstraction and that no significant progress has been made in the past three years.

The Ogoni clean-up exercise continues to face a number of challenges capable of stalling the exercise and leaving the local community in the current state of environmental degradation.

The following recommendations are therefore made:

– there is the need for the government to be more sincere with the clean-up exercise;
– the government must before anything else, put in place the emergency recommendations of UNEP which it claims are necessary for the clean-up exercise;
– government must make efforts to curb the insecurity in the Niger Delta region;
– HYPREP must make frantic efforts to build and earn the trust of Ogoni people and carry the people along;
– firms, such as Shell Petroleum must cooperate and be supportive of government's efforts to clean up Ogoniland; and
– Ogonis must see this opportunity as one in a lifetime and must thus, cooperate with the government, show patriotism, be patient with the government and shun all forms of activities re-polluting the land.

## Appendices

(See Figs. 5, 6, 7, 8, 9).

**Fig. 5.** Effect of environmental pollution on plants in Ogoniland **Source:** UNEP [22: 101]

**Fig. 6.** Evidence of environmental degradation in Ogoniland **Source:** UNEP [22: 146]

**Fig. 7.** Evidence of hydrocarbon and petroleum pollution in Ogoniland **Source:** UNEP [22: 199]

**Fig. 8.** The situation of water pollution in Ogoniland remains the same after three years of flagging off the clean-up exercise **Source:** Alabi [2]

**Fig. 9.** Plants still suffer from land pollution in Ogoniland after three years of flagging off the clean-up exercise **Source:** Ibekwe [13]

# References

1. Aaron, K.K.: Perspective: big oil, rural poverty and environmental degradation in the Niger delta region of Nigeria. J. Agric. Saf. Health **11**(2), 127–134 (2005)
2. Alabi, M.: Investigation: how Buhari administration awarded Ogoni clean up contract to unqualified firms. Premium Times, 5 May 2019. https://www.premiumtimesng.com/invest igationspecial-reports/328460-investigation-how-buhari-administration-awarded-ogoni-cle anup-contracts-to-unqualified-firms.html. Accessed 17 July 2019
3. Balouga, J.: The Niger delta: defusing the time bomb. International Association for Energy Economics (2009). https://www.iaee.org/documents/newsletterarticles/109balouga. pdf. Accessed 19 July 2019
4. Barnett, J.: Environmental security: new what? In: Seminar, Department of International Relations, Keele University, 4 December 1997
5. Belluck, D.A., Hull, R.N., Benjamin, S.L., Alcorn, J., Linkov, I.: Environmental security, critical infrastructure and risk assessment: definitions and current trends. In: Morel, B., Linkov, I. (eds.) Environmental Security and Environmental Management, pp. 3–16. Springer, Dordrecht (2006). https://doi.org/10.1007/1-4020-3893-3_01
6. Benton, T.: The Greening of Marxism. Guilford Press, London (1996)
7. Corby, E.: Ogoni people struggle with Shell Oil, Nigeria, 1990–1995. Global Nonviolent Action Database, 11 March 2011. http://nvdatabase.swarthmore.edu/content/ogoni-people-struggle-shell-oil-nigeria-1990–1995. Accessed 26 Dec 2019
8. Dobson, A.: Green Political Thought, 2nd edn. Rutledge, London (1995)
9. EGASPIN: Environmental guidelines and standards for the petroleum industries in Nigeria. Department of Petroleum Resources, Nigeria (1992)
10. Friedman, M.: The social responsibility of business is to increase its profits. In: Zimmerli, W.C., Holzinger, M., Richter, K. (eds.) Corporate Ethics and Corporate Governance. Springer, Berlin, Heidelberg (2007). https://doi.org/10.1007/978-3-540-70818-6_14
11. Friends of the Earth International: A journey through the oil spills of Ogoniland. https://www.foei.org/news/oil-spills-ogoniland-nigeria-shell. Accessed 20 July 2019
12. Gusau, T.I.: Oil corporation and the environment: the case of the Niger Delta. Ph.D. thesis, University of Leicester (2012)
13. Ibekwe, N.: Nigeria Govt. clarifies position on clean-up emergency project in Ogoniland. Premium Times, 24 April 2019. https://www.premiumtimesng.com/regional/south-south-reg ional/326770-nigerian-govt-clrifies-position-on-clean-up-emergency-projects-in-ogoniland. htm. Accessed 20 July 2019
14. Ihunwo, O.: Review of UNEP report on the environmental assessment of Ogoniland. University of Bologna (2016)
15. Ite, A.E., Ibok, U.J., Ite, M.U., Petters, S.W.: Petroleum exploration and production: past and present environmental issues in Nigeria's Niger Delta. Am. J. Environ. Prot. **1**(4), 78–90 (2013)
16. Lincoln, A.: The Gettysburg address, 1863. Abraham Lincoln online. www.abrahamlincolno nline.org/lincoln/speeches/gettysburg.htm. Accessed 11 July 2019
17. Nworu, O.S.: Ogoniland clean-up, remediation and satisfactory environment favorable to its development: obligations of the Nigeria state. World Environ. **7**(2), 31–41 (2017)
18. Parra, F.: Oil Politics: A Modern History of Petroleum. I. B. Tauris, London (2004)
19. Ratner, B.D.: Environmental security: dimensions and priorities. Scientific and Technical Advisory Panel to the Global Environment Facility. Washington DC (2018)
20. Saro-Wiwa, K.: Genocide in Nigeria, The Ogoni Tragedy. Saros International, Port Harcourt (1992)

21. Shell: The UNEP environmental assessment of Ogoniland: April 2018- recent developments to implement UNEP report recommendations. Shell, April 2018. https://www.shell.com.ng/sustainability/environment/unep-environmental-assessment-of-ogoniland.html. Accessed 17 July 2019

22. UNEP: Environmental assessment of Ogoniland. United Nations Environment Program. Nairobi, Kenya (2011)

23. US Department of Defense (1996)

24. Worldometers: Toxic chemicals released by industries this year. Worldometers (2019). https://www.worldometers.info/view/toxchem. Accessed 20 July 2019

25. Yakubu, O.H.: Addressing environmental health problems in Ogoniland through implementation of United Nations Environment Program recommendation strategies. Environments 4(28), 1–19 (2017)

26. Zurlini, G., Muller, F.: Environmental security. In: Jorgensen, S.E., Fath, B.D. (eds.) System Ecology Vol. (2) of Encyclopedia of Ecology, pp. 1350–1356. Elsevier, Oxford (2008)

# Mangroves Under Demographic Pressure and Salt Production Threats in the Municipality of Ouidah (Benin)

Sehouevi Mawuton David Agoungbome[1($\boxtimes$)], Estelle Gbenontin[2], and Moussa Thiam[3]

[1] African Institute for Mathematical Sciences,
Mbour km2 Road of Joal, Mbour, Senegal
`sehouevi.m.d.agoungbome@aims-senegal.org`
[2] Ecole d'Agriculture de Kétou, Université d'Abomey Calavi, Ketou, Benin
[3] Department of Civil Engineering, University of Ottawa,
161 Louis Pasteur Office A113, Ottawa, Canada

**Abstract.** Three coastal villages in the municipality of Ouidah (Djegbadji, Avlekete, and Houakpe-Daho), well-known for their salt production activities, are experiencing a substantial challenge regarding protection and conservation of the mangrove forest, a key component of their ecosystem. The increasing growth of these communities (more than 200% between 1992 and 2016) has led to the progressive destruction of the mangrove trees needed for firewood. This situation has dramatically threatened the sustainability of the whole ecosystem of the mangrove forest on which many other species rely on. In this work, we investigated the historical development of the situations from a demographical aspect and the possible consequences for the communities and future generations. It's has been shown based on the community growth rate that salt production which is the main activity in the region and employed more than half of the population (women and men) is the main cause for the destruction of the mangrove forest. Therefore, the town-hall services led discussions with the salt producers to find a more sustainable solution. Actions have then been taken to reduce the impact of these activities on the ecosystem, and propose some alternative solutions to the salt producers such as improved stoves which use palm nut hulls as the source of energy for their main activity.

**Keywords:** Mangrove forest · Ecosystem services · Salt production · Improved stoves · Ouidah

© ICST Institute for Computer Sciences, Social Informatics and Telecommunications Engineering 2020
Published by Springer Nature Switzerland AG 2020. All Rights Reserved
J. P. R. Thorn et al. (Eds.): InterSol 2020, LNICST 321, pp. 105–118, 2020.
https://doi.org/10.1007/978-3-030-51051-0_8

# 1    Presentation of Ouidah

## 1.1    History of Ouidah

Located in Benin (West Africa), Ouidah is a historical town that belongs to the Atlantique department (Rep. of Benin). The name Ouidah was etymologically given by the Kingdom of Abomey men who called people of the area "Xwéda". This name had been written in a different manner according to the colonizers of the area during that period. It finally becomes Ouidah with French in the XIIe century.

The population is mainly composed of Fon, Nago (Yoruba), Xwéda and Mina (Adja). The Xwéda were the first occupants of the area followed by the Fon coming mainly from Abomey to conquer the area during the reign of King Agadja and in 1727 made Ouidah their maritime gate. As Ouidah played an important role in the Bight of Benin as the main coastal gate during the Blacks slavery period, many other tribes arrived through TransAtlantic Trade. Nago and Haoussa tribes from Nigeria also came during that migration period and slave trade [1,2].

Since 1999, the decree "Loi 97-028 du 15 Janvier 1999, portant organisation des communes en Rep. du Benin" had redefined the administrative organization, and Ouidah then obtained the status of Municipality, led since August 2017 by Mme Celestine Adjanohoun. According to the last general census of population and habitat of 2013, the different communities are distributed as follows: 69.8% of Fon, 16.5% of Adja, 9.0% of Yoruba, 0.5% of Bariba, 0.4% of Dendi, and others [2].

In terms of administrative distribution, Ouidah is divided into 10 districts which are Ouidah I, II, III, and IV, Pahou, Savi, Gakpe, Djegbadji, Avlekete and Houkpe-daho as shown in Fig. 1.

## 1.2    Geographical Condition of the Area of Study

Ouidah lies between latitudes $2°N$ and $2°15'N$ and longitudes $6°15'E$ and $6°30'E$ and covers an area of $364\,km^2$. It is one of the eight Municipalities of the Atlantique department in Rep. of Benin (Fig. 1) and is about 40 km west of Cotonou, the main town of the country [2]. The sub-equatorial climate of Ouidah is soft and characterized by two rainy seasons (April to June and September to October) alternated with two dry spells of unequal duration. The average temperature and annual precipitation are 27 °C and 1 200 mm respectively [3,4]. Ouidah is considered as part of the agro-ecological zone VIII named the fishing zone. The land cover types include grassy savanna, swamp, and mangrove forest mostly located in the coastal part. The soil profile in the township is composed of hydromorphic and mineral soils or little humus-bearing with pseudo-gley which are favorable for growing cassava, tomatoes, maize, watermelon, and vegetables. The land cover shows a high proportion of agricultural areas, with some wetlands mainly located near the Atlantic ocean [5,6]. There are also many palm trees (1660 ha) and coconut trees (600 ha) plantations in the district of Gakpe, the reforested plantation of *Acacia Auriculiformis* (500 ha) and a natural forest

(225 ha) in the district of Pahou. The majority of the households are located in the urban districts of Ouidah and Pahou. However, some groups of small villages are agglomerated in Savi, Gakpe, Djegbadji, Houakpe-Daho, Avlekete, where people are still living and working traditionally.

## 1.3    Societal Distribution and Activities

The population of Ouidah has significantly increased over the past three decades. The population grew from 64 433 inhabitants in 1992 to 162 034 inhabitants in 2013, an increase of 151.48%. From 2013 to 2016, the projection of the population was estimated to reach 197 720 inhabitants, with a total increase rate of more

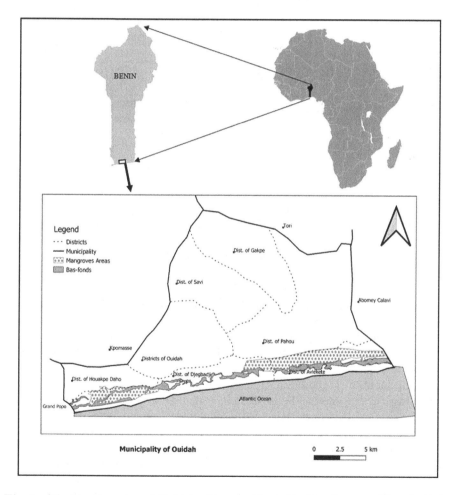

**Fig. 1.** Admistrative map of Ouidah   (Source: Township Development Plan 3, 2017–2022).

than 200% since 1992 [7]. This evolution of the population is shown in the table below per district and gender.

**Table 1.** Population of ouidah from 2002 to 2016 in the 10 districts and per gender. (Source: Plan de Development Communal 3eme Generation, 2018–2022)

| District | [a]RGPH3, 2002 | | | RGPH4, 2013 | | | [b]Pro, 2016 | | |
|---|---|---|---|---|---|---|---|---|---|
| | Male | Female | Total | Male | Female | Total | Male | Female | Total |
| Avlekete | 2725 | 2911 | 5636 | 5624 | 5829 | 11453 | 6863 | 7113 | 13976 |
| Djegbadi | 2072 | 2098 | 4170 | 2444 | 2553 | 4997 | 2982 | 3115 | 6097 |
| Gakpe | 2258 | 2518 | 4776 | 3091 | 3145 | 6236 | 3772 | 3838 | 7610 |
| Houakpe | 1454 | 1487 | 2941 | 1748 | 1725 | 3473 | 2133 | 2105 | 4238 |
| Pahou | 6877 | 7559 | 14436 | 38097 | 40377 | 78474 | 46488 | 49270 | 95758 |
| Savi | 3848 | 4340 | 8188 | 4890 | 4895 | 9785 | 5967 | 5973 | 11940 |
| Ouidah I | 6186 | 6670 | 12856 | 4493 | 4731 | 9224 | 5483 | 5773 | 11256 |
| Ouidah II | 4652 | 5228 | 9880 | 6375 | 7335 | 13710 | 7779 | 8950 | 16729 |
| Ouidah III | 3120 | 3603 | 6723 | 7320 | 7887 | 15207 | 8932 | 9624 | 18556 |
| Ouidah IV | 3477 | 3472 | 6949 | 4514 | 4961 | 9475 | 5508 | 6054 | 11562 |
| Tatal | 36669 | 39886 | 76555 | 78596 | 83438 | 162034 | 95907 | 101815 | 197722 |

[a]RPGH: Recensement General de la Population et de l'Habitat
[b]Pro: Projected population

The table shows that almost half of the population of the municipality lives in the district of Pahou, which is the biggest in area. With the districts of Ouidah I, II, III and IV, Pahou hosts the main commercial activities centers and markets, and they form the urban area of the municipality, where more than 75% of the population lives. This distribution also points to the massive exodus of the population from rural to urban areas where the economic activities take place. The district of Avlekete just follows in term of demography and with its long coast and water bodies offering the possibility for sea and lake fishing and also for Tourism. When considering the gender distribution in Ouidah, one must notice that women are slightly larger (51.50%) than men, mirroring the national gender distribution at the country level. This highlights the position of women in our society and the importance of improving gender equality as women are a large component of our communities.

The Institut National de la Statistique et de l'Analyse Economique (INSAE) (2016) reveals in its report that trading, small-scale manufacturing industries and farming accounts for 32%, 15% and 12% respectively of the major economic sector in the municipality of Ouidah. The major crops grown are cassava, maize, palm tree, tomatoes, watermelon. However, other intermediate activities are present such as fishing, livestock, tourism, and some agribusiness cooperative groups which produce palm oil and various food products [7]. Salt production mainly undertaken by women is considered to negatively affect the coastal ecosystem. Dossou et al. (2010) reported that the activity started on Benin coasts between 1420 and 1550 and has been practiced in the districts of Avlekete, Djeg-badji, and Houakpe-daho since Xwéda communities arrived in the area [8]. With the withdrawal of water from the lagoon, the production chain begins with the collection of a salted sand crust which is then mixed with the lagoon water and filtered through a traditional filter built locally, to obtain finally the brine, water with a high concentration of salt (Fig. 2).

**Fig. 2.** Traditional filter composed of a first layer of braided mangrove branches, then a second layer of thin clothing superimposed as a filter, into which the salted sand crust and the lagoon water are poured. The filter also has a pipe at the base to collect the brine (source: Nouvelle Afrique Magazine 2018/03/26).

Salt production is based on a chemical process called crystallization in which salt solution evaporates, precipitates, settles and forms the sodium chloride. The brine collected from the filtration process is crystallized by burning in mangrove woods. On average, the preparation uses 53 kg of woods to produce 3.5 kg of rough salt.

Referring to Table 1, the current evolution of the population of these three villages which doubles in the last 20 years (from 12 747 in 1992 to 24 311 in 2016), will certainly modify the environment especially the management of land cover and land use. In the three villages, mangrove trees (*Rhizophora racemosa* and *Avicennia Africana*) are the main source of energy for the fire. The past decades have witnessed increasing exploitation of mangroves for cooking as well as for energy utilisation in salt and palm oil production and also fish smoking. These populations have exploited a large domain of the mangrove forest inducing the destruction of the species if nothing is done. Continuous pressure on mangrove forests will likely increase the risks on the remaining tracts of forest, compromising wider ecosystem functionality and impacting on surrounding human populations.

That is why salt production has been the focus point of many studies, which strive to analyze their impact on the ecosystem. Many environmental institutions and some local associations such as Eco-Ecolo and Eco-Benin, highlighted the destruction of the mangrove forest due to the daily needs of the communities of these three villages who have been using the mangrove trees for many years now.

# 2   Mangrove Ecosystems in Ouidah

On a global scale, mangrove ecosystems have experienced risks of destabilization or even pronounced risks of extinction due to several natural and above all anthropogenic factors [9]. The recent population growth and the related activities to support human well-being have mainly contributed to increasing the over-exploitation of many natural resources. In this section, we will review the current state, the threats and the possible consequences.

## 2.1   Mangrove Ecosystem

The term mangrove refers to a wetland ecosystem at low tide in the intertidal zone of tropical and subtropical latitudes. The mangroves are unique plants that have evolved and adapted to survive in the interface between lands and ocean in tropical humid climate regions. They are described in various ways as coastal woodland, tidal forests, and mangrove forest, which grow as trees up to 40 m high, or as shrubs below the high spring tides level. They have developed intelligent mechanisms to cope with high salt concentrations and regular flooding over their root systems by rising tides [9]. Mangroves require freshwater inflow, which brings nutrients from upstream and silt as a support substrate. Acting as a key component in the environment of 26 Sub-Saharan African coastal countries, there are composed of 17 species that do not thrive in stagnant water. African mangroves are widespread along the western coast from Senegal to Congo and occur locally in East Africa, interlinked with highly productive coastal lagoons, tidal estuaries, and deltas. They provide these areas with essential organic nutrients as well as critical breeding grounds and nurseries for larval and juvenile stages of important fisheries species [10]. Historically mangrove has been regarded as swampy, mosquito-infested, muddy wastelands and has been cleared in the past, for the interest of public health or for conversion into other uses for high profit but short-term gains. However, it has emerged that mangroves are among the most productive terrestrial ecosystems and natural renewable resources [9].

Throughout Sub-Saharan Africa, the livelihoods of coastal populations depend heavily on access to natural resources. Mangroves fulfill important functions in terms of providing wood and non-wood forest products, coastal protection, conservation of biological diversity, provision of habitat, spawning grounds and nutrients for a variety of fish and shellfish, and salt production. Mangrove forests provide the nutritional inputs to adjacent shallow channel and bay systems that constitute the primary habitat, spawning and breeding grounds for many aquatic species of commercial importance [6,9].

## 2.2  Ecosystem Services Provided by Mangrove

The Millennium Ecosystem Assessment categorized environmental services into four groups [9,11]. Examples of the services provided by mangroves are the following:

- Regulation - shoreline protection: the complex three-dimensional structure of a 200 m band of mangrove branches, trunks, and roots can absorb 75% of the energy generated by wind-generated waves, atmospheric and climate regulation; human disease control, water-processing, flood control, erosion control;
- Provision: Use of timber for fuel (cooking, fish processing, salt production); charcoal; construction, fishing, gleaning for shellfish; and extraction of chemicals (e.g. tannins, saponins, alkaloids, flavonoids) for craft and medicines, glues;
- Cultural: Amenity, recreational/tourism of mangroves is not yet well developed (except in some areas of Angola), but it's been explored elsewhere in the world, taboo/sacred areas, education and research;
- Support: Cycling of nutrients, fish nursery habitats, sediment trapping, filtering of water, treatment of waste (e.g. sewage), biochemical, absorbing toxins.

It has been proven that the presence of mangrove ecosystems on coastline save lives and property during natural hazards such as cyclones, storm surges, and erosion [12,13]. These ecosystems are also well known for their economic importance. A recent estimate suggested on a global scale that the annual values of the benefits and services provided by one kilometer of mangrove range from US$ 200 000 to 900 000 [9]. In terms of related biodiversity, mangrove forests provide habitats for a host of animal species from endangered mammals to reptiles, amphibians and birds, and spawning grounds for a variety of fish and shellfish, including several commercial species. Mangrove forests also provide nutrients to coastal marine waters, often resulting in high fisheries yields in waters adjacent to them [9]. In Ouidah (Fig. 3), mangrove is mainly known for providing firewood to households and salt production activities especially in our study areas [2]. However, the reduction in fish species and the diminution of their size have been linked with the destruction of mangrove forests.

**Fig. 3.** Mangrove in Ouidah.

## 2.3    Threats on the Mangrove and Its Ecosystem

### 2.3.1    Global Scale Threats

Rivers are dammed, their waters diverted and the intertidal zone extensively developed for agriculture or aquaculture, resulting in the destruction of mangrove forests. Large tracts of mangrove forests have also been converted to rice fields, fish and shrimp ponds, industrial, urban and tourism development and other non-forest uses. Mangrove areas are further exploited for fuelwood and charcoal. In overpopulated and acute fuelwood-deficient areas, even small branches and saplings are removed primarily for domestic fuel [9]. Salt is produced by villagers by boiling brackish water in clay bowls on fire made using mangrove trees; this technique requires huge quantity of woods, so places a heavy demand on the mangroves. On a larger scale, salt is harvested from evaporation ponds or shallow brine-filled pits, usually built-in cleared mangrove areas. The mangroves in West Africa also face many of the conservation and development challenges emblematic of the continent as a whole. Four major drivers of change can be identified across the continent [9], (i) population growth and urban development in the coastal zone (ii) economic and political trends, (iii) climate change, (iv) changes in upstream habitat.

### 2.3.2    Local Threats

At Ouidah, the mangrove ecosystem has never been threatened as it is this last two decades. The population rate is increasing, and with more women and men in need of fuelwood. In 2014, according to the World Food Program study, the poverty rate in Benin rural areas (39.7%) was ahead of the urban area (31.4%) in 2011 [14]. Households in villages like Djegbadji and Avlékété, face many challenges to cope with their daily needs. The average living cost is under 1 USD per day per person (500F CFA/Jour/Person). Therefore, it is quite difficult or almost impossible to witness household using gas cookers. This implies that the population of these areas mainly relies on mangrove woods for fuelwood. But recent studies have shown that population use more and more mangrove, a situation which has drastically induce the state government to take a decree that prohibits the destruction of mangrove trees and moreover any ecosystem in the wetland close to the sea. Thus, at the present rate of destruction, the United Nations Environment Program – World Conservation and Monitoring estimated that $15,000 \, m^3$ of mangrove trees had been exploited per year in Benin in the past. Furthermore, they observed that the quarter of the mangrove area generally in Africa had been cut-off between 1980 and 2006 and that we shall observe the deforestation of about 70% of the total area of mangrove in Africa if no action is taken [9].

### 2.4    Consequences of the Destruction of the Mangrove Forest

Obviously, the impact of human activities clearly affects the mangrove ecosystem in Ouidah. Bearing in mind the key role played by mangrove in wetland, it appears that all the surrounded species (fishes, birds) of the ecosystem are under high vulnerability risk and more specifically species that rely on the mangrove in their life cycle. At the first level, the mangrove forests are recognized for excellent carbon sequestration and storage in the soils that surround mangrove roots and then contributes to reducing greenhouse gases effect on our planet. Secondly, the mangrove roots constitute the appropriate environment for many fish species reproduction. The local communities admit that the size and the number of fishes have decreased over the past years. This condition will get worse because of the fishing system named Acadja which functions as an artificial system of enhancing fish production by providing, through branches fixed on the bottom of the lake, additional substrate for the development of plants and animals which will serve as fish's nutrients. This system is known for reducing the depth of the body of water and decreasing the fish fauna biodiversity because few species can adapt to these new conditions [15]. Moreover, some migrant birds (*terns*) who usually migrate and dwell in the mangrove trees in their season seldom arrive in the region. This will contrast the efforts of the town-hall to promote ecological tourism and inhibit the attractiveness of regional eco-tourism.

Mangrove roots are also known to have the ability to trap sediment particles drawn from upstream channels and stabilize the coastline [9]. Its destruction leads then to the filling of the lagoon which causes the reduction of the depth of the water body and therefore causes flooding events to occur in case heavy rains.

The high illiteracy rate of those communities mainly composed of fishers and farmers makes them more vulnerable to flood events and their capacity to cope with it is then compromised. The 2010 flooding events which affected the region caused many financial losses (crops, livestock, houses, education equipment, etc.) and even humans death [2].

It then appears that the destruction of the mangroves by the population of these three villages impacts not only the mangroves and its ecosystem but also affect the community's sustainability, livelihood, and well-being. The need for adequate programs and policy, elaborated in accordance with them is urgent. Some alternative solutions moreover need to be proposed at affordable prices in such a way to effectively address the problem.

## 3    Ongoing Initiatives to Conserve the Mangrove Forest

Attempts have been made to restore the mangrove forest in Benin, between 1998 and 1999. Two hundred thousand *Rhizophora racemosa* and *Avicennia Africana* trees were planted with a survival rate of 62% after 12 months [9]. Later in 1999, a further 470 000 mangrove trees of both species were planted, although the survival rates are not reported. Supporting activities included awareness-raising and information provision to local communities living in the target areas will be beneficial and contribute to the success of such programs.

Many projects and activities had also been initiated to address the problem of destruction of mangrove trees in Ouidah, and more generally in Benin. At the national level, laws and decrees had been voted by the parliament to limit the abusive exploitation of woods in most of the forests. The risk is so high that the government decree forbids the destruction of the mangrove, an offense punishable by judicial sanctions up to imprisonment. Then, the population felt that their primary needs for firewood have not been taking into consideration because no option was given to them. In response, some NGOs and institutions have promoted alternative solutions that continue to enable economic activities, but in a manner that does not threaten the mangrove ecosystem. Some NGOs, propose new activities such as oil production, and the latest is a new and improved stove as an alternative to this community. Mainly, the alternative solutions aim to address salt production which is the major activity in the area by focusing on some types of stoves that function without woods as input. The observation is that any solution that fits with this activity could then be easily adapted to other sector or activity and replicated according to their local available materials as input.

### 3.1    Solar Salt Solution

The solar solution is a process that relies on the sunshine and its heat to evaporate the water vapor from the brine. This solution had been proposed to the population of Ouidah by UNIVER-SEL in 1998 as an alternative to cooking it. Some challenges were reported: (i) the process duration can take about 2–3 days to produce what is produced in half a day and it mainly depends on the weather and some other natural parameters (wind, humidity, ...), (ii) the system is afford-able except only the system tarpaulins (5 m × 2 m) which was estimated to 10 USD, (iii) the solution is an extensive process which requires a large surface of production to dry the brine, (iv) a training was required in order to arrange the tarpaulins in a way to foster a good production and the manipulation of tools needed for harvest or collection of the salt is special; (v) and these women considered that drying the brine will not eliminate pathogenic microbes in the salt and then cause a bad quality of salt comparing to their traditional process.

However, the project failed to bear fruit because once the project's staff left the communities, the salt producers returned to their traditional way of doing.

### 3.2   Improved Stoves

The most appreciable alternative to these communities remains the improved stove which combines local products in replacement of the mangrove woods. The objective of the improved stove is to create alternative stoves using local products but without mangrove woods or limited amounts. Until now, a total of four (04) stoves have been proposed each with its own challenges.

- Traditional stove: this is the first type of stove that the women and the population of the villages have been using for salt production. It is made with clay collected from the bottom of the lagoon and has a shape of an empty cylinder. It has one orifice for wood at the basis and has also 3–4 openings for bowls (Fig. 4). This stove uses 25 L of brine and 53 kg of wood within 120 min to produce 3.5 kg of rough salt.

**Fig. 4.** Structure of the traditional stove  (source: Nouvelle Afrique Magazine 2018/03/26).

- The Ofedi stove is the same as the traditional one but the clay here is mixed with palm kernel cake. Training is required in order to master how to use it effectively. This type of stove does not address the mangrove issue and did not get the approval of the population. However, the main issue raised by the users is the longer duration to produce the same amount of salt and more energy as a matter of fact.
- Action plus stove: this stove was produced using red clay and cement to shape the stove in the parallelepiped-shape. This combination with cement stabilizes the clay and gives it more resistance. It has two orifices for woods with two openings for bowls. The users reported that this stove is less resistant than the other and also consumes more energy and takes longer to produce salt. For instance, it requires on average 62 kg of wood to transform 25 L of brine into 3.78 kg of salt within 412 min.
- Mafoubo stove also uses clay to produce the stove in a cylinder-shape. It has only one orifice and one opening. It didn't get also the approval of the population because of the long duration of salt production. This stove uses 25 L of brine and 48 kg of wood within 325 min to produce 3.7 kg of salt.
- Mivo stove: this type of stove is the last generation of stove proposed to these communities. It has been proposed base on the prototype that the township is working on and funded by the United Nations Development Programme (UNDP). In fact, to avoid the destruction of the mangrove, the mayor in collaboration with her technical advisors try to link the palm oil production chain and it dusts which can be a good input in the replacement of the wood. Then, the system presented below, consists of the reuse of waste from a chain in other-chain as an important input. The stove is made of metal components and has a solar system for ventilation. It has four (04) openings where the palm nut hulls are dropped off as input (Fig. 5).

**Fig. 5.** Mivo stove structure using solar panel as energy source and palm nut hulls.

This solution is a good approach to the mangrove and its ecosystem conservation. As for disadvantages, this stove requires the continual presence of the user for adding the palm nut hulls. However, the Mivo stove will definitely help to address the main issue of the destruction of the mangrove.

### 3.3    Recommendation for Policy and Management

The benefits and services provided by mangrove trees are enormous and everything needs to be gathered to protect and conserve it. The mangroves forests need to be preserved in order to sustain the surrounding ecosystem. At the country level, we recommend that the law and decrees for ecological protection in general and mangrove forest, in particular, should be reinforced and made known to the general public and the people living in those areas through sensitization campaigns. Locally, the town-hall services need also to continue collaborating with the communities in order to get their input to improve the different versions of the stoves. Emphasis should be given to increase the efficiency of the stove by reducing the time duration, no or minor consumption of wood, and the resistance of the proposed stove. Moreover, a plantation of acacia auriculiformis and eucalyptus camaldulinsis should be implemented in those villages to supply additionally woods.

## 4    Conclusion

In summary, Ouidah hosts a valuable mangrove forest located in the three coastal villages of Djegbadji, Avlekete, and Houakpe-daho. Due to the actual growth of these communities coupled with the urgent demand of wood for salt production, the mangrove forest ecosystem has been enormously threatened. The services provides by such an ecosystem are many, and more actions need to be implemented to conserve it. Beyond laws and decrees, the state government needs to sensitize the communities and fund alternative solutions for salt production. Concerning the improved stoves which aim at replacing the input (mangrove woods) by palm nut hulls, new versions must include the insights of those communities in order to improve them for their well-being and moreover to preserve the ecosystem of mangrove forests.

**Acknowledgements.** We are thankful to Ouidah's Municipality staff especially the Technical service and the Planning and Local Development service responsible for providing the workspace environment and support during my internship and the writing of this paper. We are also thankful to Foutse YUEHGOH who contributed in an inestimable way and for her objective reviews.

# References

1. Law, R.: Ouidah: The Social History of a West African Slaving 'Port' 1727–1892. Nouvelle Presse (1993)
2. de Ouidah, M.: Plan de Développement Communal 3eme Generation (2018–2022). PDC-3 Ouidah (2017)
3. World Bank Database. https://donnees.banquemondiale.org/indicateur/AG.LND. PRCP.MM. Accessed Sept 2017
4. Food and Agriculture Organization. http://www.fao.org/nr/water/aquastat/data/query/results.html. Accessed Sept 2017
5. Nacoulma, J.D., Guigma, J.B.: Institutional context of soil information in Benin. Institutional Assessment Benin Country Report (2015)
6. Ministère de l'Environnement et de la Protection de la Nature (Benin): Programme d'Action National d'Adaptation aux changements climatiques du Bénin. Convention-cadre des Nations Unies sur les changements climatiques (2008)
7. Institut National de la Statistique et de l'Analyse Economique (INSAE): Cahier des villages et quartiers de ville du département de l'Atlantique (RGPH 4, 2013) (2016)
8. Dossou, J., Kpoclou, Y.E., Ballogou, V.Y., Ouikoun, G.: Amélioration des procédés traditionels de production de sel alimentaire (NaCl) par l'utilisation d'un distillateur solaire d'eau de mer. Bulletin de la Recherche Agronomique du Bénin, N 67 (2010)
9. UNEP-WCMC: Mangroves of Western and Central Africa. UNEP-Regional Seas Programme/UNEP-WCMC (2007). http://www.unep-wcmc.org/resources/publications/UNEP_WCMC_bio_series/26.html
10. Shumway, C.A.: Forgotten Waters: Freshwater and Marine Ecosystems in Africa. Strategies for Biodiversity Conservation and Sustainable Development, Boston University (1999)
11. Hejnowicz, A.P., Kennedy, H., Rudd, M.A., Huxham, M.R.: Harnessing the climate mitigation, conservation and poverty alleviation potential of seagrasses: prospects for developing blue carbon initiatives and payment for ecosystem service programmes. Front. Mar. Sci. 2, 32 (2015). https://doi.org/10.3389/fmars.2015.00032
12. Dasgupta, S., Islam, M.S., Huq, M., Khan, Z.H., Hasib, M.R.: Quantifying the protective capacity of mangroves from storm surges in coastal Bangladesh. PLoS ONE 14(3), e0214079 (2019). https://doi.org/10.1371/journal.pone.0214079
13. Blankespoor, B., Dasgupta, S., Lange, G.-M.: Mangroves as a protection from storm surges in a changing climate. Ambio 46(4), 478–491 (2016). https://doi.org/10.1007/s13280-016-0838-x
14. Programme alimentaire mondial des Nations Unies (PAM): Republique du Bénin: Analyse Globale de la Vulnérabilité et de la Sécurité Alimentaire (AGVSA) (2014). World Food Program. http://www.wfp.org/food-security
15. Niyonkuru, C., Laleye, P.A.: Impact of acadja fisheries on fish assemblages in Lake Nokoué, Benin, West Africa. Knowl. Manag. Aquat. Ecosyst. 399, 05 (2010). https://doi.org/10.1051/kmae/2010033

# Climate Change and Energy Efficiency

# Hydroclimate Analysis Under 1.5 and 2 °C Global Warming in the Faleme River Basin

Mamadou Lamine Mbaye[1(✉)], Khadidiatou Sy[1], Bakary Faty[2],
and Saidou Moustapha Sall[3]

[1] Laboratoire d'Océanographie, des Sciences de l'Environnement et du Climat (LOSEC),
Université Assane SECK de Ziguinchor, BP 523, Ziguinchor, Sénégal
mlmbaye@univ-zig.sn
[2] Direction de la Gestion et de la Planification des Ressources en Eau (DGPRE), Sphère
Ministérielle, 2ième arrondissement Diamniadio – Batiment B2, Dakar, Sénégal
[3] Laboratoire de Physique de l'Atmosphère et de l'Océan, Ecole Supérieure Polytechnique,
Université Cheikh Anta Diop, BP 5085, Dakar, Sénégal

**Abstract.** In this study, we analyze the hydroclimate of the Faleme basin which is a major tributary in the Senegal River Basin. This basin has faced hydrological droughts that have negatively affected rainfed agriculture, the economic development and have enhanced poverty. The main objective of this work is to investigate the variability and the changes of the basin hydroclimate during the past and the future under 1.5 and 2 °C global warming. Extreme precipitations analysis at Kidira (outlet of the basin) exhibit two noticeable periods 1950–1980 and 1981–2010; in the first period wet day's frequency and rainfall intensity decrease considerably. In the second period, the rainfall intensity, the consecutive dry days decrease while consecutive wet days, wet day frequency increase. Over the whole basin from 1901 to 2013, a general annual deficit is noticed with the simplified water balance, and the standardized precipitation from 1970 to 2010. As for the future changes over the basin by analyzing three regional climate models (RCA4, RACMO22, CCLM) simulations, rainfall is likely to increase under both warming conditions. Potential evapotranspiration from Penman is projected to increase with the highest magnitudes under 2 °C. Moreover, hydrological simulation with the GR4J model, project slight increase of river discharge in the coming decades. However, the simplified water balance shows drier conditions under both warming scenarios. Therefore, water saving technologies, crop resistant to higher evapotranspiration, and integrated water resources management should be developed and promoted in order to reduce the adverse effects of climate change.

**Keywords:** Hydroclimate · Faleme basin · Impacts · Global warming · Climate change

## 1 Introduction

The impact of climate change is already having an adverse effect on the stability of entire countries, regions, and continents. According to the fifth report of the Intergovernmental

J. P. R. Thorn et al. (Eds.): InterSol 2020, LNICST 321, pp. 121–133, 2020.
https://doi.org/10.1007/978-3-030-51051-0_9

Panel on Climate Change (IPCC), the impacts of extreme climate events have led to disruption of water supply and food production, alteration of ecosystems, mortality and morbidity, damage to infrastructure and settlements, and consequences human well-being and for mental health [1]. Furthermore, drought and flood are becoming more frequent worldwide. In addition, the potential changes in climate variability and in the frequency, intensity of extreme climate events are emerging as main determinants of future impacts and vulnerability [2]. In Africa, extreme weather and climate events including droughts and floods have considerable impacts on socio-economic sectors, natural resources and ecosystems, livelihoods, and human health [1].

Over West Africa, the recurrence of droughts has led to a significant decrease of streamflow in many river basins. Rivers are among the main water resources for drinking, irrigation, and industrial purposes in inland areas [3]. The Senegal River Basin has faced these conditions, its annual average flow at Bakel (reference station) has been reduced from an average of 840 $m^3.s^{-1}$ in the period 1950–1972 to only 419 $m^3.s^{-1}$ in the period 1973–2002 [4]. That hydrological drought has reduced rainfed agriculture, decreased the seasonal flooding of wetlands, limited economic development, and in the overall, enhanced poverty [5]. Such water shortage has obviously affected the main activities in the basin (agriculture, fishery, hydropower generation, etc.). Furthermore, it is well documented that hydro meteorological extremes [6, 7] will increase in the future and could have serious consequences on human societies and ecosystems. The Faleme River Basin (major tributary of the Senegal River Basin) is facing seriously the impacts of climate change and these are likely to be exacerbated in the future. It is in this context that our study aims to provide a better understanding of the potential impacts of 1.5 and 2.0 °C global warming levels (GWLs) on the hydroclimate of the basin. This will generate reliable climate change information for adequate adaptation measures in order to reduce the vulnerability of basin's people. Observed meteorological data and climate output from three regional climate models (RCA4, RACMO22, and CCLM) were used for analyzing the variability and the changes of the hydroclimate. In addition, the hydrological model GR4J has allowed us to simulate river discharge during the historical period (1984–2013), at 1.5 °C warming period (2017–2046) and at 2.0 °C warming period (2032–2061).

This paper is structured as following: after the Introduction, Data and Methodology are described in Sect. 2; the Results are presented in Sect. 3; Discussion and Conclusion are given in Sect. 4 and Sect. 5, respectively.

## 2   Data and Methodology

The Faleme basin is located in West Africa between longitudes 11°12′ and 12°15′0 W and latitudes 12°11 and 14°27 N. It is the main tributary of the left bank of the Senegal River Basin. The following stations (Fig. 1) were extracted from the Climatic Research Unit Time series (CRU TS) dataset (1901–2013) for monthly time series of precipitation and potential evapotranspiration; this dataset is gridded to 0.5 × 0.5 degree spatial resolution [8].

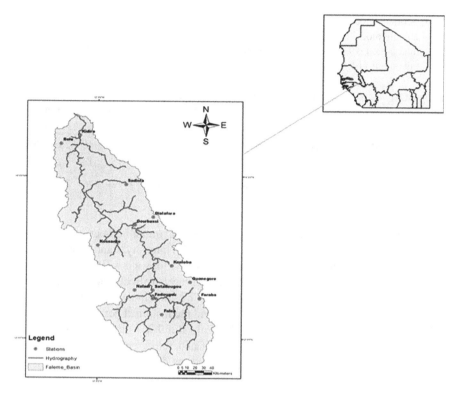

**Fig. 1.** Faleme river basin and its main stations

Then, we computed the mean values of precipitation and potential evapotranspiration over the whole basin by using the ensemble mean of all stations. We have used also daily observed rainfall at Kidira (1950–2010) from the National Agency of Civil Aviation and Meteorology of Senegal (ANACIM). Furthermore, daily climate simulations from three regional climate models (CCLM: Cosmo- Climate Limited-area Modelling Community Regional Climate Model, RCA4: Rossby Centre regional Atmospheric climate model, and RACMO22: Regional Atmospheric Climate Model) within the Coordinated Regional Climate Downscaling Experiment (CORDEX, [9]) are used. The spatial resolution of these climate models is 0.44° grid. One of the goal of CORDEX project, was to produce high regional climate simulations in order to better understand local and regional climate features over the world. These regional climate models (RCMs) are driven by the MOHC-HadGEM2 global climate model (GCM) following RCP4.5 Representative Concentration Pathways under 1.5 and 2.0 °C Global Warming Levels (GWLs). Three different periods were considered: historical (1984–2013), 1.5 °C warming period (2017–2046) and 2.0° warming period (2032–2061); these warmings are identified compared to the pre-industrial level [10]. Some characteristics of these RCMs are given in Table 1.

**Table 1.** Climate model data with the name of the driving global climate model (GCM), institute, regional climate model (RCM), and the different periods of simulations. The reference period is the historical period obtained with 0.5 °C warming, with respect to the preindustrial in the same way as both targets (1.5 °C and 2 °C) in the future.

| Driving GCM | Institute | RCM | Reference period | 1.5 °C warming period | 2.0 °C warming period |
|---|---|---|---|---|---|
| MOHC-HadGEM2-ES | SMHI | RCA4 | 1984–2013 | 2017–2046 | 2032–2061 |
| | KNMI | RACMO22T | 1984–2013 | 2017–2046 | 2032–2061 |
| | CLMcom | CCLM4–8–17 | 1984–2013 | 2017–2046 | 2032–2061 |

Hydroclimate indices are computed such as the maximum number of consecutive wet and dry days, frequency of wet and dry days, rainfall intensity, standard precipitation index (SPI), standard evapotranspiration index (SPEI), aridity index (P over PET), water balance/budget (P minus PET). The signification of these hydroclimate metrics/indices are summarized in Table 2. The changes in the basin hydroclimate are estimated by the difference between the future warming periods and the historical period.

We used the hydrological model GR4J (Génie Rural à 4 paramètres Journaliers) to simulate river discharge during the historical and future periods. GR4J is a simple rainfall-runoff model. It uses forcing data such as daily rainfall, temperature and evapotranspiration to simulate river flow at the outlet Kidira.

**Table 2.** Hydroclimate indices

| Index name | Index signification | Unit |
|---|---|---|
| Simple daily rainfall intensity index (SDII) | Let PRwj be the daily precipitation amount on wet days, PR $\geq$ 1 mm in period j. If W represents the number of wet days in j, the rainfall intensity is given by the sum of PRwj divided by W | mm |
| Maximum number of consecutive dry days (CDD) | Let PRij be the daily precipitation amount on day i in period j. Count the largest number of consecutive days where PRij < 1 mm | day |
| Maximum number of consecutive wet days (CWD) | Let PRij be the daily precipitation amount on day i in period j. Count the largest number of consecutive days where PRij > 1 mm | day |
| Water balance | Difference between precipitation and potential evapotranspiration (P-PET) | mm |

(continued)

**Table 2.** (*continued*)

| Index name | Index signification | Unit |
|---|---|---|
| Aridity index | Fraction of precipitation over potential evapotranspiration | – |
| Standardized precipitation index (SPI) | In each rainfall time step, the rainfall mean over the whole period was subtracted, and after the difference was divided by the standard deviation | – |
| Standardized evapotranspiration index (SPEI)_ | In each evapotranspiration time step, the evapotranspiration mean over the whole period was subtracted, and after the difference was divided by the standard deviation | – |
| Low flows (10P) | 10th percentile of river flows means the value above which 90% of the daily flows are found | $m^3/s$ |

More details on the functioning of this model can be found in [11, 12]. Then, the climate output from the above three regional climate models are used by GR4J to simulate stream flows in the Faleme River during the historical and the future period.

## 3   Results

### 3.1   Interannual Variability of the Past Hydroclimate

Figure 2 shows the interannual variations of precipitation characteristics at Kidira (outlet of the Faleme basin) from 1950 to 2010. The years 1970s and 1980s have the highest number of consecutive dry days (Fig. 2a) and dry day's frequency (Fig. 2c) by contrast of the consecutive wet days (Fig. 2b) and the wet day's frequency (Fig. 2d). These years correspond to the periods where the Sahel region faced the most severe droughts. However, wet periods are relatively found during the 1950s and the 2000s, this later result is confirmed by the standard precipitation index (Fig. 2f) where blue color indicates an increase and red color exhibits water deficit. As for the rainfall intensity (Fig. 2e), the more heavy rainfall are found in the 1960s.

As for the mean over the whole basin by using CRU datasets, the standardized precipitation index (Fig. 3a) shows noticeably two different periods: a relatively wet period (1901–1970), and a water deficit period (1971–2013), with high interannual variability in both periods. Regarding the SPEI from 1901 to 2013 (Fig. 3b), higher potential evapotranspiration is noticed in particular periods such as 1907-1911, 1939-1945, 1969-1972, and 1990-2013; the other periods highlighted low potential evapotranspiration. Generally, the aridity indexes (Fig. 3c) are below one, this means that the annual PET is usually higher than the annual precipitation in this basin. This later result is well seen in the simplified water balance (P-PET) in Fig. 3d, where in the whole period, negative values are found which indicated more water losses through evapotranspiration.

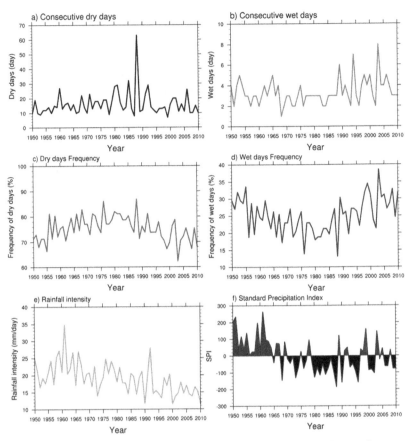

**Fig. 2.** Interannual variability of maximum number of consecutive dry days (a), maximum number of consecutive wet days (b), dry days frequency (c), wet days frequency (d), rainfall intensity (e) and standardized precipitation Index (f) at Kidira (1950–2010) (Color figure online)

## 3.2 Future Changes of the Basin Hydroclimate Under Global Warming Levels

With regard to the future hydroclimate of the basin under 1.5 and 2.0 °C global warming, the three RCMs (RCA4, RACMO22, CCLM) and their ensemble mean show mainly an increase of rainfall during the wet season (Fig. 4); even though in few months, precipitation could slightly decrease in the beginning and the end of the rainy season. This increase is more pronounced with 1.5 °C than with 2.0 °C, global warming. However, in the coming decades, potential evapotranspiration is likely to increase in all regional climate models and their ensemble mean (Fig. 5). The changes of PET are more substantial with 2.0 °C global warming. CCLM displays the greatest increase of water losses through the processes of evaporation and transpiration.

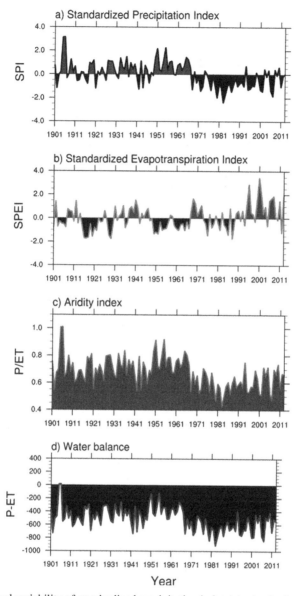

**Fig. 3.** Interannual variability of standardized precipitation index (a), standardized evapotranspiration index (b), aridity index (c) and water balance (d) over the whole basin (1901–2013)

### 3.3 Simulated River Discharge During the Past and the Future

Furthermore, we simulated river discharge at the main outlet of the basin (Kidira) by using the output of these regional climate models as forcing of the hydrological model GR4J during the historical (1984–2013), under 1.5 °C global warming (2017–2046), and under 2.0 °C global warming (2032–2061).

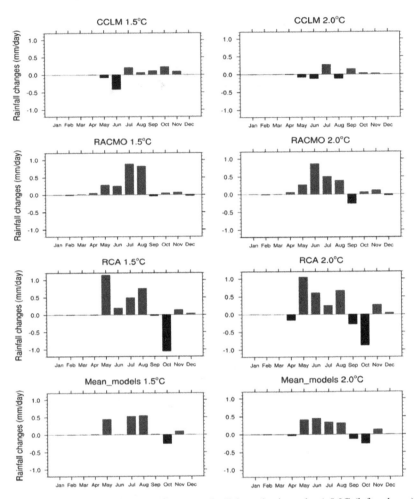

**Fig. 4.** Monthly changes of precipitation over the Faleme basin under 1.5 °C (left column) and 2.0 °C (right column) GWLs for the three RCMs and their ensemble mean. Red color indicates a decrease and blue color indicates an increase. (Color figure online)

The results are shown in Fig. 6 in the form of box-plots. It is clearly noticed that river discharge is likely to increase under both warming when compared to the historical period. This situation may be due to the probable increase of rainfall. The CCLM regional climate model exhibits the lowest increase of streamflow. The increase of river flow is highly linked to the input data, particularly precipitation that is relatively common in several rainfall-runoff models. Some characteristics of the basin hydroclimate are summarized in Table 3. The simple water balance (P-PET) is negative in all periods which means the basin may experiences in the future water stress up to −154.09 mm under 1.5 °C and −160.25 mm under 2.0 °C.

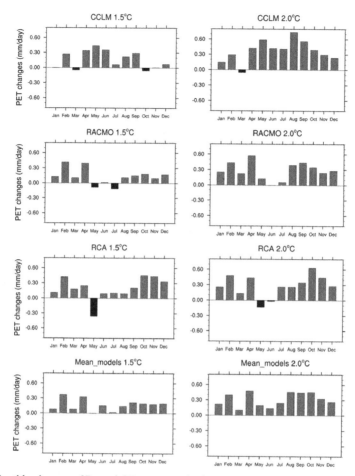

**Fig. 5.** Monthly changes of Potential Evapotranspiration over the Faleme basin under 1.5 °C (left column) and 2.0 °C (right column) GWLs for the three RCMs and their ensemble mean. Red color indicates a decrease and green color indicates an increase. (Color figure online)

Rainfall is projected to increase from historical to the future; an increase of 42.03 mm under 1.5 °C, and an increase of 36.85 mm under 2.0 °C. As well documented, temperature generally increases under both warming scenarios. Moreover, potential evapotranspiration follows obviously the same changes as temperature. However, the decline of the simple water balance while there could be a slight increase of precipitation may be due to an overestimation of the potential evapotranspiration. As found by these authors [13] smaller change is found under 1.5 °C scenario as the 2.0 °C scenario. Moreover, dry day's frequency might decrease under 1.5 °C global warming and increase under 2.0 °C global warming. In addition, the low flows characterized here by the 10th percentile, indicate a potential decrease of these river flows at 2046 and 2061 horizons.

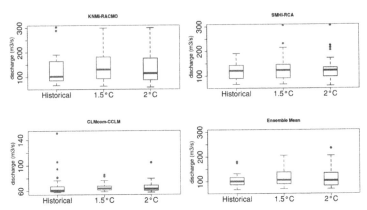

**Fig. 6.** Box plots of simulated river discharge under historical period (red color), under 1.5 °C (green color) and 2.0 °C (blue color) of the Faleme at Kidira outlet (Color figure online)

**Table 3.** Summary of the mean characteristics of the basin's hydroclimate (water balance, Rainfall, Evapotranspiration, Temperature, dry day's frequency, low flows) of the ensemble mean of all RCMs during the reference period (1984–2013), 1.5 °C warming period (2017–2046), and 2.0 °C warming (2032–2061)

| Indicators | Reference period (1984–2013) | 1.5 °C warming (2017–2046) | 2.0 °C warming (2032–2061) |
|---|---|---|---|
| Water balance (mm) | −154.09 | −155.38 | −160.25 |
| Rainfall (mm) | 689.77 | 731.8 | 726.62 |
| Evapotranspiration (mm) | 843.86 | 887.18 | 886.87 |
| Temperature (∘C) | 27.74 | 28.901 | 29.514 |
| Dry day's frequency (%) | 10.889 | 10.75 | 10.917 |
| Low flows (10th percentile) | 1.019 | 0.999 | 0.971 |

## 4 Discussion

This water shortage (Fig. 2 and 3) is within the period when the Sahel experiences its severe droughts in the 20th century which was a result of the cooling of the North Atlantic relative to the South Atlantic [14] However, some heavy rains were found in particular years; this kind of rainfall causes usually floods which affect human societies and their socio-economic activities. Substantial water is lost through evapotranspiration which is generally the most significant component of the water budget, acting to recycle much of rainfall, in particular, over the Sahel region [15]. In the coming decades, the RCA4 and RACMO22 models exhibit the most considerable changes in the future. This increase could be the result of moisture supply for convection from the North

Atlantic Ocean due the global warming which increases the atmospheric water vapor that in turn can leads to substantial precipitation over the basin. Temperature (not shown here) has similar changes that potential evapotranspiration. It generally increases in all climate models, and obviously in their ensemble mean. This is a well-known situation, as in the literature, the climate models in several studies agree in a general increase of temperature in the future due to anthropogenic greenhouse gases [16, 17]. The increase of evapotranspiration will lead to more atmospheric water vapor which generate cloud by condensation; the increase of cloudiness could in turn generate considerable rainfall. Additionally, it should also be taken into account the influence of the global tropical oceans and the North Atlantic SSTs that highly influence the Sahel rainfall [18]. In the ensemble mean, lower values of evapotranspiration during the rainy season can be explained by the fact that PET is moisture limited during the dry season and energy during the wet season. The differences in the models projections are mainly due to the physical paramctrization and the convection scheme used to simulate the hydroclimate processes of the basin. The slight increase of streamflow found in the future can be explained by an increase of precipitation resulting from more atmospheric cooling due to high evaporation and an increase of the atmospheric water holding capacity [7].

## 5  Conclusion

This study analyses the past and the future variations of the hydroclimate of the Faleme basin under 1.5 and 2.0 °C global warming. In the past, the analyses show a higher inter-annual variability of precipitation, potential evapotranspiration, their indexes and the water balance. Generally, wet period (1901–1970), and dry period (1971–2013), were identified. The annual water budget shows a water deficit over the whole basin. Furthermore, the years 1950s and the 2000s, are wetter than those in the 1970s and the 1980s. In the future, the basin is likely to experience relatively slight increase of precipitation, and considerable increase of temperature and potential evapotranspiration in the coming decades. Water losses through evaporation and transpiration are more pronounced under 2.0 °C global warming. It is projected also an increase of streamflow in future under both warming, particularly with 1.5 °C global warming. Moreover, low flows could decrease in future. These results show also that the level of warming that is related with the greenhouse gases emission, has an important impact on the projected climate change signals. According to these findings, the riparian people of the basin should develop and use water saving technologies, crop resistant to higher evapotranspiration, and integrated water resources management, smart agriculture. However, due to uncertainties related to climate simulations and the hydrological model, further investigations are needed with more regional climate simulations and uncertainty analysis. Bias correction techniques on climate model output may improve the quality of the hydrological simulation. Instead of using a simple rainfall-runoff model, physically-based hydrological models may offer better representation of the hydrological processes.

**Acknowledgments.** The authors thank the Laboratoire d'Océanographie, des Sciences de l'Environnement et du Climat (LOSEC) of the University of Assane Seck, Ziguinchor were the work has been mainly done. The authors would like to thank also Babacar Faye and the anonymous reviewers for their valuable suggestions and comments to improve the quality of the paper. We are further thankful to AWARD and the One Planet Fellowship for the scientific skills acquired during the science week in Morocco.

# References

1. IPCC: Summary for policymakers. In: Field, C.B., et al. (eds.) Climate Change 2014. Impacts, Adaptation, and Vulnerability. Part A: Global and Sectoral Aspects. Contribution of Working Group II to the Fifth Assessment Report of the Intergovernmental Panel on Climate Change, pp. 1–32. Cambridge University Press, Cambridge and NewYork (2014)
2. IPCC: Impacts, Adaptation, and Vulnerability – Contribution of Working Group II to the Intergovernmental Panel on Climate Change Third Assessment Report, 1032 p. (2001)
3. Mouri, G., Takizawa, S., Oki, T.: Spatial and temporal variation in nutrient parameters in stream water in a rural–urban catchment, Shikoku, Japan: effects of land cover and human impact. J. Environ. Manag. **92**(7), 1837–1848 (2011). https://doi.org/10.1016/j.jenvman.2011.03.005
4. Enda-TM: climate change adaptation and water resources management in West Africa. Synthesis report, WRITESHOP, Dakar, Senegal, 95 p. (2007)
5. Oyebande, L., Odunuga, S.: Climate change impact on water resources at the transboundary level in West Africa: the cases of the Senegal, Niger and Volta Basins. Open Hydr. J. **4**(1), 163–172 (2010). https://doi.org/10.2174/1874378101004010163
6. Mbaye, M.L., Diatta, S., Gaye, A.T.: Climate change signals over senegal river basin using regional climate models of the CORDEX Africa simulations. In: Kebe, C., Gueye, A., Ndiaye, A., Garba, A. (eds.) InterSol 2018. LNICST, vol. 249, pp. 123–132. Springer, Cham (2018). https://doi.org/10.1007/978-3-319-98878-8_12
7. Mbaye, M.L., Sylla, M.B., Tall, M.: Impacts of 1.5 and 2.0 °C global warming on water balance components over Senegal in West Africa. Atmosphere **10**(11), 712 (2019). https://doi.org/10.3390/atmos10110712
8. Harris, I., Jones, P.D., Osborn, T.J., Lister, D.H.: Updated high-resolution grids of monthly climatic observations the CRU TS3.10 dataset. Int. J. Climatol. (2013). https://doi.org/10.1002/joc.3711
9. Giorgi, F., Jones, C., Asrar, G.: Addressing climate information needs at the regional level: the CORDEX framework. World Meteorol. Organ. Bull. **58**, 175–183 (2009). http://wcrp.ipsl.jussieu.fr/cordex/documents/CORDEX_giorgi_WMO.pdf
10. Sylla, M.B., Faye, A., Giorgi, F., Diedhiou, A., Kunstmann, H.: Projected heat stress under 1.5 °C and 2 °C global warming scenarios creates unprecedented discomfort for humans in West Africa. Earth's Future **6**(7), 1029–1044 (2018). https://doi.org/10.1029/2018EF000873
11. Perrin, C., Michel, C., Andréassian, V.: Improvement of a parsimonious model for streamflow simulation. J. Hydrol. **2003**(279), 275–289 (2003). https://doi.org/10.1016/S0022-1694(03)00225-7
12. https://webgr.irstea.fr/modeles/journalier-gr4j-2/fonctionnement_gr4j/. Accessed 21 Dec 2019
13. Liu, L., Xu, H., Wang, Y., Jiang, T.: Impacts of 1.5 and 2 °C global warming on water availability and extreme hydrological events in Yiluo and Beijiang River catchments in China. Clim. Change **145**(1), 145–158 (2017). https://doi.org/10.1007/s10584-017-2072-3

14. Giannini, A., Salack, S., Lodoun, T., Ali, A., Gaye, A.T., Ndiaye, O.: A unifying view of climate change in the Sahel linking intra-seasonal, interannual and longer time scales. Environ. Res. Lett. **8**, 024010 (2013). https://doi.org/10.1088/1748-9326/8/2/024010

15. Ruti, P.M., et al.: The West African climate system: a review of the AMMA model inter-comparison initiatives. Atmosph. Sci. Lett. **12**, 116–122 (2011). https://doi.org/10.1029/201 8EF000873

16. Mbaye, M.L., Haensler, A., Hagemann, S., Gaye, A.T., Moseley, C., Afouda, A.: Impact of statistical bias correction on the projected climate change signals of the regional climate model REMO over the Senegal River Basin. Int. J. Climatol. (2015). https://doi.org/10.1002/joc.4478

17. Nangombe, S.S., Zhou, T., Zhang, W., Zou, L., Li, D.: High-temperature extreme events over Africa under 1.5 and 2 °C of global warming. J. Geophys. Res.: Atmos. **124**, 4413–4428 (2019). https://doi.org/10.1029/2018JD029747

18. Giannini, A., Saravanan, R., Chang, P.: Oceanic forcing of Sahel rainfall on interannual to interdecadal time scales. Science **302**, 1027–1030 (2003). https://doi.org/10.1126/science.1089357

# Supervision Strategy of a Hybrid System PV with Storage for Injection to the Electrical Network

Amadou Ba[1]([⊠]), Alphousseyni Ndiaye[1], and Senghane Mbodji[2]

[1] Research Team Energetic System and Efficiency,
Alioune DIOP University of Bambey, Bambey, Senegal
{amadou4.ba.ba,alphousseyni.ndiaye}@uadb.edu.sn
[2] Research Team Renewable Energie Materials and LASER,
Alioune DIOP University of Bambey, Bambey, Senegal
senghane.mbodji@uadb.edu.sn

**Abstract.** In photovoltaic system (PVS) hybrid, battery are often used for energy storage in order to ensure a permanent operation. Our system consists of solar panels, a boost converter which serves as an interface between the PVS and the load, and a buck-boost converter between the battery and the load. To ensure proper operation of the system, the DC bus voltage must be maintained constant. The batteries are sensitive to overcharging and deep discharge phenomena and more PVS have a low conversion efficiency. Faced with these problems the objective of this study is to maintain constant voltage bus, optimize performance of the PVS and to control the battery state of charge and discharge. The control strategy is a combination of MPPT (Maximum Power Point Tracking) control based on artificial neural networks (ANN) and an algorithm against the battery charge state. Simulation results show that the bus voltage is hold constant with the PI and PID correctors. There is also an improvement in conversion efficiency and control of the state of battery charge.

**Keywords:** ANN · Battery · Boost converter · Buck-boost convert · PVS

## 1 Introduction

The environmental protection became a very important point, since the solution is to have a cheap source of energy, sustainable and low-polluting. In recent decades utmost importance is given to photovoltaic systems to meet the global energy challenge. Photovoltaic systems are no longer limited to stand-alone systems but also contribute to increase the electricity generation facilities through PVS connected to the electrical distribution network. But the major problem of these systems is their low conversion efficiencies around 10–23% [1] and the

J. P. R. Thorn et al. (Eds.): InterSol 2020, LNICST 321, pp. 134–145, 2020.
https://doi.org/10.1007/978-3-030-51051-0_10

intermittent nature of their source. Faced with these problems photovoltaic modules must operate at their Maximum Power Point (MPP), hence the need to use commands MPPT [2] to improve performance. On the other hand to provide continuous access of energy, storage systems such as batteries are a solution. These are sensitive to overcharge and deep discharge phenomena [3]. These have a significant impact on battery lifetime. It is then necessary to associate a control system to ensure their protection. Faced with these various problems a methods have been developed to optimize the PVS conversion efficiency and control the state of charge of the battery. Traditional methods such as constant current or constant voltage have been proposed in the literature. In [4] a PI-type controller is used to maintain a constant current and the charging voltage to a variation in climatic conditions. The system consists of two converters (Boost and Buck). A MPPT control based on fuzzy logic is used to optimize the conversion efficiency and in our stady we use artificiel neuron network ANN to improuve the efficience. Simulation results show that the classical PI controller maintains the current and the voltage out of the Buck constant to charge the batteries. This objectif is achieved with the PID controller that maintains current and output voltage of the converter constant in Buck [5] and we note the good performance of the MPPT control based on logic compared to the conventional commands types P&O and INC. Other researches focuse on the control of the battery charge state to improve their lives. In [6] the approach is to control the deep charge and discharge phenomena by storing energy needs at night and the same approach is used in [7]. In [8,9] experimental implementation of a device for controling the state of charge (SOC) of a standalone PV system are presented. A control strategy for a multi-source system (Panels, Wind, battery and generator) has been developed [10]. However, the system must be equipped with a charge or discharge regulator to maintien the voltage constant and we note the good performance of a series regulator [11]. Other works deal with to the regulation of the DC voltage of the system. The latter is strongly influenced by the voltage of the PVS, the battery charge and load. This is achieved in [12] where a comparative study of a PID controller and fuzzy logic (FL) is done and there is a good performance of the FL command to maintien constant the current and voltage of the charge battery. A comparative study of a PI controller and a controller based on the predictive method for regulating the DC bus of a hybrid system is presented [13]. Autors study the regulation of the DC voltage and the control of the SOC but no one uses the ANN to improuvement the performance of the PVS and control the SOC of the battery. The main goal in this paper is to maintain constant the voltage bus and to study the implementation of an intelligent control for controlling the battery charge. As a contribution we firstly kept bus voltage constant with a PID controller that improves response time and oscillations and also developed an algorithm that improve the efficiency of PVS by ANN and simultaneously control the state of charge of the battery.

## 2  Presentation of a Hybrid System

Hybrid systems combine two or more complementary renewable sources such as wind and solar or several renewable and conventional sources such as solar and diesel generator. In our case we use PVS and batteries to feed a dc load. When PVS production is sufficient and the state of charge of the batteries is below than the minimum admissible. In this case, the PVS supplies feed the load and charge the battery through a bidirectionnel converter. The hybrid system studied in this work is used to feed a continuous load at a constant voltage. It consists of solar panels that convert light energy into electrical energy and storage battery that feed the load during the low sunlight hours. A power electronic converters are used as interface between the panels and the load and between the batteries and charge (Fig. 1). The addition of a storage battery increases flexibility in system control and enhances the overall availability of the system.

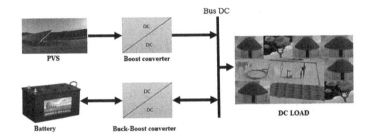

**Fig. 1.** Structure of a hybrid system.

### 2.1  Modeling Panel

In the literature several models have been developed to describe the behavior of a photovoltaic cell. The standard model consists [14, 15] of a current source associated with a diode and two resistors modeling the losses. The electrical circuit representing the electrical model of the cell is given in Fig. 2. The mathematical equation linking the current $I_{PV}$ and the voltage $V_{PV}$ of the cell is given by Eq. 1 and represents the mathematical model of the cell.

$$I_{pv} = [I_{cc}\frac{G}{G_0} + k_t(T - T_r)] - I_D - \frac{V_{pv} + R_s I_{pv}}{R_{sh}} \tag{1}$$

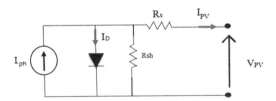

**Fig. 2.** Electric model of a solar cell.

$I_{cc}$ is the short-circuit photo current under standard conditions;

$G_0$ et $T_r$ are the reference illuminance and temperature, respectively;

$k_t = 23.10^{-3}A$ is the short-circuit photo current temperature coefficient. The current and the voltage at the terminal of a cell are low, so we associate multiple cells to obtain sufficient current and voltage to our systems.

## 2.2 Model of the Battery

Several models have been developed in the literature among which there is the simple electric model [3,16,17] or RC (Résistor Capacitor) model that are used. It consists of a fem $E_0$ representing the load voltage of the battery, a capacitor $C$ modeling the internal capacity of the battery and an internal resistance $R_b$. The mathematical equations describing the mathematical model of the battery are its state of charge (SOC) and its charging $V_{chb}$ and discharging voltage $V_{dchb}$ [18]. To protect the battery, it is essential to maintain its state of charge (SOC) between a maximum allowable state $Soc_{max}$ and a minimum state $Soc_{min}$ which must not be exceeded. The Eqs. 2, 3, 4 and 5 give the mathematical model of the battery.

$$Soc(\%) = 100(1 - \frac{I_{bat}}{C_{bat}}t) \tag{2}$$

$$V_{chb} = [2 + 0.16Soc] + \frac{I_{bat}}{C_{bat}}(\frac{6}{1 + I_{bat}^{0.86}} + \frac{0.48}{(1 - Soc)^{1.2}} + 0.36)[1 + 0.0025\Delta t] \tag{3}$$

$$V_{dchb} = [2.085 - 2.12(1 - Soc)] + \frac{I_{bat}}{C_{bat}}(\frac{4}{1 + I_{bat}^{1.3}} + \frac{0.27}{(1 - Soc)^{1.5}} + 0.02)[1 - 0.007\Delta t] \tag{4}$$

$$C_{bat}(Ah) = \frac{P_{load}t}{DOD(\%)V_{bat}} \tag{5}$$

$C_{bat}$ is the battery capacity in Ah which is a function of the power of the load, the charging time $t$, DOD (Depth Of Discharge) and the battery voltage $V_{bat}$ [19].

# 3 Description and System Control Approach

## 3.1 Control Unidirectional Converter

Boost converter is used as an interface between the PVS and the charge and the objective of the control of this converter is to maximize the power output. Several MPPT control techniques have been developed in the literature and in the case of our study we will use an MPPT control based on artificial neural networks for continued maximum power point. We develop a flowchart to implement the ANN controler. The ANN are parallel connected processors where each calculates the single output based on the information it receives. To implement an intelligent command, it is necessary to get a database which is used as learning. In our study we chose the InC to generate this database by varying the profile of sunshine and temperature. The architecture of the neural control consists of an input layer of two (02) neurons corresponding to the current and voltage of the PVS, a hidden layer of fifteen (15) neurons and output layer of one (01) neuron corresponding to the durty cycle. Figure 3 shows the algorithm of the neural control used and from the current and voltage of the panels it provide a duty ratio for controlling the converter.

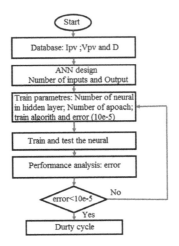

**Fig. 3.** Algorithm neuronal MPPT control.

## 3.2 Bidirectional Converter Model

The buck-boost converter Fig. 4 plays a crucial role in hybrid systems; it allows to charge and discharge the storage unit and maintain the constant DC bus. The operating principle of this converter is based on two modes. When K2 is closed K3 is open, it operates in the boost mode and the output voltage is greater than the intput voltage. When K3 is open and K2 closed, it operates in the buck mode and the output voltage is lower than the input voltage. Equation 6 gives the mathematical model this converter [20, 21].

$$\begin{cases} \frac{di_L}{dt} = \frac{V_b}{L_{bb}} - (1-d)\frac{V_{dc}}{L_{bb}} \\ \frac{dv_{dc}}{dt} = (1-d)\frac{I_L}{C_{bb}} - \frac{V_{dc}}{RC_{bb}} \end{cases} \tag{6}$$

Where $V_b$, $C_{bb}$, $L_{bb}$ and d are the voltage of the battery, the output capacitor of the converter, the inductance of the converter and the duty cycle, respectively.

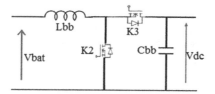

**Fig. 4.** Electrical model of a buck-boost converter.

## 3.3  Regulation of the DC Bus

The DC bus voltage depends on the power produced by PVS, the charging and discharging current of the battery and the load power [22]. To maintain it constant, generally two control loops of voltage and current are used (Fig. 5). The error between the reference voltage and the DC bus voltage is feed to a corrector and the output provides a reference current $I_{ref}$ which is compared with the current of the battery and the error produced is sent to a second corrector which its output is used to control the converter mode in charging or discharging. So when the error between the reference voltage and the the DC voltage is negative the control loop provides a negative reference current and corresponds to the battery charge. If it is positive, it generates positive reference current and corresponds to the battery discharges. Therefore, we will use the PI and PID controller to regulate the voltage and current whose transfer function is given respectively by the following Eqs. 7 and 8.

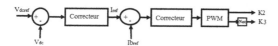

**Fig. 5.** Control loop of the voltage and current.

$$C_{PI}(p) = k_p + \frac{k_i}{p} \tag{7}$$

$$C_{PID}(p) = k_p + \frac{k_i}{p} + K_i p \tag{8}$$

From Eq. 6 the functions are found for each control loop.

$$\frac{v_{dc}(p)}{i_L(p)} = \frac{RI_L L_{bb} p + RV_{dc}(1-D)}{RV_{dc}C_{bb}p + V_{dc} + (1-D)I_L R} \tag{9}$$

$$\frac{i_L(p)}{d(p)} = \frac{RV_{dc}C_{bb}p + V_{dc} + (1-D)I_L R}{RL_{bb}C_{bb}p^2 + L_{bb} + R(1-D)^2} \tag{10}$$

In order to find the parameters of these correctors based on the phase mage method and gain where a system is stable, if the phase margin and gain are successively included between 45° and 60° and of 10 and 15 dB [23,24], we used values presented below (Table 1).

**Table 1.** Correcteur and parametres size.

| Corrector | PI | | PID | | |
|---|---|---|---|---|---|
| Parametres | $k_p$ | $k_i(s^{-1})$ | $k_p$ | $k_i(s^{-1})$ | $k_d(s)$ |
| Valus | 0.5 | 125 | 0.9 | 92.456 | $1.510^{-2}$ |

The main object if of this section is to maintain the voltage bus constant which is influenced by changes in the power of the PVS and the battery.

### 3.4    Control Strategy of the Hybrid System

The main object if is to develop an algorithm (Fig. 6) which can track the maximum power point (MMP) of the PVS and control the charging and discharging of the battery. This control strategy is the combination of a MPPT based on the ANN and a strategy of suppervion in order to protect the battery to the overcharge and deep discharge. This algorithm can be divided into four modes:

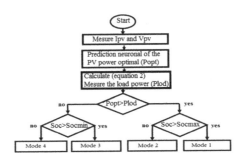

**Fig. 6.** System Control Algorithm.

**Mode 1**: when the power of the photovoltaic system is greater than the power of the load and the battery charge state is greater than equal to the maximum state of charge (85%), (S1 and S2) switch are **ON** and S3 is **OFF** to disconnect the battery and protect it to the overload.

**Mode 2**: when the power of the PVS is greater than the load power and the state of charge is less than the maximum state of charge, (S1, S2 and S3) switch are **ON** and the PVS feed the load and charges the batteries.

**Mode 3**: When the power of the PVS is less than the load power and the state of charge is greater than the maximum state of charge, S1, S2 and S3 are **ON** and the load is feed by the PVS and the battery.

**Mode 4**: when the power of the PVS is less than that of the load and the state of charge is less than the minimum state of charge (20%), switch S1 and S2 are **ON** and S3 is **OFF** to disconnect the battery in order to protect it against the deep discharge. Figure 7 shows the structure of the hybrid system with the approach of the command.

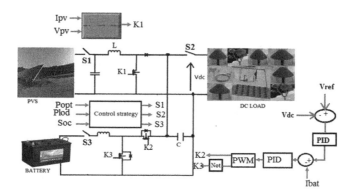

**Fig. 7.** Structure of our system stady.

## 4   Simulation Results and Discussion

The simulation is performed under the environment of Matlab/Simulink and the system consists of a PVS Twenty-seven (27) type of panel 1STH-220-P of (03) strings of (09) modules, an acid type battery set powering a DC load. The equations to design the converters elements are obtained from references [3].

Table 2 provides system parameters and the sizing results (Fig. 8).

**Table 2.** System and simulation Settings.

| Power(W) | $I_{sc}(A)$ | $V_{oc}(V)$ | $C_1(F)$ | $C(F)$ | $C_b(Ah)$ |
|----------|-------------|-------------|----------|--------|-----------|
| 218.871  | 7.97        | 36.6        | $150\ 10^{-6}$ | $22\ 10^{-6}$ | 50 |

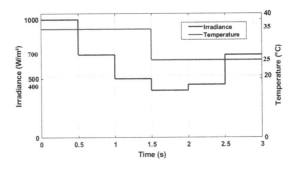

**Fig. 8.** Irradiance $(W/m^2)$ and temperature$(C)$.

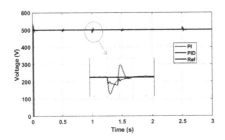

**Fig. 9.** DC bus voltage and the reference.

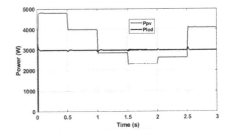

**Fig. 10.** Power PVS and load.

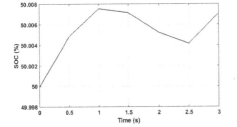

**Fig. 11.** State of charge of the battery.

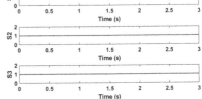

**Fig. 12.** Switchs commutation.

The objective of this study is firstly to maintain constant voltage DC bus and in the other hand to control the battery charge state and improve their lifetime. The Bus DC voltage is influenced by the variation of the voltage of PVS, the charging and discharging current of the battery and the variation of the load. For optimal operation of the system, the load supply voltage must be kept constant. A comparative study of PI and PID controller to maintain constant DC bus voltage is done. Figure 9 shows that the voltage is kept constant with the two correctors. The comparative study shows that the PID controller is better than PI in terms of response time and reduces overshoots (Table 3). The main object of this comparative study is to choose the correector who has fast speed convergence and low oscillations. That's why we choose the

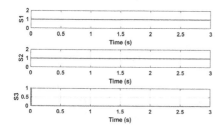 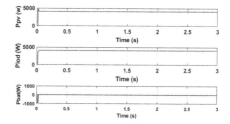

**Fig. 13.** Switchs commmutation.          **Fig. 14.** Power variation.

**Table 3.** Comparative stydy.

| Corrector | Reponse time (ms) | Overshoots (%) |
|-----------|-------------------|----------------|
| PI        | 100               | 44             |
| PID       | 60                | 20             |

PID correcteur to maintain constant the DC bus. In Fig. 10, we see that boost converter output power under standard conditions (1000 $W/m^2$ and 25 °C) corresponds to the power of the PVS proving yield optimization with neuronal MPPT control. The current and the voltage of the PVS neuronal command, provides a duty cycle for optimum operation of the boost converter. Figure 11 shows the battery state of charge and it is on mode charge when the power of the PVS is greater than the load power [0 to 1 s]. On mode discharge when the PVS power is less than the load power [1 to 2.5 s]. Figure 12 show the switchs commutation, the battery is connected. And when the power of PVS is greater than the load power, the battery state of charge reaches the maximum or minimum state of charge, S3 is turned off (Fig. 13) to protect battery to the overcharge or deep discharge. Figure 14 shows that the battery is disconnected. The load is powered continuously and the battery charge state is controlled.

## 5   Conclusion

The objective of this study is to disign a new control strategy and power management for a hybrid stand-alone PV/battery feeding a DC load. The bus voltage, kept constant is influenced by the variation of the voltage of PVS and batteries and we note a good performance of PID controller compared to a PI. The developed control strategy combining MPPT control based on ANN and battery charging state control algorithm improves the PVS conversion efficiency and contributes to the protection of the batteries against the phenomena overcharge and deep discharge. We have considered to validate our control strategy by doing a real-life implementation with all the other factors that can impact the performance of the system.

# References

1. Massalti, S., Harrag, A., Loukriz, A.: A new neural network size step variale networks MPPT controller: review, simulation and implementation hardwarde. J. Renew. Sustain. Energ. Rev. **68**, 221–233 (2017)
2. Yatimi, H., Ouberri, Y., Aroudam, E.: Enhancement of power production of an autonomous system based PV MPPT technology is robust. In: Procedia Manufacturing; The 12th International Conference Interdisciplinarity in Engineering, pp. 397–404 (2019)
3. Traore, M., et al.: Supervision of a PV system with storage connected to the power line and design of a battery protection system. Wireless Netw. **1**, 1–9 (2018). https://doi.org/10.1007/s11276-018-1886-x
4. Yilmaz, U., Kircay, A., Borekci, S.: PV system MPPT fuzzy logic method and PI control as a load controller. J. Renew. Sustain. Energ. Rev. **81**, 994–1001 (2018)
5. Pathak, P.K., Yadav, A.K.: Design of battery charging system through smart MPPT using SPV system. J. Sol. Energy **178**, 79–89 (2019)
6. Angenendt, G., Zurmühlen, S., Mir-Montazeri, R., Magnor, D., Sauer, D.U.: Enhancing battery lifetime in home PV battery storage system using forecast based operating strategies. In: 10th International Renewable Energy Storage Conference Energy Procedia, vol. 99, IRES: 15–17 March 2016, Düsseldorf. Germany **2016**, pp. 80–88 (2016)
7. Bayy, M., Rao, B.P., Rao, U.M., Moorthy, N.: Battery state estimation using AC analysis. In: Journal of Energy Procedia, 1st International Conference on Power Engineering, Computing and CONtrol, PECCON-2017, 2–4 March 2017, VIT University, Chennai Campus, vol. 117, pp. 739–744 (2017)
8. Messikh, L., Chikhi, S., Chikhi, F., Chergui, T.: Development of a charge controller/battery discharge with adaptive voltage thresholds for photovoltaic applications. J. Renew. Energy **11**(102), 281–290 (2008)
9. Viswanatha, V., Reddy, R.V.S.: Microcontroller based bidirectional buck-boost converter for photo-voltaic power plant. J. Electr. Syst. Inf. Technol. **5**, 745–758 (2018)
10. Bendary, A.F., Ismail, M.M.: Battery charge management for Hybrid PV/Wind/Fuel cell with storage battery. J. Energy Procedia **162**, 107–116 (2019)
11. Gueye, S.I. Gueye Thiaw, L., Sow, G., Ndiaye, A., Thiam, M.: Conception d'un régulateur solaire avec commande MPPT, Revue du CAMES - Sciences Appliquées et de l'Ingénieur, vol. 1(2), pp. 104–108 (2014)
12. Rai, N., Rai, B.: Control of fuzzy logic based PV-battery hybrid system for standalone DC applications. J. Electr. Syst. Inf. Technol. **5**, 135–143 (2018)
13. Jayachandran, M., Ravi, G.: Predictive power management strategy for PV/battery hybrid unit based islanded microgrid AC. J. Electr. Power Energy Syst. **110**, 487–496 (2019)
14. Yatimi, H., Oubeeri, Y., Aroudam, E.: Enhancement of power production of an autonomous PV system is based robust technical MPPT. In: 12th International Conference Interdisciplinary in Engineering on Procedia Manufacturing, vol. 32, pp. 397–404 (2019)
15. Xu, D., Dai, Y., Yang, C., Yan, X.: Adaptive fuzzy sliding mode command-filtered backstepping control for islanded microgrid with PV energy storage system. J. Franklin Inst. **00**, 1–17 (2019)
16. Hu, J., Xu, Y., Cheng, K.W., Guerrero, J.M.: A model predictive control strategy of PV-battery microgrid under variable power generations and load conditions. J. Appl. Energy **221**, 195–203 (2018)

17. Vavilapalli, S., Umashankar, S., Sanjeevikumar, P., Fedak, V., Mihet-Popa, L., Ramachandaramurthy, V.: A-buck chopper based energy storage system for the cascaded H-bride inverter in PV applications. J. Energy Procedia **145**, 534–541 (2017)
18. Malek, A., Achaibou, N., Haddadi, M.: Modeling of lead acid batteries in pv systems. J. Energy Procedia **18**, 538–544 (2012)
19. Marmouh, S., Boutoubat, M., Mokrani, L.: Performance and power quality improvement is based voltage DC bus regulation of a stand-alone hybrid energy system. J. Electr. Power Syst. Res. **163**, 73–84 (2018)
20. He, W., Rangel, C.A.S., Ortega, R., Astolfi, A.: Energy shaping control for buck-boost converters with unknown constant power load. J. Control Eng. Pract. **74**, 33–43 (2018)
21. Mirzaei, A., Forooghi, M., Ghadimi, A.A., Abolmasoumi, A.H., Riahi, M.R.: Design and construction of a load controller for stand-alone PV/battery hybrid system by using a new control strategy and power management. J. Sol. Energy **149**, 132–144 (2017)
22. Netoa, J.T.D.C., Salazar, A.O., Lock, A.S.: An analog based control scheme applied in stand-alone photovoltaic systems for DC power distribution. J. Renew. Sustain. Energy Rev. **110**, 236–246 (2019)
23. Oubrahim, R.: PID Auto Tuning by Unified and Efficient Structure, Doctoral thesis. Metz, France (1998)
24. Trochut, S., Contribution to the study of stability of monolithic switching converters: application to mobile telephony; Thesis, Lyon, France, p. 44 (2005)

# ICT and Innovative Connectivity as an Enabler for Sustainable Development

# Assessing the e-Readiness of Marginalised Communities for e-Government Services: A Case of Oniipa, Namibia

Karin Fröhlich[1(✉)], Marko Nieminen[1], and Antti Pinomaa[2]

[1] Aalto University, Konemiehentie 2, Espoo, Finland
karin.frohlich@aalto.fi
[2] Lappeenranta-Lahti University of Technology LUT, Yliopistonkatu 34, Lappeenranta, Finland

**Abstract.** A community network is highly regarded as an alternative method for extending services to marginalized communities. However, the success of community networks remains low as the host community often fails to take the ownership of such projects in a sustainable way. The literature recommends the use of baseline surveys and needs assessment to identify fundamental roles that could be played by a community network within a given society. It is argued that aligning community networks to the needs of the community could potentially contribute to their success. This study conducts a baseline survey with the aims of understanding key roles that a proposed community network could play within the context of e-Government and m-Government services provision. Community in Oniipa Town in Namibia was selected as a case study. It was found that the identified community had a poor electricity infrastructure, but an encouraging growth of mobile phone adoption, even though mobile phone credit is considered expensive. Despite these challenges, the community showed a keen interest in m-Government and e-Government services. Accordingly, the proposed community network shall engage the community through a human-centered design methodology in an effort to develop e-Government services suitable for the community. The community network shall rely on solar energy and the use of e-Government and m-Government is expected to reduce population mobility in search of government services something that could reflect positively on climate.

**Keywords:** Community network · Connectivity · Electricity · e-Government · m-Government · Information and Communication Technologies (ICTs) · Rural areas

## 1 Introduction

Information and Communication Technologies (ICTs) are a critical strategic resource that can be used to promote social and economic development initiatives in rural (marginalised) communities [1]. They keep families connected by facilitating communication and enable access to a multitude of services at a lower cost [1, 2]. However,

J. P. R. Thorn et al. (Eds.): InterSol 2020, LNICST 321, pp. 149–163, 2020.
https://doi.org/10.1007/978-3-030-51051-0_11

marginalised communities are often characterised by a poor ICT infrastructure as they are considered a less appealing market for ICTs [2]. This is partly because of the remote locations of the marginalised communities with less infrastructure, roads, and even lower literacy rates. Accordingly, researchers are contemplating various approaches for using ICTs to extend government services more equally to citizens in marginalised and rural communities. The use of mobile phones and community networks has the potential to promote "a people-centered, inclusive and development-oriented Information Society" [3, p. 118]. Stork, Calandro and Gillwald [4] reports of a steady growth in the use of mobile phones to access the internet in Africa. Ochara and Mawela [5] went on to argue that mobile government (m-Government) has the potential of bridging the digital divide between citizens of different social standing [5]. Thus, with m-Government, citizens with access to mobile phones can equally access government services through. Similarly, previous studies motivate the use of community networks as a viable way for extending the sustainability of ICTs access projects to marginal communities [2, 3, 6]. Nonetheless, community networks have recorded a low rate of success in marginalised communities of developing countries where they have been implemented [2]. Lack of project ownership by the community as a result of not using bottom-up methodologies when implementing community networks is one of the reasons that has led to the failure of community networks [2]. This is further complicated by a failure to understand fundamental needs of the local community members when deploying a community network [1].

This calls for initiating community networks with the conducting of needs or electronic readiness (e-Readiness) assessment [1, 2]. Pade-Khene, Mallinson and Sewry [1] marked the beginning of a community network (Siyakhula Living Lab) with a baseline survey to understand the context and level of e-Readiness. Similarly, the Mankosi community network had its needs assessment done prior to commencement in 2012 [2]. In addition, such efforts paves way for human-centred design Information and Technology (IT) projects. Accordingly, this study presents an e-Readiness assessment of a marginal community (Oniipa town council) that was identified as the host of a community network courtesy of the ongoing Fusion Grid research project. Fusion Grid research project focuses on extending ICTs and related supporting infrastructure, being off-grid electricity to marginalised communities. Findings from this study are expected to guide the direction for the full rollout of the community network research project. The project aims to use solar-powered ICT infrastructure for internet access and off-grid power system for electricity distribution as described in [7, 8]. The technology base used in the project is integrated with off-the-shelf components, introducing a less complex, modular, Plug and Play concept that suits rural communities that are characterized by un-skilled individuals.

## 2    Literature Review

This section explains community networks and goes on to explore measures of e-Readiness.

## 2.1  Community Networks

A community network is a decentralised information and communication network that is built, owned and/or operated by a community [3, 6]. The government; independent individuals; the private sector often come into such projects as the project sponsors who help raise funds for the infrastructure. For example, the Siyakhula Living Lab (SLL), established in 2009, is a collaboration between universities (Rhodes University and the University of Fort Hare), the South African Department of Trade and Industry (Technology and Human Resources for Industry Programme (THRIP)), the Cooperation Framework on Innovation Systems between Finland and South Africa, the Meraka Institute and the Nokia Siemens Networks [1]. SLL facilitates the provisioning of new technology and skills to a selected marginalised community in South Africa. The SLL project made available computers and internet access to schools that were selected for the project. The Mankosi community network extended the use of a wireless mesh network to Mankosi community, a marginalized community in the Eastern Cape province of South Africa. The mesh network was used to facilitate communications (Voice over IP (VoIP) calls) using internet. The network used solar energy for powering up the ICT devices. The project was initiated through the University of Western Cape. However, members of the community participated as technicians, and took part in the setting up of the network [2]. Similarly, this study focused on the provision of a community network in Oniipa town council (OTC), Namibia. The study aims to use the Oniipa community to test the viability of implementing m-Government through a community network.

## 2.2  e-Readiness

SITA GovTech (2010) in Gumbo, Jere and Terzoli [9] define e-Readiness as a measure of the extent to which an identified organisation is prepared to engage and make use of ICT.

Fathian, Hoorali and Akhavan [10] shared a similar view by stating that e-Readiness is an organisation's ability to adopt, use and benefit from ICTs. This implies that a marginalised community's e-Readiness is the degree of its preparedness to adopt and use a community network. For sustainability purposes, a community taking part in a community network would need to own the network and use it to its benefit. Measures of e-Readiness are diverse and often overlap from one to another. In general, measures of e-Readiness include the availability of the ICT infrastructure, the magnitude of the use of the ICTs, a local ICT economy, human capacity and a supportive policy framework [11]. However, Pade-Khene et al. [1] used different measures to evaluate the e-Readiness of a community to a community network. They suggested that if a community is to become a partner in a community network engagement, readiness would be determined by "existing communication patterns, information needs and values, and current technology and media use" [1, p. v]. In a community network project, findings from the initial assessment could be revisited in the future, and make comparisons to assess the impact of the community network. This study assumes measures used by Pade-Khene et al. [1] in assessing e-Readiness. The framework proposed by Pade-Khene et al. [1] was evaluated in a marginalised community that is comparable to the one considered in this study. In addition, their framework was used within the context of a community network, being something that makes it suitable for this study. Accordingly, understanding existing communication patterns, information needs and values, and current technology and media use shall help to evaluate the impact of the research project on Oniipa town council as it influences the way the community members accept and access the government services by use of their mobile phones.

## 3   Methodology

A qualitative case study research methodology was used in this research. A community was identified to pilot test ICTs for a rural community. It should be noted that the community network research project reported in this study is a result of a collaboration between the industry, university and public sector. The three main pillars of the research project are electricity provision (solar PV-based power system integrated with energy storage; Lithium-ion batteries, and power electronics), connectivity (4G LTE mobile network base station), and digital services (electronic learning (eLearning), mobile payments, and e-Government or m-Government). Oniipa was identified and selected as the community for piloting the exploratory Fusion Grid concept platform, the case for this research. The research project is a 2.5 years long. In particular to ethical concerns, related Namibian Offices/Ministries/Agencies (OMAs) were engaged to gain approval for the research project to be hosted by Oniipa town council. Table 1 shows activities that were done in preparation of the Fusion Grid concept piloting in Namibia.

**Table 1.** Fusion Grid project initiation activities.

| Dates | Activity | Outcome |
| --- | --- | --- |
| April 2018 | *Doing Business with Finland* seminar by Team Finland, visiting ministries and other beneficiaries in Namibia | Project approval, beneficiaries and key players identification |
| December 2018 | Exploration of pilot sites, visits (including Oniipa Town Council) | Baseline survey-data collection and sites evaluation |
| February 2019 | Fusion Grid Project and Oniipa Town Council Delegation Meeting | Discuss project pilot setup including electricity and connectivity provisions |

Data gathered in this project was used for research purposes alone. The identity of participants was kept anonymous.

### 3.1   Data Collection and Analysis

This study focuses on the data gathered during the baseline survey. Data was gathered using a questionnaire with open and close ended questions prepared by the research group in the study. Randomly selected respondents from the Oniipa region were targeted. Descriptive statistics were used to analyze data that was gathered using close ended questions. Qualitative data analysis techniques of content analysis was used in analyzing data that was gathered by use of open ended questions. Findings from each open ended question were categorized and grouped together. The analysis involved a comparison of views from different respondents.

## 3.2   The Study Site

Oniipa town council is located in Oshikoto region (province), north of Namibia. Oniipa town council has a population of approximately 30 000. Oniipa town council attained a town council status on the 3rd of April 2015. According to the Namibian Local Authorities Act, a town council is an urban settlement that can rely on its own financial resources to pay for part of its operations and does not have to rely on government support alone. The donor agents and the central government are expected to contribute additional funding for the operation of a town council. The status of a settlement is key to anticipating the level of service provision such as roads and infrastructure. It is important to realise that the growth of Namibian urban settlements were partly influenced by the developments in the colonial era. Oniipa town council is on the north of the Red Cordon Fence that was erected during the colonial era. During the apartheid rule by South Africa, the Red Cordon Fence divided Namibia into two, the north, dominated by villages (Bantustans) and the south dominated by urban settlements. This implied that the Bantustans, like Oniipa town council, were to be administered by Traditional Authorities with little or no government support while the southern part of Namibia was under the then homeland government. Furthermore, the Red Cordon Fence was used to control the movement of previously disadvantaged black populations to the southern urban settlements of Namibia. To date, out of Namibia's fourteen regions, it is those regions that are located in the north with a big proportion of rural areas that have the poorest people namely Kavango region (55.2%), Caprivi (50%) and Oshikoto (44%), home to Oniipa town council [13]. The level of poverty and poor infrastructure in Namibian rural areas make these regions less attractive for business investment especially those in the ICT sector. Figure 1 shows the location of Oniipa.

The overall terrain for Oniipa is mostly flat with silt to sandy soils. The environmental temperature is usually within the range of 3 to 31 °C with rainfall ranging between 400 and 450 mm per annum. The Namibia Statistic Agency [14] has suggested the Oshikoto region, home to Oniipa, to be a major player in communal agriculture. The Oshikoto region recorded the highest number of households that applied for agriculture loans between the years 2010 and 2015 [14]. This arguably explains the monthly average income of participants per month that is pegged at NAD $3761.29 (approximately US $266.18). A family based in Oniipa has an average size of six members. Furthermore, government departments that include health and education are major source of employment for the locals.

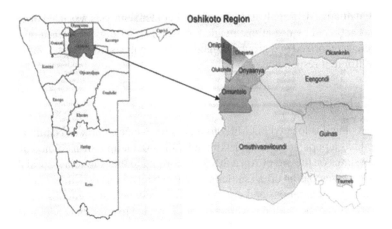

**Fig. 1.** Geographical location of Oniipa.

# 4 Results

A total of 100 questionnaires were distributed, hand delivered, and collected in Oniipa. Out of the delivered 100 questionnaires, 62 were completed (62%). In terms of gender distribution of respondents, 68% were female while the remaining were males (32%). The age distribution of respondents is shown in Fig. 2. The majority of respondents were more than 30 years old. The general trend in Namibia is that, the elderly are mostly found in the rural areas as the youth have migrated to urban settlements for educational or employment purposes [12].

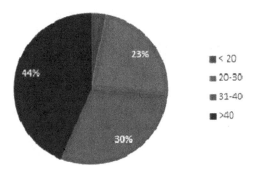

**Fig. 2.** Age distribution of respondents.

## 4.1  e-Readiness

Key findings on the level of e-Readiness of participants from Oniipa include access to education, current media and use, communication patterns, and the use of e-Government and m-Government.

**Access to Education.** The level of education in a society is considered one of the key measures of e-Readiness. Education promotes human capacity development, being something that promotes the adoption of new technologies and modern ways of doing things [11]. The majority of respondents from Oniipa town council indicated that they prefer to have access to education (61%). Approximately 83% of the respondents had formal education as shown in Fig. 3. The majority of respondents had metric (high school) and certificates or a diploma.

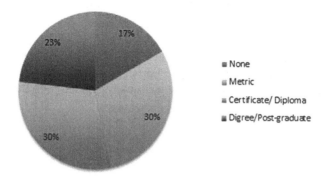

**Fig. 3.** Respondents' educational background.

**Current Media and Use.** Respondents were asked to indicate if they have access to electricity or their other source of energy, their ownership of selected household electrical goods and ICT devices. It was found that only 47% of the respondents had access to electricity. Accordingly, respondents were asked to indicate their sources of energy.

Figure 4 shows findings on source of energy for respondents from Oniipa town council. Only 38% indicated that they have access to the national electricity grid. Forty five percent of the respondents indicated that the question was not applicable suggesting that they neither use electricity, solar or a generator as a source of energy. This group most likely rely on firewood or charcoal. These results were corroborated by further findings showing that electricity access (81%) is the most preferred service by participants from Oniipa. This is followed by access to clean water (71%), healthcare (61%) and education (61%).

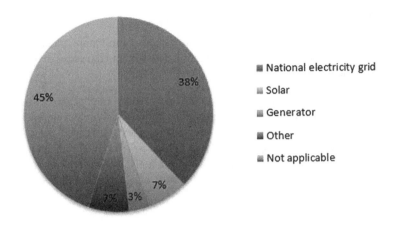

**Fig. 4.** Source of electricity.

In addition, respondents were asked to indicate electrical household goods they own. Figure 5 shows that a small proportion of the participants owned consumer appliances. This could be explained by a lack of access to electricity.

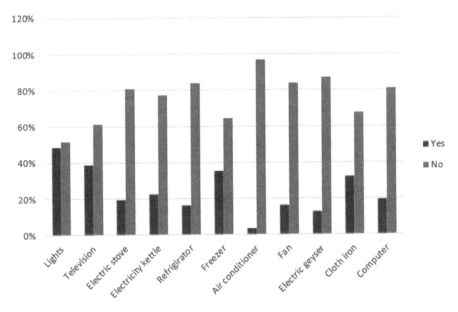

**Fig. 5.** Household goods owned by respondents.

However, respondents indicated that they either own or have access to ICT, namely radio (87%), mobile phone (74%), smart phone (58%) and a television set (52%) as shown in Fig. 6. When asked what they would prefer to own, respondents indicated that they would prefer to have lights (77%) and a mobile phone (65%). Having internet access (52%), a radio (45%), television set (35%) and laptop/computer (19%) are surprisingly among the least preferred gadgets or ICTs.

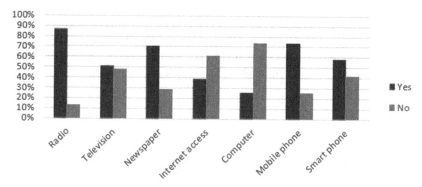

**Fig. 6.** ICT appliances and services owned or accessed by respondents.

Further data was gathered to establish how often respondents bought credit for their mobile phones. The majority (42%) of respondents indicated that they purchase credit on a weekly basis. Sixteen percent of the respondents indicated that they buy credit twice a week while the other sixteen percent indicated that they buy credit for mobile phones twice a month. Mobile phone credit is mainly (81%) used to communicate with family members, conducting business (45%) and making payments (35%), these being illustrated in Fig. 7.

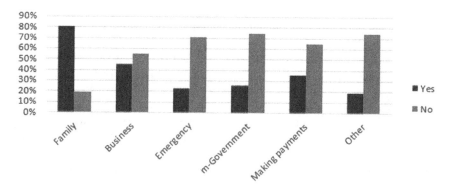

**Fig. 7.** Uses of mobile phones.

**Communication Patterns.** In addition, data was gathered to evaluate the existing communication patterns. If a community network is to be a success, project sponsors need to understand the need and use of ICTs within the community and explore ways of influencing user behaviour or seek to integrate ICTs with existing practices. Data on communication patterns 1) within a village, 2) between villages and 3) within Namibia was gathered. Findings on communication patterns in these three cases are reported next:

1) Findings suggest that communication within a village is mainly by use of a mobile phone (87%) and word of mouth (74%). Internet (35%) and meetings (32%) are not often used. These findings might suggest that the use of mobile phones within the context are mainly based on text message or voice calls. Hence, one of the objectives of the community network, suggested by the study, could be promoting the use of internet. Figure 8 shows communication patterns within a village.

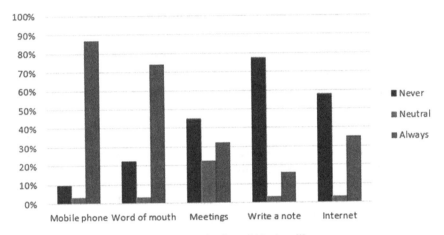

**Fig. 8.** Communication within the village.

2) Respondents were also asked to indicate communication patterns between villages. Results shows that mobile phones (87%) remained the popular form of communication followed by word of mouth (74%) and radio (74%). It has to be noted that there is a slight increase in the use of meetings for communication between villages. Respondents went on to indicate that the information on *"funerals, job opportunities, scholarship, outbreak diseases....... scholarship opportunity, jobs and terrorism news"* are examples of information often exchanged between villages. Similarly, another respondent indicated that they share *"information about health services [and] job opportunities."* Suggesting the use of word of mouth, another respondent indicated that they share *"hot gossips"*. Figure 9 show findings on communication between villages.

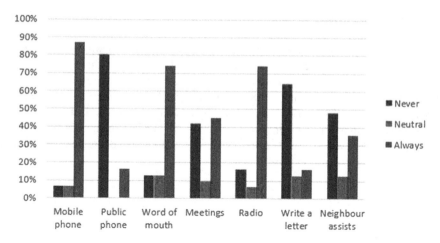

**Fig. 9.** Communication between villages.

3) Lastly, communication between people across Namibia relies on mobile phones and radio as shown in Fig. 10. News is the dominant piece of information found in communication across Namibia. One of the respondents suggested that we share *"whatever is going or happening in or out of the country"*. Another respondent adds that they share *"news, what is happening in the world and different news in my country"*.

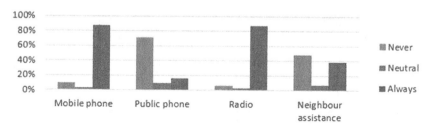

**Fig. 10.** Communication with people across Namibia.

**e-Government Use by Marginalised Community.** Data was gathered to establish e-Government and m-Government readiness of respondents. Study findings show a notable use of e-Government by respondents. For example, one of the respondents stated that he uses internet to pay *"for the municipality bills, applying for death, birth, Identification Document card/certificate"*. Similarly, another respondent stated that: *"It can be nice to pay bills online like electricity, water. Apply for services online than to go to the office for the queue"*. Another respondent stated that he access *"the government services in the internet"*. These findings suggest that some of the respondents are ready to use m-Government and e-Government services. It was also important to establish critical factors influencing one's readiness to e-Government and m-Government (Fig. 11). Social influence is shown to have an influence towards m-Government as 52% strongly agreed that they would use m-Government if those around them used it. Ironically, only 32% indicated that they would not use m-Government (m-Gov) if those around them do not use the technology. However, a lot of respondents (77%) indicated that they do not use m-Government even though 65% expect it to be easy. Furthermore, respondents would need advice on m-Government use (58%) as they feel e-Government is less complicated than m-Government (58%). This could be down to the fact that respondents have little to no experience with m-Government and e-Government. In addition, there is a perception that m-Government would be expensive (58%). 61% of the respondents are of the opinion that mobile phone credit is expensive.

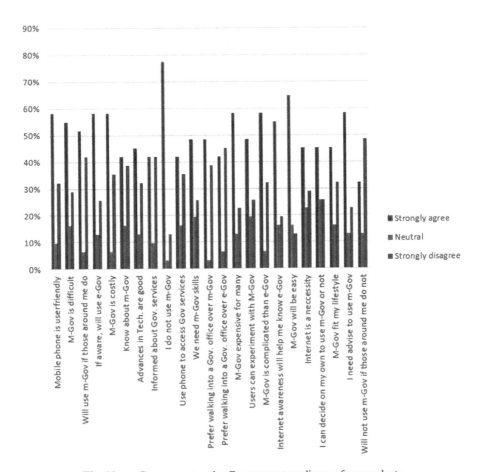

**Fig. 11.** m-Government and e-Government readiness of respondents.

## 5   Discussion

Marginalised communities are often excluded from accessing and using ICTs due to a number of factors, among them, a poor ICT infrastructure. The use of community networks is one of the ways for promoting ICTs growth and use in marginalised rural communities. This paper sought to enhance the success of a community network by conducting a pilot study in order to understand the needs of the community. The authors argue that enlisting suitable ICTs and aligning these to the needs of the community members will most likely promote sustainability of the project. Accordingly, findings from the base line survey were used to enlisting feasible services that could be extended through the community network to ensure beneficiaries to buy in. Environmental, socio-technical, economic and political factors were tabled in deliberating possible services that could be extended to Oniipa community through a community network. The following services were considered for the next steps to take in the study:

**The Provisioning of Internet Connectivity.** Results from data collection and analysis suggest a poor internet connectivity infrastructure in Oniipa and surrounding villages. So, the study proposed to offer connectivity via 4G/LTE base station, which in one key component of the Fusion Grid concept, and standard mobile phones operate as a customer end devices. *Expectations and the goal are that the concept platform continues its operation self-sustained by the community/new system operator even after the concept piloting period. To ensure self-sustainability, the systems considered in this study had respective business case models that highlighted potential benefits to the system owner/operator and/or community.* Internet connection shall be used to access other internet-based services that are available through the concept platform. A local mobile network operator; Telecom Namibia, was identified as a key partner to help with internet connectivity and later on support the sustainability of the project together with the community. The community is open to the possibility of free connectivity inside the base station coverage area. While this is interesting for a start, there are concerns that the interest towards connectivity was motivated by the fact that connectivity will be free during planned piloting period. As noted from the baseline survey, people from these rural communities have little disposable income.

**The Provisioning of Electricity.** Findings from data collection and analysis showed that electricity is the most preferred service by the Oniipa community. Thus, few participants indicated that they have access to the national electricity grid. Pade-Khene et al. [1] made a similar observation on Dwesa-Cwebe, a rural area in the Eastern Cape province of South Africa. However, it has to be noted that this finding comes as a surprise given that Oniipa is a town council where electricity provision is expected to be better. For sustainability, it was decided to engage the Oniipa town council as one of the sponsors in electricity provision. A modular off-grid system power cell, consisting of solar PV panels and Li-ion battery, with size of approximately 5 kW output power is suggested and planned to be implemented to one of the selected house of group of five houses, providing electricity to itself and four houses close by. It was noted that members of the Oniipa community owned few electric goods. Hence, power cell system with 5 kW as a starting power rating was considered adequate for basic and entry level needs of charging mobile phones and possibly local computer servers, fridge, tv, radio and fans, small consumer appliances.

**e-Government Services.** e-Government services that could benefit the community were identified. Identification (ID) card application process and registration for death certificate systems were identified as possible solutions for the planned piloting period. It should be noted that so far people are travelling long distances, hitchhiking to and from government departments when applying for ID cards. Since it has been the traditional role and way of the government to offer IDs, it was decided to engage the government as one of the key players for e-Government. Another e-Government service that could be considered was online education; eLearning systems and/or applications. The government was also considered as a key player or sponsor for educational systems. It was resolved that local entrepreneurs could participate the development of websites and applications that could facilitate e-Government services. Alternatively, crowd funding or open source could be considered as alternative sources of funding. However, the observed major challenge in application development for e-Government was a lack of coding skills. While Namibia has good programmers, it was noted that the Namibian economy is yet to reach a state where it could sustain a lot of computer programmers. As such, locals may not be interested in pursuing entrepreneurial roles within these professions.

## 6   Conclusion

This study reported a baseline survey for the implementation of a community network in a marginalized community. It was found that electricity access remains a major challenge and accordingly, the highest priority of basic services to have in Oniipa town council. Furthermore, there appears to be a less interest in using internet. The majority of residence prefer to have access to electricity and own a mobile phone. The mobile phone is widely used as a communication tool locally, across villages and within Namibia. It is encouraging that respondents showed to have an interest in using m-Government and e-Government services. Respondents showed more interest in e-Government if there is awareness and the mobile phone is deemed affordable. In addition, culture might have a role in influencing the use of e-Government and m-Government services. These findings are critical for the proposed solution and its further plans described in the study that aims to address electricity, connectivity and digital services, including government service access challenges.

## References

1. Pade-Khene, C., Mallinson, B., Sewry, D.: Sustainable rural ICT project management practice for developing countries: investigating the Dwesa and RUMEP projects. Inf. Technol. Dev. 17(3), 187–212 (2011)
2. Rey-Moreno, C., Sabiescu, A.G., Siya, M.J.: Towards self-sustaining community networks in rural areas of developing countries: understanding local ownership. In: Proceedings of the 8th International Development Informatics Association Conference, Port Elizabeth, South Africa (2014). ISBN 978-0-620-63498-4

3. Saldana, J., et al.: Alternative networks: toward global access to the internet for all. IEEE Commun. Mag. (2017). https://doi.org/10.1109/mcom.2017.1600663
4. Stork, C., Calandro, E., Gillwald, A.: Internet going mobile: internet access and use in 11 African countries. Info 15(5), 34–51 (2013)
5. Ochara, M., Mawela, T.: Enabling social sustainability of e-participation through mobile technology. Inf. Technol. Dev. 21(2), 205–228 (2013)
6. Fuchs, C.: Sustainability and community networks. Telematics Inform. 34, 628–639 (2017)
7. Demidov, I., Pinomaa, A. Lana, A., Pyrhönen, O., Partanen, J.: Techno-economic analysis of network configuration of PV-based off-grid distribution system. In: 25th International Conference on Electricity Distribution (CIRED), 3–6 June 2019, Madrid, Spain, Paper no. 1874 (2019)
8. Lana, A., Demidov, I., Pinomaa, A., Carrillo, D., Pyrhönen, O.: Energy management methodology for fusion grid. In: Proceedings of IEEE PES Innovative Smart Grid Technologies Europe, ISGT-Europe 2019, Bucharest, Romania (2019)
9. Gumbo, S., Jere, N. Terzoli, A.: A qualitative analysis to determine the readiness of rural communities to adopt ICTs: a Siyakhula living lab case study. In: Proceedings of the IST-Africa (2012)
10. Fathian, M., Hoorali, M., Akhavan, P.: E-readiness assessment of non-profit ICT SMEs in a developing country: the case of Iran. Technovation 28, 578–590 (2008)
11. Van Belle, J.P., Vosloo, S.: The influence of location on the e-readiness of South African non-profit organisations. In: Garg, R.J., Mahadeo, J. (ed.) Bridging digital divide. Macmillan Advanced Research Series, Delhi, pp. 126–139 (2007)
12. Winschiers-Theophilus, W., et al.: Moving away from Erindi-Roukambe: transferability of a rural community-based co-design. In: Proceedings of the 12th International Conference on Social Implications of Computers in Developing Countries, May, Ocho Rios, Jamaica (2013)
13. Namibia Statistics Agency: Poverty dynamics in Namibia: a comparative study using the 1993/94, 2003/04 and the 2009/10 NHIES surveys (2012). https://cms.my.na/assets/docume nts/p19dnar71kanl1vfo14gu5rpbkq1.pdf. Accessed 10 Nov 2018
14. Namibia Statistic Agency: Namibia census of agriculture 2013/2014. Communal sector report (2015). https://d3rp5jatom3eyn.cloudfront.net/cms/assets/documents/NAC_2013.pdf. Accessed 12 Aug 2019

# Vulnerability Analysis in Mobile Banking and Payment Applications on Android in African Countries

Didier Bassolé[✉], Gouayon Koala, Yaya Traoré, and Oumarou Sié

Laboratoire de Mathématiques et d'Informatique (LAMI),
Université Joseph Ki-Zerbo, Ouagadougou, Burkina Faso
dbassole@gmail.com, gouayonkoala1@gmail.com, yaytra@gmail.com,
oumarou.sie@gmail.com
http://www.univ-ouaga.bf

**Abstract.** In this paper, we analyze vulnerability of some mobile banking and payment applications on Android platforms. This analysis aims at performing vulnerability assessments, facilitating an informed assessment of the information security and privacy risks that mobile banking and payment applications face in African countries, and creating awareness in the research and practice communities. We especially try to assess the risks of attacks related to privacy and data confidentiality by checking access permissions and code vulnerability of these applications. Another purpose of our work is to enable users, businesses and governments to take advantage of the opportunities offered by mobile banking and payment applications while minimising the information security risks to which they are exposed.

**Keywords:** Vulnerability · Mobile banking · Mobile payment · Security · Android applications

## 1 Introduction

A study conducted by the international firm Deloitte [11] revealed that 660 million Africans will be equipped with a smartphone in 2020 against 336 million in 2016. This high penetration rate of smartphones in African countries will lead to an increase in the development and use of mobile applications including applications related to financial transactions.

The introduction and development of mobile banking and payment is a real alternative to the very low rate of banking in African countries. Mobile money, electronic wallet attached to an individual via a telephone number, allows to make various financial transactions without a card or a bank account. Mobile banking and payment is thus a formidable opportunity for progress for the entire value chain and its evolution must translate into a new generation of infrastructure services capable of offering customers the same level of security, availability

© ICST Institute for Computer Sciences, Social Informatics and Telecommunications Engineering 2020
Published by Springer Nature Switzerland AG 2020. All Rights Reserved
J. P. R. Thorn et al. (Eds.): InterSol 2020, LNICST 321, pp. 164–175, 2020.
https://doi.org/10.1007/978-3-030-51051-0_12

and performance regardless of the circumstances of the mobile banking and payment transaction.

More concerned about economic than security issues, companies too often pass innovation, ease of use and consumer demands before the basic safety rules. However, when vulnerability in mobile applications are exploited, critical data leaks can be very costly for the enterprise. Many factors, including the multiplicity of hardware platforms and operating systems combined with the personalization possibilities left to devices users and the vulnerabilities of devices and their applications, make mobile a high-risk payment platform.

However, the option of using mobile banking and payment services has become almost natural and it is becoming urgent for users to be made aware of potential security risks. Many users need to be reassured about the reliability and security of their banking transactions mobile. Fundamental issues arise for a secure use of mobile banking: are mobile banking applications safe? Can they be used safely? How can we conciliate innovation and security in the development process of mobile banking and payment applications?

The remainder of this paper is structured as follows: Sect. 2 discusses related works. Section 3 presents our vulnerability analysis process, Sect. 4 discusses results of our analyzes. Section 5 focus on consequences of permissions on privacy and the security of personal data, Sect. 6, provide discussions on mobile banking and payment security services and requirements. We conclude this work in Sect. 7.

## 2    Related Works

Mobile banking and payments are increasingly being adopted by organisations as a new way of doing business in the $21^{st}$ century. Thus mobile banking and payments security concerns are becoming more and more pressing as smartphones penetration, and its associated bulk of malicious apps, is increasing in developing countries. Security issues in mobile banking and payments procedure have already had a significant amount of discussion in the literature [4,5,7,10].

In [9], Paul Ruggiero and Jon Foote illustrate Cyber threats to mobile phones. There evoque the fact that the number of new vulnerabilities in mobile operating systems jumped and the number and sophistication of attacks on mobile phones is increasing, and countermeasures are slow to catch up. Vishal Goyal et al. develop a framework for analyzing the risks involved in electronic payments in developing countries [1,3]. In [2], K. Linck et al. examine security issues in mobile payment from the customer viewpoint. Their study is considered as a guideline for mobile payment service providers in order to prevent security concerns through appropriate design and communication of payment procedures and to convince customers of the security of their mobile procedures by meeting concerns in informative advertising. In [6], Bradley Reaves et al. perform security analysis of branchless banking applications in the developing World. Their analysis discovers pervasive weaknesses and shows that six of the seven applications broadly fail to preserve the integrity of their transactions. Their analysis reveals that the majority of these apps fail to provide the protections needed by financial service. Ajit Singh in [8], identify some vulnerabilities in mobile cashless transactions that can be exploited by hackers and result in the denial or theft of services for consumers, as well as the loss of revenue, brand reputation, and customer base for vendors. He also explains how mobile apps developers and end user/customers can prevent their sensitive personal information and transactions from being hacked.

In a study on vulnerabilities in mobile financial applications published in 2018, *Positive Technologies* [12] found that most of the applications analyzed in 2016 had vulnerabilities whose main threat was access to sensitive customer data. This study shows that in 2017, attacks on mobile banking applications concerned identity theft, access to customer banking data and fraudulent transactions (Fig. 1). In order to avoid these risks, the study recommends that banks pay more attention to an appropriate architecture, careful formulation of technical requirements and secure development. It is necessary to rigorously test applications and security mechanisms.

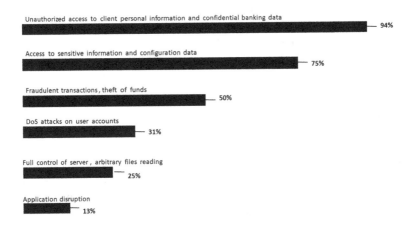

**Fig. 1.** Potential impact of attacks on mobile banks (vulnerable applications)

According to a new study published in 2019 by *Positive Technologies* [13], it appears that unsecured data storage (Fig. 3) and authentication data (Fig. 2) are gaps that offer opportunities for cyber attackers. This study also reveals that malware also comes from official app stores. Following the example of Anubis, a bank trojan horse that managed to avoid the security checks performed by Google Play and the Android security system.

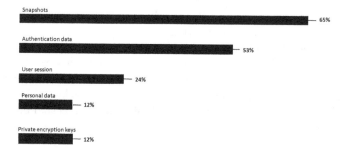

**Fig. 2.** Main leaks in client-side components (percentage of vulnerable applications)

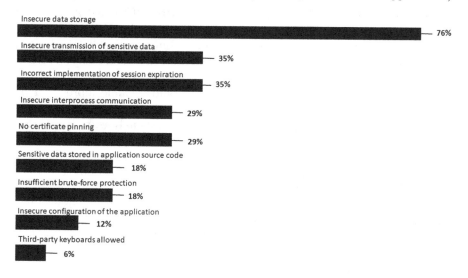

**Fig. 3.** Vulnerabilities of mobile applications (percentage of client-side components)

## 3    Vulnerability Analysis Process

### 3.1    Applications to Analyze the Degree of Data Exposure

Mobile banking and payment applications are used to provide services to the customers. The banking, financial and other payment applications are relatively more sensitive to security compared to other category of non-financial applications. Studies conducted on certain categories of applications have identified security breaches of data stored via mobile applications. Thus, through this study, we wish to place particular emphasis on the degree of data exposure with the use of financial applications in Africa. Our sample includes a total of fifty-three (53) applications from African banks or banks with subsidiaries in Africa. Our choice is motivated on the one hand by the high number of users of the Android platform making them targets for malware authors [14,15].

On the other hand, several studies report a high risk of attack risks for Android applications compared to iOS applications [12,13].

All these applications have been downloaded on Google Play. This approach allows us to have applications that have undergone Google's verification tests before being published. The objective is to assess the risk associated with financial applications, including the risk of data privacy attacks. This consists of verifying access authorizations, code vulnerability, and intellectual property protection (piggybacking) of these financial applications.

### 3.2 Analysis Process

Our study concerns mobile banking applications in Africa. This analysis concerns fifty-three (53) mobile applications of the main banking players emerging from the African market such as Ecobank, Coris Bank International, UBA (United Bank of Africa), BOA (Bank Of Africa), Diamond bank, etc. and subsidiaries of banks such as Société Générale, Standard Chartered, etc. present in Africa. For the analysis of these applications, we used the static and dynamic approach. This analysis concerns the characteristics, interactions, permissions granted and security of personal data in each application. For the static analysis, we proceeded by reverse engineering with Apktool (Fig. 4). It allowed us to obtain the source code for each application we inspected. The inspection concerned the manifest files in order to analyse the characteristics of each of the applications. It verifies the interactions of an application or its components with the system and reveals potential security threats and privacy breaches. Apktool is used to disassemble (or reassemble) the file *class.dex* in the apk and get the bytecode of the file *.dex*. It is used with the tools smali and baksmali. smali allows you to have the files in a more human-readable format and also to compile the file if you have made changes. baksmali is used to decompile the files *class.dex*. For dynamic analysis, we used the virustotal platform (with more than sixty antiviruses) for malware detection.

**Fig. 4.** Tools and procedure for decompiling/recompiling an apk.

# 4   Results of the Analysis

One of the disadvantages of the Android security model is the permissions management. Android has approximately one hundred and thirty (130) permissions, including permissions that are at risk with respect to their access to sensitive and personal information. Some permissions are new and more exploited by malware authors and are dangerous with regard to their access to sensitive personal data. As a result, they are more exploited by malware authors.

Malware developers exploit weaknesses in permissions management at several levels. For each application analyzed, we have the most dangerous access required and all permissions granted.

In the Fig. 5, we associate each permission with the number of analyzed applications with this authorization.

In the Fig. 6, we have associated the number of permissions it contains with each application analyzed.

We identified thirty-nine different permissions in all the applications analyzed. Most applications have access to networks, location data, camera, user tasks, device status, messaging, contacts, accounts, calls, voicemail, etc. We therefore checked the seriousness of these different permissions. Of the thirty-nine permissions identified, twenty-five are considered more risky. Thus, according to our analysis:

- 71.7% of the analyzed applications access precise location and write information to the memory card while 43.4% provide SD card read access;
- 45.28% of the applications analyzed provide access to the camera and 13.21% of the applications allow voice (audio) recording;
- 60.38% of the applications analyzed allow contacts to be read, 16.98% to be written and 18.87% to be used to make telephone calls;
- 35.85% of applications provide access to accounts and 3.77% of applications provide access to user activities;
- Only one application grants access to SMS (send, receive and read) and 7.55% of applications grant access to Bluetooth;
- In addition, all analyzed applications require Internet access;
- In 30.18% of Android applications that we have analyzed the android attribute: allowBackup is set to "true". This allows you to create a backup copy of the application data when the device is connected to a computer. An attacker can use this vulnerability to obtain the application data.

The results of the dynamic analysis revealed five (5) malware, including trojans in three (3) applications. Static analysis has identified applications that can be used to display account balances, transfer money, make mobile payments, etc. This analysis identified authorization abuses that could compromise the confidentiality of sensitive data.

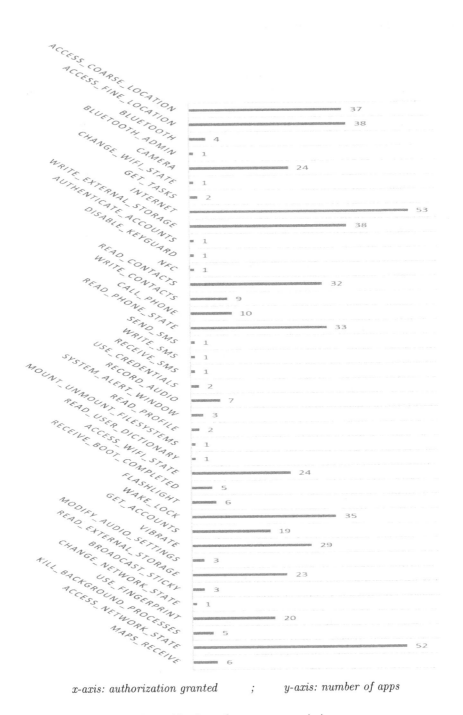

x-axis: authorization granted    ;    y-axis: number of apps

**Fig. 5.** Number of apps per permission

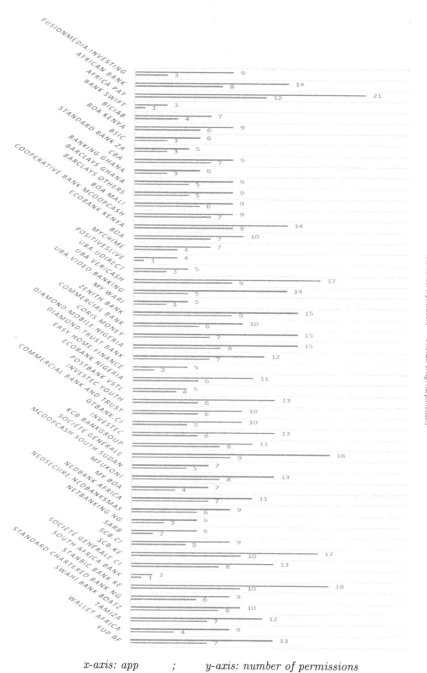

*x-axis: app     ;     y-axis: number of permissions*

**Fig. 6.** Number of permissions per app

# 5    Consequences of Permissions on Privacy and the Security of Personal Data

In our analysis, the granting of permissions is important in data protection. Although some permissions are required for the application's features, their management remains a concern for the security of the data stored on the devices. In addition to the ignorance of some users, authorizations giving access to sensitive resources expose these resources to malware threats. The need to find alternatives is essential for the protection of sensitive resources.

The particularity of these applications is Internet access. Since all these applications provide access to the Internet, any other access to a sensitive resource increases the risk of data leakage. With Internet and SMS access, a malicious application can read SMS and send overpriced SMS to third parties. Also access to the location (38 apps involved in our analysis) allows a malicious application to send the user's position to a third party. Access to the camera allows a malicious application to take image or video files and transmit them to third parties over the Internet. In addition, there is access to audio recording and memory card access, all of which compromise the confidentiality of personal data in the presence of a malicious application.

We have permissions giving access to user information, to the user's location, to produce and send personal data and having control over the device's hardware and access to the Internet. As a result, these accesses to user information make the application more vulnerable to the risks of malicious attacks. Permissions may each be harmless but granted together, the risk of exposing confidentiality can increase considerably.

# 6    Mobile Banking and Payment Security Services and Requirements

The increasing complexity of the technologies used to develop mobile applications and the lack of security expertise of multiple developers of such applications in developing countries, can largely explain the recurring vulnerabilities they present. In order to limit the risks in mobile banking and mobile payment apps, some good practices can be applied. Securing user data requires a responsible attitude from application developers and users themselves.

## 6.1    Requirements and Recommendations for Developers and Decision-Makers

In addition to the proposals made in [16,17] against the threats mentioned, we propose various preventive measures to prevent the violation of the privacy of users of mobile banking applications.

1. Do not store data on the handset to avoid exposing the device to theft or malicious application. The storage of sensitive information is a key point

of security for a mobile application. If the storage of sensitive information is absolutely necessary, the data must be encrypted. In this case, the type of encryption to be used depends on the type of sensitive information to be stored on the equipment (secure container of the equipment, third-party encryption container, etc.). No sensitive information should be stored in application logs, caches (http queries), local databases (SQLite), or, of course, in application code.

2. Restrict application permissions to what is strictly necessary to limit impacts in the event of an attack. Sensitive permissions (sending SMS, GPS positioning, etc.) must be examined carefully.

3. Secure transactions on the network, including exchanges between the application and its server. The data that passes between the server and the mobile are often sensitive (business data, personal data). We must ensure that strict management of access and user rights is carried out on the server side. All communications must be encrypted because it is not uncommon to connect to unsafe networks (public wifi).

4. Use existing cryptographic means, safe and robust, and in no way its own cryptographic algorithms. When encrypting streams by means of a certificate (for example, for HTTPS), it is essential to verify the validity of the server certificate (validity end date, no self-signed certificate, recognized certification authority, etc.).

5. Encrypt the application before distributing it via the blinds and use separate channels of communication for sensitive data.

6. Use adequate means for testing applications in order to address programming risks. The major questions for testing applications: what are apps writing to the file system? How is data stored? How are apps communicating via HTTP and Web Services? SSL? How are apps communicating over the network? TCP and Third-party APIs. Use HTTPS instead of HTTP and accept only valid SSL Certificates.

7. Injection flaws tend to be easier to discover when examining source code than via testing. Scanners and fuzzers can help attackers find injection flaws. Follow secure coding practices from respective platforms.

8. Developers need to learn more about the importance of secure storage of private and sensitive data.

9. They must disable the backup of the application by setting the android attribute: allowBackup to "false".

10. Also, more vigilance is needed during the design phase to avoid a high number of vulnerabilities created during this stage.

## 6.2   Proposals for Solutions for Users

As the main victim, users must be careful in the use of smartphones and associated mobile applications so as not to compromise their devices by extending their functionality, granting dangerous access, disabling protection, etc. To regularly integrate patches, users must update their operating system. Therefore, for application updates, they must take care to check for new authorizations added. They must limit application permissions to what is strictly necessary to limit impacts in the event of an attack. Sensitive permissions (sending SMS, GPS positioning, etc.) must be carefully examined. When applications require too wide access to features or data, users should not grant them if the authorizations requested are unreasonable in relation to the purpose of the application. They should carefully check the links received by email or SMS before opening them from any source. And if the linked address contains spelling mistakes, the email is not authentic.

## 7    Conclusion

Mobile banking and payments are an important technological innovation that increasingly impacting the financial ecosystem in African countries. Therefore, for widespread use and customer acceptance of mobile banking and payments services, both perceived and technical levels of security should be high. For customers, privacy should not be compromised and there should be no possibility of financial losses. Then, we invite engineers, designers and developers of mobile banking services and applications from African countries to integrate safety and security aspects into their development process and to strike a balance between user-friendliness and security. It is very necessary and fundamental to take account all the subtleties of implementation of security mechanisms, apply SSDLC practices, and rigorously test applications and security mechanisms.

Taking into account the future, particularly the economic challenges of information security, it is essential that the various players (users, decision-makers and practitioners) in mobile banking and mobile payment pool their efforts and experiences in order to reduce the impact of vulnerabilities in mobile applications.

## References

1. Goyal, V., Pandey, U. S., Batra, S.: Mobile banking in India: practices, challenges and security issues. Int. J. Adv. Trends Comput. Sci. Eng. **1**(2), 56–66 (2012). ISSN No. 2278–3091
2. Linck, K., Pousttchi, K., Wiedemann, D.G.: Security issues in mobile payment from the customer viewpoint. In: Ljungberg, J. (Hrsg.) Proceedings of the 14th European Conference on Information Systems (ECIS 2006), Göteborg, Schweden, pp. 1–11 (2006)
3. Pousttchi, K., Giaglis, G.M., Werthner, H., Tschammer, V., Froeschl, K.A.: Conditions for acceptance and usage of mobile payment procedures. In: Proceedings of the 2nd International Conference on Mobile Business, Austria, Vienna, pp. 201–210 (2003)
4. Harris, M.A., Patten, K.P.: Mobile device security considerations for small-and medium-sized enterprise business mobility. Inf. Manag. Comput. Secur. **22**(1), 97–114 (2014). https://doi.org/10.1108/IMCS-03-2013-0019
5. Wang, Y., Hahn, C., Sutrave, K.: Mobile payment security, threats, and challenges. In: 2016 Second International Conference on Mobile and Secure Services (MobiSec-Serv), pp. 1–5 (2016)

6. Reaves, B., Scaife, N., Bates, A., Traynor, P., Butler, K.R.B.: Mo(bile) money, mo(bile) problems: analysis of branchless banking applications in the developing world. In: The Proceedings of the 24th USENIX Security Symposium, Washington, D.C., 12–14 August 2015 (2015). ISBN 978-1-931971-232. https://www.usenix.org/node/190885
7. Krueger, M.: The future of m-payments—business options and policy issues. Electronic Payment Systems Observatory (ePSO), Institute for Prospective Technological Studies, August 2001. http://epso.jrc.es/Docs/Backgrnd-2.pdf
8. Singh, A.: Cashless India: leveraging possibilities and facing security challenges in the mobile Space. https://www.globallogic.com/gl_news/cashless-india-leveraging-possibilities-and-facing-security-challengesin-the-mobile-space/
9. Ruggiero, P., Foote, J.: Cyber threats to mobile phones. US-CERT http://www.us-cert.gov/
10. Karnouskos, S. et al.: Secure mobile payment–architecture and business model of SEMOPS. In: Evolution of Broadband Service, Satisfying User and Market Needs, EURESCOM Summit 2003, Heidelberg, Germany, 29 September–1 October 2003 (2003)
11. Les tendances 2018 du secteur des technologies, médias et télécommunications (TMT) en Afrique. https://www2.deloitte.com/fr/fr/pages/presse/2018/des-foyers-africains-connectes-a-internet-via-les-technologies-mobiles.html
12. Financial application vulnerabilities. https://www.ptsecurity.com/ww-en/analytics/financial-application-vulnerabilities/. Accessed 23 Apr 2018
13. Vulnerabilities and threats in mobile applications. https://www.ptsecurity.com/ww-en/analytics/mobile-application-security-threats-and-vulnerabilities-2019/. Accessed 19 June 2019
14. Mobile Threats Report, Juniper Networks Third Annual, March 2012 through March 2013
15. Symantec, 19 August 2013. https://www.symantec.com/security-center/writeup/2013-081914-5637-99
16. National Institute of Standards and Technology. Guidelines on Cell Phone and PDA Security (SP 800-124). http://csrc.nist.gov/publications/nistpubs/800-124/SP800-124.pdf
17. Stallings, W.: Cryptography and Network Security: Principles and Practice, 6th edn. Pearson, London (2013)

# Stakeholder Relations and Ownership of a Community Wireless Network: The Case of iNethi

Jaydon Farao(✉) (iD), Monet Burse, Hafeni Mthoko (iD), and Melissa Densmore (iD)

UCT Centre in ICT for Development, University of Cape Town, Cape Town, South Africa
frxjay002@myuct.ac.za

**Abstract.** The primary objective for this study is to investigate multi-stakeholder understanding of ownership of a community wireless network (CWN) located in Ocean View, Cape Town. This is important because ownership and stakeholder relations are components that contribute to the success of a CWN. Using the convenience and snowball sampling method, we completed 11 semi-structured interviews with stakeholders from the University of Cape Town and the Ocean View community. We consider different ways ownership is conceived between stakeholders. We found that the involvement of the community at initiation of a CWN project is imperative in establishing ownership of a CWN. We characterize some of the ways in which discordant conceptions of ownership have resulted in miscommunication within this project and offer considerations for researchers to take into account as they collaborate with communities on joint initiatives.

**Keywords:** ICT4D · Community engagement · Ownership · Stakeholders · South Africa

## 1 Introduction

A community wireless network (CWN) is a network that is created to provide free and affordable Internet access to members of a community [3]. The CWN is usually created and maintained by members of a community primarily, but often include organisations, working towards shared objectives [4]. Some of the benefits of a community-owned network include: 1) community empowerment; 2) utilisation of community resources for project development; 3) working towards addressing contextual needs within the community; and 4) the sharing of local information and expertise [5]. Community ownership of a CWN is necessary because of the nature of the project, thus how the community and other stakeholders create ownership, and how that manifests, is important to understand the success of such initiatives. Therefore, the relationship between primary and secondary stakeholders, as well as the relationships within the stakeholder groups, are a necessary focus to understand how ownership of Information and Communication Technologies (ICTs) manifests in project implementations. Beyond network and internet coverage, CWNs have the potential to provide a platform for the distribution of

© ICST Institute for Computer Sciences, Social Informatics and Telecommunications Engineering 2020
Published by Springer Nature Switzerland AG 2020. All Rights Reserved
J. P. R. Thorn et al. (Eds.): InterSol 2020, LNICST 321, pp. 176–191, 2020.
https://doi.org/10.1007/978-3-030-51051-0_13

locally created knowledge and artefacts within a community. That said, defining particular goals for a CWN project within a community can affect the success of that project along with the existing embedded community connections and relationships [1]. Participation in Information and Communication Technology and Development (ICTD) projects has become an important way in which community engagement is improved [21]. This participation is usually prioritised in order to "improve success, ownership, and acceptability" of an ICTD project [22]. There has been a movement from using participation as purely a means to meet the needs of users [23] towards Community based Co-design, which uses principles of Participatory Design and utilises community insights as an asset during the design process [24]. The involvement of the community early on in a project is a significant factor in ensuring effective ownership of an ICTD project [25]. Pade, Mallinson, and Sewry [26] describe the involvement of the community, and continuation of their commitment throughout the project, as a factor to ensuring local sustainability. This sustainability is achieved best when the community perceives the project as their own. Pade, Mallinson, and Sewry further describe local ownership as something that should be taken at the initial stages of the project, and not given.

Ownership of ICT projects is an important characteristic for achieving autonomous, or semi-autonomous community engagement [2]. Ultimately, the goal of ICTD projects is to empower the community through the use of ICTs.

### 1.1 Case Study: iNethi OV

The stakeholders for this study are involved in the iNethi deployment of a community wireless network (CWN) located in Ocean View (OV). "iNethi" is a University of Cape Town (UCT) led ICTD non-profit organisation. The primary contributors to this organisation are a team of interdisciplinary researchers who seek to utilise ICTs as a vehicle to provide low cost services for connecting communities to; the rest of the world, the internal members of the community, and the surrounding populations. The goal of iNethi, as defined by Lorini et al. [1] is to "build up infrastructure to support community-based services and content sharing," whereas the priority of the community is the provision of reasonably priced internet access. iNethi's philosophy is centred around providing agency to people in the "creation, construction, management, and cost of a wireless network" [1]. The OV CWN is one of many in the Western Cape. OV was chosen because the iNethi network is currently being deployed in some parts of the community, with prospects of expanding further and of being fully community-owned and operated. Additionally, OV residents also have an existing goal to create and distribute local content using a CWN. While the community has these ambitions, they are, however, an economically marginalized community, still affected by apartheid spatial planning and inequality. 48% of households in OV have a monthly income of 3200 rand or less, and 16% of households live in informal dwellings [1]. Previous research [1] has shown that internet access is not affordable as a result of high data costs by cellular networks. iNethi has therefore been deployed in the community as a CWN. The OV deployment is a fairly recent implementation but has shown great potential for scalability and replication. However, potential tensions between stakeholder groups, lack of necessary technical skill, and possible miscommunication between the groups has caused the project to primarily be operated and mobilised by iNethi. What transpired in this case study, we argue, is the result of multiple, and at times, conflicting understandings of ownership.

## 1.2  Background

**Stakeholder Theory and ICTs**
Stakeholder Theory seeks to explain and guide the mechanisms of an organisation, including its structure and operation [6]. The organisation is described as a unit with which a variety of participants interact to accomplish multiple purposes [7]. It considers how stakeholders benefit from a project and uses stakeholder management to coordinate the relationships between different stakeholders in order to achieve a particular goal [8]. Stakeholder Theory can be categorised into three branches, namely normative, descriptive, and instrumental. The normative perspective is concerned with the moral and philosophical obligations to work towards the common good [9]. Since human beings are affected by any decision made within the project, they should have equal opportunity to contributing to those decisions. The second perspective, descriptive, is concerned with the interaction between stakeholders and the characteristics and behaviour of these stakeholders [10]. The instrumental perspective is concerned with organisations caring for their stakeholders to provide an advantage in ensuring success [11]. Bailur [12], and Donaldson and Preston [6] acknowledge that these perspectives are difficult to distinguish in practice. Bailur further emphasises that to carry out a stakeholder approach to development, one needs to have a "desire to understand what influence stakeholders have on the organization" [12]. She uses stakeholder theory and proposes a stakeholder analysis framework to analyse a telecentre project in the Dhar district, a rural area in central India.

Stakeholders in an organisation are defined by Freeman [14] as any group or person who is affected by the outcomes of a project, those who are "vital to the survival and success of the corporation". Freeman, Wicks and Parmar [15] emphasise the importance of stakeholders in achieving the goals set out by an organisation or project team. These stakeholders can be separated into primary or secondary stakeholders, the former having a direct relationship with the organisation and its progress, while the latter include the public who are affected by the organisation and its projects [16]. The relationship between stakeholders and their participation, both primary and secondary, is important in encouraging ownership and sustainability of ICT projects [17]. The participation of community stakeholders, particularly, should be prominent in the initial stages of an ICT project in an effort to encourage leadership, while external actors, such as researchers, should attempt to limit their involvement and responsibilities as much as possible [17].

The importance and needs consideration of stakeholders when designing ICTD projects is highlighted in research done by Ho, Owusu and Aoki [18]. They sought to identify various stakeholders and their respective requirements in order to design an appropriate mobile platform for the treatment of patients with sexually transmitted diseases in Uganda. They focused on seven "key stakeholders" and how their needs, which were often conflicting, affected the design and consequent outcome of the project. Ho, Owusu and Aoki note that while all stakeholders seek to "improve sexually transmitted infection (STI) treatment and reduce the prevalence of STIs", they are still bound by different financial interests, amongst other differences. Additionally, conflicting stakeholder requirements, and the circumstances each stakeholder was in, determined how smoothly the project and operations could take place. A barrier to funding from one stakeholder inevitable resulted in stagnancy for the progress of other key stakeholders. This financial and logistical delay could affect how well ownership is taken by the community involved. With a dependent relationship, ownership may be difficult to instill. Ho, Owusu and Aoki also found that because of the disruptive nature of an ICTD project, as well as the potential disruption by other stakeholders and their internal dynamics, researchers and designers need to "position" themselves thoughtfully to consider the needs of all stakeholders, as far as possible, and not just focus on primary users.

Bailur [12] investigated the use of a stakeholder analysis framework along with existing Stakeholder Theory in an ICTD project in a rural area in India. The aim of the project was to analyse telecentres in prominent locations in rural areas. When analysing the ICTD project, Bailur found that the project had both a normative and instrumental perspective when it concerned stakeholders and their engagement. It was also found that the management of stakeholder arrangement and responsibilities was a top-down one which produced a lack of ownership of the project within the communities involved. The proposed stakeholder analysis framework is recommended to be applied on an existing project in order to better understand stakeholder relationships and engagement, as well as to determine why a project was not as successful as previously anticipated. Banda and Chigona [7] use Bailur's research to investigate stakeholders in a similar context, the analysis of a telecentre project in Malawi.

## Ownership and ICTs

An ICTD project such as iNethi is intended to be a grassroots project, seeing as it is a CWN. This kind of project is defined by Escobar [19] as a development initiative coordinated by a local community for the benefit of that community. However, since there are additional project partners that may include researchers, technical experts, and other external stakeholders to the community, additional factors lead to the management and resultant ownership of a grassroots project. The first being that the community involved; a) does not feel pressured into adopting extraneous practices, and b) allows the project to become embedded into their existing social structures [13]. The first factor acknowledges that the technologies may have been developed by external actors, but its implementation should be rooted in the natural conditions of the community. The second factor involves the continuous fluidity of the arrangement of the social structures within a community to gain momentum throughout development [13]. This means the reorganisation and dynamism by the community as a choice by that community, to act and react to ICTD projects in certain ways. Overall, a grassroots approach describes a community-driven one, and resultantly a community-owned project, and this has been interpreted by Pade-Khene, Mallinson and Sewry [20] as a key factor to the success of an ICTD project. Banda and Chigona [7] investigated the relationship between stakeholders and how it affects ownership in an ICT project carried out in a rural community in Malawi. The project they investigated sought to provide ICT services in the form of telecentres which they note have continuous barriers to sustainability. Bailur [12] describes one of the factors that act as a barrier to sustainability in ICTD projects as a lack of meaningful stakeholder engagement and this motivated Banda and Chigona to explore how stakeholders engage in the project concerned. It was found that a lack of consultation and research with the community affected various stakeholder engagements, and as a result affected ownership of the telecentre service.

There are two different kinds of ownership we consider in this paper, as defined in organisational studies. These are formal ownership and psychological ownership. Formal ownership is the legal arrangements which encompasses the possession of shares and revenue, the right to have influence and control, and the right to information about what is owned [27]. Psychological ownership is the perception and feelings of the community that the project or artefact is "theirs" [28]. The model of psychological ownership is expanded by Avey et al. [29] through the inclusion of accountability, sense of belonging, and self-identity, among others. Rey-Moreno et al. [30] use the two kinds of ownership to investigate the development of local ownership in a community network that is initiated by an external actor. They find that "ownership is a critical element to take into account when looking at externally initiated interventions." With externally initiated projects, external actors are going to be stakeholders who are not necessarily residing in the targeted community. These stakeholders bring with their contribution, their methods of developing the project along with funding which could affect how the project is owned. The components of both formal and psychological ownership are thus important to consider when investigating how stakeholder relations affect the taking of ownership of an ICTD project, especially when a stakeholder group is external to the community. Ultimately the different levels of stakeholder engagement, as well as who stakeholders are, help to shape what is understood by ownership.

## 1.3   Study Aims

The primary objective for this study is to investigate multi-stakeholder understanding of ownership of a community wireless network (CWN) located in Ocean View, Cape Town. This study focused on the Ocean View (OV) community in the Western Cape Province. The study aimed to explore how ownership is defined and created amongst stakeholders at both UCT and the OV community as it pertains to the iNethi project. To do this we epistemologically engaged with Stakeholder Theory to discuss how the different stakeholder groups organised themselves, interacted with each other, and how these interactions affected what was understood by taking ownership of the community network. This study adopted Stakeholder Theory to investigate how ownership is created in ICT4D projects such as the iNethi CWN initiative. Stakeholder Theory is used in this study in order to better understand the manner in which various participants in an organisation interact and organise themselves and how these aspects relate to ownership. It is used in an analytical way in order to identify the key stakeholders and how their knowledge, behaviour, and positions, among others, affect how ownership of a CWN is taken. This research demonstrates an introductory exploration, with preliminary results, into how stakeholder relationships affect ownership of ICT projects in Cape Town, South Africa.

## 2  Methodology

### 2.1  Study Approach

The study formed part of the social constructivist paradigm [31] and utilised a qualitative approach. We chose to utilize a qualitative approach to investigate ownership because it allowed us to; explore the relationship between ownership and stakeholder relationships, provide context for individual understanding of ownership, and present the complexity of stakeholder relationships. Much of the data collected conformed to the descriptive perspective of Stakeholder Theory in that the relationships of stakeholders were investigated as well as their behaviours within those dynamics.

The study employed a purposive, convenience sampling technique [32]. This allowed for the recruitment of participants within Ocean View; however, using these sampling methods could result in skewed responses because all participants who are users of the network reside within the same geographical area and have a similar socioeconomic status. It is important to note who the stakeholders considered in the iNethi project are, as it exists in OV. Some of the stakeholders include the directors of the "OV Com Dynamic" (the deployment of the iNethi network in OV), residents of OV, researchers at the University of Cape Town, the UCT computer science department, and Telkom, to mention a few. Samples were taken from two main stakeholder groups: UCT and the OV community. The reason to focus on these two groups is that they are the main stakeholders involved in the daily functioning of the iNethi project, including the weekly meetings they participate in. The sample size was 11, which included participants from UCT (5) and OV (6). Data was gathered through semi-structured interviews and observations; which was guided by Stakeholder Theory. The observations included taking notes during the weekly stakeholder meetings, while the interviews were with individual stakeholders.

#### 2.1.1  Interviews

Interviews were conducted with stakeholders in the Ocean View community and UCT. Interviews lasted 20–30 min and were conducted at a time and place convenient to our participants. Permission was sought from participants to audio record interviews for analysis purposes.

#### 2.1.2  Observations

Observations were carried out during three weekly stakeholder meetings. The meetings were attended by stakeholders within the management of iNethi, either in person or via video conferencing. The meetings consisted of a briefing on the agenda and discussions on the progress of the project in its various domains. During these meetings we sought to understand the relational dynamics between stakeholders such as: how stakeholders engaged during the meeting; the priority agenda items for different stakeholders; how the meetings were run and who took the lead and how decisions were negotiated. Permission was sought from all stakeholders to take part in the meetings and gain insights on how the project is progressing.

## 2.2  Data Analysis

The semi-structured interviews were carried out by two researchers, one of which noted the responses during the interview. The notes taken during the observations of meetings were analysed immediately after in order to better understand how engagements between stakeholders in different contexts affect ownership of the iNethi project within OV. Both interviews and observations were analysed through a narrative and coded through a process of thematic analysis [33]. During the interviews with the iNethi users residing in OV, the research assistant who aided recruitment was present in those meetings. At particular points during the interviews the assistant interjected when a participant was unable to answer. This may have affected participant responses for the interview, as well as created bias. It should also be noted that the results presented in this paper are preliminary.

## 2.3  Research Ethics

Approval for the study was obtained from the University of Cape Town's Ethics Committee. Informed consent was carried out prior to interviews and observations. Participants were informed that their participation was voluntary and that their responses would remain anonymous. We worked closely with a prominent member of OV in order to recruit participants for the users of this study. This member occupied a research assistant role. When requesting consent, we used verbal consent primarily because some users were uncomfortable with written consent, viewing it as a form of contract. We decided to explain the purposes of the study, including the risks and benefits of their responses to our questions, verbally.

In order to allow participants to feel as comfortable as possible, we conducted interviews at locations participants requested to have them. Some interviews were held in participants' homes, and others were held in conference rooms. Accommodating participants in these locations was an effort to allow responses to be as authentic as possible as well as to mitigate the power dynamic that exists between us as researchers, and participants, especially in the case of OV stakeholders. Researchers from UCT entering the OV environment presents a power dynamic. This dynamic may have influenced some of the responses; however, we attempted to reduce this influence by allowing participants to guide where and how they were most comfortable. Similarly, when interviewing UCT stakeholders, we had to ensure that our treatment of different stakeholder groups was appropriate and maximises participants honest engagement, while also not emphasising our role as UCT researchers in a way that promotes bias.

Another ethical factor was the reporting of anonymised data. In some cases, information gathered could be clearly linked to a particular stakeholder if the reader was involved in the project. When this data had the potential to inflict more harm to stakeholder relations than positive impact, it was considered more closely for inclusion. While it is important to include as much of the information gathered as possible, we considered the overall impact on the various stakeholders as well.

## 3   Research Findings

In analysing our data collected during interviews and observations, the following key aspects were extracted (following the interview discussions) as it relates to ownership of the iNethi network in OV: stakeholder perceptions of ownership, perception of the iNethi project, stakeholder relations, and concluding with barriers to producing ownership. This section details the preliminary results and analysis.

### 3.1   Stakeholder Perceptions of Ownership

During our interviews with stakeholders, it was important to understand how ownership is perceived and understood by stakeholders as it pertains to the iNethi project. This is aligned with psychological ownership as defined by Pierce and Kostova [28], as their perceptions could influence when and how ownership is taken. One of the UCT stakeholders defined ownership in the OV community as:

*"Taking the power back in the form of a community network."*

This stakeholder was cognizant to what that meant in relation to the positionality of the researchers in interacting with the OV community. They described the researchers as a "support system" while both stakeholder groups learnt from each other during the development of the project. Ownership, in their view, is related to empowerment. When questioned about whether OV stakeholders are empowered by iNethi, they expressed that they are, through the transferring of skills to operate the platform. This sentiment was shared with another UCT stakeholder, while noting that UCT still has more involvement than is preferable. This stakeholder defines ownership as:

*"Owning infrastructure by building it, deciding the speed and price of internet, and owning content and services by creating local social networks."*

This notion of ownership was shared by an OV director stakeholder who described it as:

*"local content creation while incorporating their own ideas that they relate to and that makes sense."*

The UCT stakeholder also described the OV stakeholders owning the iNethi network legally but that the project is not run independently, this indicated that they believed OV stakeholders had formal ownership of the project as described by Pierce and Rubenfeld [27]. This presented some conflict in the perception of ownership and legality. Having legal ownership, as found in the interviews with OV stakeholders has little bearing on their perceived ownership of the project. In other words, the formal ownership did not encourage the psychological ownership.

During the interviews with one of the directors of the iNethi network deployment in OV, the stated ownership was related strongly with the acquiring of skills, and elaborated further, that it is also related to having a qualification for those skills. The reasoning for this distinction is that they believe that the acquiring of qualifications increases the job opportunities as well as decreases the dependence on UCT for technical and business help. The emphasis on expertise and upskilling is likely due to the low availability of similar work opportunities in that area.

*"iNethi is not owned by OV yet. It is still managed by UCT and funded by UCT."*

Another director states:

*"We [OV Com directors] do not have the intellect. Since iNethi is mostly technology, training would create ownership."*

The comment on gaining skills agrees with the UCT stakeholder's comments on empowerment, but the comment that skills training is still necessary, along with relevant qualifications, suggests that the OV stakeholders believe that not enough has been done to empower them towards a sense of ownership. In this way, the formal ownership in the form of qualifications could advance psychological ownership of the project.

On the other hand, the stakeholders representing users of the iNethi network felt that there was a sense of ownership of the network as they were able to buy vouchers and connect to the network at a lower cost compared to their network providers. However, users described that there were still problems with connectivity and the occasional loss of data, which we understood as a barrier to taking complete ownership of the wireless network. Users had communicated these complaints to a director of iNethi in OV, and upon further investigation it was found that the concerns were not communicated to UCT researchers during their weekly meetings. This fragmented communication demonstrates the disconnect between stakeholders. It shows an uneven reliance on particular groups and does not portray balanced engagement.

Another component of ownership highlighted by a user stakeholder is the intention by OV Com Dynamic for the network to be distributed to the rest of the OV community. This would lead to having more users connected to the iNethi network and the stakeholder sees this as important to owning the project as a community. The user responded:

*"It needs to be built across the whole of Ocean View."*

Interestingly, one of the pitfalls of using the network has been the overwhelming demand by the number of users on the network at times, as noted by another user stakeholder:

*"The signal is bad sometimes. It takes too long because there are too many users."*

This results in slower network and was noted as a deterrent by users of the network. This means that in order to optimise ownership in OV, both the maintenance and managing of the network, and its distribution to the rest of the community should be a concern. Balancing those key components would be the challenge.

### 3.2  Perception of the iNethi Project

When asking the participants about what iNethi means to them we received a diversity of responses. This indicated some discrepancy on the understanding of iNethi. Much of this inconsistency was concerning the structure of iNethi as it relates to the OV community. One primary stakeholder, a founder of iNethi positioned at UCT, defined iNethi as:

*"the non-profit organisation to initiate infrastructure technology, to be deployed in OV".*

They elaborated that the deployment of iNethi in OV is considered as a partner project to the overall iNethi project. That project partner is called "OV Com Dynamic". This is in contrast to other stakeholders who were unsure what the scope of iNethi was. A UCT researcher indicated that the definition of iNethi has been continuously negotiated, which has resulted in some confusion as to what it entails in totality. Interestingly, one of the directors of OV Com Dynamic began describing iNethi as first what UCT says it is, and then continuing to what they believe it entails. They defined iNethi as a Wi-Fi network that is used to generate money through the sale of vouchers. This, we have found, is the definition of OV Com Dynamic. The variance in the responses indicate that there is a level of disagreement and/or misunderstanding of iNethi and what the expectations of the project are. We believe that a lack of consensus in this regard can affect how effeÞctive ownership is taken by the community. This is evident in that when stakeholders have contrasting definitions of the project they are involved in, it may lead to the conflict of various expectations for that project, as well as misunderstandings on what the project's objective is.

Similar to the differing definitions of iNethi, the expectations from stakeholders also offer contention. Stakeholders in OV, being a part of a community with a significant unemployment rate, understandably have priorities concerning the creation of jobs and the generation of income. This is seen as one of the main expectations of the project by this stakeholder group. Stakeholders from UCT acknowledge the need to prioritise the needs of the OV community; however, the need to provide the infrastructure necessary for the implementation and use of the iNethi platform is the main priority for the UCT researchers. These conflicting stakeholder expectations and the effect on the success of an ICTD project is supported by Ho, Owusu and Aoki [18]. When these expectations are in contention, the conflict can affect how well primary stakeholders in OV support and integrate within the project, and thus it affects how well ownership is taken by the community.

One of the methods used by ICTD projects to address the differences mentioned above is a formulation of a memorandum of understanding (MOU) [26, 34]. Stakeholders at UCT described the MOU to be in development and discussion, but also that this has been the case for a significant period during the project development. Additionally, UCT stakeholders seek to step out of their roles in the project, giving full agency to the OV stakeholders, by the end of 2019, within 6 months at the time of writing. Not having the roles and expectations of stakeholders outlined in a form that is understood by all stakeholders in the late stages of the project could have effects on ownership of the project. If primary stakeholders in OV are not seeing official recognition of their needs and roles through a medium they acknowledge and understand, they may not feel confident enough to take the ownership of the project that is required of them. One could question whether the use of a document such as an MOU, a document that is perhaps foreign to the OV stakeholders and proposed by the UCT stakeholders, is effective and appropriate. UCT stakeholders had mentioned that only one of the primary OV stakeholders, a director of OV Com Dynamic, was present during the development of the MOU, and this could affect how well the MOU is received by the rest of the directors in OV. An MOU can be seen as an attempt to create formal ownership of the project. Whether this evolves into psychological ownership is questionable, seeing as it is a largely foreign form of documentation to the OV community stakeholders. It has the potential to alienate and create barriers to ownership if it is not readily accepted. This negotiation between formal and psychological ownership, and who defines how these types of ownership are created, is a concern when navigating how different stakeholders operate and interact in a project.

### 3.3 Stakeholder Relations

One of the primary ways of stakeholder interaction include weekly meetings between the OV Com Dynamic directors and the UCT research team. These meetings alternate venues every week. One venue being the UCT offices and the other being at a high school in OV which serves as the offices of the OV Com Dynamic. During the observation of the meetings held at UCT it became clear that an agenda was set for each meeting, with main contributions by one of the founders of iNethi, a UCT researcher. The agenda was shared to all stakeholders before the meeting in order to allow for contributions from all concerned. The use of an agenda for a meeting was introduced by UCT stakeholders as the norm for weekly meetings. In this way it can be seen as imposed as the status quo for the running of meetings. We noted that stakeholders at OV may not be comfortable with this convention used at UCT, and upon further interviews with UCT researchers we found that when meetings are held in OV, an agenda is rarely set. We also found that UCT waited for OV to initiate the meeting (along with the sharing of the agenda), and multiple times a meeting at OV did not take place because it was not initiated. This, we observe as an attempt to allow OV to take control of one of the key structures for engaging with all stakeholders. Again, this is an attempt at instilling formal ownership. It is hinged upon conventions defined by the UCT stakeholder group, who have influence and power in the stakeholder relation by virtue of their position as researchers from a prominent university.

The lack of meetings in OV should not be concluded as a lack of initiative. Instead we would argue that the format of the meetings, including the setting of the agenda, could contribute to the lack of comfortability of the OV Com Dynamic directors with the status quo as defined by UCT. We presented this argument to one of the UCT stakeholders and they acknowledged that they had not thought of it that way and that they would not request an agenda for the next meeting at OV. This revealed that while the UCT researchers may be seeking to get OV stakeholders to take ownership, they may still be imposing methods of engagement they have normalised on a stakeholder group that have not. It should be noted that during our research period we were not able to attend an organised meeting in OV as one did not take place.

During the meetings held at UCT one of the directors in OV would usually Skype in. While this is a means of ensuring the stakeholders in OV are able to contribute to meetings, the variables associated with initiating a Skype call caused complications during meetings. During one of the meetings, the Skype call was disconnected due to a poor connection in OV. This, however, did not stop the meeting. It continued with only UCT stakeholders present. This meant that a significant portion of the meeting was involving only one group of stakeholders. Minutes were taken of the meeting; however, this is another way of operating meetings imposed by the UCT stakeholder group. While it may not be practical to conclude a meeting if a stakeholder cannot be present, the continuation of the meeting without a key group of stakeholders can influence the relationship between stakeholder groups.

Additional exclusionary aspects to the weekly meetings were found to be; the content discussed during the meeting, as well as a lack of effective communication by the OV Com Dynamic directors on the state of the project in OV to the UCT stakeholders. The content discussed during meetings observed was predominantly technical. This involved an opportunity for feedback from the OV stakeholder, and thereafter dealt with other technical issues concerning the researchers at UCT. These discussions are necessary according to a UCT stakeholder, however, a different approach to the structuring of meetings could be more effective in optimising engagement between stakeholder groups. An improved structure should highlight objectives for all stakeholders since the last meeting and establish any feedback received from users of the iNethi network. When interviewing a director at OV, many of the problems associated with the iNethi network, as well as the issues users of the network faced, were topics not communicated during meetings. This lack of openness indicates a weakness in stakeholder relations. It could lead to UCT stakeholders being unaware of issues faced by OV stakeholders and may produce expectations and progress that do not align with reality.

During a meeting in which stakeholder relations and ownership were discussed, tension arose as the OV Com Dynamic directors began sharing their feelings about ways in which they have felt isolated from the progression of the project. This included discussions around the naming of the network, as well as an understanding of what iNethi and OV Com Dynamic means to them. UCT stakeholders responded defensively at first, indicating that the concerns raised were not highlighted before, which the OV Com Dynamic directors disagreed with. This instance emphasised that: a) there was a miscommunication about the fundamentals of the CWN; b) OV Com Dynamic directors have either felt disempowered to speak openly before or UCT directors have misunderstood them; and c) stakeholder power relations remained in UCT stakeholder's favour. The meeting was felt to provide an important perspective on the CWN project, and the role each stakeholder plays in achieving shared objectives. Additional tensions that arose included how the social positions of directors within OV affect ownership.

The reality of operating a CWN such as iNethi was seen to be overlooked at times. One of these realities is how the directors in OV are positioned socio-economically. Differing positions of stakeholders can be perceived to have an influence on ownership. Not all of the directors of OV Com Dynamic reside in OV, and this has opened discussions on how the proximity to the project by location, as well as the priority of the project in a stakeholder's daily life can affect the involvement and ownership within the project. This was highlighted by both UCT and OV stakeholders and has indicated that tension exists surrounding these stakeholder characteristics. Thus, how stakeholders are positioned within the project and its location may influence how ownership is produced and should be considered when developing the project.

The interaction between stakeholders, both between and within respective groups, can create tensions and a lack of cohesion that lead to barriers to taking ownership as described by Pade and Mallinson [26].

### 3.4 Barriers to Producing Ownership

The findings presented offer some insights into how ownership can be hampered in the development of ICT4D projects, specifically a CWN. Stakeholder relations and the perceptions of ownership by stakeholders have highlighted some of the barriers to producing or taking ownership of a CWN such as iNethi, by a community, particularly because an ICT4D project of this nature should be community-owned. Stakeholder relations, both within and between stakeholder groups, affect how successfully the community stakeholder can take ownership. A cohesive and strong stakeholder group is necessary to allow for a smoother transition into ownership. A cohesive stakeholder group should be encouraged and developed during the initiation of the project, similar to ownership as stated by Ballantyne [17]. In this way, navigating stakeholder expectations, conflicting objectives, and overall understanding of the project can be addressed early in the project.

Other barriers to ownership, as described by user stakeholders and directors within OV, include the lack of awareness of the project, the limited reach of the network within the community, the technical limitations to access, and the maintenance of the network. These are not necessarily the barriers to ownership as defined by UCT stakeholders. A UCT stakeholder described one of the barriers to be the lack of initiative shown by the OV Com Dynamic and how it has been challenging not to aid when the OV directors require assistance. The power dynamic between researcher stakeholders and the OV stakeholders influence much of this barrier to ownership and it would be interesting to investigate how this dynamic would change should OV Com Dynamic directors be empowered in the way they would want i.e. the gaining of qualifications for the work they do. According to one of the directors, this would mitigate the demand for UCT's help as a regular occurrence and provide directors a sense of achievement. Managing this dynamic between stakeholders is an important component of creating the circumstances for the "taking" of ownership.

## 4   Conclusion and Future Work

This study explored how stakeholders and their positions affected the sense of ownership of a community wireless network ICT4D project. The study has shown through preliminary results that various stakeholder relations can affect how effectively ownership is created, especially if a stakeholder group is external to the community and in a position of influence and power. Consolidating the relationship between formal ownership, which is often conferred by external stakeholders, and psychological ownership, that needs to be created within community stakeholders, is a key component, and challenge, in creating ownership of a CWN. Future CWN projects should prioritise ownership and healthy stakeholder relations at the initial and throughout all stages of the project and this should include conforming to conventions within the community when developing plans and arranging engagements between stakeholders. External stakeholders should attempt to remove all bias when organizing how the project will commence. This could prevent future barriers to ownership within the community and could create the optimal path towards autonomy in the community.

Investigating the power dynamics and effects on stakeholder relations within CWNs could provide further insight into how ownership and stakeholder relations are associated; however, this is outside the scope of this study. Since this study presents preliminary findings, future work could elaborate on this study by providing a supplementary understanding of community-owned projects such as CWNs. Further research could also include an in-depth study into the components of psychological ownership, and how it manifests in ICTD projects such as iNethi. As well as expounding on the relationship between formal and psychological ownership.

**Acknowledgements.** We would like to thank the Ocean View community for their engagement, contributions, and feedback. In addition, we would also like to thank the directors of OV Com Dynamic for their assistance with fieldwork and the arrangement of interviews.

# References

1. Lorini, M.R., et al.: Localize-it: co-designing a community-owned platform. In: Krauss, K., Turpin, M., Naude, F. (eds.) IDIA 2018. CCIS, vol. 933, pp. 243–257. Springer, Cham (2019). https://doi.org/10.1007/978-3-030-11235-6_16
2. Myers, B.: Imagine, invent, program, share: a library-hosted computer club promotes 21st century skills. Comput. Libr. **29**(3), 6–9 (2009)
3. Abdelaal, A., Ali, H.H.: Community wireless networks: emerging wireless commons for digital inclusion. In: IEEE International Symposium on Technology and Society, Arizona, USA, pp. 1–9. IEEE (2009)
4. Kuchibhotla, H.N., et al.: An empirical analysis of collective actions in university anchored community wireless networks. In: IEEE Southeastcon, Jacksonville, USA, pp. 1–5. IEEE (2013)
5. Siochrú, S.Ó., Girard, B.: Community-based networks and innovative technologies: New models to serve and empower the poor. In: Making ICT Work for the Poor. United Nations Development Programme, New York, USA (2005)
6. Donaldson, T., Preston, L.: The stakeholder theory of the corporation: concepts, evidence, and implications. Acad. Manag. Rev. **20**(1), 65–91 (1995)
7. Banda, C., Chigona, W.: The impact of stakeholder management on the sense of ownership in telecenter projects: the case of Malawi. In: Choudrie, J., Islam, M.S., Wahid, F., Bass, J.M., Priyatma, J.E. (eds.) ICT4D 2017. IAICT, vol. 504, pp. 439–450. Springer, Cham (2017). https://doi.org/10.1007/978-3-319-59111-7_36
8. Fontaine, C., Haarman, A., Schmid, S.: The stakeholder theory. Edlays Educ. **1**(1), 1–33 (2006)
9. Phillips, R.A.: Stakeholder theory and a principle of fairness. Bus. Ethics Q. **7**(1), 51–66 (1997)
10. Jawahar, I., McLaughlin, G.L.: Toward a descriptive stakeholder theory: an organizational life cycle approach. Acad. Manag. Rev. **26**(3), 397–414 (2001)
11. Clarkson, M.E.: A stakeholder framework for analyzing and evaluating corporate social performance. Acad. Manag. Rev. **20**(1), 92–117 (1995)
12. Bailur, S.: Using stakeholder theory to analyse telecenter projects. Inf. Technol. Int. Dev. **3**(3), 61–80 (2006)

13. Breytenbach, J., Villiers, C.D., Jordaan, M.: Communities in control of their own integrated technology development processes. Inf. Technol. Dev. **19**(2), 133–150 (2013)
14. Freeman, E.R.: Strategic Management: A Stakeholder Approach. Cambridge University Press, New York (2010)
15. Freeman, E.R., Wicks, A.C., Parmar, B.: Stakeholder theory and "the corporate objective revisited". Organ. Sci. **15**(3), 364–369 (2004)
16. Buchholtz, A.K., Carroll, A.B.: Business & Society: Ethics and Stakeholder Management, 8th edn. Thomson/South-Western, Mason (2012)
17. Ballantyne, P.: Ownership and partnership – keys to sustaining ICT-enabled development activities. International Institute for Communication and Development, 8 (2003)
18. Ho, M.R., Owusu, E.K., Aoki, P.M.: Claim mobile: engaging conflicting stakeholder requirements in healthcare in Uganda. In: 2009 International Conference on Information and Communication Technologies and Development (ICTD), Doha, Qatar, pp. 35–45. IEEE (2009)
19. Escobar, A.: Reflections on 'development': grassroots approaches and alternative politics in the third world. Futures **24**(5), 411–436 (1992)
20. Pade-Khene, C., Mallinson, B., Sewry, D.: Sustainable rural ICT project management practice for developing countries: investigating the Dwesa and RUMEP projects. Inf. Technol. Dev. **17**(3), 187–212 (2011)
21. Mpazanje, F., Brown, I.: Participation in rural community ICT4D project initiatives: a literature review. In: International Conference on Social Implications of Computers in Developing Countries, Montego Bay, Jamaica, vol. 9, pp. 375–393 (2013)
22. Winschiers-Theophilus, H., Zaman, T., Yeo, A.: Reducing "white elephant" ICT4D projects: a community-researcher engagement. In: 7th International Conference on Communities and Technologies, Limerick, Ireland, pp. 99–107 ACM (2015)
23. Ramirez, R.: A 'meditation' on meaningful participation. J. Commun. Inform. **4**(3) (2008). http://ci-journal.net/index.php/ciej/article/view/390
24. Kapuire, G.K., et al.: Community-based co-design in Okomakuara a contribution to 'design in the wild'. In: 13th Participatory Design Conference, Windhoek, Namibia, vol. 2, pp. 207–208. ACM (2014)
25. Bridges.org: 12 Habits of Highly Effective ICT-enabled Development Initiatives (2007). http://archive.kubatana.net/html/archive/resour/070117bridges.asp?sector=RESOU. Accessed 15 May 2019
26. Pade, C., Mallinson, B., Sewry, D.: An elaboration of critical success factors for rural ICT project sustainability in developing countries: exploring the Dwesa case. J. Inf. Technol. Case Appl. Res. **10**(4), 32–55 (2008)
27. Pierce, J.L., Rubenfeld, S.A., Morgan, S.: Employee ownership: a conceptual model of process and effects. Acad. Manag. Rev. **16**(1), 121–144 (1991)
28. Pierce, J.L., Kostova, T., Dirks, K.T.: The state of psychological ownership: integrating and extending a century of research. Rev. Gen. Psychol. **7**(1), 84–107 (2003)
29. Avey, J.B., et al.: Psychological ownership: theoretical extensions, measurement and relation to work outcomes. J. Organ. Behav. **30**(2), 173–191 (2009)
30. Rey-Moreno, C., et al.: Local ownership, exercise of ownership and moving from passive to active entitlement: a practice-led inquiry on a rural community network. J. Commun. Inform. **11**(2), 1–16 (2015). http://hdl.handle.net/10566/1609
31. Vygotsky, L.S.: Mind in Society: Development of Higher Psychological Processes. Harvard University Press, Cambridge (1978)

32. Emerson, R.W.: Convenience sampling, random sampling, and snowball sampling: how does sampling affect the validity of research? J. Vis. Impairment Blind. **109**(2), 164–168 (2015)
33. Aronson, J.: A pragmatic view of thematic analysis. Qual. Rep. **2**, 1–3 (1994)
34. Tanner, M., du Toit, A.: The influence of higher education institutions on the sustainability of ICT4D initiatives in underserved communities. Electron. J. Inf. Syst. Dev. Countries **71**(1), 1–16 (2015)

# Consolidating the Right to Data Protection in the Information Age: A Comparative Appraisal of the Adoption of the OECD (Revised) Guidelines into the EU GDPR, the Ghanaian Data Protection Act 2012 and the Kenyan Data Protection Act 2019

Rogers Alunge[✉]

Joint International PhD in Law, Science and Technology (LAST-JD) CIRSFID,
University of Bologna, Bologna, Italy
alungerogers@yahoo.com

**Abstract.** The proliferation of ICTs and computational power in processing personal information has long been documented to expose individuals to risks of privacy violations and other fundamental rights abuses. This prompted calls, about five decades ago, for the development of legal regimes laying specific rules to follow when processing personal information, especially with the use of ICTs, in order to protect fundamental individual rights. Deliberations in this direction were undertaken at the OECD, and led to the adoption of the OECD Guidelines of Privacy Protection in September 1980 (revised in July 2013), which listed eight principles of data processing on which national and supranational regimes were expected to build personal data processing laws.

This paper attempts a comparative review on how these principles are consolidated in relevant European and African legislation: that is, between the EU's GDPR on the one hand and the Ghana and Kenyan data protection instruments on the other. Being a more advanced legal regime in terms of data protection, the GDPR serves here as a measuring rod to examine how the basic OECD Principles are reflected in the personal data processing rights and obligations provided in the Ghana Data Protection Act of 2012 and the Kenyan Data Protection Act of 2019. The paper concludes with a general note that while the Kenyan legislation appears mostly copied from and consolidates OECD data protection principles more or less exactly like the GDPR, the Ghanaian Act offers comparatively less rigorous protection in some areas.

**Keywords:** Data protection · GDPR · Ghana Data Protection Act · Kenya Data Protection Act · OECD

## 1 Introduction

As the world keeps adopting innovations in Information and Communication Technology (ICT) and other forms of computational machinery to facilitate human interactions, the

J. P. R. Thorn et al. (Eds.): InterSol 2020, LNICST 321, pp. 192–207, 2020.
https://doi.org/10.1007/978-3-030-51051-0_14

last few decades are equally witnessing a global shift by national, international and supranational legal regimes increasingly giving individuals some level of control over information about themselves processed by means of ICTs. Following the documentation of the ever growing risks people expose themselves to as they increasingly rely on ICTs and other technologies [1, 2, 3], the reaction by main legal frameworks has been to impose some rules to be observed and rights to be considered when processing information about individuals. We are in a time when governments and private bodies are enthusiastically investing in the use of 'Big Data' analytics to solve governance problems or study consumer behaviour respectively, and there is a high demand for 'smart' technologies as well as the unprecedented generation of personal information by every web click or online activity. In the midst of all the hype about the praiseworthiness and added value which technology and personal information processing has added to humanity, there have also been concerns about the implications of the extensive monitoring and/or surveillance of our online activities by multilateral institutions and governments [4].

These concerns began mainly following the increasing use of computational power to process information in the 1960s and 1970s, and were mainly privacy concerns [4], but soon it became apparent that the traditional right to privacy may not be adequate to guarantee the necessary safeguards for other fundamental rights of individuals in a context of easy data generation, processing and recycling with the aid of sophisticated ICTs. This led to calls for enhanced protection over personal information [5], to be implemented through imposing certain restrictive or security obligations on public or private institutions processing personal data, while simultaneously granting individuals some rights geared towards exercising some level of control over the information about them being processed by these institutions.

In light of these developments, the 1970s witnessed the emergence of a novel set of principles aimed at protecting the fundamental rights and freedoms of individuals in a context of ubiquitous ICT proliferation. These principles were first embedded in the OECD[1] Guidelines on the Protection of Privacy and Transborder Flows of Personal Data of 23rd September 1980, and are generally referred to as principles of 'personal data protection' (in Europe and later Africa) or 'information privacy' (USA) [6]. This relatively novel legal regime sought to provide safeguards whenever information about individuals is being processed, and especially where such processing is done using ICTs — based on the conviction that the extensive use of ICTs for this processing data could have far reaching effects for the rights and interests of individuals. [7]. In terms of scope, the Guidelines apply to any personal data whose processing, whether by a public or private body or through automation or manually, poses a danger to privacy and individual liberties (Article 2, OECD Guidelines). It defines personal data 'any information relating to an identified or identifiable individual (data subject)'[2], subjecting its processing to eight 'principles': the collection limitation principle, the data quality principle, the purpose specification principle, the use limitation principle, the security safeguards principle, the

---

[1] The Organisation for Economic Co-operation and Development is an intergovernmental economic organisation with 36 member countries, founded in 1961 to stimulate economic progress and world trade. See www.oecd.org. Accessed 14/9/2019.

[2] Article 1(b), OECD Revised Guidelines 2013.

openness principle, the individual participation principle, and the accountability principle. On 11 July 2013, the OECD Council adopted a revised edition of the Guidelines. The eight Principles of the original version remained unchanged, but some new principles were added, including: National Privacy strategies, Privacy management programmes, and Data security breach notification.

National and supranational legal responses to privacy and data protection risks have been developed around these Guidelines. Reason why data protection laws exist in over 120 countries worldwide including 25 African countries [8], and instruments have been introduced by international and regional institutions such as the European Union, ECOWAS[3] and the African Union[4]. It should be pointed out that legal literature has constantly discussed the relationship between the concepts of privacy and data protection in the information age, with scholars still debating as to whether they are two dimensions to the same right or two distinct rights founded on different principles. While Bignami [9] considers data protection generally as a means to guarantee the right to privacy in the information age, Lynskey [5] appears in favour of their interpretation as two separate though heavily interlinked concepts and rights, while de Hert and Gutwirth [10] acknowledge that the former was conceived to address the shortcomings of the law to guarantee the right to privacy in an increasingly digitised era, a view Solove [11] equally shares. Without dwelling much on this debate, this paper adopts, for a definition of data protection, the position of the Council of Europe's convention 108 as interpreted by Hustinx [7], as those set of rules observed when processing personal data in order to protect the fundamental rights and freedoms of persons (including privacy) from any eventual violation.

In light of the above, this paper intends to review, at a higher level of abstraction, how the data protection principles embedded in the OECD Guidelines are incorporated within the European legal framework as opposed to African national responses. In particular, it comparatively examines the consolidation of these principles in Europe's General Data Protection Regulation (GDPR) on the one hand, and their materialisation in the Ghana Data Protection Act 2012 and Kenyan Data Protection Act 2019 on the other hand. The intention is, in the end, to formulate an appraisal of the level of personal data protection available to Ghanaian and Kenyan residents as opposed to their European counterparts.

This introduction shall therefore be followed by a second section briefly reviewing the events leading to the conception, adoption and subsequent revision of the OECD Privacy Guidelines. A third section shall briefly present the GDPR, the Ghanaian and Kenyan data protection instruments. The fourth section, the main part of the paper, shall examine the consolidation of the OECD Principles of data processing under all three instruments with the aim of identifying the similarities and differences between the European and African instruments, followed by a fifth and final section dedicated to conclusive remarks.

---

[3] Economic Community of West African States (ECOWAS) Supplementary Act A/SA.1/01/10 on Personal Data Protection Within ECOWAS.

[4] African Union Convention on Cyber security and Data Protection, 2014.

## 2   The 1980 OECD Guidelines on the Protection of Privacy and Transborder Flows of Personal Data

The OECD Guidelines was the first international embodiment of international principles regulating the processing of data—a text agreed upon both by the US and European countries[5]. The build-up towards its adoption can be said to have concretely began in 1972 with the creation of a Data Bank Panel within the OECD charged with 'reflecting on the regulation of the processing of information about individuals in automated databases' [3], which organised, in 1974, an *OECD Seminar on Policy Issues in data protection and privacy*, which had on the agenda discussions on privacy as well as harmonizing the already disparate rules relating to transborder data flows among member states. Three years later, in 1977, the Data Bank Panel organised a *Symposium on Transborder Data Flows and the Protection of Privacy*, which led to the dismantlement of the Data Bank Panel, and the creation of an Expert Group in 1978, immediately charged with the task of drafting Guidelines on the Protection of Privacy and Transborder Data Flows of Personal Data for the OECD [3]. After two years of negotiation, the Guidelines were finally adopted on 23rd September 1980.

The Recommendations of the Council on the Guidelines (to which the Guidelines were attached as annex) affirms the dual intention of the OECD member states to, through the Guidelines, protect 'privacy and individual liberties' while 'advancing the free flow' of information between member states[6]. It is worth mentioning that the Guidelines repeatedly use the term 'privacy protection' rather than 'data protection', a choice of words largely in favour of the US approach which has always formally employed the term 'informational privacy' in both US law and doctrine to refer to the legal regime established under the Principles in the Guidelines, instead of 'data protection' as it is referred to in Europe [12]. A revised version was adopted on 11th July 2013.

## 3   The European GDPR[7], the Ghanaian Data Protection Act 2012 and the Kenyan Data Protection Act 2019

The following subsections briefly present the European GDPR and the current Ghanaian and Kenyan data protection instruments, as well as their objectives and subject matter.

---

[5] See the Working Party for Information Security and Privacy (WPISP). 2011. The evolving privacy landscape: 30 years after the OECD Privacy Guidelines. Directorate for Science, Technology and Industry—Committee for Information, Computer and Communications Policy, DSTI/ICCP/REG(2010)6/FINAL,6.4.2011. DSTI/ICCP/REG(2010)6/FINAL. P.12.

[6] Recommendations of the Council concerning Guidelines governing the Protection of Privacy and Transborder Flows of Personal Data (23 September 1980).

[7] Regulation (EU) 2016/679 of the European Parliament and of the Council of 27 April 2016 on the protection of natural persons with regard to the processing of personal data and on the free movement of such data, and repealing Directive 95/46/EC (General Data Protection Regulation), published in Official Journal of the European Union, L 119, 4 May 2016. Retrieved from https://eur-lex.europa.eu/eli/reg/2016/679/oj. Accessed 25th February 2020.

## 3.1  The European General Data Protection Regulation (GDPR)

Coming into force on 25th May 2018 and repealing the 1995 European Data Protection Directive[8], the GDPR is Europe's main instrument regulating the processing of personal information. It was conceived to 'ensure a robust protection of the fundamental right to data protection throughout the European Union and strengthen the functioning of the [European] Single Market'[9]. It establishes rights to guarantee and obligations to comply with when processing information about or relating to individuals located within the European Economic Area, or where such processing is done by an entity located within the latter. Being a Regulation, it is directly applicable and enforceable in EU Member States according to Article 288 of the Treaty on the Functioning of the European Union (TFEU). It is widely considered the standard to follow in terms of data protection/digital privacy, lauded as the 'most profound privacy law of our generation' for being 'majestic in its scope and ambition' due to its broad definition of personal data and its attention-grabbing penalties, among other things [13]. It however runs concurrently with the e-Privacy Directive[10] and Police Directive[11] which apply lex specialis where the processing takes place respectively over a publicly accessible telecommunication network or within the context of a criminal investigation.

## 3.2  The Ghana Data Protection Act 2012

The Ghana Data Protection Act entered into force on 16th October 2012, with the objective to protect the privacy of individuals with regard to the processing of (their) personal information[12]. It came up as a fortification of the right to privacy provided for by Article 18 of the 1992 Constitution, following concerns expressed by the Ghanaian Government of the risks of harm likely to befall Ghanaian citizens through the misuse of their personal information [14], especially when processed by means of ICTs [15]. It has

---

[8] Directive 95/46/EC of the European Parliament and of the Council of 24 October 1995 on the protection of individuals with regard to the processing of personal data and on the free movement of such data, Official Journal L281, 23/11/1995, 0031–0050. Retrieved from https://eur-lex.eur opa.eu/legal-content/en/TXT/?uri=CELEX%3A31995L0046. Accessed 25th February 2020.

[9] Communication From The Commission To The European Parliament, The Council, The European Economic And Social Committee And The Committee Of The Regions Safeguarding Privacy in a Connected World A European Data Protection Framework for The 21st Century COM/2012/09 Final (2012). Retrieved from https://eur-lex.europa.eu/legal-content/en/TXT/?uri=CELEX%3A52012DC0009. Accessed 25th February 2020.

[10] Directive 2002/58/EC of the European Parliament and of the Council of 12 July 2002 concerning the processing of personal data and the protection of privacy in the electronic communications sector (Directive on privacy and electronic communications). Retrieved from https://eur-lex.eur opa.eu/legal-content/EN/TXT/?uri=CELEX:32002L0058. Accessed 25th February 2020.

[11] Directive (EU) 2016/680 of the European Parliament and of the Council of 27 April 2016 on the protection of natural persons with regard to the processing of personal data by competent authorities for the purposes of the prevention, investigation, detection or prosecution of criminal offences or the execution of criminal penalties, and on the free movement of such data, and repealing Council Framework Decision 2008/977/JHA. Retrieved from https://eur-lex.europa.eu/legal-content/EN/TXT/?uri=CELEX%3A32016L0680. Accessed 25th February 2020.

[12] Ghana Data Protection Act 2012.

also been commented that the Act was a manifestation of the Ghanaian government's desire to give the state a positive remark in the eyes of the EU in terms of the third country adequacy requirement of the then trendy 1995 EU Data Protection Directive (Article 25), which demanded that EU countries ensure that a third country provides an adequate level of (data) protection before transferring the data of EU citizens to that state [16]. In any case, it remains one of the first national responses by an African state to digital privacy concerns.

### 3.3  The Kenyan Data Protection Act 2019

The Kenyan Data Protection Act of 2019 represents Kenya's most recent and main instrument regulating the processing of personal information of Kenyan residents. The Act's historical background can be traced back to the cyber law reform process in the East African Community (EAC) of which Kenya is a member state, which began on 28 November 2006 leading to the adoption of the EAC Framework for Cyberlaws Phase I recommending EAC member states to adopt data protection legislation based upon international best practices [17]. The country later adopted a new constitution on 27th August 2010 explicitly providing for a right to privacy to include a right not to have 'information relating to their family or private affairs unnecessarily required or revealed' or 'the privacy of their communications infringed.'(Article 31). To further consolidate this right, significant attempts were made to produce a draft bill in 2012, and 2013, with the Ministry of Information and Communication Technology finally releasing, in August 2018, the Privacy and Data Protection Policy 2018 and draft Data Protection Bill, 2018. The latter was then subject to further deliberation in Parliament and later released by the Directorate of Legal Services in July 2019 as the Data Protection Bill 2019. It was signed into law by the President of the Republic on 8th November 2019, and entered into force on 25th November 2019. It consists of 75 Articles arranged into 11 parts, offering a broad range of protection to Kenyan citizens with regard to personal data processing.

## 4  Consolidating the OECD (Revised) Principles (and Corresponding Rights and Obligations) of Data Processing in Europe, Ghana and Kenya

This section, the main focus of this paper, reviews the incorporation of the above-mentioned OECD Principles of data processing listed in the Guidelines into the GDPR, the Ghanaian Data Protection Act 2012 and the Kenyan Data Protection Act 2019.

### 4.1  Collection Limitation Principle (Paragraph 7 OECD Revised Guidelines)

Paragraph 7, laying down the first Principle of the OECD Revised Guidelines, states that 'there should be limits to the collection of personal data and any such data should be obtained by lawful and fair means and, where appropriate, with the knowledge or consent of the data subject.' Information individuals share about themselves determines the inferences society makes about their lives. This Principle hence acts like the first line of defence of individuals against inferences from data about them. With the proliferation of ICTs and social media platforms, rise of Big Data and IoT, and companies investing hugely in data analytics, all kinds of data are used to study consumer behaviour; even data which, most at times, we do not even know exist or which we generate unconsciously [18] but could nevertheless be used to make inferences and decisions about us. Under this Principle, data controllers should have a valid, proportionately reasonable and legitimate reason for collecting personal data. Also, such data should be lawfully obtained i.e. not through fraudulent means or by harassing the individual.

In Europe, the GDPR embeds this Principle in its Article 5(1)(a), requiring personal data to be processed 'lawfully' and 'fairly', while Article 5(1)(c) demands that the data collected should be relevant and limited to the exact needs for the specific processing activity. Article 6 lays down the confines within which data can be collected for processing (consent, performance of a contract, compliance with an enforceable legislation, protecting the vital interests of an individual; public interest, or on grounds of valid legitimate interest[13] of the data controller).

In Ghana, Article 19 of the Data Protection Act, titled 'Minimality' provides that personal data 'may only be processed if the purpose for which it is to be processed, is necessary, relevant and not excessive.' Article 20(1) then lists the legal grounds for processing, which are the same as in the GDPR, listed in the same order. In Kenya, Articles 25(b) to (d) of the Data Protection Act require processing to be 'fair' and 'lawful', and personal data collection should be specific, relevant and limited to the object of processing. Article 30(1) also lists the same legal basis for data processing as in the GDPR, adding processing for historical, statistical, journalistic, literature, art of scientific research (Article 30(1)(b)(viii)).

### 4.2  Data Quality Principle (Paragraph 8, OECD Guidelines)

Article 8 of the OECD Guidelines requires that personal data 'be relevant to the purposes for which they are to be used, and, to the extent necessary for those purposes, should be accurate, complete and kept up-to-date.' It aims to prevent inaccurate and unfair decisions being taken from processing individuals' personal information [19]. For example, an individual seeking a loan could find it denied if the database consulted by the bank to check his/her creditworthiness contains inaccurate or outdated details about his/her financial situation, history or behaviour. It is up to the data controller to ensure that the information based on which decisions are taken about individuals are relevant and accurate[14].

The GDPR's Recital 39 and Article 5(d) require reasonable steps to be taken to ensure that inaccurate personal data upon which decisions are or are to be taken with

---

[13] 'Legitimate interest' could exist when there is a relevant relationship between the data controller and data subject, like where the data subject is a client or is at the service of the data controller (Recital 47 GDPR).

[14] This principle founded the decision of the Ninth Circuit Court of Appeal in the famous US case of *Spokeo v. Robbins*, 867 F. 3d 1108 - Court of Appeals, 9th Circuit 2017. The Court found that Mr Robbins had grounds to sue an employment placement company for having, on his profile, and for not taking the necessary steps to update inaccurate information about his marital and employment status, age and educational background, which could have been the reason why he could not find a job through that company.

regard to individuals are rectified or deleted. It also provides individuals with a right to have rectified inaccurate or incomplete data concerning them with regard to the purpose for which the data is processed (Article 16).

In Ghana, the Data Protection Act mentions 'quality of information' as a principle in its Article 17(e), and Article 26 imposes a duty on the data controller to ensure that processed data 'is complete, accurate, up to date and not misleading having regard to the purpose for the collection or processing.' In terms of related individual rights, Article 33(1) permits an individual to request the correction or deletion of 'personal data that is inaccurate, irrelevant, excessive, out of date, incomplete, misleading or obtained unlawfully…' It is interesting to note the applicability of this right in the Act vis-à-vis unlawfully obtained data: even if such data may apparently be accurate, the individual can still request its deletion if they can show it was unlawfully collected.

In Kenya, Article 25(e) of the Data Protection Act requires personal data to be 'accurate and, where necessary, kept up to date' with reasonable steps taken to ensure 'inaccurate personal data is erased or rectified without delay.' While Article 26 (d) and (e) and Article 40(1) grant individuals a right to request the correction and deletion of false or misleading data about them.

### 4.3 Purpose Specification and Use Limitation Principles (Paragraphs 9 and 10, OECD Revised Guidelines)

Both Paragraphs 9 and 10 of the OECD Revised Guidelines place material and time-based limits on the usage of personal data by data controllers. In essence, Paragraph 9 requires that personal data collected from an individual should be processed strictly within the confines of the purpose for which it was originally collected with no further processing, unless the individual consented to it or such further processing is clearly compatible with the original purpose or is necessary for other purposes permitted by law. For example, if an individual submits their home address to a company in order to have a service delivered to them, that company should not further use that home address for another purpose e.g. to advertise other products to the individual, unless the individual expressly consents to such further use. This principle targets the limitation of non-intuitive inferences which could be generated from further processing of personal data, which currently are not uncommon occurrences [20]. Paragraph 10 on its part limits the timeframe within which personal data can be stored by the data controller i.e. personal data should not still be kept after the specified purpose for which it was processed has been completed. This reduces the risk of processed data becoming excessive, irrelevant, inaccurate or outdated, or that the data is erroneously reused to the detriment of the individual. Practically, it helps complement the accuracy principle, which is discussed later.

This Principle is manifested in Article 5(b) of the GDPR, obliging data controllers to remain within the confines of the original purpose of processing, and can only subject the data to further processing if such secondary processing is reasonably compatible with original purpose for which the data was collected. Article 5(e) GDPR on its part brings to life Paragraph 10 of the Guidelines, with what is known as a 'storage limitation' requirement: which requires personal data, as long as it can enable the identification of an individual, should not be kept for longer than necessary (i.e. it should be kept just for the time needed for the original processing purpose for which it was collected). It should be noted however that this is subject to exceptions of the data being processed for scientific research or statistical purposes. Nevertheless, there should always be appropriate safeguards in place to protect the rights of the data subject.' Also relevant in this respect is the right available to data subjects not to be subject to decisions based solely on automated processing of their data i.e. without any human intervention in the processing (Article 22). This prevents the data controller from using other data they may have previously (and lawfully) obtained from the data subjects to infer behavioural traits or generate digital profiles for other purposes. It should be noted though that such automatic processing is allowed provided the data subject consented to it, or if it is for the performance of a contract to which the data subject is a party.

In Ghana, Article 17(c) of the Ghana Data Protection Act demands 'specification of purpose' when processing personal data, while Article 25 requires the data controller to process data solely for the purpose for which it was collected, and any further processing must be in compatibility with the original purpose, or unless consented to or if required by law). As regards storage limitation, Article 24(1) states that data controllers, subject to exceptions inter alia like research or statistical purposes, 'shall not retain…personal data for a period longer than is necessary to achieve the purpose for which the data was collected and processed'. In terms of corresponding data subject rights, Article 41(1), however, grants a right against automated decision-making using personal data only upon a written request by or on behalf of the data subject asking the controller to refrain from using their data for such processing. And this, apparently, only if the decision 'significantly' affects the data subject. This conveys an interpretation that organisations could generate pure automated-decisions from individuals' data if the latter do not expressly and unilaterally request the contrary, or if the decision does not 'significantly' affect them. In any case, if the decision significantly affects the individual, they are entitled to a written notice by the controller, and a chance to challenge the decision (Article 41 (2)). But then, the Act establishes no test to determine when a result can be said to 'significantly' affect an individual.

Article 25(c) of the Kenyan Data Protection Act specifies that data be collected for 'explicit, specified and legitimate purpose and not further processed in a manner incompatible with those purposes' and Article 30(2) expressly obliges controllers to process personal data in accordance with the (original) purpose for processing. As regards storage time limits, the Act requires controllers and processors not to keep personal data 'for longer than is reasonably necessary to satisfy the purpose for which it processed unless authorised or required by law, is consented to by the individual or is processed for historical, statistical, artistic, journalistic or related research purposes (Article 39(1)). The Act also replicates the GDPR by granting to individuals a general right not to be subject to decisions arrived solely by automated decision-making systems (Article 35(1)).

### 4.4 Security Safeguards Principle (Paragraph 11 OECD Revised Guidelines)

Paragraph 11 OECD Guidelines lays down the security requirement of the personal data processing, requiring data controllers to ensure that personal data is processed securely without undesirable disclosure or compromise i.e. it should be protected 'by reasonable security safeguards against such risks as loss or unauthorised access, destruction, use, modification or disclosure of data.'

The GDPR incorporates this principle in its Article 32, demanding controllers and processors to take appropriate 'technical and organisational measures' when processing personal data. Such measures can include pseudonymisation or encryption, measures to ensure confidentiality of processing, or ability to recover data or restore processing in the event of system breakdown or malfunction in the course of processing.

In Ghana, Article 28(1) of the Ghanaian Act provides an almost identical security requirement as to Article 32 of the GDPR, also suggesting pseudonymisation and encryption as potential tools to ensure data security. This is equally the case in Kenya, as illustrated in the provisions of Article 41(4) of the Kenyan Data Protection Act.

## 4.5 Openness Principle (Paragraph 12 OECD Revised Guidelines)

Article 12 of the OECD Guidelines advocates 'a general policy of openness about developments, practices and policies with respect to personal data.' This is a very crucial data protection principle, and is geared towards establishing trust between individual and organisations which process their personal information. As de Hert et al. [21] observe, once an individual relinquishes their data, they are excluded from the processing, and have no say in how such processing may affect them in future e.g. as regards automatic inferences [21]. This principle flows from one of the main objectives of data protection legislation, namely making the data subject a participant in the outcome of their own data processing. It compels controllers to provide individuals with sufficient information on the processing being carried out, empowering them to scrutinize processing of their data through exercising rights like the right of access, modification and/or deletion of their information being processed [22].

In the GDPR, this principle is materialised in Article 5(a) as the 'transparency' principle, and is reflected in a number of obligations imposed on the data controller. For one, the controller is required to clearly inform data subjects the reason for which they are collecting and processing their information (Article 12(1)), especially when such processing requires (informed) consent from the data subject. The data controller also has to inform the data subjects of their rights to withdraw their consent at any later time if they so wish (Article 7 (1) to (3)). In terms of rights under this principle, Article 13(2)(f) notably grants data subjects the right to request that the data controller explains to them how a particular processing activity yielded a given result which affects the data subject. This right could be activated especially in cases where such decision was reached through automation i.e. with little or no human intervention in the processing.

In Ghana, Article 17(f) mentions 'openness' as one of the principles of data processing. Further consolidating this principle, Article 18 requires that the controller processes personal data lawfully and without violating individuals' privacy rights. Article 27(2) lists a relatively rather exhaustive list of information which the controller, before collecting data for processing, must ensure the data subject is aware of. These include, inter alia, the contact details of the data controller, the purpose for collection, legal grounds for the processing, whether there are or will be any third party recipients of the data, the data subject's right of access and, if need be, to request rectification of the collected and processed data. Moreover, the Act requires that when a decision which significantly affects an individual is taken by automated processing, the data controller should notify the individual, hence providing an opportunity for objection (Article 41). Unlike in the GDPR however, there is no express right available for the individual to obtain meaningful information about the logic involved in processing their data.

The Kenyan Data Protection Act on its part guarantees this principle in its Article 25(b), requiring processing transparency on the part of the data controller. He is equally required in Article 29 to inform the individual about, inter alia, their rights with regard to processing, the purpose of processing as well as the contact details of the data controller or any third party who will receive the data as part of the processing procedure. While Article 32(1) places a burden of proof on the controller to prove consent for processing. In terms of data subject rights, Article 26(a) grants a right for data subject to be informed of the use for which their data is processed. This right proves useful for regulating further unauthorised processing by the controller, hence complementing the Purpose and Use Limitation principles. It should be noted however that just like with the Ghanaian Act, the Kenyan legislation appears offer no express right to data subjects to obtain an explanation from the data controller on the logic involved in processing.

### 4.6 Individual Participation Principle (Paragraph 13 OECD Revised Guidelines)

Paragraph 13 of the OECD Guidelines recommends that individuals should have the right to 'to obtain from a data controller, or otherwise, confirmation of whether or not the data controller has data relating to them; to have [the data] communicated to them…in a form that is readily intelligible to them' and 'to challenge data relating to them and, if the challenge is successful, to have the data erased, rectified, completed or amended.' This principle falls line with the somewhat supervisory role data protection law seeks to grant individuals over the processing of their information.

Accordingly, the GDPR grants a list of rights to data subjects from Article 15 to 18. Article 15 guarantees a right of access to personal data, which in essence gives individuals the right to 'obtain from the controller confirmation as to whether or not personal data concerning him or her are being processed, and, where that is the case, access to the personal data and the following information inter alia: the purposes of the processing, categories of personal data being processed, third party recipients if any, storage period of the data, right to restrict processing, or the right to lodge a complaint with a data protection supervisory authority'[15].

Article 16 complements the right of access with a right to rectification of inaccurate data. A right to erasure (also referred to as a right to be forgotten) is introduced in Article 17, which permits the data subject to request the data controller to erase all personal data it may have about them if, inter alia, processing is no longer compatible with the purpose of processing, they have withdrawn consent to the processing, or their

---

[15] Ideally, a data protection supervisory authority is an independent public authority in charge of overseeing compliance with data protection principles in a given jurisdiction. The GDPR's Article 51 requires each EU Member state to create at least one within each territory. In Ghana, the role is fulfilled by the Data Protection Commission, created by Article 1 of the Data Protection Act. In Kenya, the 2019 Data Protection Act 2019 establishes the Office of the Data Protection Commissioner in its Article 5.

fundamental rights override the processor's legitimate interest for processing. However, this right has to be balanced with other fundamental rights listed in Article 17(3) like freedom of speech and expression or general public interest (especially if the data subject is a public personality[16]). Article 18 then consolidates a right to request restriction of processing if, inter alia, the data is no longer accurate or needed for the purpose for which it was collected. Equally related to this principle is the right to data portability introduced by the GDPR's Article 20, which is a rather peculiar right in terms of granting control over personal data. The right permits data subjects to request their data under processing by a data controller to be transferred to another controller, where such data is processed by automated means.

In Ghana, Article 17(h) of the Ghana Data Protection Act notably mentions 'data subject participation' as a personal data processing principle, while Articles 32 and 35 list a relatively exhaustive set of provisions cumulatively arranged into 18 subsections relating to the right of access to personal data. It equally confers to data subject a list of rights similar to Article 15 of the GDPR, adding, inter alia, the need for consent of any other person who may be identified from the requested data or the data controller taking measures to de-identify them (Articles 35 (4) and (7)). Article 33(1)(a) confers a right to data rectification for individuals, while Article 33(1)(b) grants a 'right to be forgotten' similar to the GDPR. However, unlike the GDPR, there is no express right to data portability in the Ghana Data Protection Act.

In Kenya, similar to the Data Quality Principle, Article 26 (d) and (e) and Article 40(1) of the Kenyan Data Protection Act grant individuals a right to request the correction and deletion of false or misleading data about them. Article 34 grants rights on restriction of processing very identical to those listed under Article18 of the GDPR, and Article 36 provides a general right for individuals to object to processing unless the data controller proves legitimate interest which overrides the individual's interest. And, as in the GDPR, the Kenyan Data Protection Act provides for a right to data portability (Article 38). However, the Act does not appear to limit the right to data processed by automatic means. Apparently therefore, all forms of personal data, as long as they are structured and in a usable format, can be subject to the right to data portability.

### 4.7 The Accountability Principle and the Implementing Accountability Principle (Paragraphs 14 and 15 (B), OECD Revised Guidelines)

Paragraph 14 of the OECD Revised Guidelines makes data controllers responsible for giving effect to the principles advanced in the Guidelines. Complementing this positon, Paragraph 15 requires that they be prepared to show, upon request, a privacy management programme giving effect to the Guidelines. In essence, the Accountability Principle requires data controllers to always be in a position to demonstrate compliance with data processing requirements. It could be viewed as a supervisory mechanism to ensure that individuals are always guaranteed their data protection rights. The Implementing Accountability Principle follows up on this by requiring data controllers to always be poised to demonstrate at any time that they are compliant with data protection obligations.

---

[16] See Paragraph 99 of the ECJ's decision in Google Spain SL, Google Inc v Agencia Española de Protección de Datos and Mario Costeja González [2014] ECLI:EU:C:2014:317.

Incorporating this principle, the GDPR's Article 5(2) provides that the data controller 'shall be responsible for and be able to demonstrate compliance' with all the above data-processing principles. Article 25 on its part requires data controllers to construct their data processing activities in avid awareness of the data protection principles of the Regulation i.e. the conception and running of data processing activities should revolve around data protection principles (Data protection by Design or by Default). Moreover, a 'Data Protection Impact Assessment' requirement (Article 35 GDPR) obliges data controllers, where processing may be risky due to the nature of the data processed (like sensitive data), to carry out an assessment to clearly identify the dangers and risks such processing could present to data subjects. If risks are imminent, the processing could be ordered to stop (by the supervisory authority) or may be permitted to continue after a verified adoption of appropriate countermeasures.

The Ghanaian Data Protection Act mentions the term 'accountability' (Article 17(a)) as a principle to ensure the privacy of individuals but unlike the GDPR, it is silent as regards the data controller's use of default compliance mechanisms i.e. no express data protection by design requirement. There also appears to be no express obligation on data controllers to carry out a prior impact assessment (in the event of risky processing): rather, the Act only grants 'affected' individuals the possibility to request the Data Protection Commission to make such an assessment on a data controller's processing activity (Article 77). The Kenyan Data Protection Act on its part does provide for a 'Data protection by Default or by Design' requirement (Article 41), as well as a data protection impact assessment (Article 31).

### 4.8 Security Breach Notification (Paragraph 15(C), Implementing Accountability, Revised OECD Guidelines)

Paragraph 15 (c) of the Revised OECD Guidelines requires data controllers, as a measure to implement the Accountability Principle, to 'provide notice…to privacy enforcement authorities or other relevant authorities where there has been a significant security breach affecting personal data.' Apparently complementing the Security Safeguard Principle, this Principle was introduced in the 2013 Revised OECD Guidelines. It is worth mentioning that by the time of this revision, data breach notification requirements were already being implemented in a handful of countries and had been introduced in the US by the state of California in 2002 [23]. Data breach notifications have been asserted to serve three purposes: providing feedback on the strengths and shortcomings of a given security measures; enabling authorities and data subjects assess the data controllers's or processors' level of security with respect to their data processing activity; and they compel data controllers and processors to assess and understand their own security measures[17].

This Principle is materialised in the GDPR's Articles 33 and 34. Article 33 demands the data controller to record and/or report personal data breaches[18] to their data supervisory authorities, depending on the severity of the breach. Article 33(5) also compels data

---

[17] European Commission, Commission Staff Working Paper SEC (2012) 72 final. Impact Assessment Accompanying the General Data Protection Regulation (2012), p. 100.

[18] A personal data breach is defined by Article 4(12) of the GDPR as a 'breach of security leading to the accidental or unlawful destruction, loss, alteration, unauthorised disclosure of, or access to, personal data transmitted, stored or otherwise processed'.

controllers to document or record the details of any eventual breach, its effects and the remedial action taken, and the documentation shall enable the supervisory authority to verify compliance with this Article. Article 34 requires that data subjects be informed in case of the breach is likely to affect them significantly, but then avails the data controller of this requirement if it had applied, on the breached data, relevant measures to render the data unintelligible (like encryption), or has taken other relevant measures to ensure that the breach does not materialise into a risk for data subjects.

In Ghana, Article 31 of the Data Protection Act requires the data controller, in event of a reasonable suspicion of a security compromise, to inform the Data Protection Commissioner and the data subject. The Act, however, does not adopt a risk-mitigating approach like the GDPR: not only does it require the reporting of mere suspicions of security compromises, it appears *all* security incidents must be reported, whether or not they are significant or the controller had encrypted the data or adopted other pre or post-mitigating measures. Contrarily, in Kenya, Article 43(1) requires notification if a breach[19] presents a 'real risk of harm' to the data subject. And just like the GDPR, it adopts a risk-mitigation approach by availing the controller or processor of the duty to notify the data subject if the latter took appropriate safeguards like encryption. A slight difference with the GDPR here though is that apparently nothing avails the data controller from notifying the Data Protection Commissioner despite adopting such post-breach mitigating measures (Article 43(6)). But then Article 43(8), just like the GDPR, requires the data controller to record the details of [every] personal data breach, its effect and the remedial actions taken.

## 5  Conclusive Remarks

This paper set out to review how the Ghanaian and Kenyan data protection legislations fare before the European GDPR in consolidating a right to personal data protection for their citizens; rights embedded in the OECD Revised Guidelines Governing the Protection of Privacy and Transborder Flows of Personal Data of 11th July 2013. First, it presented an overview of the importance of data protection as a legal regime and an essential, complementary safeguard against the fundamental rights and freedoms of individuals in today's world of ubiquitous computer and IT processing of personal information. It then briefly reviews the emergence of the 1980 OECD Guidelines (and later its revision in 2013) which laid down the essential principles of the right to data protection around which related national or supranational legislations around the globe could be developed. With the EU as well as African states like Ghana and Kenya adopting data protection legislations based on these OECD principles, this paper sought to comparatively examine the rights and obligations they confer respectively on individuals and data controllers within their jurisdiction. In this light, the incorporation of the OECD data protection principles in the GDPR was comparatively measured against the incorporation of the same principles in the Ghana Data Protection Act of 2012 and the Kenyan Data Protection Act of 2019.

---

[19] Article 2 of the Kenyan Data Protection Act adopts exactly the same definition of a personal data breach as Article 4(12) of the GDPR.

Compared to the European model, the Ghanaian and Kenyan data protection instruments have made quite commendable effort to consolidate the OECD data protection principles to their respective citizens. It can however be affirmed that the African legislations copied hugely from the European model's implementation of the OECD Principles; which can be understood from a viewpoint of colonial history as well as the desire to comply with European data protection standards for economic reasons. As has been commented [24], African data protection legislations are generally heavily influenced by European legislation, owing to colonial heritage as well as the desire to comply with the EU adequacy principle or the so-called 'Brussels effect'. Nevertheless, the Ghanaian Data Protection Act differs slightly from the GDPR and even the Kenyan Data Protection Act in the application of some of these Principles, as evidenced in the absence of a right to data portability, of an obligation to record a personal data breach, or no express requirement on the data controller to do a prior data protection impact assessment (the data subject has to seize the Data Protection Commissioner so the latter seizes the data controller to request n impact assessment). Another noticeable difference is its apparent 'laissez faire' latitude to data controllers to subject data subjects to decisions of purely automated systems unless the data subject expressly notifies the data controller not to refrain from doing so. This which could be problematic because, practically, as Africa and Ghana rapidly advance towards an Internet of Things, individuals would never be able to keep track of or even know about all the data they generate, much less the data a given data controller has about them and is ready to process for profiling and other profit-making purposes. The Kenyan Data Protection Act equally embeds all the above-selected OECD Revised Principles relating to rights and duties of individuals and data subjects respectively, literally copying Europe's GDPR for the most part.

**Acknowledgments.** This research is funded by the Erasmus Mundus program LAST-JD (Joint International Ph.D. in Law, Science and Technology) coordinated by the University of Bologna.

# References

1. Solove, D.: The new vulnerability: data security and personal information. In: Chander, A., Gelman, L., Radin, M.J. (eds.) Securing Privacy in the Internet Age. Stanford University Press (2008)
2. Xavier, C., Bosua, R., Maynard, S.B., Ahmad, A.: The Internet of Things (IoT) and its impact on individual privacy: an Australian perspective. Comput. Law Secur. Rev. **32**(1), 4–15 (2016)
3. González Fuster, G.: The emergence of personal data protection as a fundamental right of the EU. LGTS, vol. 16. Springer, Cham (2014). https://doi.org/10.1007/978-3-319-05023-2
4. Nam, T.: What determines the acceptance of government surveillance? Examining the influence of information privacy correlates. Soc. Sci. J. **56**, 530–544 (2018)
5. Lynskey, O.: The Foundations of EU Data Protection Law. Oxford University Press, Oxford (2015)
6. Bennett, C.J.: Regulating Privacy: Data Protection and Public Policy in Europe and the United States. Cornell University Press, New York (1992)
7. Hustinx, P.: EU data protection law: the Review of Directive 95/46/EC and the proposed General Data Protection Regulation. Collected courses of the European University Institute's Academy of European Law, 24th Session on European Union Law, pp. 1–12 (2013)

8. Greenleaf, G.: Global data privacy laws 2017: 120 national data privacy laws, including Indonesia and Turkey. Privacy Laws & Business International Report, 10-13, UNSW Law Research Paper No. 45. https://papers.ssrn.com/sol3/papers.cfm?abstract_id=2993035. Accessed 11 Oct 2019

9. Bignami, F.: The case for tolerant constitutional patriotism: the right to privacy before the european courts. Cornell Int. Law. J. **41**, 211 (2008)

10. De Hert, P., Gutwirth, S.: Data protection in the case law of Strasbourg and Luxemburg: constitutionalisation in action. In: Gutwirth, S., Poullet, Y., De Hert, P., de Terwangne, C., Nouwt, S. (eds.) Reinventing Data Protection?. Springer, Dordrecht (2009). https://doi.org/10.1007/978-1-4020-9498-9_1

11. Solove, D.: The Digital Person: Technology and Privacy in the Information Age, vol. 1. NyU Press, New York (2004)

12. Arzt, C.: Data protection versus Fourth Amendment privacy: a new approach towards police search and seizure. Crim. Law Forum **16**(3), 183–230 (2005). https://doi.org/10.1007/s10609-005-4143-9

13. Solove, D.: Why I Love the GDPR: 10 Reasons. https://teachprivacy.com/why-i-love-the-gdpr/. Accessed 11 Oct 2019

14. Dagbanja, D.N.: The right to privacy and data protection in Ghana. In: Makulilo, A.B. (ed.) African Data Privacy Laws. LGTS, vol. 33, pp. 229–248. Springer, Cham (2016). https://doi.org/10.1007/978-3-319-47317-8_10

15. Omane Boamah, E.K.: Minister for Communications at The Launch Of The Data Protection Commission On 18th November 2014 at The International Conference Centre (Data Protection Commission). https://dataprotection.org.gh/resources/downloads/conference/10-final-speech-of-the-hon-minister-of-communications-at-the-launch-of-the-data-protection-act/file. Accessed 11 Oct 2019

16. Agyei-Bekoe, E.: Empirical Investigation of the Role of Privacy and Data Protection in the Implementation of Electronic Government in Ghana. A Doctoral Thesis Submitted in Partial Fulfilment of the Award of Doctor of Philosophy Faculty of Technology, Centre for Computing and Social Responsibility De Montfort University, September 2013

17. Makulilo, A.B., Boshe, P.: Data protection in Kenya. In: Makulilo, A.B. (ed.) African Data Privacy Laws. LGTS, vol. 33, pp. 317–335. Springer, Cham (2016). https://doi.org/10.1007/978-3-319-47317-8_15

18. Pangrazio, L., Selwyn, N.: Personal data literacies': a critical literacies approach to enhancing understandings of personal digital data. New Media Soc. **21**(2), 419–437 (2019)

19. Fuster, G.G.: Inaccuracy as a privacy-enhancing tool. Ethics Inf. Technol. **12**(1), 87–95 (2010)

20. Wachter, S., Brent M.: A right to reasonable inferences: re-thinking data protection law in the age of big data and AI. Columbia Business Law Review (2019)

21. De Hert, P., Papakonstantinou, V., Wright, D., Gutwirth S.: The proposed Regulation and the construction of a principles-driven system for individual data protection. Innovation: Euro. J. Soc. Sci. Res. **26**(1–2), 133–144 (2013)

22. Coudert, F.: Towards a new generation of CCTV networks: erosion of data protection safeguards?. Comput. Law Secur. Rev. **25**(2), 145–154 (2009)

23. Stevens, G.M.: Data security breach notification laws. CRS Report for Congress (2012). http://dev.journalistsresource.org/wp-content/uploads/2012/04/R42475.pdf. Accessed 13 10 2019

24. Makulilo, Alex B.: "One size fits all": does Europe impose its data protection regime on Africa? Datenschutz und Datensicherheit-DuD **37**(7), 447–451 (2013)

# Computer Science and Its Applications

# A Matrix Model to Analyze Cascading Failure in Critical Infrastructures

Assane Gueye[1]([⊠]), Babacar Mbaye[1], Doudou Fall[2], Alassane Diop[3], and Shigeru Kashihara[2]

[1] University Alioune Diop of Bambey (UADB), Bambey, Senegal
{assane1.gueye, babacar.mbaye}@uadb.edu.sn
[2] Nara Institute of Science and Technology (NAIST), Ikoma, Japan
{doudou-f, shigeru}@is.naist.jp
[3] Université Virtuelle du Senegal (UVS), Dakar, Senegal
alassanediop.dfip@uvs.edu.sn

**Abstract.** Critical infrastructures are defined as systems and assets, whether physical or virtual, so vital to the nation that their incapacity or destruction would have a debilitating impact on the nation's existence. Although composed of systems that are usually designed/implemented *independently*, critical infrastructures are in reality *interdependent*: hence risks/failures will often *cascade* from one system to another. In this paper, we derive an efficient procedure to fully describe the cascading effects of a node failure in a network of interdependent systems. The procedure is solely based on operations on the adjacency matrix of graph representing the network. We have also shown that the analysis of the cascades can be based on a much smaller matrix that has a DAG structure. This matrix characterization of the cascade and the dimension reduction of the analysis open new opportunities in the study of cascading effects in interdependent networks. Although this paper focuses on the interdependence between the power grid and the communication system, the model presented herein easily generalizes to the interdependence of an arbitrary number of networks.

**Keywords:** Critical infrastructure · Interdependent networks · Cascading failures · Graph theory · Adjacency matrix

## 1 Introduction

Critical infrastructures are defined as "systems and assets, whether physical or virtual, so vital to the nation that their incapacity or destruction would have a debilitating impact on security, national economic security, national public health or safety, etc., or any combination thereof [1]". They include (but are not limited to) the communication and information systems, the power grid, the water and gas distribution systems, the transportation systems, the healthcare systems, and the financial systems. These systems can be owned and operated by

© ICST Institute for Computer Sciences, Social Informatics and Telecommunications Engineering 2020
Published by Springer Nature Switzerland AG 2020. All Rights Reserved
J. P. R. Thorn et al. (Eds.): InterSol 2020, LNICST 321, pp. 211–223, 2020.
https://doi.org/10.1007/978-3-030-51051-0_15

both public and private agents. Each system has a certain degree of autonomy, but they are usually all overseen by a common entity (the state: e.g. through laws, regulations, and funding). Although they are mostly in-country, some critical infrastructures might be located outside the country. Finally, each critical infrastructure sector has unique characteristics, operating models, and risk profiles.

More importantly, these systems share common risks and threats and constitute one big system that is globally vulnerable due to the several reasons. One of the most prevalent reasons is the fact that they are interdependent and are often physically and logically interconnected at one or more interconnection points (e.g., where the power grid provides energy to the communication system).

Given the vital role they play in our modern society, critical infrastructures must be secure and able to withstand and rapidly recover from all hazards. Achieving this will require an effective collaboration and coordinated efforts both at the strategic and operation levels, and an efficient information exchange at all levels. These, on the other hands, will need a holistic understanding of the notion of risk at the global level, as risk will often be transferred from one system to the other. The main goal of this paper is to derive models and metrics to quantify the potential impacts as well as cascading effects of an incident or threat scenario in one critical sector on other critical sectors.

The main challenge in the study of interdependent system is to understand how the failure of a particular node (or group of nodes) propagates through the global network. In this paper, we use a graph theory approach to model the interdependence between different networks. More precisely, we use an extended adjacency matrix to capture the connectivity within each network as well as the interdependencies between the networks. The graph we consider is directed, as the interdependencies might not be symmetrical.

The main contribution of this paper is the derivation of an efficient procedure to fully describe the cascading effects of a node failure in the network. The procedure is solely based on operations on the adjacency matrix of the network. We have also shown that the analysis of the cascades in a network can be based on a much smaller graph that has a DAG structure. This matrix characterization of the cascade and the dimension reduction of the analysis open new opportunities in the study on cascading effects in network.

As a use-case, this paper focuses on the interdependence of the power and the communication system. Energy and communications systems are uniquely critical due to the enabling functions they provide across all critical infrastructure sectors. We study the resilience of the combined system against arbitrary node failures.

We would like to stress the fact that the focus on the power grid and communication network is just for illustrative purpose. The model and analysis proposed in the paper easily generalize to the interdependence of an arbitrary number of networks.

The remainder of this paper is organized as follow. In Sect. 2 we present the details of our model as well as the assumptions made for the model. In Sect. 3, we provide the details of procedure to characterize cascading failure using this adjacency matrix. A brief discussion of related work is presented in Sect. 4. This paper ends with a conclusion and perspectives in Sect. 5.

# 2    Model

In this section, we discuss our assumptions in modeling the power grid, the communication, and the interdependencies between them. These models are simplifications of real-life scenarios. However, we believe that they constitute good first order approximations. More precisely, we assume that:

- The power grid (PG) consists of nodes and power lines, where the nodes are mainly: *Generators* (G) that generate power, *Loads* (L) that consume power and *Buses* (B) that allow the transmission of power through them. Each generator produces a fix quantity of energy and each load demands a fix quantity of energy. A load (L) or bus (B) cannot operate if it does not have a path to at least one generator,
- The power grid is connected to a Communication and Control Network (CCN) that allows monitoring and intelligent control actions to respond to changes in the grid conditions,
- The CCN consists of Control Centers (CC) and routers (R) that are connected by communication links. A router (R) cannot operate if it does not have a path to (at least one) CC,
- Every router (R) receives power from at least one load (L) node via a directed dependency link. When all the load nodes to which a router depend on fail, the router also fails. A router is fully operational if at least one of the load nodes to which it depends is also functional at its full capacity and it has a route to the CC,
- Every bus (B) sends/receives control signals from/to at least one router (R) via a bidirectional dependency link. When all the routers to which a bus depend on fail, the bus also fails. A bus is fully operational if at least one of the dependent routers is operational,
- A load (L) is operational if its entire demand is met by the quantity of energy it receives,
- When a failure occurs in either network, there could be a cascading effect,
- The generators and control centers are autonomous: generators have internal control and control centers have energy backup, so that they will always operate (indeed, if the sources fail, the whole system breaks down: we avoid that trivial case).

Next, we model these systems and their interdependencies using graph theory notions.

## 2.1   Model of the Power Grid

With the assumptions above, the delivery of energy on the power grid can be modeled by a network flow problem (also called supply-demand model [2]). In a network flow problem, the goal is to carry a fixed amount of goods from a nonempty subset of source nodes $G_{en}$ (the generators) to a nonempty subset $L$ of destination nodes (the loads), using the network links (transmission lines). These links transit through intermediary nodes (the buses). We assume that the subset of sources is disjoint to the subset of destinations (a generator cannot be a load at the same time) and that network links are directed.

With each node in $g \in G_{en}$ (i.e., a generator), we associate a nonnegative number $s(g)$, the "supply" at $g$; and with each node $l \in L$ (i.e, a load), we associate a nonnegative number $d(l)$, the "demand" at $l$. At the buses $(B)$, there is no production or consummation. Consequently, the entire amount of goods arriving from the incoming links of a bus are distributed to its outgoing links. In this paper, we assume that there is no capacity constraints: links can carry an arbitrary amount of goods (this assumption shall be relaxed later). Finally, we assume that there is a fixed amount of energy $(\Delta)$ to be moved from the generators to the loads and we consider a balanced network where the supply fully matches the demand (supply = demand = $\Delta$).

To analyze the model, we define the notion of a *flow* which is essentially a function that assigns a number to each link and satisfies the following properties: (1) the *conservation of flows* (at each node, the difference of incoming and outgoing flows is equal to the locally consumed/produced flow) and (2) the *capacity constraints* (each link carries a quantity of flows that is at most equal to its capacity; note that in this paper capacities of the links are assumed to be infinite), (3) *balanced network*: the total amount of supply is equal to the total amount of demand (in other terms, the total amount of energy produced by the generators is equal to the total amount of energy to be consumed by the loads).

In this paper, we only consider integer flows, where links carry only integer amounts of goods. We also assume that the total amount of goods to be carried from all sources to all destinations $(\Delta)$ is also a positive integer.

Figure 1 (left figure) shows an example of flow model for a simple power grid. The generator produces 3 units of goods and loads $L_1$ and $L_2$ have respective demand of 1 and 2 units of goods. The right figure shows an example of flow (i.e., assignment of integer values to links). Links with zero unit of goods are considered inactive and are shown in dotted-line. Notice that, in general, there is a large number of possible flows. We would like to choose one so that the resulting global interdependent system is resilient to failures.

## 2.2   Model of the Communication Network

In this section, we present the model for the communication network considered in this study. First, notice that in a real-world setting, the communication network is utilized for many different applications. However, in this study we

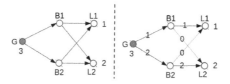

**Fig. 1.** Example of flow the power grid

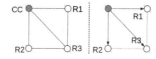

**Fig. 2.** Example of All-to-One network model

consider that it is exclusively used for the monitoring and control of the power grid. This (rather restrictive assumption) shall be relaxed later.

For the communication network (CCN), we use an All-to-One communication network model [3]. In an All-to-One model, the primary goal of the network (operator) is to enable all routers to communicate with a designated node (the CC for this study). To get all routers connected to the CC, the network (operator) chooses a collection of links that forms a spanning tree. Since the objective with the CCN is to get each router connected to the CC, we can transform the (undirected) spanning tree to a directed one rooted at the CC (with all the links going away from the CC).

Figure 2 shows an example of All-to-One network. The right figure shows an example of rooted spanning. Notice that there is a large number of possible spanning trees. We would like to choose one so that the resulting global interdependent system is resilient to failures.

### 2.3 Interdependence Model

For their respective operations to be possible, each network needs the other one: the CCN needs energy (for the routers) that is provided by the PG, while the PG needs remote control and monitoring that is enabled by the CCN. Figure 3 shows an example with interdependence links. In real-life situations, these links depends on many factors such as physical co-location and financial options.

### 2.4 Cascading Failures

For the *global* (interdependent) network to work at its full capacity, the flow chosen for the power grid must be able to carry the total quantity of produced energy and the spanning tree chosen for the communication network must connect all routers to the CC. When a link/node from either network fails, all the nodes in its downstream also fail. This leads to a cascading effect that takes place in the network.

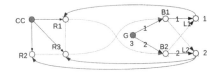

**Fig. 3.** Example of interdependence

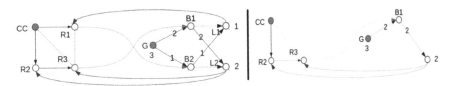

**Fig. 4.** Example of interdependence with partial cascade

For instance, in the (global) system in Fig. 3, if router $R_1$ fails, it will cause bus $B_2$ to lose control and monitoring, hence will not operate normally (i.e., fails). This will then cause load $L_2$ to fail. But $L_2$ provides energy to router $R_3$, which will then fail and cause bus $B_1$ and load $L_1$ to fail. At the end of this process, only the generator and the control center (which are considered to be autonomous) are still functioning. This is an example of full cascade in the network.

Figure 4 shows another choice of PG, CCN for the same interdependencies (top figure). In this case, a failure that starts from router $R_1$ will cascade to only part of the network. The bottom figure shows the residual network after cascade. This network configuration is clearly preferred to the one in Fig. 3.

At the end of the cascade, some part of the flow ($f_{lost}$) might be lost, and a number of communication nodes ($n_{lost}$) might become disconnected from the CC. We assume that the cost associated with the failure is a function of these two quantities $H(f_{lost}, n_{lost})$.

Our goal is to derive a procedure that describes the cascading process. Next, we present the mathematical tools needed for such a derivation.

## 2.5 Adjacency Matrix

Once a (global) network configuration is fixed, we can represent it as a graph whose node set contains the CCN nodes and the nodes from the PG. The links of the graph are composed with the links from those two networks and the interdependence links. The graph is directed, as the interdependencies might not be symmetrical. Equation 1 shows the adjacency matrix of the network configuration shown in Fig. 3. In the next section, we show how to characterize the cascade process by only using operations on this matrix.

$$\mathbf{A} = \begin{bmatrix} 0\ 1\ 1\ 1 & 0\ 0\ 0\ 0\ 0 \\ 0\ 0\ 0\ 0 & 0\ 0\ 1\ 0\ 0 \\ 0\ 0\ 0\ 0 & 0\ 1\ 0\ 0\ 0 \\ 0\ 0\ 0\ 0 & 0\ 0\ 0\ 0\ 0 \\ \overline{0\ 0\ 0\ 0} & 0\ 1\ 1\ 0\ 0 \\ 0\ 0\ 0\ 0 & 0\ 0\ 0\ 1\ 0 \\ 0\ 0\ 0\ 0 & 0\ 0\ 0\ 0\ 1 \\ 0\ 1\ 0\ 0 & 0\ 0\ 0\ 0\ 0 \\ 0\ 0\ 1\ 1 & 0\ 0\ 0\ 0\ 0 \end{bmatrix} \tag{1}$$

## 3   Analysis

The main challenge in the study of interdependent systems is to understand how the failure of a particular node (or group of nodes) propagates through the global network. In this section, we show how to fully describe the cascading effects of the failure of a node by only using operations on the adjacency matrix. To our knowledge, this is the first derivation of cascades in interdependent networks that is solely based on operations on the adjacency matrix. The method is also very efficient as it reduces the dimension of the computations.

### 3.1   Closed Cascade Domains

First, we define the notion of closed cascade domain (CCD) of a network, as *a set of nodes S such that for each pair of nodes* $(i, j) \in S$, *a failure at i will propagate to j, and vice-versa, a failure at j will propagate to i.*

The following lemma gives a one-to-one correspondence between the CCDs of a network and the strongly connected components (SCCs) of its graph.

**Lemma 1.** *Every SCC of the graph constitutes a CCD of the network, and vice-versa.*

The proof of the lemma is straightforward. Since a failure at $i$ leads to a failure at $j$ only if there is a path from $i$ to $j$, SCCs are equivalent to CCDs. In what follows, we will use CCD and SCC interchangeably.

Building upon this correspondence, we now describe the different steps of a cascade process in the network. The general idea is that a failure of some node will eventually cascade to all nodes in the same CCD. It will also then subsequently reach a node belonging to another CCD that is reachable from a node in the first CCD. Once a node in a new CCD is reached, the cascade continues from that node onwards and the same process is repeated.

### 3.2   Computing the SSC of the Network

The first step is to determine the different CCDs by using the adjacency/configuration matrix $A$. For that, we use operation in a new *semiring* whose members are the set of matrices with entry values $\{0, 1\}$. We define the operations $\vee$ (the element-wise OR function) and $\wedge$ (the element-wise AND function) (please see [4] for more details). Notice that the adjacency matrix is an element of this semiring. We define a matrix $\mathbf{C}$ (the infinite sum of powers of $\mathbf{A}$) as follow:

$$\mathbf{C} \equiv I \vee \mathbf{A} \vee \mathbf{A}^2 \vee \mathbf{A}^3 + ..., \tag{2}$$

where $\vee$ is the element-wise OR function satisfying $a \vee b = 0$ when both $a$ and $b$ are zero, and $a \vee b > 0$ (which we consider to be 1) if either $a$ and $b$ is nonzero.

The matrices $\mathbf{A}^k$ are the $k^{th}$ powers of the matrix $\mathbf{A}$. Entry $(i,j)$ of the $\mathbf{A}^k$ is positive if there exists a path of length $k$ from $i$ to $j$ (actually, it is the number of paths of length $k$ between $i$ and $j$). Hence, $\mathbf{C}(i,j) > 0$ if and only if there exists a path from $i$ to $j$.

It is worth noting that the OR-summation in the definition of $\mathbf{C}$ does not need to go to infinity. However, let us, for the time being, keep the summation infinite for convenience reasons. Later (in Sect. 3.6), we will show an efficient way to compute $\mathbf{C}$.

Now consider the matrix $\mathbf{C} \wedge \mathbf{C}^T$, where $\wedge$ is the element-wise AND function, satisfying $a \wedge b = 0$ when either $a$ or $b$ is zero, and $a \wedge b > 0$ (which we consider to be 1) only when both $a$ and $b$ are nonzero. The following lemma gives a relation between nodes belonging to the same SCC. The lemma is solely based on $\mathbf{C} \wedge \mathbf{C}^T$.

**Lemma 2.** *Entry $(i,j)$ of $\mathbf{C} \wedge \mathbf{C}^T$ is positive if and only if nodes $i$ and $j$ belongs to the same SCC.*

**Corollary 1.** *Rows of $\mathbf{C} \wedge \mathbf{C}^T$ corresponding to the nodes belonging to the same SCC are identical.*

The proof of the lemma is quite straightforward. Indeed, if $\mathbf{C} \wedge \mathbf{C}^T(i,j) = \mathbf{C}(i,j) \wedge \mathbf{C}(j,i) > 0$, then each term of the "product" must be positive. This means that there exists a path between $i$ and $j$ and a path between $j$ and $i$, which implies that $i$ and $j$ belongs to the same SCC. On the other hand, if $i$ and $j$ belongs to the same SCC, both terms of the product are nonzero, and so is the product.

For the corollary, we use the fact that the SCCs are equivalence classes: if $i$ and $j$ belongs to the same SCC and $j$ and $k$ belongs to the same SCC, then $i$ and $k$ belongs to the same SCC. In other terms, if $\mathbf{C}(i,j) \wedge \mathbf{C}(j,i) > 0$ and $\mathbf{C}(j,k) \wedge \mathbf{C}(k,j) > 0$ then $\mathbf{C}(i,k) \wedge \mathbf{C}(k,i) > 0$. By considering all nodes in the same SCC, we can easily use the above lemma to show that their corresponding rows in $\mathbf{C} \wedge \mathbf{C}^T$ have same entry patterns (i.e., are zero in the same entries and nonzero in the same entries).

From the product matrix $\mathbf{C} \wedge \mathbf{C}^T$, we define the matrix $\mathbf{S}$ as its *reduced row echelon form*. Matrix $\mathbf{S}$ is of dimension $K \times N$, where $K$ is the number of SCCs and $N$ is the number of nodes of the network. It can be obtained by performing a series of elementary operations on the rows of $\mathbf{C} \wedge \mathbf{C}^T$. It has a number of nice properties that we list next.

First, remember that each row of the matrix $\mathbf{S}$ corresponds to one SSC of the graph. Let each SCC be indexed by its corresponding row in $\mathbf{S}$ (row 1 corresponds to SCC 1, row 2 to SSC 2, ... and so on). Then, the following lemma gives us a way to label each node with the index of the SSC it belongs to.

**Lemma 3 (Labelling nodes with the index of their SCC).** *Let $l(i)$ be a function that labels a node with the index of its SCC. Then,*

$$l(i) = [1 : K]\mathbf{S}1_i, \tag{3}$$

*where $[1 : K]$ is the row vector $[1, 2, 3, \ldots, K]$ and $1_i = [0 \ldots 1 \ldots 0]^T$ is the column vector with entries equal to zero, except for entry $i$ which is 1.*

**Corollary 2.** *The labels of all nodes are given by the vector*

$$l = [1 : K]\mathbf{SI}, \tag{4}$$

*where $\mathbf{I}$ is the identity matrix.*

The arguments behind the lemma are as follows: First, notice that each column of $\mathbf{S}$ contains only one nonzero entry (actually a 1). This is the case because each node belongs to one and only one SCC. Also, the product $\mathbf{S}1_i$ is equal to column $i$ of $\mathbf{S}$ (which contains only one nonzero entry at the row corresponding to the SCC containing $i$). Thus, $l(i)$ is equal to the index of the SCC that contains node $i$.

### 3.3 Defining the (Much Smaller) Cascade DAG

Since all the nodes in the same CCD (or SCC) have the same cascading effects, we can group all such nodes in one super-node to form a new residual graph $\tilde{G}$ as follow: contract all edges in the SCC and remove duplicates and multi-edges. The resulting graph $\tilde{G}$ is a directed acyclic graph (DAG). We will call it the cascade DAG. The adjacency matrix of the cascade DAG can be derived as follows.

**Lemma 4.** *Let the matrix $\mathbf{A}'$ be definded as $\mathbf{A}' = \mathbf{SAS}^T$.*
*Then, $\mathbf{A}'(i, j)$ is the number of links (of the original graph) from SCC $i$ to SCC $j$.*

After removing all loops and multi-edges, we obtain the adjacency matrix $\tilde{\mathbf{A}}$ of $\tilde{G}$ as follow:

**Lemma 5.** $\tilde{\mathbf{A}} = (\mathbf{A}' > 0) - \mathbf{I} = 1_{\mathbf{A}' - diag(\mathbf{A}') > 0}.$

Since the failure of a network node will eventually cause failure of each node in its CCD, we can consider the failure of a super-node in the cascade DAG. Such failure, will propagate to the entire 'descendance' of that super-node (its children, the children of these children, and so on...). Hence, to characterize the effects of a failure of a node, we just need to compute its descendance in the cascade DAG. For that, we define the (cascade) consequence matrix $\mathbf{E}$ as follow:

**Definition 1.** $\mathbf{E} \equiv \mathbf{I} \vee \tilde{\mathbf{A}} \vee \tilde{\mathbf{A}}^2 \vee \tilde{\mathbf{A}}^3 + \cdots \vee \tilde{\mathbf{A}}^k.$

As was observed earlier with the matrix $\mathbf{C}$, Sect. 3.6 gives an efficient way to compute the matrix $\mathbf{E}$.

The entry of matrix $\mathbf{E}$ verifies the property: $\mathbf{E}(i,j) > 0$ if super-node $j$ is a descendant of super-node $i$. In other terms, $\mathbf{E}(i,j) > 0$ if a failure of a node in CCD $i$ will cause failure of all the nodes in CCD $j$. Hence,

**Lemma 6.** *Matrix $\mathbf{E}$ describes the cascading effect of the failure of each node.*

### 3.4  Computing Loss Related to Cascade

Now suppose that there is a loss associated with the failure of each node. Let the vector $L$ be the loss vector of the network, such that $L(i)$ is the loss associated with node $i$. We assume that the loss associated to the failure of a set of nodes $S$ is equal to the sum of the losses of the nodes

$$L(S) = \sum_{i \in S} L(i). \tag{5}$$

Then the losses associated with the failure of the different CCDs are given by

$$L_{DAG} = \mathbf{S}L. \tag{6}$$

In other terms, $L_{DAG}(k)$ is the sum of the losses associated with the failure of all the nodes belonging to the $CCD_k$ (remember that a failure of one node in the CCD will eventually propagate to all the nodes in the CCD).

Now, the losses associated with a cascade that starts from any node on the global network are given by the vector $L_{Net}$, where the vector $L_{Net}$ is equal to:

**Lemma 7 (cascade losses).** $L_{net} = \mathbf{E}L_{DAG} = \mathbf{E}\mathbf{S}L.$

$L_{net}(k)$ is the total loss incurred after a cascade that starts from any node belonging to the $CCD_k$. This loss can be written as

$$L_{net}(k) = 1_k L_{net} = 1_k \mathbf{E}L_{DAG} = 1_k \mathbf{E}\mathbf{S}L. \tag{7}$$

### 3.5  Summary of the Cascade Characterization Procedure

Now we summarize the procedure to compute the cascading effects of node failures in the network.

- From the Adjacency matrix $\mathbf{A}$, compute the matrix $\mathbf{C}$ (the next subsection shows an efficient way to compute $\mathbf{C}$)
- Compute the SCC matrix $\mathbf{C} \wedge \mathbf{C}^T$ and compute its reduced row echelon $\mathbf{S}$ to identify the different SCC (hence CCD) of the network
- Label each node of the network with the index of the CCD to which it belongs using: $l(i) = [1:K]S1_i$,
- Compute the adjacency matrix of the cascade DAG

$$\tilde{\mathbf{A}} = (\mathbf{A}' > 0) - \mathbf{I} = 1_{\mathbf{A}'-diag(\mathbf{A}')>0} \tag{8}$$

where $\mathbf{A}' = \mathbf{S}\mathbf{A}\mathbf{S}^T$.

- Compute the consequence matrix $\mathbf{E}$ (next subsection shows an efficient way to compute $\mathbf{E}$)
- Compute the cascade loss vector: $L_{net} = \mathbf{E}L_{DAG} = \mathbf{ESL}$
- For (network) node $i$, compute its associated cascade losses as:

$$L_{net}(i) = 1_{l(i)}L_{net} = 1_{l(i)}\mathbf{E}L_{DAG} = 1_{l(i)}\mathbf{ESL} \tag{9}$$

### 3.6  Efficient Computation of the Matrix C

Now we provide an efficient method to compute the matrix $\mathbf{C}$. The same method can be used to compute the matrix $\mathbf{E}$.

First, notice that since $\mathbf{C}$ is an infinite sum, directly computing it may be complex. Instead, we define a new matrix $\mathbf{D}$ as follow:

$$\mathbf{D} = \mathbf{I} + (\alpha\mathbf{A}) + (\alpha\mathbf{A})^2 + (\alpha\mathbf{A})^3 + ... \tag{10}$$

We will soon comment on the real number $\alpha$, but for the time being, just assume that it is a strictly positive number chosen to be sufficiently small.

It is not hard to see that $\mathbf{D}$ has 0 where $\mathbf{C}$ has 0, and $\mathbf{D}$ has nonzero positive entry where $\mathbf{C}$ has 1 (i.e., $\mathbf{C}(i,j) = \mathbf{D}(i,j) > 0$). So, if we can efficiently compute $\mathbf{D}$, we instantly have $\mathbf{C}$. We use the following trick for the computation of $\mathbf{D}$. Let matrix $\mathbf{F}$ be defined as follows:

$$\mathbf{F} = \mathbf{D} - (\alpha\mathbf{AD}) \tag{11}$$
$$= \mathbf{I} + (\alpha\mathbf{A}) + (\alpha\mathbf{A})^2 + (\alpha\mathbf{A})^3 + ... \tag{12}$$
$$- (\alpha\mathbf{A}) - (\alpha\mathbf{A})^2 - (\alpha\mathbf{A})^3 - ... \tag{13}$$

Hence,

$$\mathbf{F} = \mathbf{D} - (\alpha\mathbf{AD}) = \mathbf{I} \tag{14}$$

By factorizing with $\mathbf{D}$, we get

$$\mathbf{D} = (\mathbf{I} - (\alpha A))^{-1} \tag{15}$$

Now, the matrix $(\mathbf{I} - (\alpha A))^{-1}$ is not always invertible. However, if we choose a value of $\alpha$ sufficiently small, we can always make it invertible. A similar argument can be used for the computation of the consequence matrix $\mathbf{E}$.

In conclusion, the operations on the semiring mentioned earlier were just introduced for convenience reasons. To compute the cascading effects of failure of the nodes, we will only perform classical operations on real-valued matrices.

## 4  Related Work

Due to the vital role they play in modern societies, there has recently been a surge in the interest to understanding critical infrastructures [1], which are known to be interdependent systems [5].

The authors in [6] present a survey of U.S. and International Research in Critical Infrastructure Interdependency Modeling. The report presents a holistic view that includes political, economic, and social aspects. A more recent survey [7] presents an overview on some modeling approaches and models used to analyze critical infrastructures interdependencies.

Models used to analyze critical infrastructures are largely dominated by *random graphs* [8]. Due to their limitations to capture real-world networks, some authors have turned into simulation models [9]. Hybrid models [5] have also been proposed that combine both random graphs and simulations. The authors in [10] focuses on the interdependence between the power grid and the communication network. The present paper uses some of their assumptions.

Most of these models make assumptions that are often more realistic that the ones we make in this paper. However, because of their advanced models, most of the papers fail to provide a simple way to characterize cascades, and as a consequence, they often end up turning to simulations to analyze cascades. Instead, our paper is a topology-based analysis that considers only the structures of the interconnections of the nodes within and between the different networks. We have purposely taking a step back to look at the system in a more fundamental way and we have derived an efficient characterization of cascades that is solely based on operations on the adjacency matrix. To our knowledge, the is the first result of the kind in the study of cascades in interdependent network.

## 5    Conclusion

In this paper, we have studied the cascading effects of the failure of a node in an interdependent network. We have presented the derivation of an efficient procedure to fully describe the cascading effects of a node failure in the network. The procedure is solely based on operations on the adjacency matrix of the network. We have also shown that the analysis of the cascades in a network can be based on a much smaller matrix that has a DAG structure.

This matrix characterization of the cascade and the dimension reduction of the analysis open new opportunities in the study of cascading effects in network. In perspective, we plan to leverage our results to propose methods for the design and optimization of resilient interdependent networks.

**Acknowledgement.** This work was partially accomplished under NIST Cooperative Agreement No.70NANB19H063 with Prometheus Computing, LLC. The authors would like to thank Paul Patrone and Brian Cloteaux (NIST ACM Division) for their useful advice and suggestions.

## References

1. US Dept. Homeland Security: Critical infrastructure sectors (2014). https://www.cisa.gov/critical-infrastructure-sectors
2. Smith, D.K., Gueye, A.: Network flows: theory, algorithms, and applications. J. Oper. Res. Soc. **45**, 1340 (1994). https://doi.org/10.1057/jors.1994.208

3. Laszka, A., Gueye, A.: Quantifying All-to-One network topology robustness under budget constraints. ACM SIGMETRICS Perform. Eval. Rev. **41**(4), 8–11 (2014)
4. Kepner, J., Gilbert, J.: Graph Algorithms in the Language of Linear Algebra. Society for Industrial and Applied Mathematics, Philadelphia (2011)
5. Havlin, S.: Catastrophic cascade of failures in interdependent networks. Nature **464**, 1025–1028 (2010)
6. Idaho National Laboratory: Critical infrastructure interdependency modeling: a survey of US and international research (2006). https://www.osti.gov/servlets/purl/911792
7. Banerjee, J., Das, A., Sen, A.: A survey of interdependency models for critical infrastructure networks. In: Examining Robustness and Vulnerability of Networked Systems (2014)
8. D'Souza, R.M., Brummitt, C., Leicht, E.A.: Modeling interdependent networks as random graphs: connectivity and systemic risk. In: D'Agostino, G., Scala, A. (eds.) Networks of Networks: The Last Frontier of Complexity. Understanding Complex Systems, pp. 73–94. Springer, Cham (2014). https://doi.org/10.1007/978-3-319-03518-5_4
9. Rigole, T., Deconinck, G.: A survey on modeling and simulation of interdependent critical infrastructures, January 2006
10. Parandehgheibi, M., Modiano, E.: Robustness of interdependent networks: the case of communication networks and the power grid. In: 2013 IEEE Global Communications Conference (GLOBECOM), pp. 2164–2169 (2013)

# Clusters Construction Mechanism for Strictly Linear Wireless Sensor Networks

Abdourakhmane Fall, Moussa Dethié Sarr$^{(\boxtimes)}$, and Cheikh Sarr

Université de Thiès, BP 967 Thiès, Sénégal
{abdourakhmane.fall,mdsarr,csarr}@univ-thies.sn

**Abstract.** A wireless sensor network (WSN) is a set of interconnected sensors arranged in a given topology. When these sensors are arranged in a linear form, they are called linear wireless sensors networks. These particular cases of Linear WSN are today the subject of several applications like for instance monitoring border, watercourse, oil, road or rail infrastructure, gas pipe etc.

Several self-construction clusters algorithms for WSN have been proposed in the literature, these solutions, for the most part of them, are not adapted to a linear topology because having been thought under the base of nonlinear topologies. On the other hand, solutions allowing the organization in clusters for the linear WSN have been proposed. However, they do not work completely autonomously and require human intervention such as the choice of Cluster Head (CH) or the membership cluster in advance by the network administrator.

In this paper, we propose a new mechanism for self-construction clusters for strictly linear wireless sensor networks. This approach allows clustered wireless sensor organization to facilitate the routing of collected data to the sink.

The algorithm was tested on the Castalia/Omnet++ simulator and the results obtained provide a linear WSN with zero orphan node and zero singleton cluster, whatever the linear WSN cardinality, the results were also compared with the LEACH algorithm applied to a linear topology that gives a very large number of singletons nodes.

**Keywords:** Linear wireless sensor networks · Clustering algorithms · Automatic topology construction

## 1 Introduction

A wireless sensor network (WSN) is a collection of interconnected sensors for a given application. These sensors, after data collection, route them to a base station for operation. These WSN, today, are applied in several fields such as environmental (meteorology, ocean acidification, dispersion of pollutants, etc.), commercial [1], medical (implantation of micro-sensors in the human body), military (detection of chemical, biological or radiation agents) [2], etc. The WSN are arranged in a given way depending mainly

© ICST Institute for Computer Sciences, Social Informatics and Telecommunications Engineering 2020
Published by Springer Nature Switzerland AG 2020. All Rights Reserved
J. P. R. Thorn et al. (Eds.): InterSol 2020, LNICST 321, pp. 224–237, 2020.
https://doi.org/10.1007/978-3-030-51051-0_16

on their application. Thus, there are several topologies of wireless sensor networks. Cluster topologies are probably the best organization in terms of energy optimization of sensors [5].

Linear wireless sensor networks constitute a special case of WSN where the nodes are arranged in a linear pattern. These types of WSNs are subject of several applications: monitoring of bridges, road, rail, gas, oil and water streams [3, 4]. Linear WSNs are subject to the same constraints than non-linear WSNs. Consequently, the topologies of WSN (cluster topology among others) that have been proposed are also applicable in principle.

Regarding the self-construction algorithms proposed in the literature [5], they all rely on nonlinear topologies. Therefore, even if they are applicable to linear topologies, they are, however, not adapted to linearity. With these constraints, caused by linearity, new self-construction mechanisms in clusters specially adapted to the linear WSNs must be designed.

In this paper we propose a self-constructioning mechanism for strictly linear wireless sensor networks while avoiding the creation of orphan nodes and singletons clusters. The rest of the document will be organized as follows. In Part 2, we will present some clustering algorithms that have been proposed in the literature. In Part 3, we present the different topology proposals that have been made for linear WSNs. In Part 4, we will detail our algorithm. In Sect. 5, we will present the different simulation results we obtained. Finally in Part 6, we will end with the conclusion and perspectives for our research.

## 2  Clustering Algorithms in WSN

In a clustered topology, the nodes are organized into groups of nodes, each group constituting a cluster. In each cluster a node is designated as CH (Cluster Head) which role is to coordinate the cluster, to aggregate the data coming from the other nodes of the cluster, to serve as a gateway for inter-cluster transmissions etc.

WSNs are classified into two categories according to the nature of the nodes that compose them. We distinguish the homogeneous WSNs, in which all the sensors are of the same type, initially, they have the same capacities, the same responsibilities, the same reserve of energy, and we have with them the same probability of becoming CH. In these types of WSN, the CHs can periodically be changed according to selection criteria of the CHs defined by the algorithms. The second category concerns heterogeneous WSNs in which nodes do not all have the same capabilities. In these types of WSN, the CHs are chosen from among the nodes of high capacities, the other nodes are considered as simple nodes.

The clustering algorithms proposed are mainly aimed at increasing the lifetime of the WSNs. The CHs are chosen either randomly or, under the parameter base such as the residual energy of the nodes, the distance between the Sink and the nodes, the size of the clusters, etc.

In [7] the authors propose LEACH, an algorithm using a probabilistic method, composed mainly of two phases, a phase of construction of set-up phase clusters and a phase of steady-phase transmission. In the set-up phase, the CHs are randomly elected as follows: each node randomly choose a number that it compares to a threshold value $T(n)$

(1), if the number chosen is less than T(n) (1) the node becomes CH. The CHs send broadcast messages with maximum power, the non-CH nodes receiving these messages choose their home cluster by joining the CH with the highest transmission power.

$$T(n) = \begin{cases} \dfrac{P}{1-P*\left(r mod \frac{1}{P}\right)} & \text{if } n \in G \\ 0 & \text{otherwise} \end{cases} \tag{1}$$

P represents the desired percentage of clusters, r is the current round, G represents the set of nodes that have not yet been elected CH on the last 1/P rounds. In [9], LEACH-C was proposed which is an extension of LEACH. In LEACH-C all the nodes, send, initially, their position and their energy reserve to the Sink which is based on this information to elect the CHs and determine, thus, the nodes members of each cluster. With this approach the selection of CHs is done centrally. Among the extensions of LEACH are LEACH-V [10], LEACH-R [11], LEACH-M [12], TL-LEACH [15], ACTH-LEACH [17] and LEACH-WDN [18]. In [16], the authors propose HEED, where the CHs are selected according to two criteria: the residual energy of the node and the cost of CH. HEED takes place in three phases: an initialization phase, a repetition phase and a finalization phase. In the initialization phase, each node calculates the probability of becoming CH based on a probabilistic parameter and its residual energy. In the repetition phase, each node goes through several iterations until it finds the least cost of CH. In the finalization phase, the nodes decide whether they will be CH or join a cluster. In [6], the authors propose EEHC. With EEHC we have two types of CHs, necessarily selected CHs and other CHs which have volunteered, the latter are selected probabilistically. In [8], the authors propose MHRPUC in which the selection of CHs is essentially based on the residual energy of the nodes. In [13] the authors propose P-LEACH. The P-LEACH algorithm partitions the WSN into several sectors through a calculation system performed by the Sink. Indeed with P-LEACH the Sink calculates an optimal value which will constitute the number of CH of the WSN and thus the number of sectors. All sectors contain the same number of nodes, the distance between the CHs and the nodes of the same cluster is less than the radius of the network. The same sectorization concept of the WSN is used with the PASCAL algorithm [14].

In [19], the authors carry out a detailed and comparative study on the set of clustering algorithms proposed in the literature for both homogeneous and heterogeneous WSNs. In [20] also, the authors classify the different algorithms studied based on criteria such as data aggregation, the CHS rotation system, the equalization of the size of the clusters, the centrality of the CHs, the energy consumption of nodes.

However, all these clustering algorithms are essentially based on nonlinear topologies, which makes them unsuitable for linear topology WSNs. Indeed, with these types of WSNs we have additional constraints that do not exist in classical topologies. Faced with this, it becomes necessary to think about new mechanisms more adapted to these types of WSNs.

## 3   Topologies in Linear WSN

Several types of topologies have been proposed for the linear WSN in order to provide them with a better organization. The WSNs are categorized into two types (Fig. 1): We have strictly linear WSNs (a), in these networks we have a single linear line to sink direction. The second category of networks constitutes the linear WSNs with junction zones (b) where we have several linear lines with or without direction of the Sink.

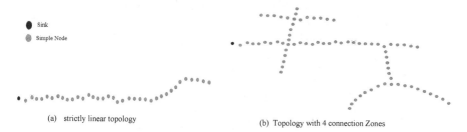

(a)   strictly linear topology

(b)  Topology with 4 connection Zones

**Fig. 1.** Linear wireless sensor network topologies

## A k-Redundant Topology

In [21] the authors propose topologies based on a k-redundant architecture in which each node of the k-neighbor network in the sense of Sink and in the opposite sense if it is a strictly linear network each node has at most 2 * k neighbors and at least k neighbors (Fig. 2). In this type of topology the availability of the WSN strongly depends on the value of k the more this value is large, the better is the network in terms of availability.

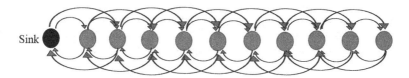

**Fig. 2.** 2-redondant topology [21]

## B N-Level Hierarchical Topologies

In hierarchical topologies [22] not all nodes have the same functionality so we have a heterogeneous network. In [22] the authors propose a three-level hierarchical topology (Fig. 3) in which we have three types of nodes: Single sensors (NCS) that act as a data sensor only, these nodes send their data to Relay Nodes (NRD) of which role is to collect data from NCS in their vicinity. The NCSs, after collection, send the aggregated packets to Data Routing Nodes that forward the data to the Sink.

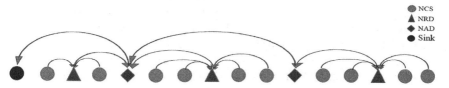

**Fig. 3.** Hierarchical topology with 3 levels [22]

**C Cluster Topology**

In [23] the authors propose a topology in logical grouping of clusters called Long Thin Wireless Sensor Network (LT-WSN). In this type of topology the linear WSN is clustered, each cluster consists of single nodes, a Cluster Head (CH) and a cluster bridge (PC). The cluster bridge and the CH define the cluster (Fig. 4). The cluster bridge is the only one capable of hosting data entering the cluster. The CH is the closest node to the Sink in terms of the number of jumps.

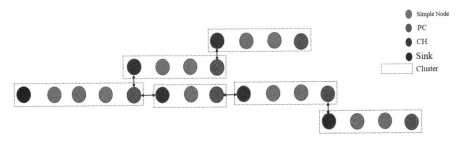

**Fig. 4.** Long Thin Wireless Sensor Networks [23]

The major disadvantage with cluster tree topologies is that CHs and PCs are manually selected by the network administrator.

In this session we presented the different topologies proposed for the linear WSN. This article proposes a cluster self-construction mechanism for linear WSNs that regulates among other things the problem of manual deployment of CHs.

## 4  Mechanism for Clusters Construction

All clustering algorithms studied in the literature (to our knowledge) are all based on non-linear architectures. Cluster tree topology proposals made in the literature require human interventions such as the choice of CHs by the network administrator. In this article, we propose **M2CRL**, a cluster self-construction mechanism for strictly linear WSNs. The algorithm assumes a 2-redundant topology where all nodes are of the same type and initially have the same capabilities and functionality.

The M2CRL algorithm comprises two phases: a first phase called the Discovery phase and a second phase called the Cluster Construction phase.

In the discovery phase (Algorithm 1), the sink discovers its neighbors and classifies them according to their proximity. Initially the sink sends in broadcast, a Hello message, in order to trigger the process of discovery, these messages are received by the neighbors of the sink. These ones in turn broadcast Hello messages that will be acknowledged, which will allow the nodes to know exactly the number of neighboring nodes v they have. After determining $v$, neighbor nodes of sink send a response to sink with the value $v$. The sink is based on the different values of v received, to evaluate the proximity with its neighbors. After the discovery phase, the sink sends a construction message to its nearest neighbor to initiate the cluster construction phase.

In the cluster construction phase, all clusters are constructed in a linear fashion. Nodes choose their cluster of membership thanks to three values: a constant Pi which constitutes the maximum number of nodes per cluster (defined by the sink), Cid which is the identifier of the cluster and Pn which constitutes the position of the node in its cluster. The construction is done thanks to a construction packet containing the three values Pi, Pn and Cid. All issued construction packets are acquitted.

Initially (Algorithm 2) the sink defines Pi that it takes in the interval [3, N/2] N being the cardinality of the WSN, it fixes Cid and Pn to 1. After defining the values it sends to the closest node a constructioning packet with the values Pi, Pn and Cid. As soon as it receives the acknowledgment from this node, it arms a new construction packet which it sends to the second closest node with the values Pi, Cid and Pn + 1. After receiving the construction packet issued by the sink, the neighbors of the sink put their Pi Pn and Cid to the values contained in the construction packet and broadcast a construction packet with the values Pi, Cid and Pn + 1. After choosing its home cluster, each node broadcasts a construction packet to its neighbors with the values Pi, Cid and Pn + 1. The other Linear WSN nodes choose their home cluster using the three principles of the following algorithm:

1. First principle of the algorithm (Algorithm 3): the position Pn of the node is equal to the maximum of Pn contained in the received construction packets Pn = max (Pn_received) and the Cid of the node is equal to the received Cid, Cid = Cid_received. This first principle is executed by the node if and only if all the received Pn are different from Pi.
2. Second principle of the algorithm (Algorithm 3): executed if one of the received Pn is equal to Pi. This principle says that if the node receives a Pn equal to Pi, it then compares the Cid contained in the packets, two scenarios are possible.

   a. if the packets contain the same Cid then the node auto-elects as Cluster Head (CH), puts its Pn to 1 and broadcast a construction packet to its neighbors with the values Pi, Cid and Pn + 1.
   b. If the received packets do not contain the same Cid then the node in question is the first neighbor of the CH, it puts its Pn to 2, keeps the maximum of Cid received Cid = max (Cid_received) and broadcasts a construction packet to its neighbors with the values Pi, Cid and Pn + 1.

3. Third principle of the algorithm (Algorithm 4): It aims to avoid singleton clusters. Indeed, after having broadcast a construction packet, the node triggers a timer which stops upon receipt of an acknowledgment. When the Timer is exhausted, i.e. no acknowledgment is received, the node self-elects as Cluster Tail (CT). If the latter is a CH, then it is a singleton Cluster, therefore the node is positioned at the father cluster by decreasing its Cid and putting its Pn to Pi + 1.

Figures 5 and 6 respectively illustrate the discovery and construction phases of the algorithm executed on a topology of eleven linearly arranged nodes.

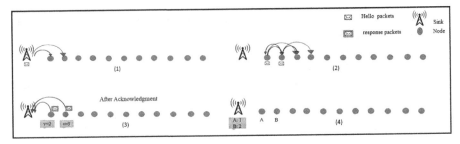

**Fig. 5.  M2CRL:** discovery phase

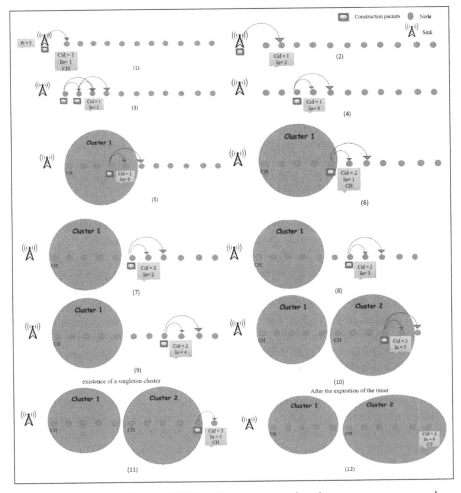

**Fig. 6.  M2CRL:** clusters construction phase

---

**Algorithm 1:** Discovery phase

---

**Result:** First phase: Allow the Sink to discover its neighbors and
their degree of proximity

**Data:** neighbor: Sink_neighbors[ ] int: v

1  Initialization: v=0
2  **struct** {
3  | **MACAddress** source
4  | int v
5  } *neighbor*
6  **begin**
7  | **if** *(isSINK == true)* **then**
8  | | Pcst=Packet(Discovery)
9  | | Send(Pcst, Broadcast)
10 | | **if** *(Receive_Response_Discovery)* **then**
11 | | | neighbor x
12 | | | x.source= Address_Packet
13 | | | x.v= v_Packet
14 | | | Add(x, Sink_neighbors)
15 | **else**
16 | | **if** *(Receive_Packet_Discovery)* **then**
17 | | | Pcst=Packet(Hello)
18 | | | Send(Pcst, Broadcast)
19 | | | start(neighborhood_discovery_Timer)
20 | | **if** *(Receive_Hello)* **then**
21 | | | Pcst=Packet(Ack_hello)
22 | | | Unicast(Pcst, Sender_Packet)
23 | | **while** *(Receive_Ack_Hello)* **do**
24 | | | v + +
25 | | **if** *(End of neighborhood_discovery_Timer)* **then**
26 | | | Pcst=Packet(Response_Discovery)
27 | | | Unicast(Pcst, SINK)

---

**Algorithm 2:** Cluster construction phase

---

**Result:** This phase makes the creation of the clusters it starts
immediately after the discovery phase of the Sink

**Data:** Int:$3 < max \leq N/2$ (N is the number of nodes in WNS) ack,
max, Pi, Pn, Cid, neighborsID[2], neighborsCid[2]

**Data:** $MACAddress : neighbors\_List[]$

1  Initialization: ack=0
2  **begin**
3  | **if** *(isSINK == true)* **then**
4  | | $Pi = random(3, max)$
5  | | $Cid = 1$
6  | | $Pn = 1$
7  | | Pcst=Packet(Pi,Pn,Cid)
8  | | Send(Pcst, A) // A is the first closest node to SINK:
        with the greatest value of v
9  |
10 | | **if** *(Receive Ack)* **then**
11 | | | Pcst=Packet(Pi,2,Cid)
12 | | | Send(Pcst, B)     // B is the second closest node to
            SINK
13 | |
14 | **else**
15 | | **if** *(Receive_Construction_Packet)* **then**
16 | | | EXECUTE Algorithm 3
17 | | **if** *(Receive_Ack)* **then**
18 | | | $ack = 1$
19 | | | $Cancel(Ack\_Timer)$

---

**Algorithm 3:** Behavior of a node following a receipt of a Construction Packet(Pcst)

---

```
1  begin
2  |   Add(MACAddress_Packet, voisinList)
3  |   if (ID_Receive_Packet == idSINK) then
4  |   |   cpt = 0
5  |   |   Pi = Pi(Pcst)
6  |   |   Pn = Pn(Pcst)
7  |   |   Cid = Cid(Pcst)
8  |   |   if (Pi == Pn) then
9  |   |   |   isCH=true
10 |   |   |   Send(Ack, SINK)
11 |   |   Pcst=Packet(Pi,Pn+1,Cid)
12 |   |   Send(Pcst, Broadcast)
13 |   else
14 |   |   if (cpt == 0)              // the node already belongs to a
   |   |   cluster
15 |   |   then
16 |   |   |   break
17 |   |   else if (cpt == 1)                // second packet received
18 |   |   then
19 |   |   |   neighborsID[2]=Packet(Pn)
20 |   |   |   neighborsCid[2]=Packet(Cid)
21 |   |   |   if (neighborsID[1] == Packet(Pi))||(neighborsID[2] ==
   |   |   |   Packet(Pi)) then
22 |   |   |   |   if neighborsCid[1]==neighborsCid[2] then
23 |   |   |   |   |   Pn = 1
24 |   |   |   |   |   Cid = Packet(Cid) + 1
25 |   |   |   |   |   isCH = true
26 |   |   |   |   |   Pi = Packet(Pi)
27 |   |   |   |   else
28 |   |   |   |   |   Pn = 2
29 |   |   |   |   |   Cid = max(neighborsCid[1], neighborsCid[2])
30 |   |   |   |   |   Pi = Pi(pcst)
31 |   |   |   |   Pcst=Packet(Pi,Pn + 1,Cid)
32 |   |   |   |   Send(Pcst, Broadcast)
33 |   |   |   |   Send(Ack)
34 |   |   |   |   cpt = cpt - 1
35 |   |   |   |   start (Ack_Timer)
36 |   |   |   else
37 |   |   |   |   Pn= max(neighborsID[1], neighborsID[2])
38 |   |   |   |   Cid= Packet(Cid)
39 |   |   |   |   Pi=Packet(Pi); Pcst=Packet(Pi,Pn + 1,Cid)
40 |   |   |   |   Send(Pcst, Broadcast)
41 |   |   |   |   Send(Ack)
42 |   |   |   |   cpt = cpt - 1
43 |   |   |   |   start (Ack_Timer) 3
44 |   |   else if (cpt == 2) then
   |   |   |                              // first packet received
45 |   |   |   cpt = cpt - 1
46 |   |   |   neighborsID[1] = Packet(Pn)
47 |   |   |   neighborsCid[1] = Packet(Cid)
48 |   |   |   Send(Ack)
```

---

**Algorithm 4:** Behavior of a node at the end of Ack Timer

---

**Result:** This process aims to eliminate singleton clusters

1 **begin**
2     **if** *(End of Ack Timer)* **then**
3        **if** *(ack == 0)* **then**
4           isCT=true
            `// Custer Tail(CT) is the most distant node of`
            `the chain`
5           **if** *(Pn == 1)* **then**
6             Pn= Pi+1
7             Cid − −

---

The cluster number of the Linear WSN is given by Nc (2) and the position of a node in the linear WSN is given by Ps (3).

$$N_c = \frac{N}{P_i} \qquad (2)$$

$$P_S = P_i * (C_{id} - 1) + P_n \qquad (3)$$

N is the cardinality of the Linear WSN.

## 5 Simulations and Results

To evaluate our mechanism, we performed our simulations on the Castalia environment, which is a wireless sensor network simulator based on the OMNet++ platform. The simulation parameters used are listed in Table 1.

**Table 1.** M2CRL: simulation parameters

| Distance between nodes | Number of nodes in different topologies | MAC protocol | Routing protocol | Radio module | Power Tx | Simulation time |
|---|---|---|---|---|---|---|
| 25 m | [5, 10, 15, 20, 25, 30, 35, 40] | TMAC | M2CRL | CC2420 | 0 dBm | 100 s |

We performed M2CRL on eight linear topologies ranging from five to forty nodes. The topology used is 2-redundant. Pi is set to 5 in all topologies. The results obtained give a good construction of homogeneous clusters (5 nodes per cluster) with zero singleton cluster. The linear WSN contains zero orphan nodes, each node belongs to a cluster.

We compared M2CRL with LEACH to highlight the inadaptability of existing cluster construction algorithms with a linear topology. The same linear topologies used with M2CRL were used with LEACH. The results obtained confirm the thesis of inadaptability. The construction of the clusters is not complete which implies the existence of several orphan nodes.

Figure 7 gives the number of cluster Head (CH) and thus the number of cluster per topology running the LEACH and M2CRL algorithms. It shows that our M2CRL mechanism creates clusters for the entire network regardless of size. In Fig. 8, LEACH creates many orphan nodes, unlike our M2CRL mechanism, which succeeds in putting all the nodes in the different clusters, without giving orphan nodes, that is to say, nodes that belong to no cluster. Figure 9 gives us the evolution of the construction time of M2CRL on the different topologies used. The results obtained show a decreasing evolution of the construction time of M2CRL clusters on different topologies. Indeed, with the first topology (5 nodes), the construction time is 9.8 s, that is to say, the cardinality of the network, Nc, increased by 4.8 (4). Formula (4) is used to determine the reference time

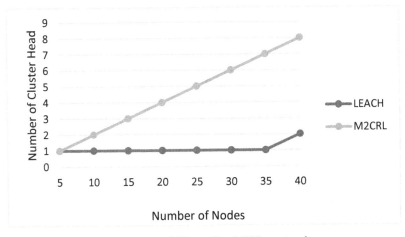

**Fig. 7.** Number of Cluster Head (CH) per topology

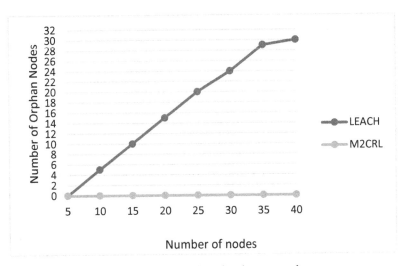

**Fig. 8.** Number of orphaned nodes per topology

in terms of constructioning clusters on a topology. This reference time will be compared to the different construction times of M2CRL on the different topologies. The graph of Fig. 9 shows that the construction times of M2CRL on the different topologies gradually decrease with respect to the established reference time.

$$Time_{reference} = N_c + 4.8 \qquad\qquad (4)$$

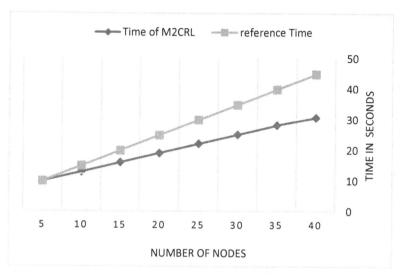

**Fig. 9.** Evolution of the M2CRL construction time

## 6  Conclusion and Perspectives

In this paper we have proposed M2CRL, a mechanism of self-construction of clusters for strictly linear networks, which is, to our knowledge, the first mechanism for self-construction of clusters for strictly linear WSNs. Comparative simulations with the previous algorithms have shown perfectly the inadaptability of the latter with linear topologies, and the important need to reflect on mechanisms that are perfectly suited to the particular case of Linear WSNs.

In perspective we plan to improve the algorithm in order to extend its possibilities so that it can take into account linear topologies with junction zones. We also plan to set up an addressing mechanism for these types of junctional linear networks. The algorithm will be improved to foresee the cases of additions of new nodes and deletions of nodes it will be necessary to set up, in the algorithm, systems of automatic reactions in case of topological modification. We also expect a round-robin system of the algorithm to avoid fixed clusters. So in each round of new clusters will be created.

# References

1. Kacimi, R., Dhaou, R., Beylot, A.-L.: Using energy-efficient wireless sensor network for cold chain monitoring. In: IEEE Consumer Communications and Networking Conference (CCNC 2009), Las Vegas, Nevada, USA, pp. 1–5. IEEE (January 2009)
2. Sentilles, S.: Architecture logicielle pour capteurs sans-fil en réseau Rapport de recherche, Université de Pau et des Pays de l'Adour, juin 2006
3. Kim, S., et al.: Health monitoring of civil infrastructures using wireless sensor networks. In: Proceedings of the 6th International Conference on Information Processing in Sensor Networks, IPSN 2007, pp. 254–263. ACM Press (2007)
4. Pan, M.-S., Fang, H.-W., Liu, Y.-C., Tseng, Y.-C.: Address assignment and routing schemes for zigbee-based long-thin wireless sensor networks. In: IEEE Vehicular Technology Conference 2008, Spring 2008, pp. 173–177 (2008)
5. Stoianov, I., Nachman, L., Madden, S., Tokmouline, T.: Pipenet: a wireless sensor network for pipeline monitoring. In: ACM IPSN (2007). http://db.csail.mit.edu/pubs/ipsn278-nachman.pdf
6. Abbasi, A.A., Younis, M.: A survey on clustering algorithms for wireless sensor networks. Comput. Commun. **30**, 2826–2841 (2007)
7. Bandyopadhyay, S., Coyle, E.: An energy efficient hierarchical clustering algorithm for wireless sensor networks. In: Proceedings of the 22nd Annual Joint Conference of the IEEE Computer and Communications Societies (INFOCOM 2003), San Francisco, California (April 2003)
8. Heinzelman, W.R., Chandrakasan, A., Balakrishnan, H.: Energy efficient communication protocol for wireless microsensor networks. In: 2000 Proceedings of the 33rd Annual Hawaii International Conference on System Sciences, vol. 2, p. 10, 4–7 January (2000)
9. Li, B., Gong, L., Wang, S., Zhou, X.: Multihop routing protocol with unequal clustering for wireless sensor networks. In: International Colloquium on Computing, Communication, Control, and Management (ISECS 2008), pp. 552–556 (2008)
10. Heinzelman, W.B., Chandrakasan, A.P., Balakrishnan, H.: An application-specific protocol architecture for wireless microsensor networks. IEEE Trans. Wirel. Commun. **1**(4), 660–670 (2002)
11. Ahlawat, A., Malik, V.: An extended vice-cluster selection approach to improve V LEACH protocol in WSN. In: 2013 Third International Conference on Advanced Computing and Communication Technologies (ACCT). IEEE (2013)
12. Li, Y.-Z., Zhang, A.-L., Liang, Y.-Z.: Improvement of leach protocol for wireless sensor networks. In: 2013 Third International Conference on Instrumentation, Measurement, Computer, Communication and Control (IMCCC). IEEE (2013)
13. Mhatre, V., Rosenberg, C.: Homogeneous vs heterogeneous clustered sensor networks: a comparative study. In: International Conference on Communications, vol. 6. IEEE (2004)
14. Young, H., Wan, Y., Haosong, G., Zeng, H.: A partition based LEACH algorithm. In: IEEE Ninth International Conference on Computer and Information Technology, pp. 40–45 (2009)
15. Mirza, M.A., Garimella, R.M.: PASCAL: power aware sectoring based clustering algorithm for wireless sensor networks. In: The International Conference on Information Networking (ICOIN), Chiang Mai, Thailand, January 2009 (2009)
16. Loscri, V., Morabito, G., Marano, S.: A two-level hierarchy for low-energy adaptive clustering hierarchy. Proc. Veh. Technol. Conf. **03**, 1809–1813 (2005)
17. Fahmy, S., Younis, O.: HEED: a hybrid energy-efficient distributed clustering approach for AdHoc sensor networks. IEEE Trans. Mob. Comput. **3**, 366–379 (2004)
18. Guo, L.-Q., Xie, Y., Yang, C.-H., Jing, Z.-W.: Improve by LEACH by combining adaptive cluster head election and two-hop transmission. In: International Conference on Machine Learning and Cybernetics (ICMLC), vol. 4, pp. 1678–1683 (2010)

19. Gupta, G., Younis, M.: Fault-tolerant clustering of wireless sensor networks. In: Proceedings of the IEEE Wireless Communication and Networks Conference (WCNC 2003), New Orleans, Louisiana, March 2003 (2003)
20. Wang, A., Yang, D., Sun, D.: A clustering algorithm based on energy information and cluster heads expectation for wireless sensor network. Comput. Electr. Eng. **38**, 662–671 (2012)
21. Rostami, A.S., Keshavarz, H., Mohanna, F., Hosseinabadi, A.A.R.: Survey on clustering in heterogeneous and homogeneous wireless sensor networks. J. Supercomput. (2017). https://www.researchgate.net/publication/319155887
22. Wei, D., Chan, H.A., Kaplan, S.: Energy efficient clustering algorithms for wireless sensor network. Conference Paper. IEEE (June 2008). https://doi.org/10.1109/ICCW.2008.50
23. Ndoye, E.H.M., Jacquet, F., Misson, M., Niang I.: Using a token approach for the MAC layer of linear sensor networks: impact of the node position on the packet delivery. In: 2014 IFIP Wireless Days (WD), pp. 1–4 (2014). (cf. 38, 70)
24. Jawhar, I., Mohamed, N., Agrawal, D.P.: Linear wireless sensor networks: classification and applications. J. Netw. Comput. Appl. **34**(5), 1671–1682 (2011). (cf. p. 3, 5, 35, 38, 39, 59, 70)
25. Pan, M.-S., Fang, H.-W., Liu, Y.-C., Tseng, Y.-C.: Address assignment and routing schemes for zigbee-based long-thin wireless sensor networks. In: IEEE Vehicular Technology Conference 2008, Spring 2008, pp. 173–177 (2008). (cf. p. 1, 3–5, 35, 40, 56, 66, 67)

# On the Treewidth of Planar Minor Free Graphs

Youssou Dieng[1(✉)] and Cyril Gavoille[2]

[1] LI3, Assane Seck University of Ziguinchor, Ziguinchor, Senegal
ydieng@univ-zig.sn
[2] LaBRI, University of Bordeaux, Bordeaux, France
gavoille@labri.fr
https://sites.google.com/a/univ-zig.sn/ydieng/

**Abstract.** We study in this article, the treewidth of planar graphs excluding as minor a fixed planar graph. We prove that the treewidth of every planar graph excluding a graph having a poly-line $p \times q$-grid drawing is $O(p\sqrt{q})$. As consequences, the treewidth of planar graphs excluding as minor the cylinder $\mathscr{C}_{2,r}$ or its dual $\mathscr{C}_{2,r}^*$ is $O(\sqrt{r})$, where $\mathscr{C}_{2,r}$ denotes the cylinder of height 2 and circumference $r$. This bound is asymptotically optimal. The treewidth is $O(\sqrt{r \log r})$ if the excluded graph is any outerplanar graph with $r$ vertices.

**Keywords:** Planar graph · Graph Minor · Treewidth · Graph drawing

## 1 Introduction

*Tree-decomposition* is one of the most general and effective technique for designing efficient graph algorithms. Roughly speaking a tree-decomposition of an input graph $G$ is a collection of subgraphs of $G$, called *bags*, that cover $G$ in a tree-like manner (see Fig. 1 and Sect. 2 for precise definitions). *Treewidth-k* graphs are graphs having a tree-decomposition of *width* $k$, i.e., into bags of at most $k + 1$ vertices. It has been shown (see for instance [Arn85, AP89, Bod96, Cou90]) that many optimization problems on graphs, including NP-hard ones, can be solved by the use of dynamic programming techniques based on tree-decompositions and whose efficiency is directly related to the size of the bags. So, identifying graphs of small treewidth is of great interests.

The problem to decide whether the treewidth of a graph is $k$ is NP-complete [ACP87], but there are linear time algorithms for each fixed $k$. The best polynomial time approximation algorithm achieves $O(\sqrt{\log k})$ performance ratio where $k$ is the treewidth [FHL08]. For planar graphs, approximation algorithms with performance ratio 1.5 do exist [ST94, GT05].

The work of Cyril Gavoille is partially funded by the French ANR projects ANR-16-CE40-0023 (DESCARTES) and ANR-17-CE40-0015 (DISTANCIA).

J. P. R. Thorn et al. (Eds.): InterSol 2020, LNICST 321, pp. 238–250, 2020.
https://doi.org/10.1007/978-3-030-51051-0_17

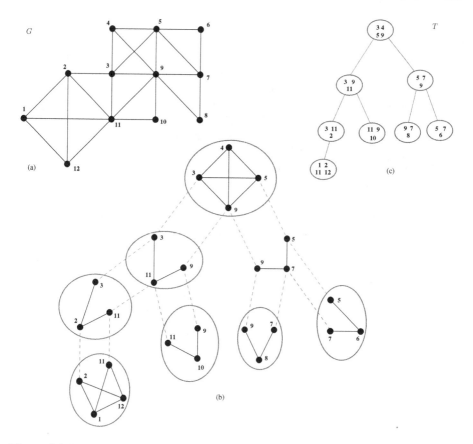

**Fig. 1.** (a) A graph $G$; (b) a tree-like representation of $G$; and (c) a tree-decomposition $T$ of $G$ of width 3.

A seminal work about tree-decompositions is the one of Robertson and Seymour and their Graph Minor Theorem that has been proved in a more than twenty paper serie spanning over 20 years, from [RS83, RS86, RS03, RS04]. Along their proof, they gave a decomposition theorem [RS03] capturing the structure of graphs excluding a fixed *minor* (see Sect. 2 for precise definitions). Informally, the theorem says that every graph excluding some fixed graph $H$ as minor has a tree-decomposition into bags that can "almost" be embedded on a surface on which $H$ cannot be embedded.

A keystone in the proof of the Graph Minor Theorem is the grid-minor theorem [RS86] which says that every graph of treewidth large enough is guaranteed to have a large grid as minor. In other words, if a graph $G$ excludes a $r \times r$ grid as minor, then the treewidth of $G$ is at most $g(r)$ for some function $g$. The current best upper bound is $g(r) \le r^{9+o(1)}$ [CT19], whereas the best lower bound is $g(r) \ge r^{2+o(1)}$ as proved in [RST94]. In this latter paper, it has been conjectured that the best possible bound is in fact $r^{2+o(1)}$, whereas [DHK09] have conjectured $\Theta(r^3)$.

This grid-minor theorem played also a key role for the important Disjoint Paths Problem [KW10], in several other deep meta-theorems and applications as mentioned in [Gro07]. For some applications, efficient solutions can be still computed for graphs having specific tree-decompositions, and not only those of small width. For instance, [DG03, DG07] have studied graphs having a tree-decomposition whose bags contain vertices, possibly many, that are close to each other. Graphs of bounded *tree-length*, i.e., having a tree-decomposition into bags of bounded diameter, admit additive *spanners*, *compact routing schemes*, and *distance labeling schemes* with short labels [BvLTT97, GKK+01, DG04, Dou05, DDGY07, CDE+12], that are important applications for Distributed Computing. Note that many graphs with unbounded treewidth have bounded tree-length. Chordal graphs, interval graphs, split graphs, AT-free graphs, permutation graphs, and many others, are such examples. Further developments on tree-length can be founded in [CDE+08, UY09, Lok10].

In this paper, we study the question about the treewidth of graphs excluding as minor a planar graph. The paper is organized as follows. We start in Sect. 2 with a formal description of minors, tree-decompositions and graph drawings. Section 3 presents our contribution with an overview of the main ingredients for our results. Section 4 gives the proof of the main theorem.

## 2    Minor, Tree-Decomposition and Drawing

Let $G$ be a simple connected undirected graph with vertex-set $V(G)$ and edge-set $E(G)$. An edge between two vertices $u$ and $v$ of $G$ is denoted by $\{u, v\}$. The *contraction* of $\{u, v\}$ in $G$ is the result of identifying the vertices $u$ and $v$ and removing from $G$ all resulting loops and multiple edges. A *minor $H$* of $G$ is a subgraph of a graph that can be obtained from $G$ by a sequence of edge contractions (see Fig. 2).

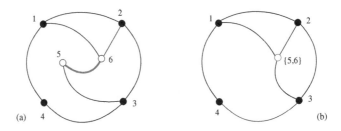

**Fig. 2.** (a) A graph $G$; and (b) a minor of $G$ obtained by contracting edge $\{5, 6\}$.

We say that $G$ *excludes* $H$ if $H$ is not a minor of $G$. By transitivity of the minor relation, if $G$ excludes $H$, then $G$ excludes every graph having $H$ as minor.

We now present the basic notions of *tree-decomposition* and *treewidth*. See Fig. 1 for an illustration.

**Definition 1.** *A* tree-decomposition *of a graph $G$ is a tree $T$ whose nodes, called* bags, *are subsets of $V(G)$, and such that:*

1. $\bigcup_{X \in V(T)} X = V(G)$;
2. $\forall \{u, v\} \in E(G)$, $\exists X \in V(T)$ *such that* $u, v \in X$; *and*
3. $\forall u \in V(G)$, *the set of bags containing $u$ induces a subtree of $T$.*

*The* width *of a tree-decomposition $T$ is* $\max_{X \in V(T)} \{|X| - 1\}$. *The* treewidth *of a graph $G$ is the minimum width over all possible tree-decompositions of $G$.*

The notions of *path-decomposition* and *pathwidth* are defined similarly, except that in Definition 1, $T$ must be a path. It is not difficult to see that if $H$ is a minor of $G$, then the treewidth (resp. pathwidth) of $H$ is no more than the treewidth (reps. pathwidth) of $G$.

Our results rely on plane embeddings of graphs. More precisely, a *drawing* of a graph $G$ maps each vertex of $G$ to a point of the plane and each edge to a simple open Jordan curve between its endpoints. A drawing divides the plane into topologically connected regions, called *faces*; the infinite region is called the *outerface*. A *planar graph* is a graph that can be drawn in the plane without crossing edges. The *dual* of a graph drawn $G$ is the graph denoted by $G^*$ whose the vertices are faces of $G$, and the edges connect faces having a common edge of $G$ on their borders.

In this paper, we consider *grid-drawings* where vertices of the graph have integer coordinates and edges between adjacent vertices are poly-line whose bends have integer coordinates too. Such drawings were developed by de Fraysseix et al. in [dFPP88, dFPP90] and Schnyder in [Sch90].

More precisely, a graph has a *poly-line $p \times q$-grid* drawing if it has a drawing such that vertices are plotted at the vertices of the $p \times q$ grid, and edges are contiguous sequences of segments, each segment being a straight-line between two vertices of the $p \times q$ grid. The grid-drawing is *orthogonal* if edges can be drawn as path of the grid, i.e., represented as sequences of horizontal or vertical segments only. The drawing is *flat* if every vertex is represented by a horizontal line segment. Finally, the drawing is *straight-line* if each edge consists of one segment only. The $p \times q$ *grid* is the graph whose vertex-set $\{(i, j) : i \in [0, p), j \in [0, q)\}$ and for which two vertices $(i, j)$ and $(i', j')$ are adjacent if and only if $|i - i'| + |j - j'| = 1$. The $p \times q$-cylinder, denoted by $\mathscr{C}_{p,q}$, is the graph with same vertex-set of the $p \times q$-grid and such that $(i, j)$ and $(i', j')$ are adjacent if and only if there are adjacent in the $p \times q$-grid or $i = i'$ and $|j - j'| = q - 1$. In other words, $\mathscr{C}_{p,q}$ is the Cartesian product of a path of $p$ vertices by a cycle with $q$ vertices. We refer to [dBETT99] for a wide overview of grid-drawings, and Fig. 3 for illustrations.

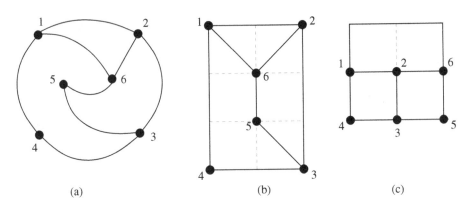

**Fig. 3.** (a) A planar graph $G$; (b) a $4 \times 3$-grid straight-line drawing of $G$; and (c) a poly-line orthogonal $3 \times 3$-grid drawing of $G$.

## 3   Our Contributions

Bounding the treewidth of a graph by a function of a minor it excludes is one of the most surprising property of the Graph Minor Theory. As previously discussed, if a graph $G$ excludes some planar graph $H$, then the treewidth of $G$ is at most some constant depending on $H$. The best current upper bound on the treewidth is $r^{9+o(1)}$ where $r = |V(H)|$. In fact, the bound holds even if $H$ is the $r \times r$ grid. The treewidth bound can be reduced to $O(r)$ if the excluded minor is a $K_{2,r}$ [BvLTT97], a forest [BRST91] or a cycle [FL89] of $r$ vertices. It is also known that the treewidth of graphs excluding a $3 \times 3$ grid (resp. a $4 \times 4$ grid) is at most respectively 7 [BBR09] (resp. 7 262 [BBR07]).

We investigate the question of the treewidth of a graph $G$ that excludes a planar graph $H$ whenever $G$ is itself planar. It is known [RST94] that the treewidth of a planar graph excluding an $r$-vertex planar graph, or an $r \times r$ grid, is only $O(r)$. The most accurate bound on the term $O(r)$ can be derived from [GT12] and [RST94], as explained later in the Lemma 4.

Our main result is (see Sect. 4 for the proof):

**Theorem 1.** *The treewidth of every planar graph excluding as minor a graph having a poly-line $p \times q$-grid drawing is $O(p\sqrt{q})$.*

Because $\mathscr{C}_{2,r}$ and its dual $\mathscr{C}_{2,r}^*$ have $4 \times r$-grid drawings (see Fig. 4), and that $K_{2,r}$ is a minor of $\mathscr{C}_{2,r}^*$, we derive directly from Theorem 1 that:

**Corollary 1.** *Let $H \in \{\mathscr{C}_{2,r}, \mathscr{C}_{2,r}^*, K_{2,r}\}$. The treewidth of every planar graph excluding $H$ as minor is $O(\sqrt{r})$.*

This bound significantly improves upon the $r + 2$ upper bound of [Thi99]. As we will see later, the bound of $O(\sqrt{r})$ is actually asymptotically optimal.

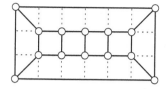 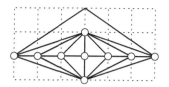

**Fig. 4.** A straight-line $4 \times r$-grid drawing of the $2 \times r$-cylinder $\mathscr{C}_{2,r}$ and a poly-line drawing of its dual $\mathscr{C}_{2,r}^*$, here for $r = 7$.

We now derive a similar bound if the excluded graph is outerplanar. Theorem 1 allows us the plug results from literature of Graph Drawing Theory. For instance, using the result of [Bie14][Th. 9], every outerplanar graph $H$ with $r$ vertices and pathwidth $k$ has straight-line $O(k) \times O(r)$-grid drawing. From Theorem 1, the treewidth of every planar graph excluding $H$ is $O(k\sqrt{r})$.

However, this latter bound can be slightly improved as follows:

**Proposition 1.** *Every planar graph excluding as minor an outerplanar graph with $r$ vertices and pathwidth $k$ has treewidth $O(\sqrt{kr})$, which is at most $O(\sqrt{r \log r})$.*

*Proof.* Let $H$ be the excluded minor. We observe that the straight-line $O(k) \times O(r)$-grid drawing of the minor $H$ as built in [Bie14][Th. 9] is actually based on a flat orthogonal drawing due to [Bie12][Th. 1]. The property of this drawing is that, if $H$ is 2-connected, then it has a flat orthogonal $(4k-3) \times \lceil 3(r-2)/2 \rceil$-grid drawing.

The connectivity condition on $H$ can be overcome, because as proved in [BBCR14], any outerplanar graph can be made 2-connected while increasing its pathwidth by a constant factor. We also remark that if $H$ has a flat orthogonal $p \times q$-grid drawing, then $H$ is a minor of the $p \times q$-grid (simply contract the horizontal segments representing the vertices). By Lemma 1 $H$ is also a minor of the $O(\sqrt{pq}) \times O(\sqrt{pq})$-grid. And, by Lemma 4(ii), the treewidth of a planar graph excluding such a grid, and thus $H$, is $O(\sqrt{pq})$. Overall, plugging $p = O(k)$ and $q = O(r)$, we get that the treewidth of a planar graph excluding $H$ as minor is $O(\sqrt{kr})$.

We concluding by noting that $k = O(\log r)$, because the treewidth of $H$ is at most two, and the pathwidth of any graph with $r$ vertices is at most its treewidth plus one times $O(\log r)$ [KS93][Theorem 6]. $\square$

The end of this section is devoted to a discussion about the optimality of the treewidth bounds we have obtained.

If $H$ is a general planar graph, then the $O(r)$ bound of [RST94] is optimal (asymptotically). This is because there are planar graphs $H$ with $O(r)$ vertices that are not minor of the $r \times r$ grid. In other words, if $G$ is the $r \times r$ grid, then $G$ is planar and has treewidth[1] $r$, whereas it excludes $H$, an $O(r)$-vertex planar

---

[1] It is well-known the $p \times q$ grid has treewidth $\min\{p, q\}$.

graph. For concreteness, consider $H = \mathscr{C}_{3,r+2}$, the $3 \times (r+2)$-cylinder. It is easy to show that: (1) any drawing of $H$ contains at least $\delta \geq r/2 + 1$ disjoint nested cycles[2]; and (2) $H$ cannot be a minor of a graph having a drawing with less than $\delta$ disjoint nested cycles, since edge contraction and taking subgraph cannot increase the number of disjoint nested cycles. Unfortunately, the $r \times r$ grid has only $r/2 < \delta$ disjoint nested cycles. So, $H$ that has $3r + 6 = O(r)$ vertices is not a minor of a planar graph $G$ of treewidth $r$ (the $r \times r$ grid).

However, as demonstrated by Corollary 1, the $O(r)$ bound can be reduced if we restrict furthermore the family of excluded minors. To formalize this idea, let us consider an infinite graph family $\mathscr{H}$ closed under taking subgraphs. And, let $\theta_{\mathscr{H}}(r)$ be the function defined as the smallest $t$ such that every planar graph excluding any graph $H \in \mathscr{H}$ with at most $r$ vertices has treewidth at most $t$. The main question we have addressed in this paper is to find a large family $\mathscr{H}$ of planar graphs such that $\theta_{\mathscr{H}}(r) = o(r)$.

Observe that Lemma 4(ii) implies that $\theta_{\mathscr{H}}(r) \leq 9r$ for each family $\mathscr{H}$ of planar graphs. Function $\theta_{\mathscr{H}}$ must be linear in general, since from the discussion above, if $\mathscr{C}_{3,r+2} \in \mathscr{H}$, then there are planar graphs excluding $\mathscr{C}_{3,r+2}$ and of treewidth at least $r$. Thus $\theta_{\mathscr{H}}(|V(\mathscr{C}_{3,r+2})|) = \theta_{\mathscr{H}}(3r+6) \geq r$.

On the other hand, it is easy to see that $\theta_{\mathscr{H}}(r) = \Omega(\sqrt{r})$ for every graph family $\mathscr{H}$. Indeed, for any $H \in \mathscr{H}$, by denoting $r = |V(H)|$, the $\lceil \sqrt{r} - 1 \rceil \times \lceil \sqrt{r} - 1 \rceil$ grid has $< r$ vertices, so it excludes $H$. However, this grid has treewidth $\lceil \sqrt{r} - 1 \rceil$.

From the above discussions, we have therefore:

**Proposition 2.** *For every family $\mathscr{H}$ of planar graphs, $\sqrt{r} - 1 \leq \theta_{\mathscr{H}}(r) \leq 9r$. Furthermore, if $\mathscr{C}_{3,\lfloor r/3 \rfloor} \in \mathscr{H}$, then $\theta_{\mathscr{H}}(r) \geq r/3$.*

So, from Proposition 2, the $O(\sqrt{r})$ bound of Corollary 1 is optimal. And more generally, the family $\mathscr{H}_p$ composed of all $r$-vertex graphs having a poly-line $p \times O(r/p^2)$-grid drawing have $\theta_{\mathscr{H}_p}(r) = O(\sqrt{r})$ which is optimal.

## 4    Proof of the Main Theorem

The goal of the section is to prove Theorem 1 that we recall the statement:

**Theorem 1.** *The treewidth of every planar graph excluding as minor a graph having a poly-line $p \times q$-grid drawing is $O(p\sqrt{q})$.*

We start with a simple lemma:

**Lemma 1.** *The $p \times q$ grid is a minor of the $\lfloor (2 + \sqrt{2})\sqrt{pq} \rfloor \times \lfloor (2 + \sqrt{2})\sqrt{pq} \rfloor$ grid.*

---

[2] Note that if a triangle is chosen as outerface of $\mathscr{C}_{3,r+2}$, then the resulting drawing has $r + 2$ nested triangles. However, a drawing with the minimal number of nested disjoint cycles can be obtained by choosing a quadrangle of $\mathscr{C}_{3,r+2}$ as outerface.

*Proof.* W.l.o.g., assume that $p \leq q$. The construction is illustrated on Fig. 5. The $p \times q$ grid $H$ is first split into squares, each one being a $p \times p$ grid. There are $s = \lceil q/p \rceil$ such squares, the last one may be completed by some columns if $p$ does not divide $q$.

Let $k = \lceil \sqrt{s+1} \rceil + 1$. Observe that $k$ is the smallest integer such that $k \cdot (k-2) \geq s$, since $k \cdot (k-2) \geq (\sqrt{s+1}+1) \cdot (\sqrt{s+1}-1) = s$. In the illustration on Fig. 5, $s = 8$ and $k = 4$.

Now, the $s$ squares are organized into $k$ strips, each containing $k-2$ squares. Extra squares may be added to complete the last strip. Then, each such strip is surrounded by two extra squares: one at the beginning and one at the end (cf. the red squares on Fig. 5). The final grid $M$ is composed of the $k$ strips each of $k$ squares. Therefore $M$ is a $pk \times pk$ grid.

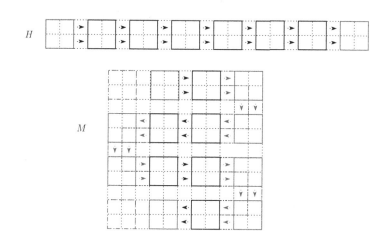

**Fig. 5.** From a $3 \times 24$ grid $H$ to a $12 \times 12$ grid $M$. (Color figure online)

Grid $M$ contains $H$ as a minor, since the edges between two adjacent squares in $H$ exist also in $M$ either horizontally, if the squares belong to the same strip, or vertically and then horizontally to make the turn between consecutive strips. We have $pk = p \cdot (\lceil \sqrt{s+1} \rceil + 1)$. Using the fact that $\lceil \sqrt{\lceil x \rceil} \rceil = \lceil \sqrt{x} \rceil$, we have $\lceil \sqrt{s+1} \rceil = \lceil \sqrt{\lceil q/p \rceil + 1} \rceil = \lceil \sqrt{\lceil q/p + 1 \rceil} \rceil = \lceil \sqrt{q/p+1} \rceil$. It follows that $pk = p \cdot \lceil \sqrt{q/p+1} \rceil + p < p\sqrt{q/p+1} + 2p = \sqrt{pq + p^2} + 2p$. Since $p \leq q$, $p = \sqrt{p^2} \leq \sqrt{pq}$, and it follows that $pk < \sqrt{pq + pq} + 2\sqrt{pq} = (\sqrt{2}+2)\sqrt{pq}$. Thus, $M$ is a $\lfloor (2+\sqrt{2})\sqrt{pq} \rfloor \times \lfloor (2+\sqrt{2})\sqrt{pq} \rfloor$ grid. This completes the proof. $\square$

The proof of our second lemma, relies on a special drawing transformation preserving height due to [Bie14].

**Lemma 2.** ([Bie14], **Theorem 5**). *Any poly-line $p \times q$-grid drawing can be transformed into a flat orthogonal $p \times w$-grid drawing with $w \leq \max\{n, m\} + b$,* *where n and m are respectively the number of vertices and edges of the graph, and b is the maximum number of local minima and maxima of polygonal curves in the poly-line drawing.*

We are now ready to prove:

**Lemma 3.** *Every graph having a poly-line $p \times q$-grid drawing is minor of the $p \times (3pq)$ grid.*

*Proof.* Let $G$ be a graph having a poly-line $p \times q$-grid drawing $\Gamma$. Transform $\Gamma$ into a flat orthogonal $p \times w$-grid drawing $\Gamma'$ thanks to Lemma 2, where $w \leq \max\{n, m\} + b$ with $n = |V(G)|$ and $m = |E(G)|$. The number $b$ can be upper bounded by the number of bends of any edge drawn as poly-line in $\Gamma$. Each bend occupies a point of the grid in $\Gamma$. Therefore, the number of vertices of $G$ is $n \leq pq - b$. From the planarity of $G$, $m < 3n = 3(pq - b)$. It follows that $w \leq \max\{n, m\} + b \leq 3(pq - b) + b \leq 3pq$, and thus $\Gamma'$ is a flat orthogonal $p \times (3pq)$-grid drawing of $G$.

We conclude the proof by observing that the grid supporting $\Gamma'$, say the graph $M$, contains $G$ as minor. Indeed, in $M$, original vertices and edges of $G$ are represented has sequences of horizontal or vertical segments. These sequences of segments are connected subgraphs of $M$, and actually internally disjoint paths as they can meet only at vertices of $G$. Thus, contracting in $M$ vertices of $G$ into single vertices, and edges of $G$ into single edges, provides a graph $G'$ containing $G$ as subgraph. Therefore, $G$ is a minor of $M$ minor, completing the proof.    □

To conclude the proof of Theorem 1, we will use an accurate bound of the excluded grid-minor theorem of [RST94].

**Lemma 4.** ([GT12, RST94]). *Every planar graph $G$ excluding a planar graph $H$ as minor has treewidth at most:*

i. *$9r/2 - 4$, if $H$ is the $r \times r$ grid with $r \geq 2$; and*
ii. *$9r - 22$, if $H$ has $r \geq 3$ vertices.*

*Proof.* It has been proved in [GT12, Theorem 1.4, pp. 419] that every planar graph either contains a $h \times k$-cylinder $\mathscr{C}_{h,k}$ as minor or has branchwidth at most $k + 2h - 2$ (for $k \geq 3$ and $h \geq 1$). In particular, if a planar graph $G$ excludes a $r \times r$ grid as minor, then its branchwidth is at most $r + 2r - 2 = 3r - 2$ (since, if $G$ excludes an $r \times r$ grid, then it excludes an $r \times r$-cylinder as well). It is also well known that the treewidth of $G$ is at most $\max\{3b/2 - 1, 1\}$, where $b$ is the branchwidth of $G$. It follows that the treewidth of $G$ is at most $3(3r-2)/2 - 1 = 9r/2 - 4$ if $G$ is planar and excludes an $r \times r$ grid as minor, for $r \geq 3$. Observe that if $H$ is a $2 \times 2$ grid (i.e., a cycle $C_4$) then $G$ must be an outerplanar graph (since it cannot contains neither a $K_4$ nor a $K_{2,3}$ as minor that both contains a $C_4$). Thus $G$ has treewidth $2 \leq 9 \cdot 2/2 - 4 = 5$. Therefore, the bound holds also for $r = 2$, proving the first point.

It is known that every Hamiltonian planar graph with $r$ vertices is contained as minor in a $r \times r$ grid [RST94, Theorem (1.3)]. Moreover, every $r$-vertex planar graph is contained as minor in a Hamiltonian planar graph with $2r - 4$ vertices for $r \geq 4$. The graph is obtained by replacing one edge per separating triangle by a degree-4 vertex (cf. [RST94, Theorem (1.4)]). It follows that every planar graph $H$ with $r$ vertices is contained as minor in a $(2r - 4) \times (2r - 4)$ grid.

Therefore, if a planar graph $G$ excludes an $r$-vertex planar graph $H$ as minor with $r \geq 4$, then $G$ excludes an $(2r - 4) \times (2r - 4)$ grid as minor, and thus has treewidth at most $9 \cdot (2r - 4)/2 - 4 = 9r - 22$. Observe that if $H$ has $r = 3$ vertices, then $G$ must be a forest and thus has treewidth $1 \leq 9 \cdot 3 - 22 = 5$. Therefore, the bound holds also for $r = 3$, proving the second point.    □

By combining Lemma 3 and Lemma 1, we get that a graph $H$ having a poly-line $p \times q$-grid drawing is the minor of the $O(p\sqrt{q}) \times O(p\sqrt{q})$ grid. By Lemma 4(i), the treewidth of a planar graph excluding such a square grid, and thus $H$, has treewidth $O(p\sqrt{q})$, which completes the proof of Theorem 1.

Using the constants in Lemma 3, 1, and 4(i), we can obtained a more accurate upper bound on the treewidth for Theorem 1, namely of $9 \lfloor (2 + \sqrt{2})\sqrt{p \cdot 3pq} \rfloor /2 - 4 \approx 27p\sqrt{q}$.

## 5   Conclusion

In this paper, we establish a connection between the treewidth of a planar graph $G$ excluding as minor a graph $H$ and the ability of poly-line grid-drawing of $H$ with small height. One of the consequences of our main result is that the treewidth of every planar excluding such graph $H$ is $O(\sqrt{r})$ where $r = |V(H)|$, which is optimal. We also show that if $H$ is outerplanar, then the bound increases to $O(\sqrt{r \log r})$, leaving open the question of the optimality of this bound.

## References

[ACP87] Arnborg, S., Corneil, D.G., Proskurowski, A.: Complexity of finding embeddings in a $k$-tree. SIAM J. Algebr. Discrete Methods **8**, 277–284 (1987). https://doi.org/10.1137/060802410.1137/0608024

[AP89] Arnborg, S., Proskurowski, A.: Linear time algorithms for NP-hard problems restricted to partial $k$-trees. Discrete Appl. Math. **23**, 11–24 (1989). https://doi.org/10.1016/0166-218X(89)90031-0

[Arn85] Arnborg, S.: Efficient algorithms for combinatorial problems on graphs with bounded decomposability - a survey. BIT Numer. Math. **25**, 2–23 (1985). https://doi.org/10.1007/BF01934985

[BBCR14] Babu, J., Basavaraju, M., Chandran, L.S., Rajendraprasad, D.: 2-connecting outerplanar graphs without blowing up the pathwidth. Theor. Comput. Sci. **554**, 119–134 (2014). https://doi.org/10.1016/j.tcs.2014.04.032

[BBR07] Birmelé, É., Bondy, J.A., Reed, B.A.: Brambles, prisms and grids. In: Bondy, A., Fonlupt, J., Fouquet, J.L., Fournier, J.C., Ramírez Alfonsín, J.L. (eds.) Graph Theory in Paris, pp. 37–44. Springer, Basel (2007). https://doi.org/10.1007/978-3-7643-7400-6_4

[BBR09]   Birmelé, É., Bondy, J.A., Reed, B.A.: Tree-width of graphs without a $3 \times 3$ grid minor. Discrete Appl. Math. **157**, 2577–2596 (2009). https://doi.org/10.1016/j.dam.2008.08.003

[Bie12]   Biedl, T.C.: A 4-approximation for the height of drawing 2-connected outer-planar graphs. In: Erlebach, T., Persiano, G. (eds.) WAOA 2012. LNCS, vol. 7846, pp. 272–285. Springer, Heidelberg (2013). https://doi.org/10.1007/978-3-642-38016-7_22

[Bie14]   Biedl, T.: Height-preserving transformations of planar graph drawings. In: Duncan, C., Symvonis, A. (eds.) GD 2014. LNCS, vol. 8871, pp. 380–391. Springer, Heidelberg (2014). https://doi.org/10.1007/978-3-662-45803-7_32

[Bod96]   Bodlaender, H.L.: A linear time algorithm for finding tree-decompositions of small treewidth. SIAM J. Comput. **25**, 1305–1317 (1996). https://doi.org/10.1137/S0097539793251219

[BRST91]  Bienstock, D., Robertson, N., Seymour, P.D., Thomas, R.: Quickly excluding a forest. J. Comb. Theory Ser. B **52**, 274–283 (1991). https://doi.org/10.1016/0095-8956(91)90068-U

[BvLTT97] Bodlaender, H.L., van Leeuwen, J., Tan, R.B., Thilikos, D.M.: On interval routing schemes and treewidth. Inf. Comput. **139**, 92–109 (1997). https://doi.org/10.1006/inco.1997.2669

[CDE+08]  Chepoi, V.D., Dragan, F.F., Estellon, B., Habib, M., Vaxès, Y.: Diameters, centers, and approximating trees of delta-hyperbolic geodesic spaces and graphs. In: 21st Annual ACM Symposium on Computational Geometry (SoCG), pp. 59–68. ACM-SIAM, June 2008. https://doi.org/10.1145/1377676.1377687

[CDE+12]  Chepoi, V.D., Dragan, F.F., Estellon, B., Habib, M., Vaxès, Y., Xiang, Y.: Additive spanners and distance and routing labeling schemes for hyperbolic graphs. Algorithmica **62**, 713–732 (2012). https://doi.org/10.1007/s00453-010-9478-x

[Cou90]   Courcelle, B.: The monadic second-order logic of graphs. I. Recognizable sets of finite graphs. Inf. Comput. **85**(1), 12–75 (1990). https://doi.org/10.1016/0890-5401(90)90043-H

[CT19]    Chekuri, C., Tan, Z.: Towards tight(er) bounds for the excluded grid theorem. In: 30th Symposium on Discrete Algorithms (SODA), pp. 1445–1464. ACM Press, January 2019. https://doi.org/10.1137/1.9781611975482.88

[dBETT99] di Battista, G., Eades, P., Tamassia, R., Tollis, I.G.: Graph Drawing: Algorithms for the Visualization of Graphs. Prentice Hall, Upper Saddle River (1999)

[DDGY07]  Dourisboure, Y., Dragan, F.F., Gavoille, C., Yan, C.: Spanners for bounded tree-length graphs. Theor. Comput. Sci. **383**, 34–44 (2007). https://doi.org/10.1016/j.tcs.2007.03.058

[dFPP88]  de Fraysseix, H., Pach, J., Pollack, R.: Small sets supporting Fary embeddings of planar graphs. In: 20th Annual ACM Symposium on Theory of Computing (STOC), pp. 426–433. ACM Press (1988). https://doi.org/10.1145/62212.62254

[dFPP90]  de Fraysseix, H., Pach, J., Pollack, R.: How to draw a planar graph on a grid. Combinatorica **10**, 41–51 (1990). https://doi.org/10.1007/BF02122694

[DG03]  Dourisboure, Y., Gavoille, C.: Tree-decomposition of graphs with small diameter bags. In: Fila, J. (ed.) 2nd European Conference on Combinatorics, Graph Theory and Applications (EuroComb), pp. 100–104, September 2003

[DG04]  Dourisboure, Y., Gavoille, C.: Sparse additive spanners for bounded tree-length graphs. In: Královič, R., Sýkora, O. (eds.) SIROCCO 2004. LNCS, vol. 3104, pp. 123–137. Springer, Heidelberg (2004). https://doi.org/10.1007/978-3-540-27796-5_12

[DG07]  Dourisboure, Y., Gavoille, C.: Tree-decompositions with bags of small diameter. Discrete Math. **307**, 2008–2029 (2007). https://doi.org/10.1016/j.disc.2005.12.060

[DHK09] Demaine, E.D., Hajiaghayi, M., Kawarabayashi, K.-I.: Algorithmic Graph Minor Theory: improved grid minor bounds and Wagner's contraction. Algorithmica **54**, 142–180 (2009). https://doi.org/10.1007/s00453-007-9138-y

[Dou05] Dourisboure, Y.: Compact routing schemes for generalised chordal graphs. J. Graph Algorithms Appl. **9**, 277–297 (2005). https://doi.org/10.7155/jgaa.00109

[FHL08] Feige, U., Hajiaghayi, M., Lee, J.R.: Improved approximation algorithms for minimum-weight vertex separators. SIAM J. Comput. **38**, 629–657 (2008). https://doi.org/10.1137/05064299X

[FL89]  Fellows, M.R., Langston, M.A.: On search, decision and the efficiency of polynomial-time algorithms. In: 21st Annual ACM Symposium on Theory of Computing (STOC), pp. 501–512, ACM Press, May 1989. https://doi.org/10.1145/73007.73055

[GKK+01] Gavoille, C., Katz, M., Katz, N.A., Paul, C., Peleg, D.: Approximate distance labeling schemes. In: auf der Heide, F.M. (ed.) ESA 2001. LNCS, vol. 2161, pp. 476–487. Springer, Heidelberg (2001). https://doi.org/10.1007/3-540-44676-1_40

[Gro07] Grohe, M.: Logic, graphs, and algorithms. In: Electronic Colloquium on Computational Complexity (ECCC), vol. TR07-091, September 2007. http://eccc.hpi-web.de/eccc-reports/2007/TR07-091/

[GT05]  Gu, Q.-P., Tamaki, H.: Optimal branch-decomposition of planar graphs in $O(n^3)$ time. In: Caires, L., Italiano, G.F., Monteiro, L., Palamidessi, C., Yung, M. (eds.) ICALP 2005. LNCS, vol. 3580, pp. 373–384. Springer, Heidelberg (2005). https://doi.org/10.1007/11523468_31

[GT12]  Gu, Q.-P., Tamaki, H.: Improved bounds on the planar branchwidth with respect to the largest grid minor size. Algorithmica **64**, 416–453 (2012). https://doi.org/10.1007/s00453-012-9627-5

[KS93]  Korach, E., Solel, N.: Tree-width, path-width, and cutwidth. Discrete Appl. Math. **43**, 97–101 (1993). https://doi.org/10.1016/0166-218X(93)90171-J

[KW10]  Kawarabayashi, K.-I., Wollan, P.: A shorter proof of the Graph Minor Algorithm - the unique linkage theorem. In: 42nd Annual ACM Symposium on Theory of Computing (STOC), pp. 687–694. ACM Press, June 2010. https://doi.org/10.1145/1806689.1806784

[Lok10] Lokshtanov, D.: On the complexity of computing treelength. Discrete Appl. Math. **158**, 820–827 (2010). https://doi.org/10.1016/j.dam.2009.10.007

[RS83]   Robertson, N., Seymour, P.D.: Graph minors. I. Excluding a forest. J. Comb. Theory Ser. B **35**(1), 39–61 (1983). https://doi.org/10.1016/0095-8956(83)90079-5

[RS86]   Robertson, N., Seymour, P.D.: Graph minors. v. Excluding a planar graph. J. Comb. Theory Ser. B **41**, 92–114 (1986). https://doi.org/10.1016/0095-8956(86)90030-4

[RS03]   Robertson, N., Seymour, P.D.: Graph minors. XVI. Excluding a non-planar graph. J. Comb. Theory Ser. B **89**, 43–76 (2003). https://doi.org/10.1016/S0095-8956(03)00042-X

[RS04]   Robertson, N., Seymour, P.D.: Graph minors. XX. Wagner's conjecture. J. Comb. Theory Ser. B **92**, 325–357 (2004). https://doi.org/10.1016/j.jctb.2004.08.001

[RST94]  Robertson, N., Seymour, P.D., Thomas, R.: Quickly excluding a planar graph. J. Comb. Theory Ser. B **62**, 323–348 (1994). https://doi.org/10.1006/jctb.1994.1073

[Sch90]  Schnyder, W.: Embedding planar graphs on the grid. In: 1st Symposium on Discrete Algorithms (SODA), pp. 138–148. ACM-SIAM, January 1990

[ST94]   Seymour, P.D., Thomas, R.: Call routing and the ratcatcher. Combinatorica **14**, 217–241 (1994). https://doi.org/10.1007/BF01215352

[Thi99]  Thilikos, D. M.: Quickly excluding a $K_{2,r}$ from planar graphs. In: 6th Twente Workshop on Graphs and Combinatorial Optimization. Electronic Notes in Discrete Mathematics, vol. 3, pp. 189–194. Elsevier, May 1999. https://doi.org/10.1016/S1571-0653(05)80054-X

[UY09]   Umezawa, K., Yamazaki, K.: Tree-length equals branch-length. Discrete Math. **309**, 4656–4660 (2009). https://doi.org/10.1016/j.disc.2009.01.009

# BACP+: A More Efficient Beacon Analysis-Based Collision Prevention Protocol

Sidiya Dieng$^{(\boxtimes)}$, Youssou Faye, and Marius Dasylva

Department of Computer Sciences, UASZ University, Ziguinchor, Senegal
s.dieng20140909@zig.univ.sn, {yfaye,mdasylva}@univ-zig.sn

**Abstract.** As in traditional wireless networks and Wireless Sensor Networks (WSN), Medium Access Control (MAC) in RFID (Radio Frequency IDentification) networks is a real challenge. RFIDs are increasingly being used for a variety of applications in several fields such as agriculture, industry, commerce, monitoring. Thus, providing MAC solution while preserving the resources (bandwidth, energy, storage, computing and transmission capacities) and ensuring scalability is very challenge. To avoid collisions that may occur between readers, anti-collision protocols use two approaches. The centralized approach based on Time Divisible Multiple Access (TDMA). The decentralized approach is based on the Carrier Sense multiple Access (CSMA) and uses notifications. That's why we offer Called Beacon Analysis-based Collision Prevention more (BACP+) to provide better performance for Called Beacon Analysis-based Collision Prevention (BACP) which uses the centralized approach by optimizing resources, and promoting the greatest number of reading with less interference. BACP+ makes full use of available resources, and frequency channels to ensure proper collision management and coverage time.

**Keywords:** Radio Frequency IDentification · Anti-colision protocol · Reader-tag

## 1 Introduction

RFIDs networks are increasingly used in several fields. The development and exponential growth of new information and communication technologies makes it possible to consider many applications distributed in space and a clear evolution towards the Internet of Things (IoT). However, because of the inherent characteristics of RFID readers and tags (energy, computing, storage and transmission capacities are limited), RFID networks do not adapt to the MAC communication protocols (MAC layer and network) proposed for wireless networks (mobile, ad-hoc, sensor) because of the significant costs generated and the variety of types of communication. Thus, for RFID specific approaches have been developed in recent years to resolve collisions, especially those between readers. In this way

© ICST Institute for Computer Sciences, Social Informatics and Telecommunications Engineering 2020
Published by Springer Nature Switzerland AG 2020. All Rights Reserved
J. P. R. Thorn et al. (Eds.): InterSol 2020, LNICST 321, pp. 251–263, 2020.
https://doi.org/10.1007/978-3-030-51051-0_18

that CSMA-based decentralized protocols use a multichannel approach [2, 4, 8–12, 16–18] to resolve reader-tag and reader-reader collusion. Those based on the TDMA [3–7, 14, 15] use a single-channel approach to adjust only reader-reader collusion. Their main disadvantage is the low reading rate and the relatively high energy consumption. Most protocols based on the centralized approach are derived from [14, 15]. BACP is proposed to be a protocol that solves problems in GDRA [16] and DRCA [17], allocates resources to readers in order to ensure a maximum use of available resources while activating the largest number of readers in a round so that they can read the tags with minimal interference. However, BACP has a default on the random choice of time intervals and the activation of the maximum of reader. That's why we offer Called Beacon Analysis-based Collision Prevention more (BACP+) to provide better performance for BACP by optimizing resources, and promoting the greatest number of readings while minimizing interference. BACP+ makes full use of available resources, frequency channels to ensure good collision management and coverage time. The rest of the paper is as follows. Section 2 presents the state of the art on reader anti-collision protocols, including centralized protocols. A description of BACP [18] and its limitations are provided in Sect. 3. BACP+ solution is presented in Sect. 4. We make performance analysis and evaluation in Sect. 5. Finally, we conclude the paper and identify research perspectives in the section.

## 2   State of Art

Collisions degrade the performance of RFID systems. Thus, to ensure the necessary coordination between readers and avoid collisions, a Medium Access Control (MAC) must be established between readers and/or tags. For this, we distinguish two existing approaches [1]. The decentralized approach in which available system resources such as frequencies and time are distributed among the readers to prevent them from collisions [2–12]. This approach can effectively reduce the risk of readers collisions. However, its protocols are based on TDMA [3–7] or CSMA mechanisms [2, 8–12]. In RFID, most distributed protocols based on TDMA approaches are derived from an earlier algorithm called Distributed Color Selection. They use a dedicated communication channel between readers to organize their activity [2]. They solve effectively the problem of reader collisions. However, the actual communication takes place between the reader and tag. This type of protocol does not take into account the problems of collision between reader and tag, which reduces RFID performance. As a result, with decentralized protocols, reader collisions persist, throughput and computation are generally very low, but mobility and equity are taken into account. In centralized approach where protocols are usually based on the TDMA, readers require a coordinator (a Central Server) for the RFID network, which manages and allocates resources to readers [14–18]. Readers can communicate by wired or wireless to the server. In the case of wireless, frequency between the readers and the central server is different from the frequency that readers use to communicate with the tags [13]. These protocols are less responsive to reader mobility, but they come over the problem of throughput, equity and sometimes reader-tag collision for which decentralized protocols suffer from. The single-channel approach was first developed to allow readers to discuss the medium with less interference [14, 15]. So, in dense deployments where multiple readers are nearby and lead to increasing collisions, multichannel solutions are implemented [16, 20]. It provides readers with four different channels to query tags, making tag readings less competitive and less prone to collisions. However Geometric Distribution Reader Anti-collision solution (GDRA) [16] has the disadvantage of poor resource management. To reduce collisions and promote maximum reading notion of changing channel is introduced by the Distance Based RFID Reader Collision Avoidance (DRCA) protocol [17]. But, channel abandonment still persists and prevent channel loss by introducing read priority to separate conflict in a channel. Nevertheless, BACP has shortcomings related to time slots lost at the beginning of the execution of the protocol, consistent collisions in high time slots and quite a lot of inactivated drives in a cycle. Thus, we propose BACP+ to overcome these problems.

# 3    Review of BACP Protocol

## 3.1    Problem in GDRA and DRCA

In GDRA, when collision happen between two readers, they leave the channel and select another random channel and wait for the next round. As a result, the abandoned channel is unused and resources are wasted. Although GDRA is a multichannel protocol, it does not use this function correctly, because it is possible for a reader to read the tags with another reader in the channel without any interference. However, this question is not taken into account in this protocol and readers leave the channel as soon as it is busy. The DRCA protocol makes improvements to the problem of abandoning the channel and waiting for the next round. Thus, when the readers detect that the channel is busy, if they are not around the active reader, then they increment their time interval to one and choose another channel. Indeed, they can try to participate again in the current round. On the other hand, the problem with the DRCA is that readers which have the ability to access the channel again are allowed to randomly select one of the four existing channels. Therefore, with a probability of 25%, a reader chooses his previous channel. However, it wastes energy because it caused the reader to unsuccessfully attempt to access the channel [18]. Thus, the problem of GDRA is not solved in some cases. It is in this sense that the BACP was introduced to correct this weakness.

## 3.2    Description of BACP

BACP aims to resolve weakness in GDRA and DRCA by allocating resources to readers in ways that ensure maximum use. It also tries to activate more readers in round so that they can read the tags with minimal interference. In BACP, readers communicate with a central server. The server announces the start of each round by sending an AC (Arrangement Command) message to the readers. The duration of each AC is considered to be 2.83 ms and each round is divided into two phases. The contention phase, during which readers are in contention to access the channel by sending a tag message. The contention phase is divided into K slots, the duration of each time interval is Tslot = 5 ms. The readers are equipped with a bistatic antenna and can therefore send a beacon message in each time interval. In addition to listening to the channel. The duration of sending a tag message is TBeacon = 0.3 ms. In the BACP protocol, each time slot is divided into 16 sub-slots, and each reader selects in its time interval to send a tag message randomly. The duration of each time interval is the time it takes to send a beacon message. Each reader sends a beacon message during the selected sub-slots from its time slot and listens for the channels to receive beacon messages from the neighboring readers. In the same time interval if a large number of neighboring readers are there, then a collision occurs between the tag messages sent in the sub-slots, but with a very low probability. In the BACP protocol, each reader sends a tag called Preference_Code (PC). Each Preference_Code contains Reader_ID and a bit called Prev_state. Each network drive to a specific unit called Reader_ID. Prev_state is a bit (the last bit from the left) that refers to the readers state in the previous turn If the reader was able to read the tags of the previous round, then the value of Prev_state is zero (0); otherwise, it's one (1). To better illustrate BACP, we consider the scenario of Fig. 1-(a) and Fig. 1-(b) which show respectively the deployment topology of readers and their behavior during a round. The readers randomly select time slots and frequency channels after the central server sends the AC message. After selection, the readers are divided into the following four categories: channel 1={L3, L9, L4}, channel 2 ={L1, L8}, Channel 3={L2, L7} and Channel 4={L5, L6}.

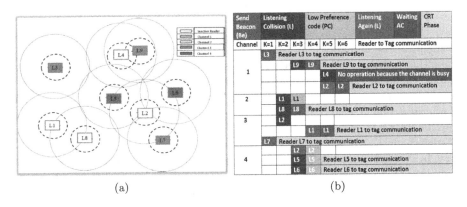

(a)                                              (b)

**Fig. 1.** Example: scenario for BACP

At the beginning of the first interval, k = 1, readers L3 and L7 send respectively their Preference_Code (PC) to the channels 1 and 3. Then they listen to the channel until the end of the first time slot, since they do not receive any PC from the neighboring readers, so they use the channel and start reading the tags.

When the second time interval (TI) begins, the readers L1, L8 and L2 listen to the channel. Since the reader L7 reads the tags, reader L2 understands that the channel is busy and therefore calculates its distance to the reader L7. Since the reader L2 is in the interference range of the reader L7 and moreover the distance between the two readers is greater than 2 * drt (distance reader-tag) then L2 increases his TI by one unit and selects randomly another channel (channel 4, k = 4).

After the end of the second TI, k = 2, the readers L1 and L8 compare the PCs received from each other. Since the L8 reader's PC is bigger, it occupies the channel (it is assumed that Prev_state of all drives is zero in this round) and L2 will change channels. He randomly chooses channel 3 and increments his TI to k = 5.

At the beginning of the fourth TI, then in the third TI the readers L2, L5 and L6 have identified that the channel is free. They start sending their PC to the selected sub-slots. At the end of the fourth time slot, L2 compares the codes received from L5 and L6 with his PC, as his PC is smaller, he changes channels. The reader L5 also compares his PC with the received codes. Since L5 has only received the L2 PC and its PC is larger than L2, it can access the channel. The same goes for the L6 reader. The BACP protocol enables more readers in one round. In the BACP protocol, no reader needs to continually listen to the channel. If the reader has selected the time interval k, it only listens to the channel during the time interval (k−1), this reduces the power consumption. The evaluation of BACP with other protocols indicates that it has a good throughput.

### 3.3   Limits of BACP

The random selection of time intervals is a real problem in BACP. When readers have the opportunity to have a new channel, this means that the probability of interference in the highest TI, increases and possibly more drives are inactive. This is due to the use of the sift function [19] defined by probability formula: $pk = \delta * \dfrac{1}{\alpha^k}$ by this protocol. This function makes it possible to select with a high probability intervals: $\delta = \dfrac{(1 - \alpha) + \alpha^k}{1 - \alpha^k}$, where $\alpha$ is a constant between 0 and 1 and $\delta$ is a computable constant and K is the number of TI and k is a values between 1 and K. However, BACP presents some weakness that we will try to correct later:

if the reading area of two readers is in interference, then they will have to wait for the next AC if they have chosen the same slot.

if the coverage area of two readers overlaps, then the reader with hight priority will keep the channel and the other will change channels in the next time slot. On the other hand, if the collision occurs in the hight time intervals, then readers may wait for the next round. Applying equity for readers that are in the same channel and time-slot can reduce the chance of reading multiple readers in this time-slot. For example, if L2 was more important than L5 and L6 then they would have to leave the channel. In this case we lose two readings for a single reading as shown in Fig. 2.

The delay is long because the readers did not start their interrogations very early.

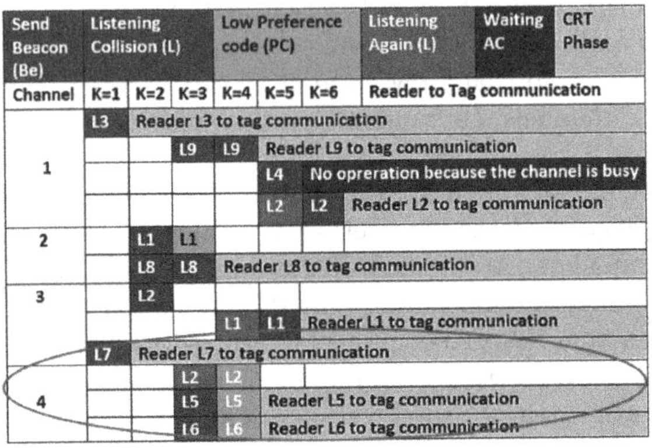

| Send Beacon (Be) | Listening Collision (L) | | | Low Preference code (PC) | | | Listening Again (L) / Waiting AC / CRT Phase |
|---|---|---|---|---|---|---|---|
| Channel | K=1 | K=2 | K=3 | K=4 | K=5 | K=6 | Reader to Tag communication |
| | L3 | | | | | | Reader L3 to tag communication |
| | | | L9 | L9 | | | Reader L9 to tag communication |
| 1 | | | | | L4 | | No opreration because the channel is busy |
| | | | | | L2 | L2 | Reader L2 to tag communication |
| 2 | | L1 | L1 | | | | |
| | | L8 | L8 | | | | Reader L8 to tag communication |
| 3 | | L2 | | | | | |
| | | | | L1 | L1 | | Reader L1 to tag communication |
| | L7 | | | | | | Reader L7 to tag communication |
| 4 | | | L2 | L2 | | | |
| | | | L5 | L5 | | | Reader L5 to tag communication |
| | | | L6 | L6 | | | Reader L6 to tag communication |

Fig. 2. Collisions in BACP

# 4    BACP+

## 4.1    Solve the Problem of Lost Time Slots

In BACP all readers randomly choose a time-slot, if there are readers that interfere, then they will randomly choose sub-slots from the 16 available in the same slot. Then they will compare their PC. The reader which has the largest PC will keep the channel and the others will change channel and the TI will be incremented by one. We can note that this can lead to empty TI at the beginning of the round and others overloaded because it is possible that no reader chooses the beginning slots due to the randomness of the choice. To bring a solution for this, we propose in BACP+ to solve collisions of readers very early. In this case all readers must start sending their tags to k = 1 in order to scan the network. If collision is detected between readers then they compare their PC and the one with the biggest will read the tags and the others will increment their time-slot by 1. So all the TI will be busy. Figure 3 shows the slots time lost in BACP.

However in BACP+, since all the readers will try to communicate at the time interval k = 1 to avoid losing TI, this can lead to collisions (at the beginning of the TI) that we will try to solve in Sect. 5.2.

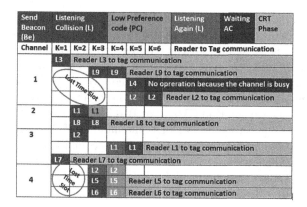

**Fig. 3.** Lost slots time in BACP

## 4.2 Deal with the Loss of the Channel Due to the Same Slot

In BACP if several readers have chosen the channel and the same time-slot as the distance between the readers is less than 2 times drt as it is the case between L4 and L9 (see Fig. 1-(a)), they wait for the next round and the channel is lost because their communications may collide with the response of a tag. In order to keep the channel, BACP+ compares the PC of the two readers, and reader with biggest priority will keep the channel and the other one expects the next AC.

## 4.3 Make Compromise Between the Density of Readers and the Number of Time Slots

If the density of the readers is very high then we will have a lot of collision in the TI. Thus, we can provide a solution that will make a compromise between the time slots and the number of readers. This will reduce collisions in time intervals.

# 5  Analysis and Evaluation

In this section we make evaluation and analysis of BACP+ and BACP to determine and justify its performances. To do this, we use in the first reader reading throughput as a comparison metric.

## 5.1 Comparison of Reading Throughput

In the scenario of Fig. 4, we can see that BACP+ increases the read throughput compared to BACP. This is generally due to the exploitation of free slots time at the beginning which will allow all readers to compete during the contention phase and avoid the congestion at the end of the round which makes some readers to wait for the next AC if they do not do not win the channel. If we know that the time slot is 5 ms and that the reading period of the readers on the tags is 0.46 s, we can quantify the read throughput d of each solution depending of the read throughput of one reader per ms using the formula below: D= d (T_slot * N_slot + T_com), where D is the read throughput of a reader; d is the quantification throughput of each solution (BACP or BACP+); T_slot is the duration of a time interval, it is equal to 5 ms; N_slot is the number of time slots occupied by the reader in his communication and T_com is the communication time between reader and tags. Thus, we have determined the total reading throughput BACP and BACP+ in Table 1 based on this formula: the reading throughput of reader L5 is $D_5$ = d(t5.10 − 3 ∗ 5 + 0.46) = 0.485d bits/s.

**Table 1.** Reading throughput in d bits/s

| Reader | L1 | L2 | L3 | L4 | L5 | L6 | L7 | L8 | L9 | Total throughput |
|--------|------|------|------|------|------|------|------|--------|-------|------------------|
| BACP | 0,475 | 0,475 | 0,475 | 0,485 | 0,485 | 0,475 | 0,46 | 0,4853 | 0,485 | 4,266 bits/s |
| BACP+ | 0,485 | 0,485 | 0,485 | 0,485 | 0,485 | 0,485 | 0,485 | 0,485 | 0,485 | 4, 365 bits/s |

The total read throughput is equal to the sum of the throughputs $\sum_{L=1}^{n} D$ for each reader, is 4,266d bits/s for BACP and 4,365d bits/s for BACP+. This is achieved by this formula $\sum_{L=1}^{n} D_i$ with n the number of readers. From Table 1, throughput of BACP+ is 0.099d bits/s higher than that of BACP. Similarly, it has been found that the BACP+ flow throughput remains higher than that of the BACP in the others Figs. 4, 6 and 8.

## 5.2  Analysis Based on Channels Without Interference

In this section, we try to implement the deployment effect of non-interference readers through Figs. 4-(a) and Fig. 4-(b) to measure the behavior of both solu-

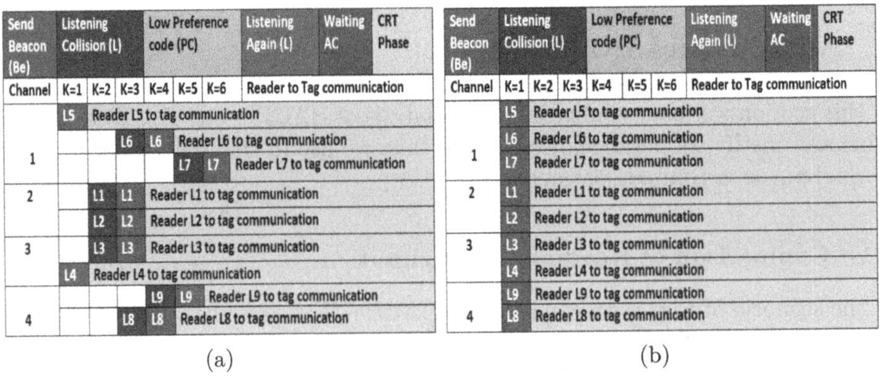

(a)                                              (b)

**Fig. 4.** Channels without interference

tions. The readers randomly chose channels as follows: Channel 1 = {L5, L6, L7}, Channel 2 = {L1, L2}, Channel 3 = {L3, L4} and Channel 4 ={L8, L9}.

If the choice of channels is such that there is no interference, then BACP+ is more efficient than BACP because at the beginning of slot all readers have reads without collision. This helps to reduce the cycle time compared to that of the BACP protocol. While we find that there is no collision on either side of the two protocols but in terms of cycle time, we find that BACP+ takes less time than BACP. This is due to the random choice of time intervals in BACP. Thus we have a read throughput of 98.98% in BACP+ and 96.73% in BACP.

## 5.3 Density-Based on Mobility

Here, we try to implement reader density to justify the solutions' performance. We can see that there is less reading in both solutions because many readers wait for the next AC. However, in high-density where the reading areas of multiple readers overlap, as shown in Figs. 9 and 10, BACP+ has a better read throughput than BACP. In this case, BACP prevents the activation of all these interfering readers while BACP+ chooses one readers which increases the reading throughput. After random channel selection the readers are distributed as follows: Channel 1 = {L6, L7, L8}, Channel 2 = {L1, L2}, Channel 3 = {L3, L4} and Channel 4 = {L5, L9}. Figures 5 and Fig. 6-(a) and Fig. 6-(b) highlight the scenario in Fig. 7. If the system is dense then BACP+ activates more readers than BACP with a time less than that of the BACP. For BACP and BACP+, we determine from Table 2, the total read throughput:

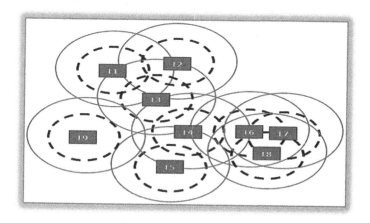

**Fig. 5.** Hight density of readers

It can be seen that the read throughput in BACP+ (2.9 bit/s) is 0.063d bit/s higher than that of BACP (2.837d bit/s). Thus, we reach a reading throughput of 98.47% in BACP+ against 96.33% in BACP. With mobility, we try to implement reader mobility to justify the performance of solutions. We see that the

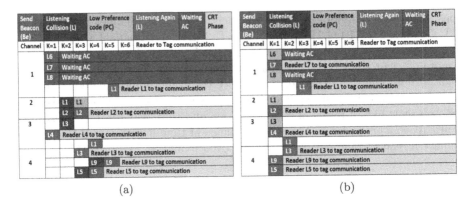

(a)                                                    (b)

**Fig. 6.** Hight density without mobility

**Table 2.** Reading throughput

| Reader | L1 | L2 | L3 | L4 | L5 | L6 | L7 | L8 | L9 | Total throughput |
|--------|------|------|------|------|------|----|-------|----|-------|------------------|
| BACP   | 0,466 | 0,475 | 0,475 | 0,485 | 0,47 | 0 | 0 | 0 | 0,466 | 2,837 bits/s |
| BACP+  | 0,475 | 0,485 | 0,475 | 0,485 | 0,485 | 0 | 0,485 | 0 | 0,485 | 2, 9 bits/s |

trend is basically the same because there are many readers waiting for the next AC. However, in high mobility situations where the reading areas of multiple readers overlap, as shown in Fig. 7, BACP+ has a better read throughput than BACP. Indeed, in such circumstances, BACP prevents the activation of all these interfering readers, while BACP+ chooses one of these readers.

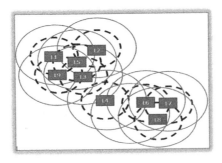

**Fig. 7.** Hight density deployment of reader

After random channel selection the readers are distributed as follows: Channel 1 = {L9, L5, L1, L2}, Channel 2 = {L3, L4}, Channel 3 = {L6, L7} and Channel 4 = {L8}. For a high density of mobile readers, we find that the BACP+ protocol activates more readers than the BACP protocol in a round. For example in BACP the reader L4 is at the end of the cycle he can not because he is in the last time slot. While in BACP+ this problem does not happen because L4 participated very early in the cycle so he will have time to change channel and be active. In addition, the TI is more shorter in BACP+ than in BACP (Fig. 8).

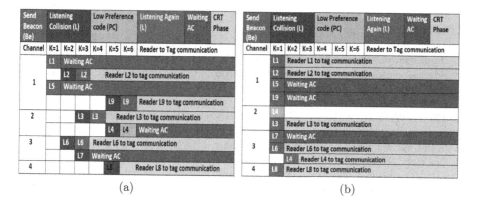

(a)                                    (b)

**Fig. 8.** Hight density with mobility

## 6  Conclusion

In this paper, after having developed a state of the art in which the distributed and centralized reader anti-collision protocols are presented, we have turned to multichannel protocols that offer a higher reading throughput via simultaneous readings. But they nevertheless exhibit more interference than single-channel protocols. Even if GDRA, DRCA can manage these interferences, BACP, a last proposed solutions, is more efficient. We have proposed BACP+, a BACP enhancement that tries to keep all its benefits while increasing its reading speed. Manual simulation scenarios based on concrete and precise examples allowed us to detect some trend criteria related to interference, density and mobility. We have been able to determine that if neighboring readers choose different channels so that they do not interfere, then even if the number of reads is the same for BACP as for BACP+, the reading time is shorter in BACP+ than in BACP. In this way, we have to find a channel selection or allocation algorithm in order to prevent interference between neighbors. We have also shown that the higher the density of the readers, the lower the read throughput in both protocols. However, the bit throughput will be lower in BACP+. We have seen that mobility favors reader-tag collisions. Therefore, a wait for the next AC by readers is common in these cases. In addition, the degree of activity is higher in BACP+ than in BACP at the beginning of the contention period, which may impact energy consumption. It will then be a question of making the compromise between flow of reading and preservation of the energy. We also want to lead in BACP+ a reuse policy of the released channel before the end of the round. We continue to work on the theoretical analysis to better justify the performance of our BACP+ contribution compared to the BACP. We also plan to do simulation taking into account other parameters such as energy consumption to better justify the performance of each solution.

# References

1. Jamieson, K., Balakrishnan, H., Tay, Y.C.: Sift: a MAC protocol for event-driven wireless sensor networks. In: Römer, K., Karl, H., Mattern, F. (eds.) EWSN 2006. LNCS, vol. 3868, pp. 260–275. Springer, Heidelberg (2006). https://doi.org/10.1007/11669463_20
2. Kim, S.W., Joshi, G.P.: Reducing interference in RFID reader networks. In: RFID Systems, vol. 297(2010)
3. ETSI, E. 302,208–2 v1. 1.1, September 2004. CTAN. http://www.Etsi.Org
4. Nasri, N., Kachouri, N., Samet, M., Andrieux, L.:. Radio Frequency Identification (RFID) working, design considerations and modelling of antenna. In: 5th International Multi-Conference on Systems, Signals and Devices, IEEE SSD 2008, pp. 1–6. IEEE, July 2008
5. Leong, K.S., Ng, M.L., Cole, P.H.: The reader collision problem in RFID systems. In: IEEE International Symposium on Microwave, Antenna, Propagation and EMC Technologies for Wireless Communications, MAPE 2005, vol. 1, pp. 658–661. IEEE, August 2005
6. Klair, D.K., Chin, K.W., Raad, R.: A survey and tutorial of RFID anti-collision protocols. IEEE Commun. Surv. Tutor. **12**(3), 400–421 (2010)
7. Bueno-Delgado, M.V., Pav-n-Mari-o, P.: A maximum likelihood based distributed protocol for passive RFID dense reader environments. J. Supercomput. **476**, 1–456 (2013). https://doi.org/10.1007/s11227-012-0779-5
8. Olaleye, O.G., et al.: Modeling and performance simulation of PULSE and MCMAC protocols in RFID-based IoT network using OMNeT++. In: 2018 IEEE International Conference on RFID (RFID). IEEE (2018)
9. Garcia-Alfaro, J., Navarro-Arribas, G.: Foreword from the program chairs of DPM 2010 (2011)
10. Safa, H., El-Hajj, W., Meguerditchian, C.: A distributed multi-channel reader anti-collision algorithm for RFID environments. J. Comput. Commun. **64**, 44–56 (2015)
11. YuJing, Z., Yinghua, C.: EDMC: An enhanced distributed multichannel anti-collision algorithm for RFID reader system. In: Proceedings of American Institute of Physics Conference (2017)
12. Jiang, Y., et al.: An efficient multi-channel reader collision avoidance protocol in RFID systems. In: Proceedings of Wireless Communications and Networking Conference (WCNC). IEEE (2016)
13. Assarian, A., et al.: A beacon analysis-based RFID reader anti-collision protocol for dense reader environments. Comput. Commun. **128**, 18–34 (2018)
14. Nawaz, F., Jeoti, V.: NFRA-C, neighbor friendly reader to reader anti-collision protocol with counters for dense reader environments. J. Network and Computer Applications **49**, 60–67 (2015)
15. Polastre, J., Hill, J., Culler, D.: Versatile low power media access for wireless sensor networks. In: Proceedings of the 2nd International Conference on Embedded Networked Sensor Systems, pp. 95–107. ACM, November 2004

16. Bueno-Delgado, M.V., Vales-Alonso, J.: On the optimal frame-length configuration on real passive RFID systems. J. Network Comput. Appl. **34**(3), 864–876 (2011)
17. Golsorkhtabaramiri, M., Issazadehkojidi, N.: A distance based RFID reader collision avoidance protocol for dense reader environments. Wireless Pers. Commun. **95**(2), 1781–1798 (2017)
18. Assarian, A., Khademzadeh, A., HosseinZadeh, M., Setayeshi, S.: A beacon analysis-based RFID reader anti-collision protocol for dense reader environments. Comput. Commun. **128**, 18–34 (2018)
19. Delgado, B., et al.: A geometric distribution reader anti-collision protocol for RFID dense reader environments. IEEE Trans. Autom. Sci. Eng. **10**(2), 296–306 (2013)
20. ETSI EN 302 208. Radio Frequency Identification Equipment operating in the band 865 MHz to 868 MHz with power levels up to 2 W and in the band 915 MHz to 921 MHz with power levels up to 4 W; Harmonised Standard covering the essential requirements of article 3.2 of the Directive 2014/53/EU (2016)

# Enriching Geolocalized Dataset with POIs Descriptions at Large Scale

Ibrahima Gueye[1(✉)], Hubert Naacke[2], and Stéphane Gançarski[2]

[1] Ecole Polytechnique de Thiès, LTISI, Thies, Senegal
igueye@ept.sn
[2] Sorbonne Université, CNRS, Laboratoire d'Informatique de Paris 6, LIP6,
75005 Paris, France
{hubert.naacke,stephane.gancarski}@lip6.fr

**Abstract.** We present an efficient method to enrich a geolocalized dataset with contextual description about Points of Interest (POI). We implemented our solution using two large scale datasets: YFCC [14] and Geonames [2]. A practical problem we have encountered is the size of the manipulated data. Actually, the YFCC geolocalized dataset accounts for 45 million entries that we propose to cross with 12 millions of Geonames POIs. We show that using the Apache Spark cluster computing platform and the GeoSpark [18] spatial join library as-is lead to inefficient computation because of the important bias in the data. We propose a method to distribute the data non uniformly according to the data bias, which greatly improves the spatial join performance. Moreover, we propose a method to select among a set of close POIs, those which are the most relevant with the YFCC entries. The resulting enriched dataset will be made publicly available and should contribute to better validate future works on large scale POI recommendation.

**Keywords:** YFCC large scale dataset · Distributed query processing · Spatial join · Apache Spark · POI recommendation

## 1 Introduction

Photos and videos extracted from social media are used in many contemporary studies and research that are as varied as they are numerous. These works range from the Point Of Interest (POI) recommendation system for tourist tours [6–8,13] to helping systems for destination promotion [1]. These photos and videos are also used as training data for unsupervised deep neural networks [11] or supervised classifications [5]. Such data originating from social media is usually provided with some contextual information: at least every photo has a geo-location (GPS coordinates), a user id, and a timestamp.

However, there is an increasing demand for richer contextual information that could be captured in new recommendation models, expecting to improve

© ICST Institute for Computer Sciences, Social Informatics and Telecommunications Engineering 2020
Published by Springer Nature Switzerland AG 2020. All Rights Reserved
J. P. R. Thorn et al. (Eds.): InterSol 2020, LNICST 321, pp. 264–273, 2020.
https://doi.org/10.1007/978-3-030-51051-0_19

the overall quality of recommendation systems. It appears that recent research efforts about POI recommendation fall into two distinct lines of works, depending on the model complexity and the dataset scale. There are either complex (sophisticated) models validated using rich but small-scale datasets, or simpler models validated through large-scale datasets but containing few contextual information [3]. We are not aware of much work that would explore the two abovementioned dimensions together, *i.e.*, works that would propose a sophisticated model taking into account rich semantic information and validated at large scale using millions of POI from several continents all around the world. If a complex recommendation model have a low theoretical complexity that qualify it as scalable, its large scale performance validation remains an open issue as long as there is no publicly available rich and large dataset for such validation.

Our goal is to contribute to the research community about POI recommendation and deliver a rich and large-scale dataset. This will help to improve both the training phase as well as the test phase of new POI recommendation models. We consider a large-scale dataset about geo-located photos originating from social media, and focus on enriching it with contextual POI descriptions. We intend to join two large-scale datasets on their geo-location, which raises two difficult problems: (1) a photo location almost never exactly match any POI location, it generally requires to approximately match 0 or many POIs within a fixed radius. (2) Among all the possible close POIs that approximately match a photo location, only few of them are relevant with the photo.

We show that using the Apache Spark cluster computing platform and the GeoSpark [18] spatial join library as-is lead to inefficient computation because of the important bias in the data. We propose a method to distribute the data non uniformly according to the data bias, which greatly improves the spatial join performance. Moreover, we propose a method to select among a set of close POIs, those which are the most relevant with the photo tags. We implemented our solution using two large scale datasets: YFCC [14] and Geonames [2].

In the following Sect. 2, we provide some background knowledge. Section 4 details our enrichment method. Section 3 gives an overview of related works.

## 2 Background: YFCC100M, Geonames Datasets and Spatial Queries

### 2.1 Yahoo Flickr Creative Commons 100M : YFCC100M

The exponential growth of Instagram has brought photo sharing to the mass, generalizing the use-case that Flicker early initiated through its photo sharing platform. By now, Flicker contains an impressive amount of photos that users published since 2004, and it still remains an active platform for sharing photos over the Internet and to manage personal galleries on the cloud. In particular, the availability of Flicker's data has made it academically recognized as a source of pictorial research [7]. In July 2015, Yahoo released and made available a visual content dataset for researchers called "Yahoo Flickr Creative Commons

100M" *YFCC100M* [14]. The Dataset contains more than 100 million multimedia metadata published on Flickr between 2004 and 2014, consisting of 99.2 million photos and 0.8 million videos. Each entry of the YFCC100M dataset contains the user ID, the date when the photo was taken, and up to 24 optional fields among them the most relevant for our work are the geo-location as GPS coordinates, and the users' tags. The YFCC dataset comes with 3 kinds of supplementary information: attributes related to the camera that took the picture such as the photo definition, or the camera brand; auto-generated concepts (*e.g.*, people, animal, food, outdoor) obtained by an unsupervised image processing approach, and geographic attributes (*e.g.*, street, town, country) associated with the GPS coordinates of a photo. Photos taken with digital devices usually carry descriptive information, called metadata. This information often appears as the exchangeable image contained in the JPG photos. Metadata can be parsed and saved when the photo is uploaded to a website.

### 2.2 Geonames Dataset

The YFCC dataset does not contain detailed information about the POI categories, which is what we aim to add by matching the photo locations with the POI categories included in the Geonames dataset [2].

The Geonames is a geographical database that covers all countries and contains over eleven million unique features (see Fig. 1) whereof 4.8 million populated places and 13 million alternate names. These place names correspond to Point of Interest (POI). All features are categorized into one out of nine feature classes and further sub categorized into one out of 645.

The usefulness of the dataset of Geonames with respect to the YFCC100M is that their crossing will allow to find the points of interest associated with each photo, or those which are closest. But most importantly, it gives us the ability to access the POI categories; rarest data and most difficult to obtain.

### 2.3 Spatial Queries and Quadtree

When crossing these two large datasets, we need to process spatial queries that require specific methods.

A spatial query is a set of spatial conditions characterized by spatial operators that form the basis for the retrieval of spatial information from a spatial database system. Moreover, we express some combination (longitude and latitude) for extracting specific information from the datasets without actually changing these data. Considering this, we aim dealing with spatial queries.

To efficiently process spatial queries, we will rely on indexes. Spatial indices are used by spatial databases to optimize spatial queries by accessing a spatial object efficiently. Conventional index types do not efficiently handle spatial queries such as how far two points differ, or whether points fall within a spatial area of interest. Without indexing, any search for a feature would require a sequential scan of every record in the data, resulting in much longer processing time. In a spatial index construction process, the minimum bounding rectangle serves as an object approximation [16]. Many common spatial index methods exist [10,16]. In our work, we choose the Quadtree [16].

**Fig. 1.** GeoNames feature density map  (source: www.geonames.org)

## 3   Related Work

The YFCC Dataset release opened many possibilities in data-driven research fields. It gave new opportunities exploiting geolocalized data and crossed with identified existing POIs for recommendation [4,6,7,9,17].

We motivate our work by reminding that recent works on POI recommendation using YFCC dataset enriched with POI categories is restricted to small scale data:

[7] considers 250 POIs located in 8 towns, and 153 K visits (*i.e.*, posts). [6] considers 118 POI in one city, and 332 K visits. This is 10 to 100 order or magnitude less than the dataset scale we are considering.

In [7] authors present PERSTOUR, an algorithm for recommending personalized tours. This recommending uses POIs and existing real-life travel sequences to align with users interests. They formulate the problem using orienteeriing problem and consider two mains constraints: time budget and specific starting and ending POIs. The authors validate their proposition using the YFCC100M dataset and show promising results. They enhanced the PERSTOUR algorithm in [8] by updating user interests through visit recency and visit duration of their POIs. The authors propose other extensions. In [6] they propose an other enhanced personalized itinerary recommendation that considers queuing times at recommended POIs, while in [15] they propose a Personalized Crowd-aware Trip recommendation.

The YFCC data is also used in many other case studies. In [1], the authors used it in a context of photo recommendation for posters of touristic destination promotions. The authors highlight the dual character of information about photos and videos posted on social networks. On the one hand there is the metadata which is the set of information that describes the media; for example a title, some tags, a description. On the other hand, there is all comments published by social network users. These comments have the particularity of containing explicit emotions on the media, but also sometimes tags. Based on this observation, the authors propose following two concepts: This duality in the characterization of photos and videos is related to their metadata and their comments. Authors of this contribution propose a model between these two concepts, using a naive Bayesian classifier, which is a machine learning algorithm. The purpose of this model is to help the management agents of the tourist destination promotion to choose the most suitable photo for the promotion of a destination. For their experimental validation, the authors used a final dataset containing 21 K posts in New York city; which is a quite small scale.

Many other works focusing on POIs for touristic or travel recommendation are available. But they use other datasets [12, 19] in their experimental validation. While these datasets are different from YFCC, they still are at relatively small scale.

## 4    Enriching a Photo Dataset with POI Categories

Consider the simplified schemas for the two datasets to be joined: **YFCC***(user, date, photoID, latitude, longitude)*, and **GN***(POI, latitude, longitude, categories)*. We aim to process the query $J$ that associates a photo $y$ with a POI $o$ if the distance $d$ between $y$ and $o$ is less than a given upper bound $b$. We have:

$$J = \{(y,o)|y \in YFCC, o \in GN \land d(y,o) \le b\} \tag{1}$$

We investigate three methods to process $J$ in a distributed environment such as Apache Spark.

**The *Cartesian* Method.** The first baseline method named *Cartesian* is to translate $J$ in SQL and submit it to the Spark framework which is able to process $J$ in parallel. This requires to define $d$ as a user defined function, to compute the cartesian product between $YFCC$ and $GN$ then to apply $d$ and select the $(y, o)$ couples that satisfy the condition. This method has a high complexity: the number of $d$ invocations is $|YFCC| \times |GN|$, which is the order of $10^{14}$ in our case.

**The *IndexJoin* Method.** The second method named *IndexJoin* relies on the GeoSpark [18] additional library to compute the spatial join. Note that GeoSpark is a dedicated library for processing large-scale spatial data in a cluster computing system. GeoSpark extends Apache Spark/SparkSQL with a set of out-of-the-box Spatial Resilient Distributed Datasets (SRDDs)/ SpatialSQL that efficiently load, process, and analyze large-scale spatial data across machines. The spatial IndexJoin is computed in a parallel and distributed way as follows:

– The $GN$ dataset is partitioned based on the GPS locations of POIs, using a quad-tree like approach. Each partition boundary covers a specific rectangular area of the world. The area assigned to a partition has a lower bound that depends on the distance $b$ of the join operation to process. Therefore even in dense areas with many POIs, the smallest partition area still has edges of minimal size around $2 * b$. As a consequence, some partitions are rather unbalanced in terms of number of POIs they contain.

- The $YFCC$ dataset is partitioned using the partitioning that has been defined for the $GN$ dataset. This means that $YFCC$ has the same partitions as $GN$ in terms of geometry.
- The two spatial-partitioned datasets are distributed over the machines such that each $YFCC$ partition is located on the same machine as the corresponding $GN$ partitions that contains POIs in the same area or close areas (less than $b$ meters).
- Each machine computes the $YFCC/GN$ join a distinct set of $YFCC$ partitions.

We empirically observed that the $J$ spatial join processing had the expected degree of parallelism (*i.e.*, 200 cores are fully utilized) during the processing of 995 partitions out of 1000. However, processing the last 5 partitions raised important performance degradation as it was highly unbalanced: most of the query time was spent in processing those last 5 partitions, using only 5 CPU cores out of 200 available ones. Therefore the *indexJoin* method suffers from an unbalanced partitioning which is due to data bias. Indeed, few famous small areas (having an edge size lesser than $b$) actually contain most of the POIs and photos. The vast majority of other areas have very few POIs and photos.

We solve this major performance issue by proposing the next method.

**The *Bias-aware* Method.** This method aims to balance a join workload in the case of high data skew on the join attribute values. It relies on the idea to partition the dataset according to the expected result size within a partition. This differs from the previous method which partitions the data according to the partition size. It enables to handle data skew in an efficient way by ensuring that the number of $(y, o)$ results is rather uniform among the partitions.

We divide the photo dataset into two parts: a bias-free part denoted $Y_{free}$ and a biased part denoted $Y_{bias}$. We defined the biased areas as the top-N world most visited cities denoted $C$. Notice that in the following section, we empirically tune $N$. We use the city information contained in the dataset to put into $Y_{bias}$ the photos located in $C$; the remaining part of the dataset is put in $Y_{free}$. We process $Y_{free}$ using the above *IndexJoin* method. Then to process $Y_{bias}$ efficiently, we re-distribute it into 1000 partitions and process it using the *Cartesian* method.

## 5   Experiments

### 5.1   Experimental Set Up

We implemented the above described join methods and ran them on the Spark cluster of the LIP6 Lab, which consists of 1 driver machine and 10 worker machines. Each worker machine has 20 CPU cores (Intel Xeon processors with hyperthreading) and 50 GB memory, totaling 200 cores and 500 GB memory in use for join processing.

We had to clean the YFCC dataset. We only kept entries with valid GPS coordinates and date.

## 5.2   Join Performance with Spatial Index

We first run the YFCC/Geonames join on the entire dataset. It lasts 2 h. Then we study the impact of most visited cities on the performance. We successively removed from the YFCC dataset the top-N most visited cities. We report the response time on Fig. 2, the x-axis gives the number of cities that have been skipped, it has a log scale. For example, we see that when we removed 20 cities the response time is 322 s. It decreases below 50 s when more than 200 most visited cities have been removed. The index should only be used for the remaining cities (approx 32 800). We explain the poor performance for most visited cities as follows. When using the spatial index to join YFCC with Geonames location on the condition that they are distant of less than 500 m, the spatial partitioning keeps some dense areas (with a radius about 500 m). The join computation within each area is sequential which explains the high response time.

Therefore, the most visited cities must be treated apart, as detailed in next section.

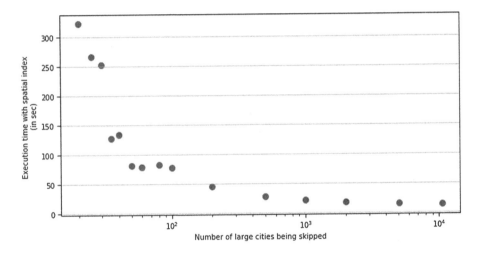

**Fig. 2.** Execution time for YFCC/Geonames join with spatial index. Log scale

## 5.3   Join Performance Without Index for the Most Visited Cities

We now target on computing the YFCC/Geoname join for the 200 most visited cities. Indeed, we observe that cities with a lot of visits also have the highest number of POIs.

We run the YFCC/Geonames join for each city with many visits using the cartesian method explained in Sect. 4. We report the response time on Fig. 3. For readability we only show the top-80 most visited cities, the response time being less than 0.5 s for the remaining cities. We observe that even for New-York, the most visited city, the response time is rather low (11.8 s), thanks to the high degree of parallelism. The total response time for processing the 200 most visited cities is less than 125 s. This means that we can proceed the full set of 33000 cities in less than 175 s.

In comparison, we also measured the performance using a single join method. The response time to join the entire dataset is 2 h (respectively 157 h) for the spatial index method (resp. the cartesian join method). Thus our *Bias-aware* method is at least 40 times more efficient than when using a single join method.

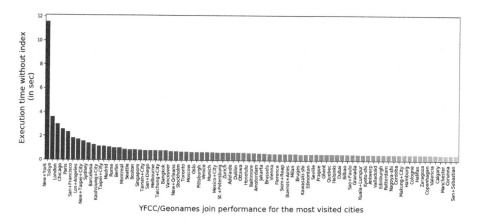

**Fig. 3.** YFCC/Geonames join execution time without index, for the top 80 cities with the highest number of visited locations. Cities are ordered by decreasing join time

## 6  Conclusion and Future Works

Considering the lack of publicly available rich and large-scale dataset for POI recommendation research, we have proposed an efficient method to join YFCC with Geonames datasets. We propose a efficient approximate spatial join method that performs on top of Apache Spark and takes into account the important bias on the spatial distribution of locations to better distribute the join workload on a cluster of machines.

The main use we will make of this enriched dataset is to extract more accurately users' information and define a new method for POI recommendation that is expected to leverage on rich and world-wide travel information to improve the recommendation quality. To achieve this goal, we are improving our POI selection method. Actually, We are facing the problem of choosing, for a given photo $y$ a small set of best matches among a possible large set of $(y, o)$ resulting from the spatial join described in Sect. 4. The $d$ distance function might not help here since every $o$ candidate is close to $y$ (by definition of $J$ we have $d(y, o) \leq b$). Therefore, we are investigating a method to select the best matches among a set of close candidate POIs, by comparing the photo tags with the POI description.

# References

1. Deng, N., Li, X.R.: Feeling a destination through the "right" photos: a machine learning model for dmos' photo selection. Tour. Manag. **65**, 267–278 (2018)
2. Geonames: The geonames dataset. http://www.geonames.org/export. Accessed 26 Nov 2019
3. Griesner, J., Abdessalem, T., Naacke, H., Dosne, P.: Algeospf: a hierarchical factorization model for POI recommendation. In: IEEE/ACM International Conference on Advances in Social Networks Analysis and Mining, ASONAM, pp. 87–90 (2018)
4. Griesner, P.-B.: Scalable models for Points-Of-Interest recommender systems. Ph.D thesis, Telecom ParisTech, Paris, tel-02085091, 7 2018. Artificial Intel-ligence [cs.AI] (2018)
5. Joulin, A., Grave, E., Bojanowski, P., Mikolov, T.: Bag of tricks for efficient text classification. In: Proceedings of the 15th Conference of the European Chapter of the Association for Computational Linguistics: Volume 2, Short Papers, Valencia, Spain, April 2017, pp. 427–431. Association for Computational Linguistics (2017)
6. Lim, K.H., Chan, J., Karunasekera, S., Leckie, C.: Personalized itinerary recommendation with queuing time awareness. In: ACM SIGIR Conference on Research and Development in Information Retrieval, pp. 325–334 (2017)
7. Lim, K.H., Chan, J., Leckie, C., Karunasekera, S.: Personalized tour recommendation based on user interests and points of interest visit durations. In: International Joint Conference on Artificial Intelligence, IJCAI, pp. 1778–1784 (2015)
8. Lim, K.H., Chan, J., Leckie, C., Karunasekera, S.: Personalized trip recommendation for tourists based on user interests, points of interest visit durations and visit recency. Knowl. Inf. Syst. **54**(2), 375–406 (2017). https://doi.org/10.1007/s10115-017-1056-y
9. Liu Shudong, G.V.L.J.: User modeling for point-of-interest recommendations in location-based social networks: the state of the art. Mob. Inf. Syst. (2018)
10. Manolopoulos, Y., Theodoridis, Y., Tsotras, L., Vassilis, J.: Spatial indexing techniques. In: Liu, L., Özsu, M.T. (eds.) Encyclopedia of Database Systems, pp. 2702–2707. Springer, Boston (2009). https://doi.org/10.1007/978-0-387-39940-9
11. Ni, K., et al.: Large-scale deep learning on the YFCC100M dataset. CoRR, abs/1502.03409 (2015)
12. Tang, L., Cai, D., Duan, Z., Ma, J., Han, M., Wang, H.: Discovering travel community for poi recommendation on location-based social networks. Complexity, 2019:8503962:1–8503962:8 (2019)
13. Taylor, K., Lim, K.H., Chan, J.: Travel itinerary recommendations with must-see points-of-interest. In: Companion Proceedings of the The Web Conference 2018, WWW 2018. International World Wide Web Conferences Steering Committee, pp. 1198–1205 (2018)
14. Thomee, B., et al.: Yfcc100m: the new data in multimedia research. Commun. ACM **59**(2), 64–73 (2016)
15. Wang, X., Leckie, C., Chan, J., Kwan Hui, L., Vaithianathan, T.: Improving personalized trip recommendation to avoid crowds using pedestrian sensor data. In: Proceedings of the 25th ACM International Conference on Information and Knowledge Management (CIKM 2016), pp. 25–34 (2016)
16. Xiaoyi Zhang, Z.D.: Spatial index. Geographic Information Science and Technology Body of Knowledge (2017)
17. Yonghong Yu, X.C.: A survey of point-of-interest recommendation in location-based social networks. In: Workshops at the Twenty-Ninth AAAI Conference on Artificial Intelligence. AAAI (2015)

18. Yu, J., Wu, J., Sarwat, M.: Geospark: a cluster computing framework for processing large-scale spatial data. In: SIGSPATIAL International Conference on Advances in Geographic Information Systems, pages 70:1–70:4 (2015)
19. Zhao, S., Zhao, T., Yang, H., Lyu, M.R., King, I.: Stellar: spatial-temporal latent ranking for successive point-of-interest recommendation. In: AAAI 2016: Proceedings of the Thirtieth AAAI Conference on Artificial Intelligence. AAAI Press (2016)

# Building Word Representations for Wolof Using Neural Networks

Alla Lo[1], Cheikh M. Bamba Dione[2], Elhadji Mamadou Nguer[3(⊠)],
Sileye O. Ba[4], and Moussa Lo[3]

[1] Université Gaston-Berger, Saint-Louis, Senegal
`lo.alla@ugb.edu.sn`
[2] University of Bergen, Bergen, Norway
`dione.bamba@uib.no`
[3] Université Virtuelle, Dakar, Senegal
`{elhadjimamadou.nguer,moussa.lo}@uvs.edu.sn`
[4] Dailymotion, Paris, France
`sileye.ba@dailymotion.com`

**Abstract.** Because a large portion of population in rural areas in sub Saharan Africa understand only local languages, they do not have access all to content available in the World Wide Web. Most content are available in English, Spanish, French, etc. Content in low-resource languages such as Wolof, which is mostly spoken in Senegal, are scarce. Automatic systems for natural language understanding such as machine translation systems that can transform information from common to low-resource languages would allow people in rural areas to access relevant scientific or health content.

Nowadays, word representation is the preliminary step of natural language understanding models. This paper presents investigations we conducted to build Wolof words representation using a corpus gathered from Internet. We applied neural word embedding models to the Wolof language corpus. These models are known to be able to capture into the embedding space semantic an syntactic relations between words. Experiments we conducted suggest that, despite a limited corpus size, our models successfully captures relations between words.

**Keywords:** Neural network · Word embedding · Low resource language · Wolof

## 1 Introduction

According to UNESCO, in 2012, only 20% of children in rural sub-Saharan African countries were enrolled in primary school [1]. Thus, a large portion of the population, specifically elderly people, only communicate in local languages.

Authors thank the CEA MITIC for funding this work.

J. P. R. Thorn et al. (Eds.): InterSol 2020, LNICST 321, pp. 274–286, 2020.
https://doi.org/10.1007/978-3-030-51051-0_20

These people cannot access all relevant information about agriculture, health, available into digitized documents on the internet.

Nowadays, machine learning models such as neural networks can be used to automatically extract information from digitized documents [3,18].

Although languages such as English, Chinese, French, Spanish, Arabic are dominant in the digitized world, digital documents are also available for low-resource languages such as Wolof, Pulaar which are among the mostly spoken languages in sub-Saharan Africa. These aforementioned low-resource languages have been investigated by linguists in term of their syntactical and grammatical structures [16]. Also, dictionaries relating these languages to French and English exist [17]. However, because of data scarcity, these low-resource languages have not been explored with machine learning methods to address natural language understanding tasks. Building machine learning models, such as neural machine translation systems, that can automatically extract information from audio and text data will have a strong impact in regions of the world where those languages are dominant. This will allow people from rural areas of sub-Saharan Africa, specifically elderly people, to access relevant information about health, they would not otherwise.

In this paper, we present investigations we have conducted on building word representations for Wolof. For efficient processing, words that are discrete tokens have to be represented in a numeric format that is amenable to algebraic calculations. The basic word representation is the so called one-hot encoding: for a vocabulary of $N$ words, the $n$'th word is encoded as an $N$ dimension vector filled with 0 except for the $n$'th component which is 1. The issue with this representation is that every word is at equal distance to every other word. More precisely, distances between words encode neither syntactic nor semantic information. Another possible representation is the so called bag-of-words model which consists in representing the $n$'th word as an $N$ dimension vector whose $m$'th component is the counts of the number of time word $m$ co-occurs with word $n$ [19]. This model allows to capture information about word co-occurrences: two words that co-occur with the same words will have similar vector representation. A problem with this model, however, is that it generates very high dimensional word representation.

Recently, more sophisticated models to word representation based on neural networks have been proposed [4]. These models are able to predict a word using its context (i.e. words around it) as input or, vice versa, predict the context using the word as input. The internal representation of these networks allows to generate lower dimensional word embedding that captures a richer semantic information than the bag-of-words.

In our research work, we have gathered a corpus of Wolof documents from the web. The corpus is used to train neural network-based models for word representation. In this paper, we discuss how we have applied word embedding models to this low-resource language and present our results. To our knowledge, this is the first time Wolof language is the topic of such a study. In our investigations, we built three models: the continuous bag-of-word model (CBOW, [4]) that predicts a word given its local context, the skip-gram model that predicts a word local context given the word (skip-gram, [4]), and the global vector model that predicts a word given its global context (GloVe, [6]). We have conducted various experiments to assess the effectiveness of our models. The results show that despite the limited corpus size, constructed word embedding models successfully capture semantic structure that can be recovered using distances between words in the embedding spaces.

The remainder of this paper is organized as follows. Section 2 discusses related work. Section 3 gives details about the word embedding models we have investigated so far. Section 4 presents the corpus we used to learn the models parameters. Section 5 describes the experiments we have conducted. Section 6 concludes the discussion and outlines future work.

## 2   Related Work

Because of the importance of language in human interaction, natural language understanding has been widely investigated in computer science. Natural language understanding can be approached either from speech or text inputs. In this paper our focus is on text inputs. Without being exhaustive, natural language understanding can have as object parts-of-speech tagging, named entity recognition, text classification, automatic translation, etc. [3, 18].

Natural language understanding requires representing word tokens as elements of a vector space so that algebraic calculations can be applied to them. The simplest representation is the one-hot encoding vector which does not allow to capture relationships between words, as every word is at the same distance to every other one. The bag-of-words representation allows to capture co-occurrence relations between words and thus some form of syntactic and semantic relationships [19]. The main drawback of this representation is that it is very high dimensional. Using word-document occurrences matrix factorization allows to obtain lower dimensional representation of the bag-of-words vector while maintaining relations between words [19].

In [5], word embedding with the skip-gram and the continuous bag-of-words (CBOW) were proposed. Furthermore, experimental evidences were given about the abilities of these embedding models to capture semantic and syntactic relationships between words. These relations could then be recovered by computing the distances between word vectors in the embedding space. We may note in passing that word embeddings with neural network have been implicitly used in other works. In [3], although not explicitly stated, Collobert et *al.* used neural network generated word embeddings to jointly solve some natural language understanding tasks. In [2], neural word embedding was implicitly used for language modelling tasks. However, the effectiveness of neural word embedding to capture word semantic relationships was explicitly pointed out by Mikolov et al. in [5].

The purpose of this paper is to provide a representation of Wolof words using neural network embeddings. So far, investigations about Wolof have mostly been about building dictionaries [11], and studying the grammatical structures [8–10] of the language. Other African languages such as Swahili (Southern Africa) and Amharic (Eastern Africa) have been subject of research about automatic statistical based machine translation [12–14]. However, to our knowledge, this work is the first to address Wolof (Western Africa) word representation.

# 3   Word Embedding Models

Let us introduce notations we use in the remainder of this article. We define $\mathcal{V} = \{v_1, v_2, ..., v_N\}$ as the Wolof vocabulary, more precisely the set of words occurring in the corpus. Every element of the vocabulary $v_n$ can be represented by a one-hot encoded vector $H(v_n) = (\delta_{nm})$, $m = 1, ..., N$ where $\delta_{nm}$ is the Kronecker delta symbol which is 1 when $n = m$ and 0 otherwise. Our corpus is split into phrases. If we define the size of our context to be the integer $C$, from every phrase, we can extract sequence of words $w_{t-c}, w_{t-c+1},..., w_{t-1}, w_t, w_{t+1},..., w_{t+c-1}, w_{t+c}$. Given this sequence of words, the target word is the central word $w_t$. The other words $w_{t-c}, w_{t-c+1},..., w_{t-1}, w_{t+1},..., w_{t+c-1}, w_{t+c}$ represent the context of the target.

Given the target words and their contexts, neural word embeddings are all based on the same principle: build a neural network that predicts the target word from its context, or vice versa. Parameters obtained during training of the neural networks associated to every vocabulary words are taken as their embedding. In the following sections, we describe the continuous bag-of-words (CBOW) first, then the skip-gram, and finally the global vector (GloVe) model.

## 3.1   Word Embedding with CBOW

In the CBOW model, word embedding is obtained using a three-layer neural network comprised of an input, a hidden layer, and an output layer.

The input layer takes the words of the context in their one-hot encoded forms $H(w_{t-c})$. Then every one-hot encoded word is projected into the embedding space using an embedding matrix $E$. The embedding matrix $E$ is of dimension $N \times D$ where $N$ is the number of words of the vocabulary, and $D$ is the dimension of the embedding space. The embedding dimension $D$ is an hyper-parameter to be set. Multiplying the one-hot encoding vector of a word with the embedding matrix consists simply in selecting from the embedding matrix the row corresponding to the word. Then projected words representations are averaged. The average representation is fed into a logistic regression layer with parameter $W$ to predict the target word. Figure 1 gives a graphical representation of the CBOW model architecture.

Learning the CBOW is achieved by optimizing the following cost:

$$J(E, W) = \frac{1}{T} \sum_{t=1}^{T} \log p(w_t | w_{t-c}, c = -C, ..., C, c \neq 0, E, W) \qquad (1)$$

where $T$ is the total number of target words in the training corpus. The model is named continuous bag-of-words, because the word one-hot encoding averaging step removes all information related to the words ordering.

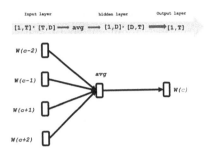

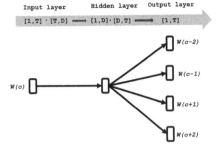

**Fig. 1.** CBOW model architecture.    **Fig. 2.** Skip-gram model architecture.

## 3.2    Word Embedding with the Skip-Gram

The skip-gram model is essentially the inverse of the CBOW model. In skip-gram, the target word $w_t$ is used as input, and context words as predicted outputs. Represented in the one-hot encoding format, the input word is projected into the embedding space using the embedding matrix $E$. As for the CBOW, projecting the word's one-hot encoding vector consists in selecting from the embedding matrix the row corresponding to the target word. Then, the projected word vector is fed into a logistic regression layer with parameter $W$ to predict words belonging to the target word's local context. Figure 2 gives a graphical representation of the skip-gram architecture.

Learning the skip-gram from a training corpus consists in optimizing the following cost function:

$$J(E, W) = \frac{1}{T} \sum_{t=1}^{T} \sum_{c=-C,...,C,c\neq0} \log p(w_{t+c}|w_t, E, W) \tag{2}$$

with respect to the embedding matrix $E$ and the regression parameters $W$. The skip-gram is named as is because words of the context are predicted from the one that is skipped, in reference to language models where $n$-gram is the name of model predicting a word from its $n$ predecessors.

## 3.3    Word Embedding with GloVe

The global vector (GloVe) introduced in [7] combines two approaches, count-based matrix factorization and neural network-based embedding. GloVe is based on the construction of global co-occurrence matrix $X$ between words, by processing the entire training corpus using a sliding context window. Each element $X_{nm}$ represents the number of times word $v_n$ of the vocabulary appears in the context of word $v_m$. In contrast to the CBOW and skip-gram models which are trained from target words' local contexts, GloVe takes into account all the aggregated local target words contexts. Thus, the co-occurrence matrix $X$ contains the words' global context.

Once the co-occurrence matrix $X$ is computed, least squares regression is used to build vector representations $E_n$ for word $v_n$. It has to be noticed that vectors $E_n$ are rows of an embedding matrix $E$. Learning GloVe using a training corpus is achieved by minimizing the following cost:

$$J(E, W, b) = \sum_{n,m=1}^{N} f(X_{nm})(E_n W_m^{\perp} + b_n + b_m - \log X_{nm})^2 \tag{3}$$

where $f(.)$ is a function weighting words contributions to the cost $J(E, W, b)$ according to co-occurrence counts $X_{nm}$ and $b, b_n, b_m$ are bias. The weight function $f$ is defined as:

$$f(X_{nm}) = \begin{cases} \left(\frac{X_{nm}}{\tau}\right)^{\alpha} & \text{if } X_{nm} < \tau \\ 1 & \text{Otherwise} \end{cases} \tag{4}$$

where $\tau = 100$ and $\alpha = 3/4$ [7]. The main role of the weight function is to reduce the effect of very frequent words such as the stop words.

## 4   Wolof Corpus

Wolof is mainly spoken by 14 million people in Senegal, Gambia, and Mauritania, three countries located in West Africa. Wolof texts are written either in Arabic or Latin alphabets. In this work, we only consider texts written in Latin alphabet. To give the reader a flavour about what Wolof looks like, we provide a very short extract from a classical Senegalese literary text *Bataaxal bu gudde nii* which translates in English as *So long a letter* [20]:

*"Aysatu, Jot naa sa bataaxal, fekk ma ci nattu. Ni ma lay tontoo mooy, wéttalikoo kaye bii, lu ma xalaat def ci; ndax, yàgg a déeyook yow, tax na maa xam ni, «waxtaan ay dund bi gor», day giifal naqar. Aysatu, sunu diggante, dug tandle. Sunuy maam a jélloo woon i sàkket, daan diisoo bés bu Yàlla sàkk. Sunu yaay ya, ku ca masaan a am rakk, yaak say moroom a koy xéccoo boot. Maak yow noo jàngandoo Alxuraan, daan ànd ca mbeddum xeer mooma aayoon lool ciy dàll ak sér. Bën sax, bu ñu ko masaan a foq, nooy bokk pax mu nu koy suul te naan: «Jinax, am bën bu rafet, te jox nu bën bu ñaaw!»Su at yi demee, nimse yi naaxsaay yit, pàttalliku yi, dara jógu fi, ñoom laay bànneexoo, ñoo tax sama àddina saf xorom. Di la fàttaliku nag; la woon lépp delsi, teewaat ci sama kanam. Ma gëmm, sama xol dekki, may yëg, ñuy dem, di ñëw: tàngaay baak leeraayu taalu matt ya, màngo xayli bu saf sàpp ak kaani, ku xàmp tàqamtiku jox sa moroom."*

Figure 3 displays the corpus word cloud. This figure shows that in the corpus, stop-words such as *ci* or *ak* (meaning *in* or *with* in English) have the highest occurrences.

The corpus contains about a hundred documents covering various topics about society, religion, politics, history, agriculture, art, culture, justice, health, science, etc. The corpus contains 47457 phrases, and a total of 867951

**Fig. 3.** Wolof corpus word cloud. Words are displayed according to their occurrence in the corpus, the more frequent, the larger the word will be displayed.

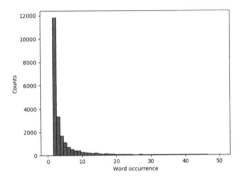

**Fig. 4.** Corpus word occurrence histogram depicting the number of words that have a given occurrence count.

repeated words. The vocabulary consists of 24232 unique words, with only thirty percent of the words occurring more than five times.

Figure 4 shows the histogram of the word occurrence frequencies in the corpus following the classical Zipf law: most words occur rarely, and few words, such as stop-words, occur very frequently [15].

## 5   Experiments

We have built three word embedding models based on the aforementioned algorithms using the Wolof corpus presented in Sect. 4. The raw texts of the corpus are preprocessed by lower-casing words, and removing accents. We restricted the vocabulary only to words occurring more than five times. We also added to the vocabulary an unknown word token to account for words in the corpus ignored in the restricted vocabulary. We then extracted phrases, and for each phrase, we build a training corpus by gathering the target words along with their contexts. Our models use the following hyper-parameters: the vocabulary size, the context size, and the embedding dimension. The vocabulary involved 7942 words comprising the unknown word token. The context size was set to 10 words. More precisely, around each target word, five words to the left and to the right are taken to be the context. We experimented various context sizes (6, 8), however, 10 was the best experimental settings. To set the embedding space dimension we tested many values ranging from 100 to 300. Because this value did not significantly affect the final results, the embedding dimension was set to 300.

The models were implemented in TensorFlow and trained using back propagation. Training neural networks involve defining learning parameters such as the learning rate, the batch size, and the number of epochs.

For all the models, the learning rate was set to 0.001. This value ensures stable convergence of the models with a regular decrease of the optimized cost. The number of epochs was set to 10 for all the models. One reason for this is that, at around this number of epochs, the cost was no longer significantly decreasing. The batch size was set to 512 for the skip-gram and the CBOW to speed up the training: the number of samples to train was very large (i.e. million of samples) and the models were trained with local context information. For GloVe, the size of the training samples is equal to the vocabulary size. Accordingly, GloVe was trained with a smaller batch size of 32 samples.

## 5.1   Qualitative Analysis

Having trained the models, we qualitatively assessed the word embedding validity by selecting a sample set of words from the vocabulary and displaying their five nearest neighbours in the embedding space. Neighborhood was taken with respect to the euclidean distance. These results are provided in Tables 1, 2 and 3. In these tables, we provide Wolof words together with their English translation for indicative purposes. Our models only exploit Wolof word occurrences. The results show that the obtained neighbours are semantically related to the target words. If we consider for example the word *bànk* (meaning *bank* in English), for the CBOW model, its nearest neighbours are *leble* (to lend), *leb* (to borrow), *cfa* (acronym for financial african community francs), *kopparu* (her/his/its money), *tayle* (pledge). Using the skip-gram model, the neighbours of the word *bànk* are *dugal* (to put), *kont* (bank account), *jàngi* (to go to school), *monjaal* (worldwide), *xareñal* (to educate). For the GloVe model, neighbours of the word *bank* are *fmi* (acronym for international world fund), *kont* (bank account), *nafa* (purse), *monjaal* (worldwide), *xaalisu* (her/his/its money). Similar analysis can be conducted for other target words in Tables 1, 2 and 3. This qualitative analysis suggests that the GloVe model produces more semantically related neighbours than the other models.

We further qualitatively verified the validity of our models by training the GloVe model on a corpus composed of 350000 Wikipedia French articles. Table 4 shows that in this large-scale French corpus, words and their nearest neighbours are semantically related. For example, the first three neighbours of the word uranus (uranus in English), are *jupiter* (jupyter), *saturne* (saturn), and *pluton* (pluto). Similarly, the nearest neighbors of the word *boudhisme* (buddhism), *hindhouisme* (hindhuism), *brahmanisme* (brahmanism), *jainisme* (jainism).

**Table 1.** Examples of Wolof words (in bold) with their five nearest neighbours according to CBOW embedding. It should be noted that Wolof words English translation (non bold) are only given for indicative purposes. Our models only exploit Wolof words occurences.

| Word | $n_1$ | $n_2$ | $n_3$ | $n_4$ | $n_5$ |
|---|---|---|---|---|---|
| **afrig** | **patiriis** | **kongo** | **lumumbaa** | **reyee** | **goney** |
| africa | patrice | Congo | lumumba | killed | youth of |
| **bànk** | **leble** | **leb** | **cfa** | **koppar** | **tayle** |
| bank | to lend | borrow | cfa | money | pawn |
| **banaana** | **xollitu** | **rattax** | **roose** | **kemb** | **delluseek** |
| banana | peel | slippy | to water | peanut | come back with |
| **aajo** | **fajug** | **regg** | **mbaax** | **solaay** | **mànke** |
| need | resolve | sate | kindness | clothing | lack |
| **bamba** | **barke** | **maam** | **ibra** | **seex** | **rasululaay** |
| bamba | grace | grand-pa | ibra | sheikh | prophet |

**Table 2.** Examples of Wolof words (in bold) with their five nearest neighbours according to skip-gram embedding. Note that the English translations (non bold) are only given for indicative purposes. Our models only exploit Wolof words occurrences.

| Word | $n_1$ | $n_2$ | $n_3$ | $n_4$ | $n_5$ |
|---|---|---|---|---|---|
| **afrig** | **oseyaani** | **asi** | **saalumu** | **sowwu** | **tugal** |
| africa | oceania | asia | south | west | france |
| **bànk** | **dugal** | **kont** | **jàngi** | **monjaal** | **xareñal** |
| bank | put in | account | go to school | world-wide | to teach |
| **banaana** | **soraas** | **màngo** | **guava** | **xollitu** | **koko** |
| banana | orange | mango | guava | peel of | coconut fruit |
| **aajo** | **fajug** | **aajowoo** | **faj** | **faji** | **drepanositoos** |
| need | resolution | want | to resolve | resolve | sickle cell disease |
| **bàmba** | **matub** | **taalubey** | **lumumbaa** | **seex** | **bijaahi** |
| bamba | completeness | student | lumumba | Sheikh | from his grace |

## 5.2   Quantitative Analysis

One of the classical procedures to quantitatively evaluate word embeddings is to solve word analogy tasks. It consists in considering a set of words and a set of semantic relations, and selecting a set of word pairs where the words in each pair are related by one of the considered relations. Then, a set of questions are stated as follows: considering two pairs $(word_k, word_l)$ and $(word_n, word_m)$, the question "word $k$ is to word $l$ as word $n$ is to word __?", where according to the considered relation, the expected response is word $m$. Because the embedding space is linear, assuming that relation between words are represented as

**Table 3.** Examples of Wolof words (in bold) with their five nearest neighbours according to GloVe embedding. Again, English translations (non bold) are only given for indicative purposes. Our models only exploit Wolof words occurrences.

| Word | $n_1$ | $n_2$ | $n_3$ | $n_4$ | $n_5$ |
|------|-------|-------|-------|-------|-------|
| **afrig** | **oseyaani** | **asi** | **gànnaaru** | **sowwu** | **tefesi** |
| africa | oceania | asia | north | south | shore of |
| **bànk** | **fmi** | **kont** | **nafa** | **monjaal** | **xaalisu** |
| bank | imf | account | wallet | world-wide | money of |
| **banaana** | **soraas** | **màngo** | **guyaab** | **xob** | **kànja** |
| banana | orange | mango | guava | leaf | gumbo |
| **aajo** | **fajug** | **tekki** | **faju** | **lew** | **réeral** |
| need | resolve | mean | resolved | legal | lose |
| **bàmba** | **xaadimu** | **rasuul** | **coloniales** | **seex** | **murid** |
| bamba | Khadim | prophet | colonial | sheikh | mourid |

**Table 4.** French Wikipedia GloVe words neighbours. The first column gives the target words and the three other columns give the first, second, and third nearest neighbours. These sample results show that neighbours are semantically related to the target word.

| Target word | $n_1$ | $n_2$ | $n_3$ |
|-------------|-------|-------|-------|
| atom | atomes | isotope | cathode |
| mathématique | mathematiques | axiomatique | probabilites |
| art | contemporain | deco | abstrait |
| peinture | figurative | picturaux | picturales |
| agriculture | arboriculture | cerealieres | cerealiere |
| boudhisme | hindouisme | brahmanisme | jainisme |
| uranus | jupiter | saturne | pluton |
| planete | extraterrestre | lointaine | orbitant |
| mer | caspienne | baltique | ocean |
| fleuve | baikal | fleuves | embouchure |

translations, we expect in the embedding space linear relation word vectors of the form

$$E_l - E_k = E_m - E_n \tag{5}$$

where we remind that $E_k$, $E_l$, $E_m$, $E_n$ are the embedding vectors of words $k, l, m, n$. Questions about relations between words can be stated as finding the word $\hat{u}$ verifying:

$$\hat{u} = \arg\min_u ||E_l - E_k - E_u + E_n||_2 \tag{6}$$

where $||.||_2$ is the $D$-dimensional euclidean distance. Then, if the embedding vector of word $m$ is among the ten word vector closest to $E_l - E_k + E_n$ we consider the system has provided the correct answer, otherwise the response is considered false.

To quantitatively assess the effectiveness of our models, we measured to which extent, for a given selected quadruple words $k, l, m, n$, one of the selected semantic relations is verified. We mainly focus our analysis on relations such as, male-female, derivative, synonym, country-capital. Table 5 gives the selected relations and word pairs, and the performances achieved by each model of the benchmark.

**Table 5.** Word analogy tasks and scores of the CBOW, skip-gram, and GloVe models. The first column specifies relations to be discovered from Wolof word pairs given in the second column. The third column gives the English translation of the word pairs. The fourth, fifth, and sixth columns give the models' results on the task (1 for correct answers and 0 otherwise).

| Relations | Word pairs (Wolof) | English translation | CBOW | SG | GloVe |
|---|---|---|---|---|---|
| Country-capital | (senegaal, dakaar) | (senegal, dakar) | 1 | 0 | 1 |
| Country-capital | (faraas, pari) | (france, paris) | 0 | 0 | 0 |
| Male-female | (janq, waxambaane) | (girl, boy) | 0 | 0 | 1 |
| Male-female | (jigéen, góor) | (female, male) | 0 | 0 | 0 |
| Male-female | (yaay, baay) | (mother, dad) | 1 | 1 | 0 |
| Male-female | (jëkkër, jabar) | (husband, wife) | 0 | 0 | 0 |
| Synonym | (rafet, taaru) | (pretty, beautiful) | 1 | 1 | 1 |
| Synonym | (teey, yem) | (prudent, cautious) | 1 | 1 | 1 |
| Synonym | (tàmbale, sumb) | (to start, to begin) | 1 | 1 | 1 |
| Synonym | (metit, naqar) | (pain, grief) | 0 | 0 | 1 |
| Synonym | (suux, diig) | (sink, ) | 1 | 1 | 1 |
| Synonym | (taarix, cosaan) | (history, story) | 1 | 1 | 1 |
| Derivation | (xam, xami) | (know, to know) | 0 | 1 | 1 |
| Derivation | (ajoor, kajoor) | (cayor resident, cayor) | 0 | 1 | 1 |
| Derivation | (jàng, jàngale) | (to learn, to teach) | 0 | 0 | 1 |
| Model performances | | | 47% | 53% | 73% |

The scores in Table 5 show that among the tested models, GloVe achieves best performances, followed by the skip-gram model. This corresponds to the conclusions of the qualitative analysis conducted in Sect. 5.1.

## 6    Conclusion

In this paper, we presented preliminary investigations we conducted to build vector representations of Wolof words from a corpus gathered from the internet. We considered three word embedding models: the CBOW, the skip-gram, and the GloVe. Our experiments demonstrate that the models are able to build effective representations that encode semantic relations between words in the embedding spaces. These relations can be recovered using euclidean distance between word embedding vectors.

In the future, we plan to extend the corpus in two directions. First, we are looking forward to significantly enlarge the corpus from 47000 to 200000 phrases. Also, we will make the corpus bilingual by pairing the Wolof phrases with their corresponding French translations. This dataset will be used to build neural machine translation models.

# References

1. AAI State of Education in Africa Report 2015. http://www.aaionline.org/wp-content/uploads/2015/09/AAI-SOE-report-2015-final.pdf
2. Bengio, Y., Ducharme, R., Vincent, P., Janvin, C.: A neural probabilistic language model. J. Mach. Learn. Res. **3**, 1137–1155 (2003)
3. Collobert, R., Weston, J.: A unified architecture for natural language processing: deep neural networks with multitask learning. In: Proceedings of the ICML (2008)
4. Mikolov, T., Sutskever, I., Chen, K., Corrado, G., Dean, J.: Efficient estimation of word representations in vector space. In: ICLR (2013)
5. Mikolov, T., Sutskever, I., Chen, K., Corrado, G., Dean, J.: Distributed representations of words and phrases and their compositionality. In: NIPS (2013b)
6. Pennington, J., Socher, R., Manning, C.: Glove: global vectors for word representation. In: EMNLP (2014)
7. Arora, S., Li, Y., Liang, Y., Ma, T., Risteski, A.: A latent variable model approach to PMI-based word embeddings. Trans. ACL **4**, 385–399 (2016)
8. Dione, C.B.: LFG parse disambiguation for Wolof. J. Lang. Model. **2**(1), 105–165 (2014)
9. Dione, C.B.: Valency change and complex predicates in Wolof: an LFG account. In: LFG Conference (2013)
10. Dione C.B.: An LFG approach to Wolof cleft constructions. In: LFG Conference (2012)
11. Khoule, M., Thiam, M.N., Nguer, E.M.: Towards the establishment of a LMF-based Wolof language lexicon. Traitement Automatique des Langues Africaines (TALAf) (2014)
12. Pauw, G.D., Wagacha, P.W., de Schryver, G.-M.: Towards English - Swahili machine translation. In: Research Workshop of the Israel Science Foundation (2011)
13. Ombui, E.O., Wagacha, P.W., Ng'ang'a, W.: InterlinguaPlus machine translation approach for under-resourced languages: Ekegusii & Swahili. In: Workshop on the Use of Computational Methods in the Study of Endangered Languages (2014)
14. Gebreegziabher, M., Besacier, L.: English-Amharic statistical machine translation. In: Workshop on Spoken Language Technologies for Under-Resourced Languages (2012)
15. Sichel, H.S.: On a distribution law for word frequencies. J. Am. Stat. Assoc. **70**, 542–547 (1975)
16. Pathe, D.: Grammaire de wolof moderne, Edition Presence Africaine (1971)
17. Cisse, M.T., Diagne, A.M., Campenhoudt, M.V., Muraille, P.: Mise au point d'une base de données lexicale multifonctionnelle : le dictionnaire unilingue wolof et bilingue wolof-français. Journées LC (2007)
18. Young, T., Hazarika, D., Poria, S., Cambria, E.: Recent trends in deep learning based natural language processing. arXiv:1708.02709 (2018)

19. Wild, F., Stahl, C.: Investigating unstructured texts with latent semantic analysis. In: Decker, R., Lenz, H.-J. (eds.) Advances in Data Analysis. SCDAKO, pp. 383–390. Springer, Heidelberg (2007). https://doi.org/10.1007/978-3-540-70981-7_43
20. Ba, M.: So long a letter. Nouvelles Editions Africaines. https://en.wikipedia.org/wiki/So_Long_a_Letter (1979)

# Author Index

Agoungbome, Sehouevi Mawuton David
105
Ahouandjinou, Sèmèvo Arnaud R. M.   20
Alhaji, Mohammed Mustapha   64
Alunge, Rogers   192
Amoussouga Badoussi, Prince E. N.   20
Assogba, Kokou M.   20

Ba, Amadou   134
Ba, Sileye O.   274
Bassolé, Didier   164
Bere, Wend-Panga Régis Cédric   52
Burse, Monet   176

Camara, Gaoussou   52

Dasylva, Marius   251
Densmore, Melissa   176
Despres, Sylvie   52
Dieng, Sidiya   251
Dieng, Youssou   238
Dione, Cheikh M. Bamba   274
Diop, Alassane   211

Fall, Abdourakhmane   224
Fall, Doudou   211
Farao, Jaydon   176
Faty, Bakary   121
Faye, Youssou   251
Fröhlich, Karin   149

Gançarski, Stéphane   264
Gavoille, Cyril   238
Gbenontin, Estelle   105
Gueye, Assane   211
Gueye, Ibrahima   264

Idowu, Harrison Adewale   89

Kashihara, Shigeru   211
Kiki, Manhougbé P. A. F.   20
Koala, Gouayon   164

Lo, Alla   274
Lo, Moussa   52, 274

Malo, Sadouanouan   52
Mambo, Abdulhameed Danjuma   64
Masinde, Muthoni   3, 77
Mbaye, Babacar   211
Mbaye, Mamadou Lamine   121
Mbele, Mpho   77
Mbodji, Senghane   134
Mthoko, Hafeni   176
Musa, Abdullahi Yahaya   64
Musa, Alhassan   64

Naacke, Hubert   264
Ndiaye, Alphousseyni   134
Nguer, Elhadji Mamadou   274
Nieminen, Marko   149
Nyetanyane, John   3

Ouaro, Stanislas   52

Pinomaa, Antti   149

Sall, Saidou Moustapha   121
Sano, Ismail   89
Sarr, Cheikh   224
Sarr, Moussa Dethié   224
Sié, Oumarou   164
Sy, Khadidiatou   121

Taiye, Waheed Adejumo   64
Thiam, Moussa   105
Thorn, Jessica P. R.   33
Traoré, Yaya   164

Printed in the United States
By Bookmasters